AFCAT
TOPIC-WISE
SOLVED PAPERS
(2011-2019) WITH 5 PRACTICE SETS

- **Corporate Office :** 45, 2nd Floor, Maharishi Dayanand Marg, Corner Market, Malviya Nagar, New Delhi-110017
  Tel. : 011- 49404757/ 49404758/ 49404768

Typeset by Disha DTP Team

DISHA PUBLICATION

For further information about the books from DISHA,
Log on to **www.dishapublication.com** or email to **info@dishapublication.com**

CONTENTS

Instructions for candidates

TIME ALLOTTED – 2 HRS.

1. Total No. of Questions–100. Each Question is of three marks.
2. One mark will be deducted for every wrong answer.

NUMERICAL ABILITY

1. Car A is travelling at 60 kmph towards northwest creating an angle 42^0 to north and Car B is travelling towards South West at 80 kmph creating an angle 48^0 degree to South. Both are started from same point. Find distance between A and B after one hour?
   - (a) 100 km
   - (b) 120 km
   - (c) 150 km
   - (d) 90 km

2. Average age of n students who promoted in class VIII is Y years. Three more students included in class whose ages are Y-1, Y-2 and Y+3 years. Find their average age when they promoted in class Xth.
   - (a) Y
   - (b) Y-3
   - (c) Y+2
   - (d) Y+5

3. Difference between two stations X and Y is 500 km one train starting from X move toward Y with 20 km/h and another train move toward X from Y with the speed 30km/h. What is the distance of the point where both train cross each other from point X.
   - (a) 400 km
   - (b) 200 km
   - (c) 300 km
   - (d) 100 km

4. The average monthly rainfall is 2.7inch, the average of first 7 months rainfall is 1.1 less than the average of yearly rainfall and rainfall of other four months is 20.3 what is the average rainfall of the last month?
   - (a) 0.9
   - (b) 10
   - (c) 2.1
   - (d) 1.3

5. X, Y and Z have some monkey in the ratio 4:3:8. If 2 monkey run away from X and 4 monkey run away Z than the ratio become 3:3:8 how many monkey they initially had?
   - (a) 10
   - (b) 20
   - (c) 40
   - (d) 30

6. A is 5 times efficient as of B. A completes a piece of work in 60 days less than B, how many time will they take individually?
   - (a) 15 days,75 days
   - (b) 13 days, 65 days
   - (c) 15 days, 60 days
   - (d) 17 days, 85 days

7. A man bought watch and pen-drive at 1564 each. And one sold for 23% profit and other sold for 23% loss. What is overall profit or loss?
   - (a) 0%
   - (b) 23%
   - (c) 46%
   - (d) 0%

8. A and B earn in the ratio 2:1. They spend in the ratio 5:3 and save in the ratio 4:1. If the total monthly savings of both A and B are Rs.5000, the monthly income of B is-
   - (a) Rs. 7,000
   - (b) Rs. 14,000
   - (c) Rs. 5,000
   - (d) Rs. 10,000

9. 240 men can finish a work in 20 days working 5 hours a day. To finish the work within 10 days working 8 hours a day, the minimum number of men required is-
   - (a) 310
   - (b) 300
   - (c) 315
   - (d) 312

10. While selling, a businessman allows 40% discount on the marked price and there is a loss of 30%. If it is sold at the marked price, profit per cent will be –
   - (a) 10%
   - (b) 20%
   - (c) 16.68%
   - (d) 16.25%

11. The average salary of all the staff in an office of a corporate house is Rs. 5,000. The average salary of the officers is Rs. 14,000 and that of the rest is Rs. 4,000. If the total number of staff is 500, the number of officers is–
    - (a) 10
    - (b) 15
    - (c) 25
    - (d) 50

12. 60% of the cost price of an article is equal to 50% of its selling price. Then the percentage of profit or loss on the cost price is-
    - (a) 20% loss
    - (b) $16\frac{2}{3}\%$ profit
    - (c) 20% profit
    - (d) 10% loss

13. There are in all, 10 balls; some of them are red and the others white. The average cost of all balls is Rs. 28. If the average cost of red balls is Rs. 25 and that of white balls is Rs. 30, the number of white balls is:
    - (a) 3
    - (b) 5
    - (c) 6
    - (d) 7

14. Either 8 men or 17 women can paint a house in 33 days. The number of days required to paint three such houses by 12 men and 24 women working at the same rate is :
    - (a) 44
    - (b) 43
    - (c) 34
    - (d) 66

15. The difference between simple and compound interest on a sum of money at 5% p.a. for 2 years. is Rs. 100. The sum of money must be.

   (a) Rs. 35,000   (b) Rs. 41,000

   (c) Rs. 40,000   (d) Rs. 45,000

16. If $\sqrt{2} = 1.4142$, find the value of

   $$2\sqrt{2} + \sqrt{2} + \frac{1}{2+\sqrt{2}} + \frac{1}{\sqrt{2}-2}$$

   (a) 1.4144   (b) 2.8284

   (c) 28.284   (d) 2.4142

17. An alloy contains copper, zinc and nickel in the ratio of 5 : 3 : 2. The quantity of nickel in kg that must be added to 100 kg of this alloy to have the new ratio 5 : 3 : 3 is

   (a) 8   (b) 10

   (c) 12   (d) 15

18. The ratio of the ages of Ram and Rahim 10 years ago was 1 : 3. The ratio of their ages five years hence will be 2 : 3. Then the ratio of their present ages is

   (a) 1 : 2   (b) 3 : 5

   (c) 3 : 4   (d) 2 : 5

REASONING AND MILITARY APTITUDE TEST

DIRECTIONS (Qs. 19–21) : *In each of the following questions, select the related letter/word/ figure/ number from the given alternatives.*

19. Microphone : Loud :: Microscope : ?

   (a) Elongate   (b) Investigate

   (c) Magnify   (d) Examine

20. Sound : Medium : : Light : ?

   (a) Air   (b) Vacuum

   (c) Water   (d) Glass

21. Democracy : India : : Communism : ?

   (a) France   (b) China

   (c) Britain   (d) America

22. In the following figure, rectangle represents Opticians, circle represents Art critics, triangle represents Riders and square represents Boxes. Which set of letters represents Art critics who are not Riders?

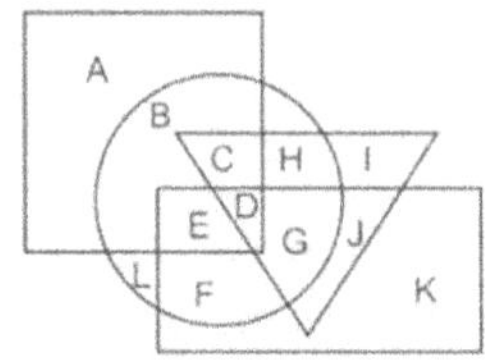

   (a) BLEF   (b) IJ

   (c) CHDG   (d) EDGJ

DIRECTIONS (Qs. 23-24): *In the following question, select the related word pair from the given alternatives.*

23. School : Education : : ? : ?

   (a) Scalpel : Teacher   (b) Hospital : Treatment

   (c) Teacher : School   (d) Class : College

24. 5 : 125 : : 7 : ?

   (a) 343   (b) 512

   (c) 243   (d) 729

DIRECTIONS (Qs. 25-26): *In the following question, select the one which is different from the other three responses.*

25. (a) Daring : Timid   (b) Beautiful : Pretty

   (c) Clear : Vague   (d) Youth : Adult

26. (a) Fish : Shoal   (b) Cow : Herd

   (c) Sheep : Flock   (d) Man : Mob

DIRECTIONS (Qs. 27-29): *For the following questions Find the odd word / letter / number from the given alternative.*

27. (a) Rival   (b) Opponent

   (c) Foe   (d) Ally

28. (a) POCG   (b) KLIZ

   (c) BUDX   (d) FQMV

29. (a) Farmer   (b) Blacksmith

   (c) Cobbler   (d) Helper

30. Which one of the following diagram represents the correct relationship among

   Professor, Male and Female.

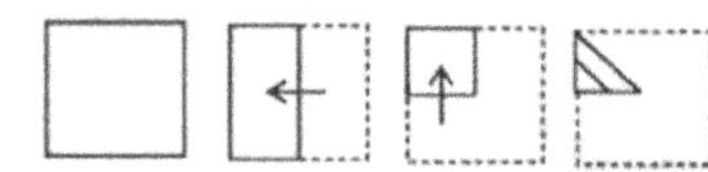

31. A's birthday is on Friday 30th June. Find the day of the week on which B's birthday in the same year if B was born 15th November ?

   (a) Tuesday   (b) Wednesday

   (c) Monday   (d) Sunday

32. A piece of paper is folded and cut. From the figures given, indicate how it will appear when opened

33. Which answer figure will complete the pattern in the following question figure?

(a) 

(b) 

(c) 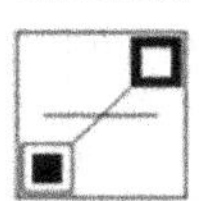

(d) 

34. Which one of the following diagram represents the correct relationship among

Pink, Blue and Fruit.

(a) 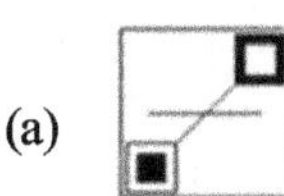

(b) 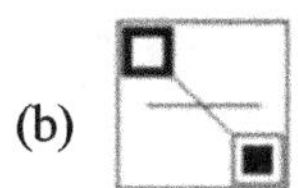

(c) 

(d)

35. Which one of the following diagram represents the correct relationship among

Brain, Cerebrum, Liver and Human body.

(a)

(b)

(c)

(d)

36. Which figure completes the statement?

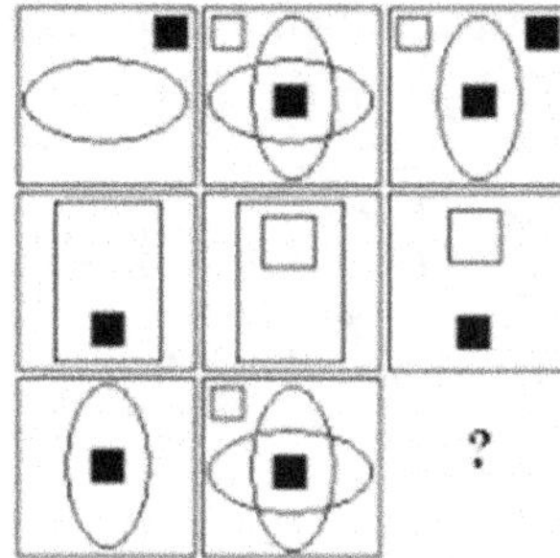

(a)

(b)

(c)

(d)

37. Look at the patterns in the squares and understand their relationship to one another so as to fill in the square with missing symbols.

(a) 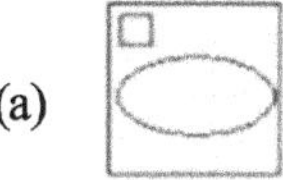

(b) 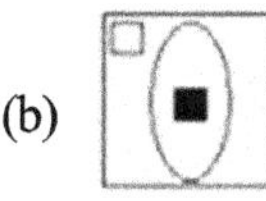

(c) 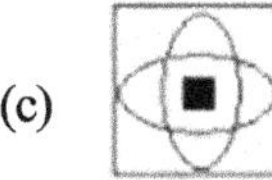

(d)

38. Replace '?' by the appropriate figure from the given options.

(a) 

(b) 

(c) 

(d) 

39. Which answer figure will complete the question figure?

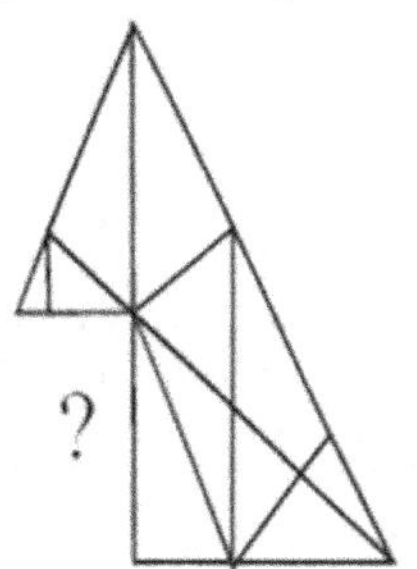

(a) 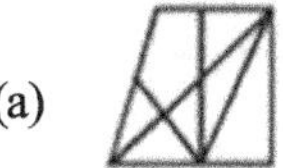

(b) 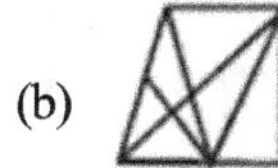

(c) 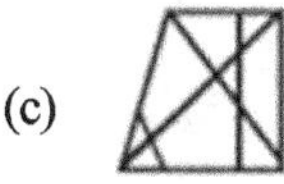

(d) 

40. Which answer figure will complete the question figure?

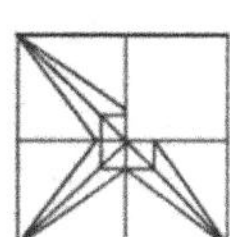

(a) 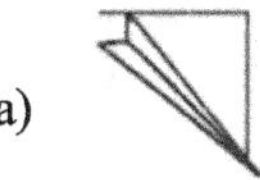

(b) 

(c) 

(d) 

DIRECTIONS (Qs. 41-43): *Complete the series of figures, by selecting correct answer figure from the given responses.*

41. **Question Figures:**

Answer Figures:

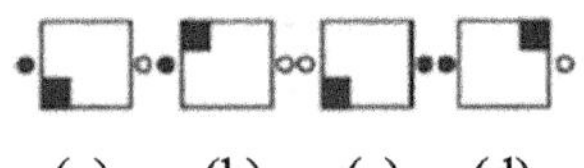

(a) (b) (c) (d)

42. **Question Figures:**

Answer Figures:

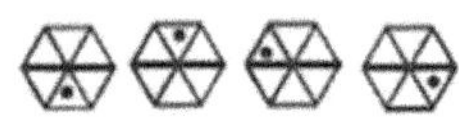

(a) (b) (c) (d)

43. **Question Figures:**

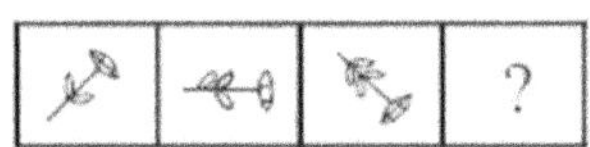

Answer Figures:

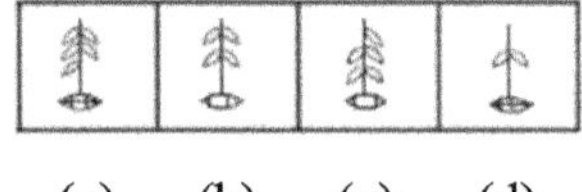

(a) (b) (c) (d)

DIRECTIONS (Qs. 44-46): *Choose a right figure from the set of answer figures which would replace the question mark (?)*

44. **Question Figures:**

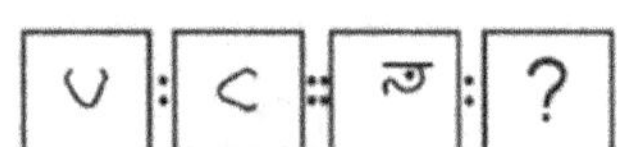

Answer Figures:

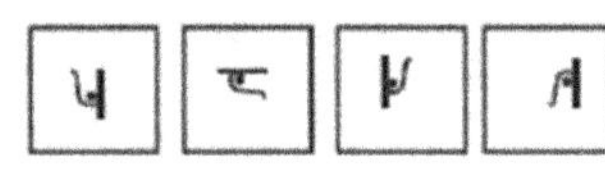

(a) (b) (c) (d)

45. **Question Figures:**

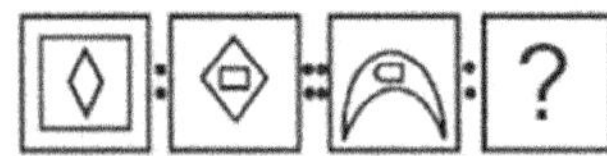

Answer Figures:

(a) (b) (c) (d)

46. **Question Figures:**

Answer Figures:

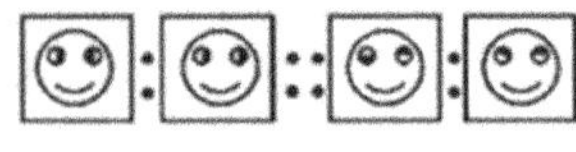

(a) (b) (c) (d)

DIRECTIONS (Qs. 47–48): *In each question below are given some statements followed by two conclusions numbered I and II. You have to take the given statements to be true even if they seem to be at variance with commonly known facts. Read all the conclusions and then decide which of the given conclusions logically follows/follow from the given statements, disregarding commonly known facts.*

Give answer

 (a) If only conclusion I follows.

 (b) If only conclusion II follows.

 (c) If either conclusion I or II follows.

 (d) If neither conclusion I nor II follows.

47. **Statements:**

All shirts are skirts.

No skirt is top.

All tops are kurta.

Conclusions:

I. All shirts are kurta

II. Some kurta are skirts.

48. **Statements:**

All September are October.

No October is November.

No November is December.

Conclusions:

I. Some September are not Novembers

II. No October is December.

DIRECTIONS (Qs. 49-50): *In each of the following questions, you are given a figure (X) followed by four alternative figures (1), (2), (3) and (4) such that figure (X) is embedded in one of them. Trace out the alternative figure which contains fig. (X) as its part.*

49. Find out the alternative figure which contains figure (X) as its part.

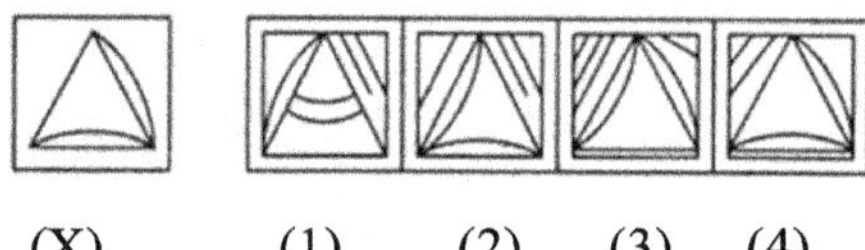

 (X) (1) (2) (3) (4)

(a) 1   (b) 2

(c) 3   (d) 4

50. Find out the alternative figure which contains figure (X) as its part.

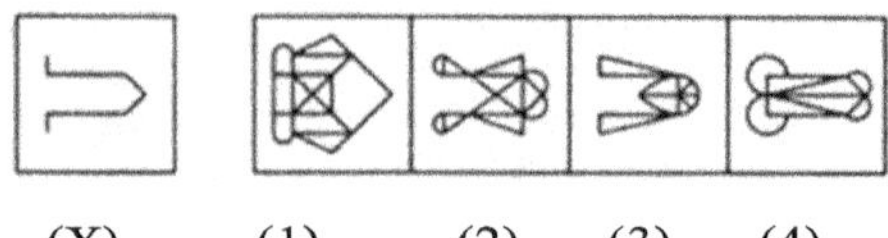

 (X) (1) (2) (3) (4)

(a) 1   (b) 2

(c) 3   (d) 4

VERBAL ABILITY

DIRECTIONS (Qs. 51-53): *Out of the four alternatives, choose the one which best expresses the meaning of the given word.*

51. POLTROON
    - (a) Pusillanimous
    - (b) Gallant
    - (c) Gutsy
    - (d) Wearied

52. ROSTRUM
    - (a) Guardian
    - (b) Podium
    - (c) Device
    - (d) Scheme

53. PROROGUE
    - (a) Adjourn
    - (b) Convene
    - (c) Rally
    - (d) Continue

DIRECTIONS (Qs. 54-56): *In the following questions, choose the word opposite in meaning to the given word.*

54. LUCRE
    - (a) Debt
    - (b) Elegance
    - (c) Outlaw
    - (d) Sissy

55. RABBLE
    - (a) Rag
    - (b) Nobility
    - (c) Scanty
    - (d) Sanction

56. COTERIE
    - (a) Loner
    - (b) Socialize
    - (c) Elite
    - (d) Indecent

DIRECTIONS (Qs. 57-60): *In the following question, some part of the sentence may have errors. Find out which part of the sentence has an error and select the appropriate option. If a sentence is free from error, select 'No Error'.*

57. It was being hard to believe (A)/that my brother could be (B)/involved in anything so sinister. (C)/No error(D)
    - (a) A
    - (b) C
    - (c) C
    - (d) D

58. The average age at which (A)/people die of heart diseases (B)/are decreasing. (C)/No error (D)
    - (a) A
    - (b) B
    - (c) C
    - (d) D

59. Hardly had I stepped (A)/out of my house when (B)/I saw them coming towards my house. (C)/No error(D)
    - (a) A
    - (b) B
    - (c) C
    - (d) D

60. The last Mughal emperor was (A)/send into exile (B)/by the British. (C)/ No error (D).
    - (a) A
    - (b) B
    - (c) C
    - (d) D

DIRECTIONS (Qs. 61-63): *Read the passage carefully and choose the best answer to each question out of the four alternatives.*

In the world have we made health an end in itself? We have forgotten that health is really a means to enable a person to do his work and do it well. A lot of modern medicine is concerned with promotion of good health. Many patients as well as many physicians pay very little attention to health; but very much attention to health makes some people imagine that they are ill. Our great concern with health is shown by the medical columns in newspaper, the health articles in popular magazines and the popularity of the Television programme and all those books on medicine we talk about health all the time. Yet for the most only result is more people with imaginary illnesses. The healthy man should not be wasting any time talking about health, he should be using health for work, the work he does and the work that good health makes possible.

61. Modern medicine is primarily concerned with:
    - (a) promotion of good health
    - (b) people suffering from imaginary illnesses
    - (c) people suffering from real illnesses
    - (d) increased efficiency in work

62. A healthy man should be concerned with:
    - (a) his work which good health makes possible
    - (b) looking after his health
    - (c) his health which makes work possible
    - (d) talking about health

63. Our great concern with health is shown by?
    - (a) free medicine distribution in hospitals
    - (b) free education to medical students
    - (c) taking yoga classes
    - (d) the health articles in popular magazines

DIRECTIONS (Qs. 64-67): *In the following questions four alternatives are given for idioms/phrases in now. Choose the one that best expresses the meaning of the given idiom/phrase.*

64. Brain sauce
    - (a) Foolish
    - (b) Wisdom
    - (c) Mentally ill
    - (d) Head full of thoughts

65. Lynch law
    - (a) Law imposed by the government
    - (b) Law of the mob
    - (c) A law that is supposed to be useless
    - (d) A rule that no one follows

66. Globetrotters
    - (a) Travellers around the world
    - (b) Sick people in hospital
    - (c) The people living in asylum
    - (d) World champions

67. Dole out
    - (a) Allocate
    - (b) Be effective
    - (c) Turn up
    - (d) Mismanage

DIRECTIONS (Qs. 68-70): *In the following passage some of the words have been left out. Read the passage carefully and select the correct answer for the given blank out of the four alternatives.*

Some scholars, while exploring the forests of America, discovered some buildings that were in ruins. These buildings were **(68)**_________ ruined by encroaching forest. They were remnants of a **(69)**_________ civilization. The scholars got interested. They excavated more and discovered **(70)**___________ their utmost surprise the remains of a flourishing civilization-the Mayas as they named it.

68. (a) reasonably   (b) surely
    (c) apparently   (d) perfectly
69. (a) great   (b) invisible
    (c) static   (d) ordinary
70. (a) at   (b) for
    (c) by   (d) to

DIRECTIONS (Qs. 71-75): *In the following questions, sentences are given with blanks to be filed in with an appropriate word(s). Four alternatives are suggested for each question. Choose the correct alternative out of the four as your answer.*

71. Grandmother has a good memory; she can remember things which __________ many years ago.
    (a) had happened   (b) have happened
    (c) happened   (d) happens to be
72. I _________ her among the crowd just now.
    (a) have glimpsed   (b) had glimpsed
    (c) have been glimpsing   (d) glimpsed
73. Lost time is _________ again, and what we call time enough always proves little enough.
    (a) found never   (b) find never
    (c) never found   (d) never been found
74. To such a degree ___________ that people rebuked him.
    (a) he made a noise   (b) did he make a noise
    (c) he had made a noise   (d) did he make noise
75. I'm going to adopt her as _________ as Julie and I get married.
    (a) sooner   (b) quickly
    (c) earlier   (d) soon

GENERAL AWARENESS

76. In 4 × 100 m race, which nation holds the record?
    (a) Nigeria   (b) USA
    (c) Kenya   (d) Jamaica
77. Which Continent has the largest coastline?
    (a) Asia   (b) North America
    (c) South America   (d) Africa

78. Which game is Geet Sethi associated with?
    (a) Squash   (b) Table Tennis
    (c) Billiards   (d) Golf
79. In which state of India "Than Ta Dance" is related?
    (a) Meghalaya   (b) Manipur
    (c) Assam   (d) Sikkim
80. When our Constitution was adopted?
    (a) 26 November 1949   (b) 26 January 1949
    (c) 26 January 1950   (d) 26 November 1950
81. The Hardest substance on the Earth?
    (a) Iron   (b) Silver
    (c) Diamond   (d) Lead
82. The language of Ashoka's Inscription?
    (a) Sanskrit   (b) Tamil
    (c) Prakrit   (d) Parthian
83. Who was awarded first Bharat Ratana?
    (a) M. Visvesvaraya
    (b) Sarvepalli Radhakrishnan
    (c) Govind Ballabh Pant
    (d) Rajendra Prasad
84. The first Modern Olympic held where and which city?
    (a) France   (b) Britain
    (c) Cuba   (d) Greece
85. Oldest Mountain range in India?
    (a) Himalaya   (b) Aravali
    (c) Satpura   (d) Nilgiri
86. Number of Players in Basket Ball?
    (a) 11   (b) 9
    (c) 7   (d) 5
87. Shuddhi Movement was run by?
    (a) Arya Samaj   (b) Brahmo Samaj
    (c) Prarthana Samaj   (d) None of these
88. ISRO's Satish Bahwan Space Center is located at which place?
    (a) Andhra Pradesh   (b) Telangana
    (c) Tamil Nadu   (d) Odisha
89. The Author of the book "The Golden Threshold"?
    (a) R.K Narayan   (b) Sarojini Naidu
    (c) Jhumpa Lahiri   (d) Arundhati Roy
90. The founder of Stavahana Dynasty?
    (a) Satakarni   (b) Simuka
    (c) Pulumavi   (d) Kanha
91. Who is the Father of the Indian Space Program?
    (a) Vikram Ambalal Sarabhai   (b) A. P. J. Abdul Kalam
    (c) Homi Jehangir Bhabha   (d) Satyendra Nath Bose

92. Uber cup is related to which sport?
    - (a) Cricket
    - (b) Badminton
    - (c) Football
    - (d) Tennis

93. Who is the youngest grandmaster in India?
    - (a) Parimarjan Negi
    - (b) D. Gukesh
    - (c) Krishnan Sasikiran
    - (d) Surya Shekhar

94. From which country India bought C-17 transport aircraft?
    - (a) Iran
    - (b) France
    - (c) USA
    - (d) Germany

95. Asian games maximum number of times?
    - (a) Japan
    - (b) China
    - (c) Thailand
    - (d) India

96. Agra city was founded by -
    - (a) Sikandar Lodhi
    - (b) Babar
    - (c) Akbar
    - (d) Shah Jahan

97. The visible part of the sun is called –
    - (a) Chromosphere
    - (b) Photosphere
    - (c) Corona
    - (d) Core

98. Ozone layer located in which layer -
    - (a) Stratosphere
    - (b) Troposphere
    - (c) Mesosphere
    - (d) Exosphere

99. Who is the chairman of the constitution drafting committee–
    - (a) Alladi Krishnaswami Ayyar
    - (b) N. Gopalaswami
    - (c) B.R. Ambedkar
    - (d) K.M Munshi

100. UN was established on?
    - (a) 1944
    - (b) 1945
    - (c) 1942
    - (d) 1946

ANSWER KEY

1	(a)	11	(d)	21	(b)	31	(b)	41	(c)	51	(a)	61	(a)	71	(c)	81	(c)	91	(a)
2	(c)	12	(c)	22	(a)	32	(c)	42	(d)	52	(b)	62	(a)	72	(d)	82	(c)	92	(b)
3	(b)	13	(c)	23	(b)	33	(c)	43	(c)	53	(a)	63	(d)	73	(c)	83	(c)	93	(b)
4	(a)	14	(c)	24	(a)	34	(d)	44	(b)	54	(a)	64	(b)	74	(b)	84	(d)	94	(c)
5	(d)	15	(c)	25	(b)	35	(d)	45	(d)	55	(b)	65	(b)	75	(d)	85	(b)	95	(a)
6	(a)	16	(b)	26	(d)	36	(b)	46	(d)	56	(a)	66	(a)	76	(d)	86	(d)	96	(b)
7	(d)	17	(b)	27	(d)	37	(a)	47	(d)	57	(a)	67	(a)	77	(a)	87	(a)	97	(b)
8	(a)	18	(b)	28	(d)	38	(c)	48	(a)	58	(c)	68	(c)	78	(c)	88	(a)	98	(a)
9	(b)	19	(c)	29	(d)	39	(c)	49	(d)	59	(d)	69	(a)	79	(b)	89	(b)	99	(c)
10	(c)	20	(b)	30	(a)	40	(b)	50	(b)	60	(b)	70	(d)	80	(a)	90	(b)	100	(b)

HINTS & SOLUTIONS

1. (a)

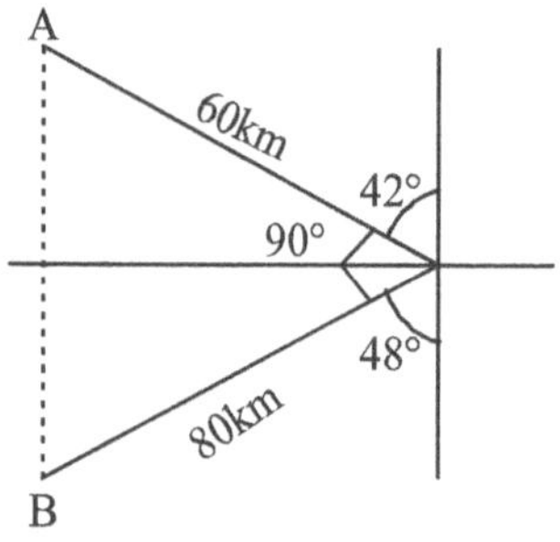

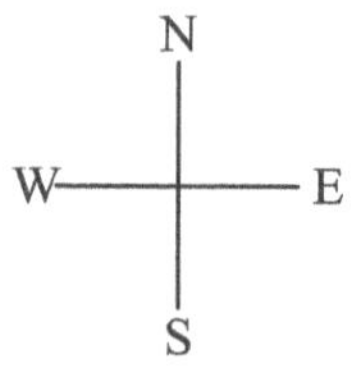

Distance travelled by A in one hour = 60 km

Distance travelled by B in one hour = 80 km

Angle between them = 90°

Using Pythagoras theorm.

Distance between A & B after one hour = $\sqrt{60^2+80^2}$

$= \sqrt{3600+6400}$

$= \sqrt{10000}$

$= 100\text{km}.$

2. (c) Total age of students who promoted in class VIII is = n. Y years.

When 3 more students included this college.

$= n.Y + Y - 1 + Y - 2 + Y + 3$

$= ny + 3y$

After two years when they are in X^{th} total age

$= n(Y+2) + 3(Y+2)$

$\text{Avg age} = \dfrac{n(Y+2)+3(Y+2)}{(n+3)}$

$= \dfrac{(n+3)(Y+2)}{n+3} = Y+2$

3. (b)

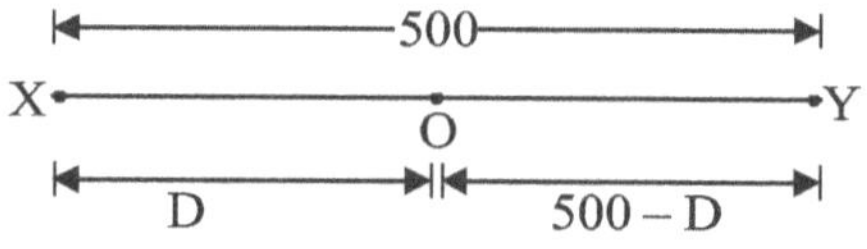

Suppose they meet at point 'O' at the same time

$\text{Time} = \dfrac{D}{20} = \dfrac{(500-D)}{30}$

$\Rightarrow$ $30D = (500-D) \times 20$

$\Rightarrow$ $50D = 500 \times 20$

$D = 200\text{ km}$

Both the train meet 200 km from point 'X'.

4. (a) Total Rain fall of 12 months = $2.7 \times 12 = 32.4$

Total Rain fall of first 7 months = $7 \times (2.7 - 1.1) = 11.2$

Rain fall of last month

$= 32.4 - (11.2 + 20.3)$

$= 32.4 - 31.5$

$= 0.9$

5. (d)

X	:	Y	:	Z
4	:	3	:	8

$\dfrac{4k-2}{3k} = \dfrac{3}{3}$

$4k - 2 = 3k$

$k = 2$

Initially monkey = $(4+3+8)k = 15k = 15 \times 2 = 30$

6. (a) According to question,

	A	:	B
Efficiency	5	:	1
Time	1	:	5

$5x - x = 60$

$4x = 60$

$x = 15$

Time take by A = 15 days

B = 75 days

7. (d) CP = 1564 + 1564 = 3128

$$SP = \frac{1564 \times 123}{100} + \frac{1564 \times 77}{100}$$

$$= \frac{1564 \times 200}{100} = 3128$$

CP = S.P

So, no profit no loss.

8. (a) Let the monthly income of B be Rs. x.

Then, Monthly income of A = Rs. 2x and

Saving of A = 5000 × 4/(4 + 1)

= Rs. 4000

Saving of B = Rs. 1000

Now, we have

(2x − 4000)/(x − 1000) = 5/3

=> 6x − 12000 = 5x − 5000

x = Rs. 7000

So, Monthly income of B = 7000

9. (b) $M_1 D_1 H_1 = M_2 D_2 H_2$

Required no. of men = (240 × 5 × 20)/(8 × 10)

= 300

10. (c) Let the M.P. be Rs. 100.

We know S.P = (100−40) = Rs. 60

and C. P. = 60 × 100/(100−30) = Rs. 600/7 = 85.7

So, Required % profit = (100−85.7)/85.7 × 100

= 14.3/85.7 × 100 = 16.68%

11. (d) Let the number of officers be x.

∵ 5000×500 = 14000x + 4000(500−x)

∴ 2500000 = 14000x + 2000000 − 4000x

∴ x = 500000/10000 = 50

12. (c) Let the cost price be Rs. 100.

∵ S.P × 50/100 = 100 × (60)/100

∴ S.P = (60×100)50

= Rs. 120

∴ Required % profit = (120 − 100)/100 × 100 = 20%

13. (c) Let the number of white balls be x.

∴ Number of red balls = (10 − x)

∴ 10 × 28 = x × 30 + 25 (10 − x)

⇒ 280 = 30x + 250 − 25x

= 280 = 5x + 250

⇒ 5x = 280 − 250 = 30

⇒ x = 6

So, The number of white balls = 6

14. (c) ∴ 8 men = 17 women

$$\Rightarrow 12 \text{ men} \equiv \frac{17}{8} \times 12 = \frac{51}{2} \text{ women}$$

∴ 12 men + 24 women

$$= \frac{51}{2} + 24 = \frac{99}{2} \text{ women}$$

By $\dfrac{M_1 D_1}{W_1} = \dfrac{M_2 D_2}{W_2}$

$$\Rightarrow \frac{17 \times 33}{1} = \frac{99 \times D_2}{2 \times 3}$$

$$D_2 = \frac{17 \times 33 \times 6}{99} = 34 \text{ days}$$

15. (c) Difference = $\dfrac{Pr^2}{(100)^2}$

$$\Rightarrow 100 = \frac{P \times 5 \times 5}{100 \times 100}$$

$$\Rightarrow \frac{P}{400} = 100$$

$$\Rightarrow P = Rs. 40000$$

16. (b) Expression:

$$= 2\sqrt{2} + \sqrt{2} + \frac{1}{2 + \sqrt{2}} + \frac{1}{\sqrt{2} - 2}$$

$$= 2\sqrt{2} + \sqrt{2} + \left(\frac{1}{2 + \sqrt{2}} + \frac{1}{\sqrt{2} - 2} \right)$$

$$= 2\sqrt{2} + \sqrt{2} + \left(\frac{-2 + \sqrt{2} + 2 + \sqrt{2}}{\left(2 + \sqrt{2}\right)\left(\sqrt{2} - 2\right)} \right)$$

$$= 2\sqrt{2} + \sqrt{2} + \frac{2\sqrt{2}}{2-4}$$

$$= 2\sqrt{2} + \sqrt{2} - \sqrt{2} = 2\sqrt{2}$$

$$= 2 \times 1.4142 = 2.8284$$

17. (b) Let x kg of nickel be mixed.

$$\therefore \frac{20+x}{100+x} = \frac{3}{11}$$

$$\Rightarrow 220 + 11x = 300 + 3x$$

$$\Rightarrow 11x - 3x = 300 - 220$$

$$\Rightarrow 8x = 80$$

$$\Rightarrow x = 10\,kg$$

18. (b) Let the ages of Ram and Rahim 10 years ago be x and 3x years respectively.

After 5 years from now,

$$\Rightarrow \frac{x+15}{3x+15} = \frac{2}{3}$$

$$\Rightarrow 6x + 30 = 3x + 45$$

$$\Rightarrow 3x = 45 - 30 \Rightarrow 3x = 15$$

$$\Rightarrow x = 5$$

∴ Ratio of their present ages

$$= (x+10) : (3x+10)$$

$$= 15 : 25 = 3 : 5$$

19. (c) As, Microphone makes sound louder. Similarly, Microscope makes the object magnified.

20. (b) Sound requires medium to travel and light can travel in vacuum.

21. (b) Country and its type of governance.

22. (a) B L E F

23. (b) We get education in school, Similarly Treatment is done in hospital.

24. (a) $5^3 = 125$

$7^3 = 343$

25. (b) In all other pairs, the two words are antonyms of each other.

26. (d) In all other pairs, second is a collective group of the first.

27. (d) Ally is different in nature.

28. (d) FQMV is different because there is no vowel in word.

29. (d) Helper may be of any profession.

30. (a)

31. (b) According to question,

Required day $= (31 + 31 + 30 + 31 + 15) \div 7 = 5$ days

Hence, B's birthday was on 5 days later of A's birthday

Hence, Wednesday is the required day.

32. (c) **33. (c)** **34. (d)** **35. (d)** **36. (b)**

37. (a)

38. (c) Similar figure reappears in every fourth step and each time a figure reappears, it rotates through 90°ACW.

39. (c) **40. (b)** **41. (c)** **42. (d)** **43. (c)**

44. (b) **45. (d)** **46. (d)**

47. (d) 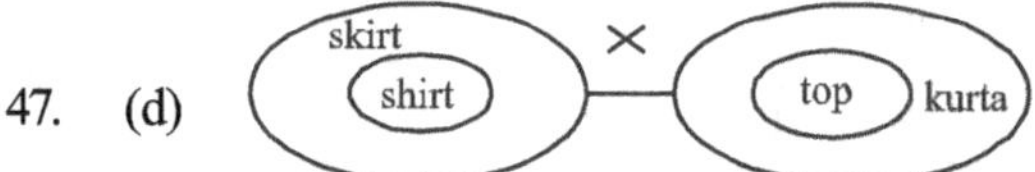

So neither conclusion I nor II follows.

48. (a) 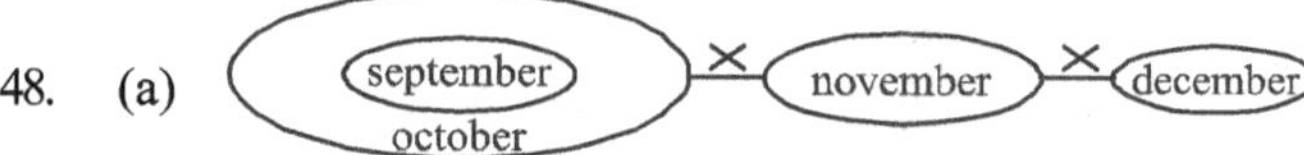

So only conclusion I follows.

49. (d) 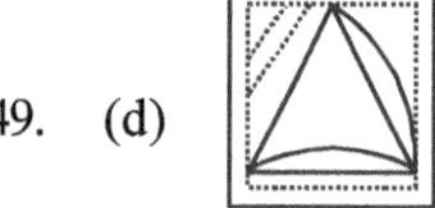

50. (b) 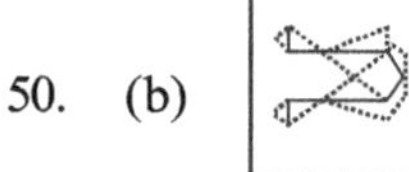

51. (a) Poltroon: having or showing a shameful lack of courage.

Pusillanimous: showing a lack of courage or determination; timid.

Gutsy: having or showing courage, determination, and spirit.

Hence Poltroon and Pusillanimous are synonyms to each other.

52. (b) Rostrum: a level usually raised surface.

Podium: a small platform on which a person may stand to be seen by an audience.

Hence Rostrum and Podium are synonyms to each other.

53. (a) Prorogue: to bring to a formal close for a period of time.

Adjourn: break off (a meeting, legal case, or game) with the intention of resuming it later.

Convene: come or bring together for a meeting or activity.

Hence Prorogue and Adjourn are synonyms to each other.

54. (a) Lucre: monetary gain.

Debt: a sum of money that is owed or due.

Outlaw: a person who has broken the law.

Sissy: a person regarded as effeminate or cowardly.

Hence 'Debt' is the correct antonym.

55. (b) Rabble: a disorderly crowd; a mob.

Nobility: the quality of being noble in character; integrity.

Hence 'Nobility' is the correct antonym.

56. (a) Coterie: a small group of people with shared interests or tastes, especially one that is exclusive of other people.

Loner: a person that prefers not to associate with others.

Hence 'Loner' is the correct antonym.

57. (a) "Being" should be removed because two forms of "be" in a complement should not be used.

58. (c) When we talk about "age" and if we need to talk about the context related to lessening, the word "reduce" should be used.

59. (d) No Error

60. (b) As the sentence is in passive and in passive voice structured sentence, we use "be + v3" and the 3rd form of "send" is "sent" thus "sent" should be used in place of "send".

61. (a) Refer to, "A lot of modern medicine is concerned with promotion of good health."

62. (a) Refer to, "The healthy man should not be wasting any time talking about health, he should be using health for work, the work he does and the work that good health makes possible.

63. (d) Refer to, "Our great concern with health is shown by the medical columns in newspaper, the health articles in popular magazines and the popularity of the Television programme and all those books on medicine we talk about health all the time".

64. (b) 65. (b) 66. (a) 67. (a) 68. (c)

69. (a) 70. (d)

71. (c) Subject + V2(past form of verb) + Object……………..+ ago.

72. (d) When 'just now' means a very short time ago. It takes past form of the verb i.e. V2.

73. (c) 'Never', 'Seldom', 'Always' are used before the 'Main verb'. Also the sentence is in 'passive voice'. Hence option C is the correct choice.

74. (b) Sentences beginning with 'To such a point, 'To such a degree', 'To such an extent' take inversion form i.e. "To such a degree + H.V. (auxiliary) + Subject + M.V."

Moreover 'make a noise' is the correct idiomatic expression not 'make noise'.

75. (d) Soon means 'a short time after then' i.e. in or after a short time.

Early means 'near the beginning of a period of time we are talking about'. Early does not mean soon. Moreover, comparative degree is not needed.

While we use quickly to refer to the speed with which something is done.

Hence option D is the correct choice.

76. (d)

77. (a) Asia, the largest continent, stretches from the eastern Mediterranean Sea to the western Pacific Ocean. There are more than 40 countries in Asia. Some are among the most-populated countries in the world, including China, India, and Indonesia.

78. (c) 79. (b) 80. (a) 81. (c)

82. (c) Prakrit, Greek, and Aramaic

83. (c) Rajagopalachari, Sarvepalli Radhakrishnan, C. V. Raman were awarded the Bharat Ratana Award in the year 1954, after the effect of the constitution.

84. (d) In 1896, the first modern Olympic was played in Athens, Greece.

85. (b) The Aravalli Range is the oldest range of fold mountains in India. The estimated age of Aravalli Range according to geologists is about 350 million years. As for now the Aravalli Range of mountains is approximately 692 km in the north–west part of India. It starts from Delhi and pass through southern Haryana and across the states of Rajasthan which ends in Gujarat.

86. (d) Basketball is a team sport in which two teams, most commonly of five players each, opposing one another on a rectangular court. The only major sport strictly of U.S. origin, basketball was invented by James Naismith (1861–1939) on or about December 1, 1891.

87. (a) Arya samaj was founded by the sannyasi Dayanand Saraswati on 10 April 1875. Members of the Arya Samaj believe in one God and reject the worship of idols. It is an Indian Hindu reform movement.

88. (a) Sriharikota is a barrier island off the Bay of Bengal coast located in the Nellore district of Andhra Pradesh, India. It houses the Satish Dhawan Space Centre, one of the two satellite launch centres in India.

89. (b)

90. (b) Simuka was an Indian king belonging to the Satavahana dynasty. He is mentioned as the first king in a list of royals in a Satavahana inscription at Nanaghat.

91. (a) Vikram Ambalal Sarabhai was an Indian scientist and innovator widely regarded as the father of India's space programme. Sarabhai received the Shanti Swarup Bhatnagar Medal in 1962. The nation honoured him by awarding Padma Bhushan in 1966 and Padma Vibhushan in 1972.

92. (b)

93. (b) As per the latest data of the World Chess Federation; D. Gukesh has become India's youngest Grandmasters at 12 years, 7 months and 17 days with this achievement, Gukesh has overtaken Praggnanandhaa who held the record at 12 years and 10 months in June 2018.

94. (c) 95. (c)

96. (a) Modern Agra was founded by Sikandar Lodhi in the 16th century. Emperor Akbar built the Agra fort and Fatehpur Sikri near Agra.

97. (b) The boundary between the Sun's interior and the solar atmosphere is called the photosphere. It is what we see as the visible "surface" of the Sun.

98. (a) Stratosphere extends upwards from the tropopause to about 50 km. It contains much of the ozone in the atmosphere. The increase in temperature with height occurs because of absorption of ultraviolet (UV) radiation from the sun by this ozone.

99. (c) The Drafting Committee had seven members: Alladi Krishnaswami Ayyar, N. Gopalaswami; B.R. Ambedkar, K.M Munshi, Mohammad Saadulla, B.L. Mitter and D.P. Khaitan. At its first meeting on 30th August 1947, the Drafting Committee elected B.R Ambedkar as its Chairman.

100. (b)

AIR FORCE COMMON ADMISSION TEST (AFCAT) II/2018

(Held on 18ᵗʰ Aug.- 2018) (Based on Memory)

Instructions for candidates

TIME ALLOTTED – 2 HRS.

1. Total No. of Questions–100. Each Question is of three marks.
2. One mark will be deducted for every wrong answer.

NUMERICAL ABILITY

1. The difference between compound interest and simple interest accrued on an amount at the end of 3rd year at a rate of 10% is 77.5 rupees. What is amount?
   - (a) 2600
   - (b) 2500
   - (c) 2800
   - (d) 2950

2. A person sells two horses for rupees 1200/ each. On the first at a profit of 20% and second at a loss of 20%. The overall profit/loss in percentage is__ ?
   - (a) 4% loss
   - (b) 4% profit
   - (c) 5% loss
   - (d) 5% profit

3. The average of 5/16 and 3/8 is__?
   - (a) 0.5425
   - (b) 0.2585
   - (c) 0.3475
   - (d) 0.4385

4. Efficiency of A, B and C is in the ratio 4:5:6. What is the ratio of the time in which they complete the work?
   - (a) 5:4:3
   - (b) 15:12:10
   - (c) 15:10:12
   - (d) 10:12:15

5. Someone purchase 5 dozen of egg in ₹ 100. Out of which 20% eggs were found broken. At what rate he should sell eggs so that he gets 10% profit?
   - (a) 2.29
   - (b) 3.25
   - (c) 2.75
   - (d) 3.75

6. A bank give 16% interest per annum compounded semi annually. What interest a man get on amount of ₹ 10000 in 2 years?
   - (a) 12665
   - (b) 13205
   - (c) 14515
   - (d) 13605

7. Find the value of $\sqrt{0.0081} + \sqrt{0.0064}$?
   - (a) 0.27
   - (b) 0.7
   - (c) 0.17
   - (d) 0.4

8. Find the value of $216^{0.16} \times 16^{0.18}$?
   - (a) 4
   - (b) 6
   - (c) 8
   - (d) 2

9. If there is 25% increase in the cost of sugar by what % consumption should be decreased in order to maintain expenditure?
   - (a) 25%
   - (b) 20%
   - (c) 32.5%
   - (d) 15%

10. Average marks of a class are 70. If average marks of fail students are 40 and pass students are 80 marks. Find percentage of pass students?
    - (a) 25%
    - (b) 50%
    - (c) 65%
    - (d) 75%

11. The population of a village increase 5% per annum. It's population at the end of 2016 was 1852200. What was its population in 2014?
    - (a) 1680000
    - (b) 1640000
    - (c) 1720000
    - (d) 1560000

12. 250 ml of mixture contains milk and water in the ratio of 7:2. How much more milk must be added to get a new mixture containing milk and water in the ratio of 4:1?
    - (a) 50 ml
    - (b) 42 ml
    - (c) 28 ml
    - (d) 32 ml

13. The average age of 25 students is 16 years. If a teacher is added the average age becomes 18 years. What is the age of teacher?
    - (a) 68 years
    - (b) 62 years
    - (c) 64 years
    - (d) 70 years

14. A and B can do a piece of work in 10 days. B and C can do it in 12 days. A and C can do it in 15 days. How long will A take to do it alone?
    - (a) 20 days
    - (b) 24 days
    - (c) 30 days
    - (d) 40 days

15. If $3^{(a+8)} = 27^{(2a+1)}$, then find 'a'?
    - (a) 1
    - (b) 0
    - (c) −1
    - (d) 0.5

16. A bus started its journey from Pune and reached Mumbai in 44 minutes at its average speed of 50 km/hr. If the average speed of the bus is increased by 5 km/hour, how much time will it take to cover the same distance?
    - (a) 40 minutes
    - (b) 38 minutes
    - (c) 36 minutes
    - (d) 31 minutes

17. The price of onions has been increased by 50% in order to keep the expenditure on onions the same, the percentage of reduction in consumption has to be.
    - (a) 50%
    - (b) $33\frac{1}{3}$
    - (c) 33%
    - (d) 30%

18. The ratio of the numbers of males and females in a club is 5 : 6. If 22 females leave the club, the ratio becomes reversed. The number of males in the club is

   (a) 40   (b) 50

   (c) 55   (d) 60

REASONING AND MILITARY APTITUDE TEST

DIRECTIONS (Qs. 19-21): *Each of the questions below contains three elements. These three elements may or may not have some linkage. Each group of the elements may fit into one of the diagrams at (a), (b), (c) and (d). You have to indicate groups of elements in each of the questions fit into which of the diagrams given below. The letter indicating the diagram is the answer.*

(a) 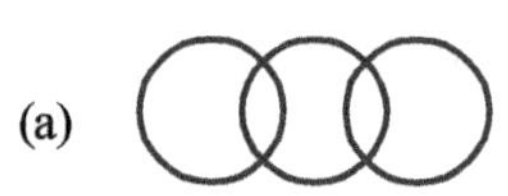   (b) 

(c) 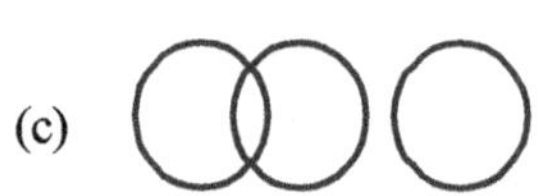   (d) 

19. Brick , House, Bridge
20. Student of law, Student of science, Men
21. Antisocial, Pickpockets, Kidnappers
22. The following diagram represents the students who are singers, dancers and poets.

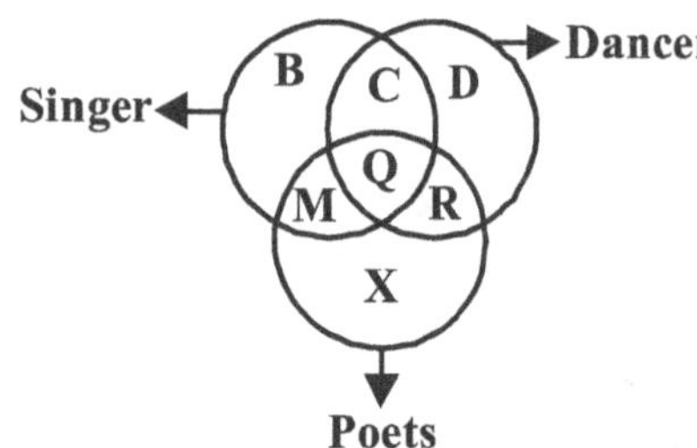

Study the diagram and identify the region which represents the students who are both poets and singers but not dancers.

   (a) B + C + D   (b) M

   (c) Q + R   (d) R + X

DIRECTIONS (Qs. 23-25) : *In each of the following questions find out the alternative which will replace the question mark.*

23. Sheep : Lamb :: Insect : ?

   (a) Cub   (b) Larva

   (c) Bull   (d) Tadpole

24. Monk : Nun :: Bachelor : ?

   (a) Spinster   (b) Woman

   (c) Lady   (d) Man

25. Dark : Fear :: Honesty : ?

   (a) Personality   (b) Money

   (c) Treachery   (d) Trust

DIRECTIONS (Qs. 26-27): *The following questions consist of two words each that have a certain relationship to each other, followed by four pairs of words. Select the pair that has the same relationship as the original pair of words.*

26. Food : Hungry

   (a) Thought : Politics   (b) Water : River

   (c) Rest : Weary   (d) Wine : Intoseication

27. Ampere : Current

   (a) Sound : Waves   (b) Newton : Force

   (c) Speed : Time   (d) Distance : Mile

DIRECTIONS (Qs. 28-30): *Choose the odd man from the words given below in the question.*

28. (a) APRIL   (b) JUNE

   (c) JULY   (d) SEPTEMBER

29. (a) Hill Myna   (b) House Sparrow

   (c) Emerald Dove   (d) Imperial Eagle

30. (a) Anther   (b) Retina

   (c) Ovary   (d) Petal

DIRECTIONS (Qs. 31-32): *In the following question, select the one which is different from the other three responses.*

31. (a) Mason : Wall   (b) Cobbler : Shoe

   (c) Farmer : Crop   (d) Chef : Cook

32. (a) Bottle : Wine   (b) Cup : Tea

   (c) Pitcher : Water   (d) Ball : Bat

33. Identify the figure that will complete the pattern.

   Question Figure

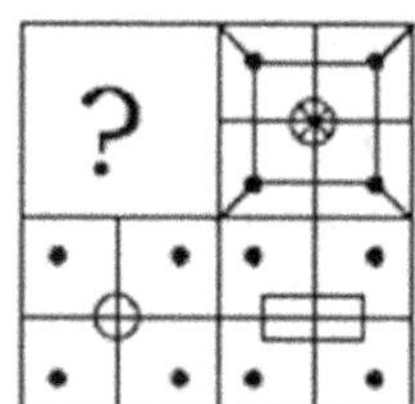

(a) 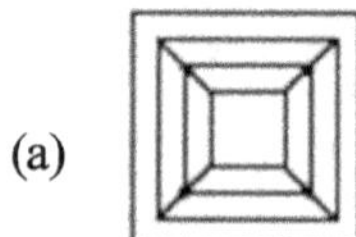   (b) 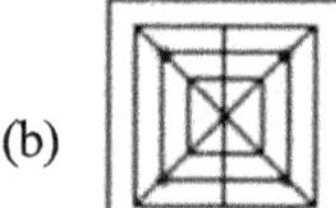

(c) 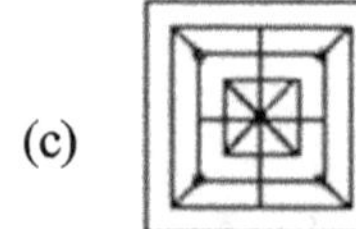   (d) 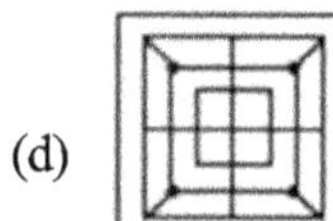

34. In a row of 64 girls, Anu is 17th from the left. Jagrati is 11th to the right of Anu. What is Jagrati's position from the right end of the row?

   (a) 36th   (b) 37th

   (c) 38th   (d) 40th

35. Consider the following figure:

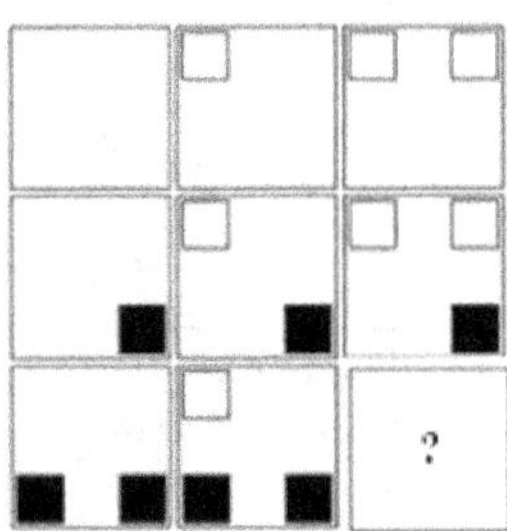

Which of the following alternatives should replace the question mark ?

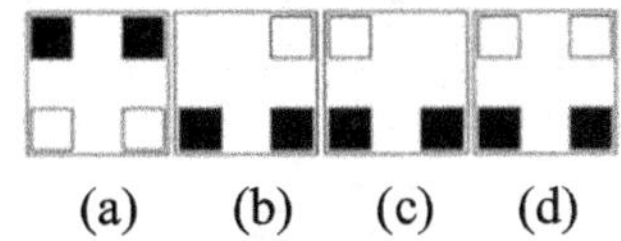

(a)   (b)   (c)   (d)

36. Which figure completes the statement?

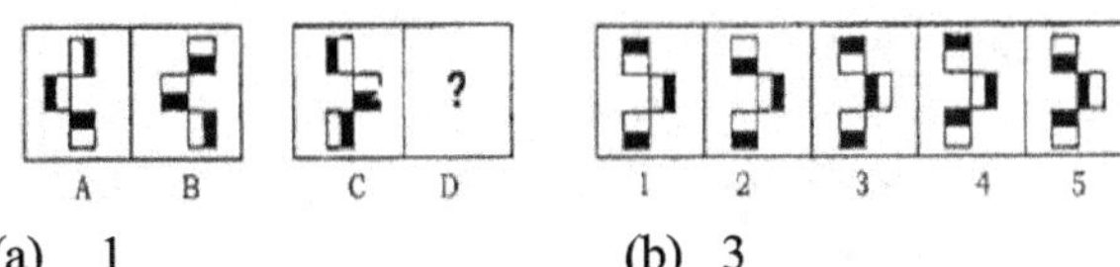

(a) 1   (b) 3
(c) 4   (d) 5

37. Find the missing figure from the given responses.

Question Figures:

Answer Figures:

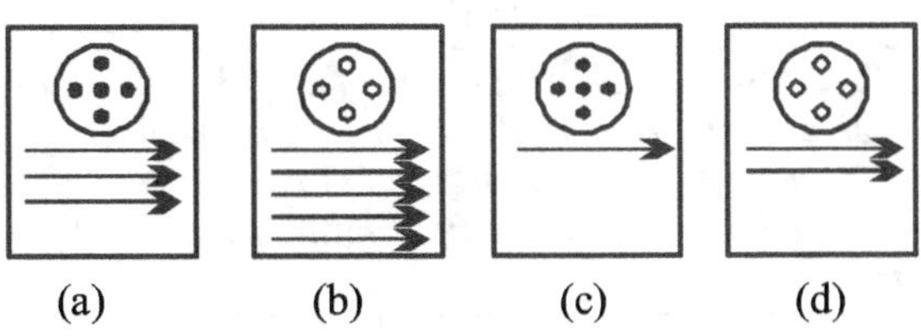

(a)   (b)   (c)   (d)

38. Which one of the Answer Figures shall complete the given question figure?

Question Figures:

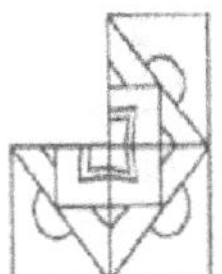

Answer Figures:

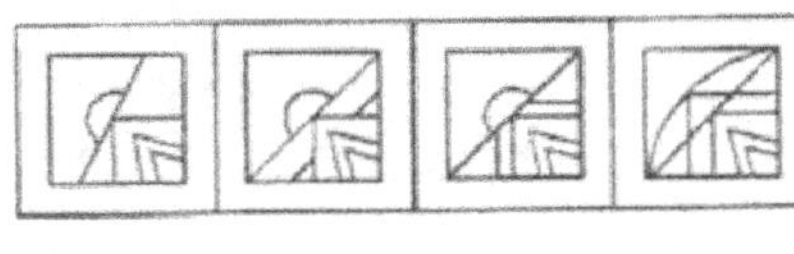

(a)   (b)   (c)   (d)

39. Which answer figure will complete the pattern in the question figure?

Question Figure:

Answer Figure:

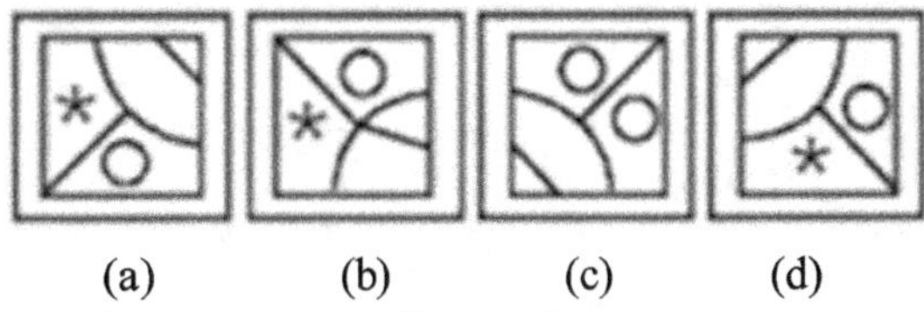

(a)   (b)   (c)   (d)

40. Which answer figure will complete the pattern in the question figure?

Question Figure:

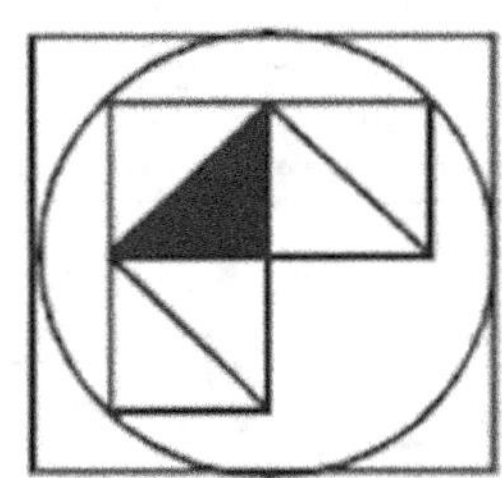

Answer Figure:

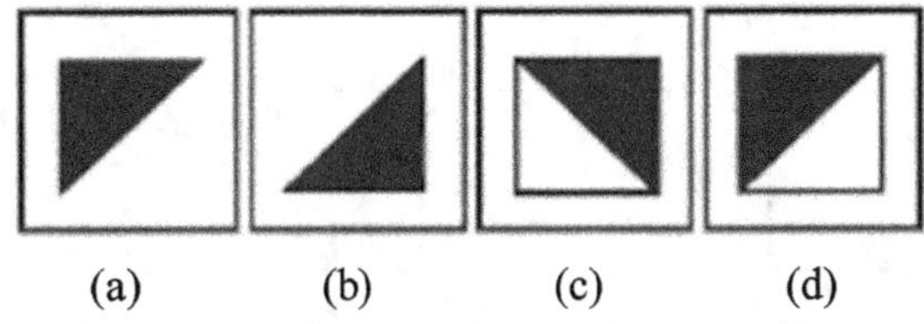

(a)   (b)   (c)   (d)

DIRECTIONS (Qs.41-43): *Find the missing figure in the series from the given answer figures.*

41. **Question Figure:**

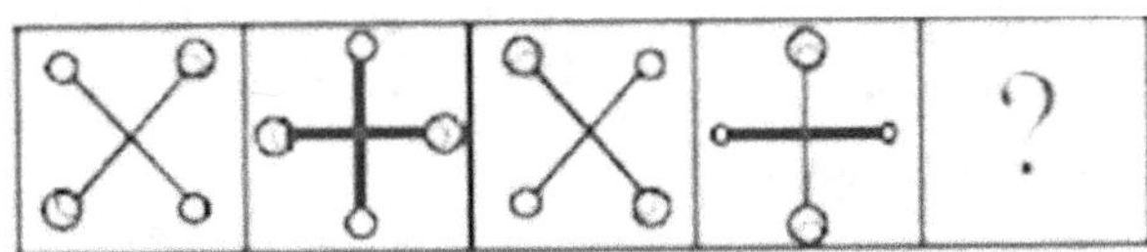

Answer Figure:

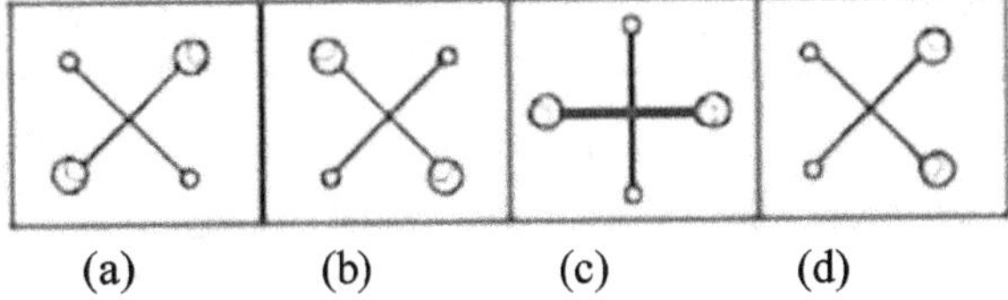

(a)   (b)   (c)   (d)

42. **Question Figure:**

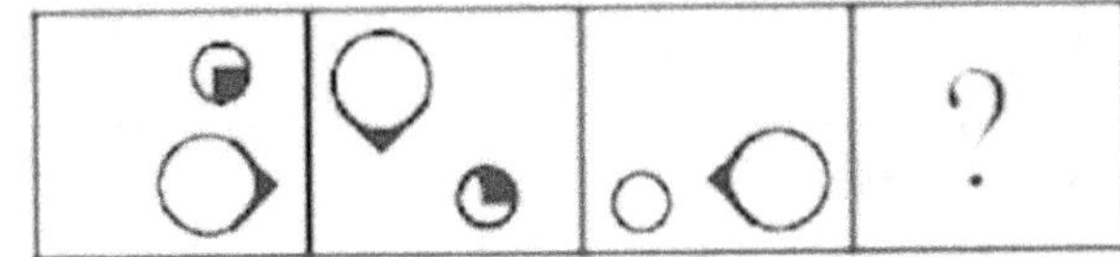

Answer Figure:

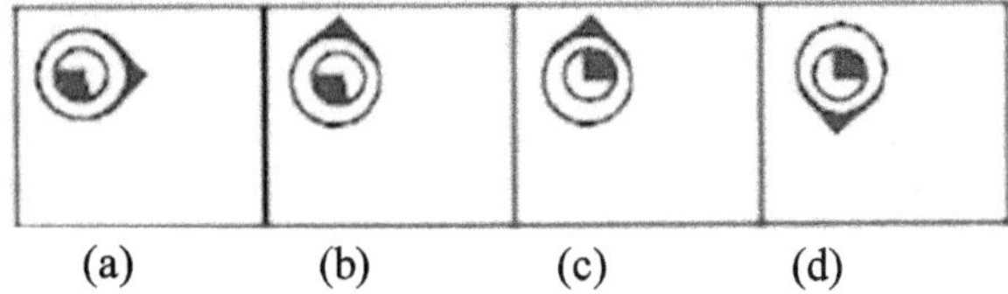

(a)   (b)   (c)   (d)

43. **Question Figure:**

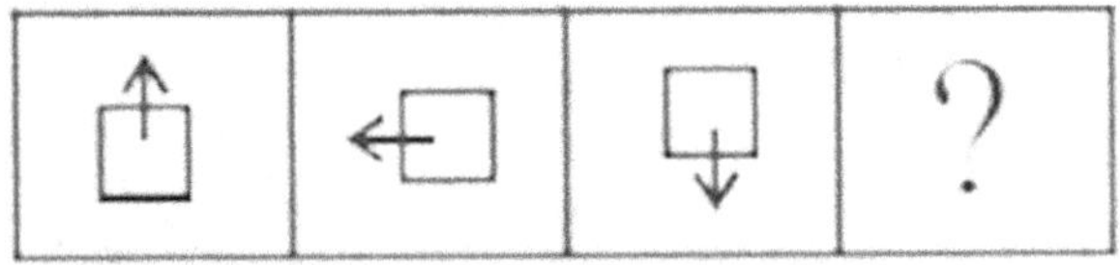

Answer Figure:

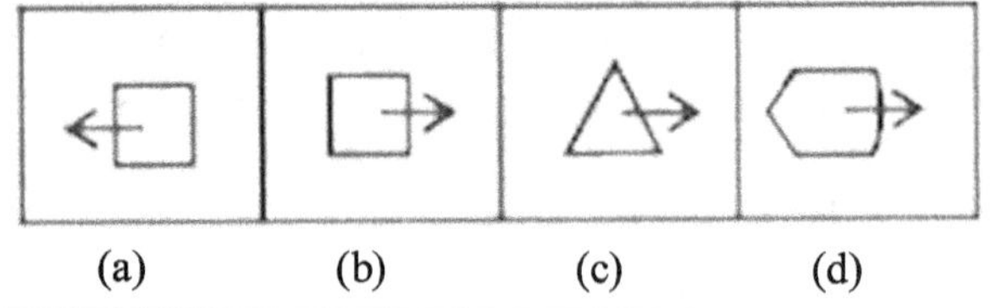

(a)   (b)   (c)   (d)

DIRECTIONS (Qs. 44-46): *Choose a right figure from the set of answer figures which would replace the question mark (?)*

44. **Question Figure:**

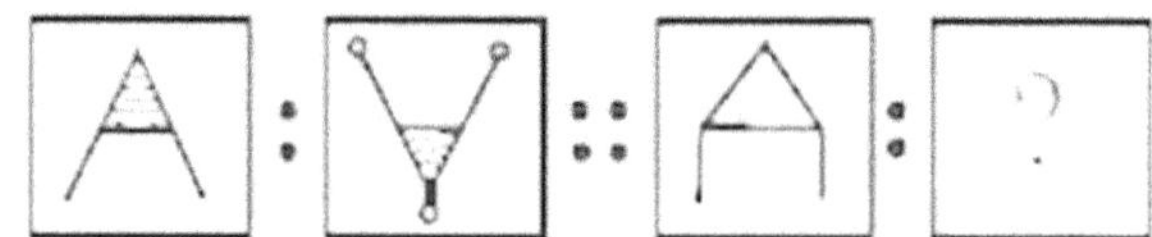

Answer Figure:

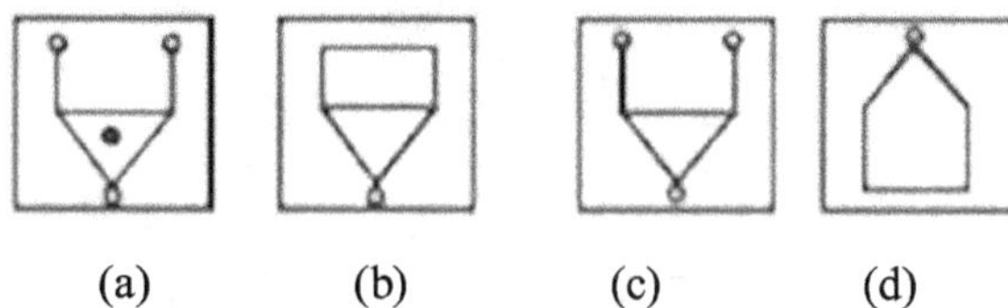

(a)   (b)   (c)   (d)

45. **Question Figure:**

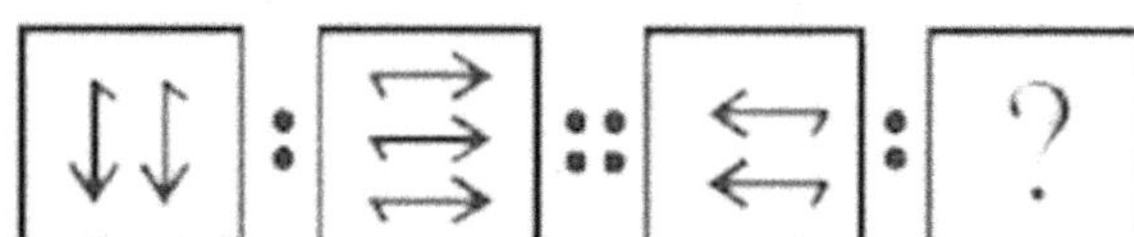

Answer Figure:

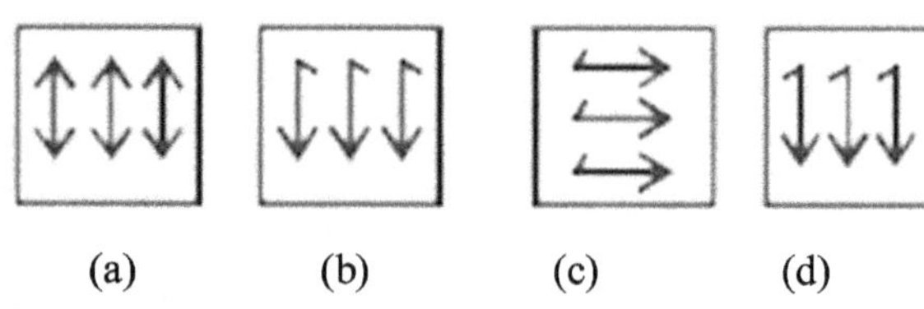

(a)   (b)   (c)   (d)

46. **Question Figure:**

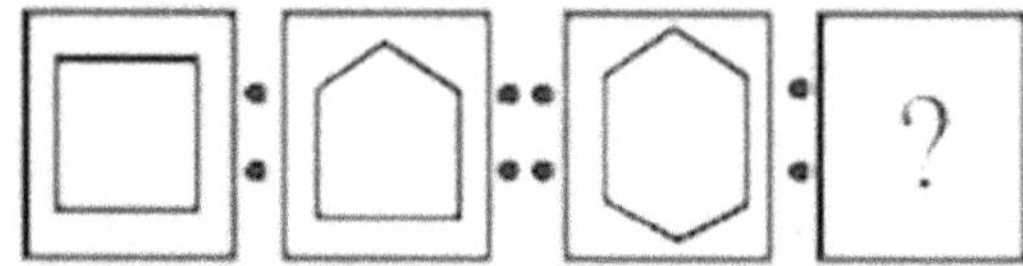

Answer Figure:

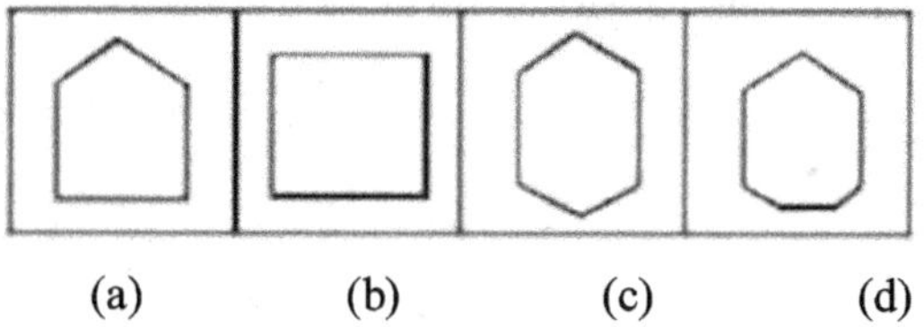

(a)   (b)   (c)   (d)

DIRECTIONS (Qs. 47 - 48): *In this question two/three statements followed by two conclusions numbered I and II have been given. You have to take the given statements to be true even if they seem to be at variance with commonly known facts and then decide which of the given conclusions logically follows the given statements disregarding commonly known facts.*

(a)   Only conclusion I is true
(b)   Neither conclusion I nor II is true
(c)   Only conclusion II is true
(d)   Both conclusions I and II are true

47. **Statement:**
No right is a left.
All up are left.
Some down are up.
Conclusions:
I.   No up is a right.
II.   At least some down are left.

48. **Statements:**
Some cricketers are footballers
All footballers are boxers.
Some boxers are players.
Conclusions:
I.   At least some boxers are cricketers.
II.   No player is a cricketer.

DIRECTIONS (Qs. 49-50): *In each of the following questions, you are given a figure (X) followed by four alternative figures (1), (2), (3) and (4) such that figure (X) is embedded in one of them. Trace out the alternative figure which contains fig. (X) as its part.*

49. Find out the alternative figure which contains figure (X) as its part.

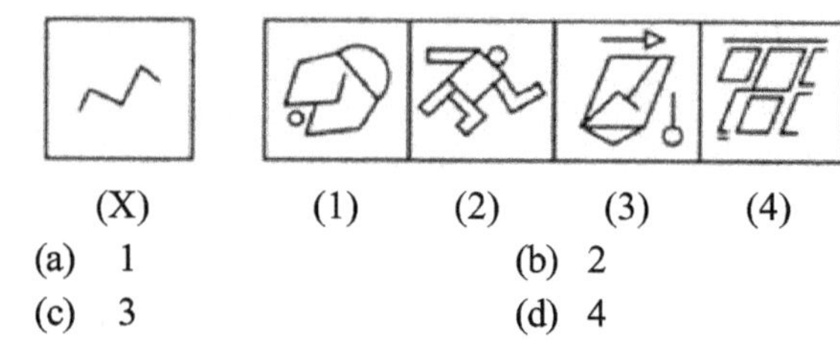

(X)   (1)   (2)   (3)   (4)

(a)   1   (b)   2
(c)   3   (d)   4

50. Find out the alternative figure which contains figure (X) as its part.

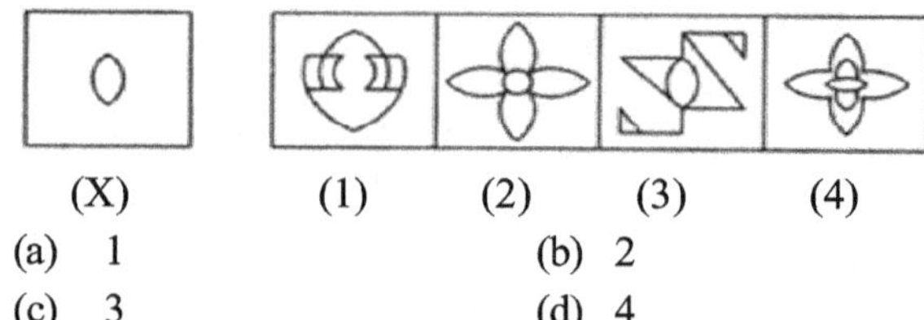

(X)   (1)   (2)   (3)   (4)

(a)   1   (b)   2
(c)   3   (d)   4

VERBALABILITY

DIRECTIONS (Qs. 51-53): *Study the paragraph and answer the questions that follow:*

Judiciary has become the centre of controversy, in the recent past, on account of the sudden 'Me' in the level of judicial intervention. The area of judicial intervention has been steadily expanding through the device of public interest litigation. The judiciary has shed its pro-status-quo approach and taken upon itself the duty to enforce the basic rights of the poor and vulnerable sections of society, by progressive interpretation and positive action. The Supreme Court has developed new methods of dispensing justice to the masses through the public interest litigation. Former Chief Justice PN. Bhagwat, under whose leadership public interest litigation attained a new dimension comments that "the Supreme Court has developed several new commitments. It has carried forward participative justice".

51. The steady expansion of judicial intervention is the result of
    (a) excessive laws
    (b) public interest litigation
    (c) Supreme Court's new methods of dispensing justice
    (d) new commitments of Supreme Court

52. According to the author, judiciary has become the center of controversy because of
    (a) problems arising in dispensing justice in the recent past
    (b) public interest litigation
    (c) sudden 'Me' in the level of judicial intervention
    (d) Supreme Court's supremacy

53. According to Justice PN. Bhagwat, Supreme Court has developed
    (a) judicial intervention
    (b) various new commitments
    (c) participative judicial approach to dispense justice
    (d) public interest litigation

DIRECTIONS (Qs. 54-58): *Given below are sentences with a blank in each. Identify the most suitable alternative among the five given that fits into the blank to make the sentence logical and meaningful.*

54. In the same amount of time it would take me to correct all the ________________ in your report, I could write a better report myself.
    (a) mistakes
    (b) problems
    (c) accuracies
    (d) obstacles

55. I have recently used the services of his ________________ agency to book a cruise in the Mediterranean.
    (a) progress
    (b) deportation
    (c) travel
    (d) transfer

56. They would like local authorities to be given greater ________________ as to how the money is spent.
    (a) affairs
    (b) function
    (c) omission
    (d) discretion

57. In a 10-billion-year-old galaxy there should have been ample ________________ for at least one species to escape its own mess, and to spread across the stars, filling every niche.
    (a) negligence
    (b) opportunity
    (c) surveillance
    (d) supply

58. A true ________________ of the resources involved in sport would include the unpaid labour services.
    (a) growth
    (b) consideration
    (c) guidance
    (d) estimation

DIRECTIONS (Qs. 59-61): *In the following passage some of the words have been left out. Read the passage carefully and select the correct answer for the given blank out of the four alternatives.*

Tibet **(59)** ________ up images of a mystic land. Snow-capped mountain peaks pierce the blue sky and fierce chilly winds sweep the rolling grasslands. Maroon-robed Buddhist monks pray in remote monasteries and **(60)** ________ horsemen pound the rugged earth. People in this high plateau perform punishing rituals like prostrating hundreds of miles in tattered clothes on pilgrimage. Spirits, spells and flying apparitions are part of the Tibetan world. In short, Tibet remains an **(61)**.

59. (a) molds
    (b) conjures
    (c) puts
    (d) toil

60. (a) sturdy
    (b) wobbly
    (c) devilish
    (d) drained

61. (a) inspiration
    (b) abhorrent
    (c) exotica
    (d) heaven

DIRECTIONS (Qs. 62-65): *In these questions some of the sentences have errors and some have none. Find out which part of a sentence has an error and indicate it corresponding to the appropriate letters. If there is no error, indicate corresponding to the option of No Error.*

62. The Allahabad High Court on Monday dismissed a plea from private power producers seeking relieve from (A)/ an RBI diktat to banks to take cognizance of a stressed loan (B)/ if repayments were missed even by a day. (C)/ No Error (D)
    (a) A
    (b) B
    (c) C
    (d) D

63. The Turkish lira, which has lost (A)/ almost half its value this year, is (B)/ another currency in doldrums. (C)/ No Error (D)
    (a) A
    (b) B
    (c) C
    (d) D

64. The mandate of emerging market central banks in (A)/the current scenario should be to let their currencies find (B)/ their true value in a smooth manner. (C)/ No Error (D)
    (a) A
    (b) B
    (c) C
    (d) D

65. Developmental activities of the (A)/ government come to a standstill (B)/ due to paucity of funds (C)/ No Error (D)
    (a) A
    (b) B
    (c) C
    (d) D

DIRECTIONS (Qs. 66-69): *In the following questions four alternatives are given for idioms/phrases in now. Choose the one that best expresses the meaning of the given idiom/phrase.*

66. Take the spear
    - (a) To drink in the company of others
    - (b) To make an exaggerated statement
    - (c) To fight fiercely till the end
    - (d) To accept full blame for something

67. Grist to one's mill
    - (a) Harmful to somebody
    - (b) Useful to somebody
    - (c) Useless to somebody
    - (d) Dreadful to somebody

68. In a lather
    - (a) Encouraged
    - (b) Tired
    - (c) Distressed
    - (d) Refreshed

69. Mop down
    - (a) To clean something
    - (b) To misinterpret a statement
    - (c) To be dejected
    - (d) To be uncertain

DIRECTIONS (Qs. 70-72): *In the following questions, choose the word opposite in meaning to the given word.*

70. UPEND
    - (a) Overbear
    - (b) Subdue
    - (c) Flourish
    - (d) Lose

71. TURF
    - (a) Shelter
    - (b) Oust
    - (c) Injure
    - (d) Evict

72. SPLEEN
    - (a) Caprice
    - (b) Cheer
    - (c) Sway
    - (d) Boisterous

DIRECTIONS (Qs. 73-75): *Out of the four alternatives, choose the one which best expresses the meaning of the given word.*

73. BARGE
    - (a) Shove
    - (b) Shout
    - (c) Interpret
    - (d) Plead

74. CHERUBIC
    - (a) Elderly
    - (b) Lowness
    - (c) Adorable
    - (d) Hardheaded

75. HUMMOCK
    - (a) Tranquility
    - (b) Slab
    - (c) Hammer
    - (d) Knoll

GENERAL AWARENESS

76. What is the maximum Number of timeouts in Volleyball that a team can take?
    - (a) Maximum of 1
    - (b) Maximum of 2
    - (c) Maximum of 3
    - (d) Maximum of 4

77. Who was the captain Indian hockey team in 1928?
    - (a) Lal shah Bokhari
    - (b) Dhyan Chand
    - (c) Kishan Lal
    - (d) Jaipal Singh

78. What is the Radcliffe Line?
    - (a) Boundary demarcation line between India and Pakistan.
    - (b) Boundary demarcation line between India and Nepal.
    - (c) Boundary demarcation line between India and China.
    - (d) Boundary demarcation line between Indian and Afghanistan.

79. Who among the following was the first posthumous recipient of Bharat Ratna?
    - (a) B.R. Ambedkar
    - (b) Lal Bahadur Shastri
    - (c) K. Kamraj
    - (d) M.G. Ramachandran

80. In which year Goa is taken by India?
    - (a) November 1949
    - (b) December 1961
    - (c) August 1962
    - (d) July 1963

81. Baltic cup is related to which game?
    - (a) Football
    - (b) Hockey
    - (c) Volleyball
    - (d) Badminton

82. Hook pass is related to which of the following game?
    - (a) Football
    - (b) Hockey
    - (c) Volleyball
    - (d) Basketball

83. Who wrote Hindu Sanskrit Book Natya Shastra?
    - (a) Bharata Muni
    - (b) Manu Rishi
    - (c) Yagyawalak
    - (d) Ashwagosh

84. When did the Jallianwala Bagh Massacre take place?
    - (a) 24 February 1919
    - (b) 10 March 1919
    - (c) 13 April 1919
    - (d) 24 July 1927

85. What was the term used for measurement of land in the Delhi Sultanate period?
    - (a) Kismat-i-Ghalla
    - (b) Ghalla Bakshi
    - (c) Masahat
    - (d) Ghazi

86. Riga is the capital of which country?
    - (a) Latavia
    - (b) Estonia
    - (c) Lithuania
    - (d) Belarus

87. Who was the founder of Brahmo Samaj?
    - (a) Debendranath Tagor
    - (b) Rammohan Roy
    - (c) Keshab Chandra Sen
    - (d) Dayanand Saraswati

88. Where is Indira Point located?
    - (a) Nicobar Islands
    - (b) Lakshadweep
    - (c) Kerala Coast
    - (d) Tamil Nadu Coast

89. JAXA is an aerospace agency of which of the following country?
    - (a) Russia
    - (b) China
    - (c) United Kingdom
    - (d) Japan

90. When did India become a member of Asian Development Bank?

    (a) 1966   (b) 1972

    (c) 1978   (d) 1982

91. Which of the given Vitamin is responsible for blood clotting?

    (a) Vitamin K   (b) Vitamin A

    (c) Vitamin E   (d) Vitamin C

92. Which of the following act is known as the Black Act?

    (a) Regulating Act of 1773

    (b) Charter Act of 1813

    (c) Vernacular Press Act 1878

    (d) Rowlatt Act 1919

93. Taseometer is an instrument to measure?

    (a) Intensity   (b) Strains

    (c) Sea waves   (d) Speed of Storm

94. Which island is located between Russia and Japan?

    (a) Kuril Islands   (b) St Helena Island

    (c) Ascension Island (d) Curieuse Island

95. "Double fault" is related to which of the following sport?

    (a) Rugby   (b) Tennis

    (c) Basket ball   (d) Football

96. 'Lona' is the term associated with which sports?

    (a) Kho Kho   (b) Kabaddi

    (c) Lawn Tennis   (d) Badminton

97. Which is the capital of Estonia?

    (a) Tallinn   (b) Vilnius

    (c) Minsk   (d) Riga

98. Which war was fought between Sher Shah and Humayun in the year 1540AD?

    (a) Battle of Chausa (b) Battle of Bhojpur

    (c) Battle of Guzargh (d) Battle of Kannauj

99. Women who won first medal in Olympic in India was?

    (a) Mary Kom   (b) Jwala Gutta

    (c) Karnam Malleswari (d) Sakshi Malik

100. Who is the author of the book "Underground"?

    (a) Colson Whitehead (b) Khaled Hosseini

    (c) Nora Roberts   (d) Dean Koontz

ANSWER KEY

1	(b)	11	(a)	21	(b)	31	(d)	41	(a)	51	(b)	61	(c)	71	(a)	81	(a)	91	(a)
2	(a)	12	(c)	22	(b)	32	(d)	42	(b)	52	(c)	62	(a)	72	(b)	82	(d)	92	(d)
3	(c)	13	(a)	23	(b)	33	(c)	43	(b)	53	(b)	63	(c)	73	(a)	83	(a)	93	(a)
4	(b)	14	(b)	24	(a)	34	(b)	44	(c)	54	(a)	64	(d)	74	(c)	84	(a)	94	(a)
5	(a)	15	(a)	25	(d)	35	(d)	45	(d)	55	(c)	65	(b)	75	(d)	85	(c)	95	(b)
6	(d)	16	(a)	26	(c)	36	(a)	46	(d)	56	(d)	66	(d)	76	(b)	86	(a)	96	(b)
7	(c)	17	(b)	27	(b)	37	(c)	47	(d)	57	(b)	67	(b)	77	(d)	87	(b)	97	(a)
8	(a)	18	(d)	28	(c)	38	(b)	48	(a)	58	(d)	68	(c)	78	(a)	88	(a)	98	(d)
9	(b)	19	(a)	29	(b)	39	(d)	49	(b)	59	(b)	69	(a)	79	(b)	89	(d)	99	(c)
10	(d)	20	(b)	30	(b)	40	(a)	50	(c)	60	(a)	70	(d)	80	(b)	90	(a)	100	(a)

HINTS & SOLUTIONS

1. **(b)** From formula, difference between C.I. and S.I. at the end of 3 years.

$$D = \frac{Pr^2}{(100)^2}\left(\frac{300+r}{100}\right)$$

$$\therefore\ 77.5 = P\left(\frac{10}{100}\right)^2\left(\frac{300+10}{100}\right)$$

$$77.5 = \frac{P}{100}\left(\frac{31}{10}\right)$$

$$\therefore\ P = \frac{77.5 \times 1000}{31} = ₹2500$$

2. **(a)** Cost price of first horse

$$= 1200 \times \frac{100}{120} = 1000$$

Cost price of second horse

$$= 1200 \times \frac{100}{80} = 1500$$

Sum of cost price of two horses

$$= 1000 + 1500 = 2500$$

Sum of selling price of two horses

$$= 1200 + 1200 = 2400$$

Loss $= 2500 - 2400 = 100$

Overall percentage loss $= \dfrac{100}{2500} \times 100 = 4\%\,(\text{loss})$

3. **(c)** Average $= \dfrac{\dfrac{5}{16} + \dfrac{3}{8}}{2}$

$$= \frac{\dfrac{5+6}{16}}{2} = \frac{11}{32} = 0.3475.$$

4. **(b)** We know that efficiency is inversely proportional to the time

So, ratio of time in which they complete the work

$$= \frac{1}{4} : \frac{1}{5} : \frac{1}{6}$$

$$= 15 : 12 : 10$$

So, ratio of time $= 15 : 12 : 10$

5. **(a)** 5 dozen $= 60$

Now, cost price of 60 eggs $= ₹100$

Number of unbroken eggs $= 60 \times \dfrac{80}{100} = 48$

to get 10% profit selling price of 48 eggs

$$= 100 \times \frac{110}{100} = 110$$

Selling price of each egg $= \dfrac{110}{48} = 2.292\,/\,\text{eggs}.$

6. **(d)** Rate of interest (semi annually) $= \dfrac{16}{2}\% = 8\%$

Time (in semi year) $= 4$

Now, compound interest $= P\left(1 + \dfrac{r}{100}\right)^t$

$$= 10000\left(1 + \frac{8}{100}\right)^4$$

$$= 13605$$

7. (c) $\sqrt{0.0081} + \sqrt{0.0064}$

$= \sqrt{(0.09)^2} + \sqrt{(0.08)^2}$

$= 0.09 + 0.08 = 0.17$

8. (a) $256^{0.16} \times 16^{0.18}$

$(2^8)^{0.16} \times (2^4)^{0.18}$

$(2)^{1.28} \times (2)^{0.72}$

$= 2^{1.28+0.72}$

$= 2^2 = 4$

9. (b) Let cost price of 1 kg sugar is ₹100

After increase in cost price by 25%

Cost price of 1 kg sugar = 125

Amount of sugar we can purchase in ₹100

$= \dfrac{100}{125} = \dfrac{4}{5} \text{kg}$

Percentage decrease in consumption

$= \left(\dfrac{1 - \dfrac{4}{5}}{1}\right) \times 100 = 20\%$

10. (d) Let number of students fail and pass in the class are x and y respectively.

ATQ,

$70(x + y) = 40x + 80y$

$30x = 10y \Rightarrow y = 3x$

Now, $\dfrac{y}{x} = 3$

$\dfrac{y}{x + y} = \dfrac{3}{1 + 3}$ {By componendo & devedendo}.

∴ Percentage of pass students $= \dfrac{3}{4} \times 100 = 75\%$

11. (a) Let population of the village in 2014 is N.

Then, $1852200 = N\left(1 + \dfrac{5}{100}\right)^2$

$\therefore N = \dfrac{1852200}{1.05 \times 1.05} = 1680000.$

12. (c) Amount of milk in the mixture

$= 250 \times \dfrac{7}{9} = 194.4 \,\text{ml}$

Amount of water in the mixture = 55.6

Let x ml of milk is added in the mixture then, Ratio of milk to water.

$= \dfrac{194.4 + x}{55.6} = \dfrac{4}{1}$

$(194.4 + x) = 55.6 \times 4$

$194.4 + x = 222.4$

$x = 28 \,\text{ml}.$

13. (a) Let the Teacher's age is x year.

ATQ,

$18 \times 26 = 16 \times 25 + x$

$468 = 400 + x$

∴ Teacher's age $= 468 - 400$

$= 68$ years.

14. (b) (A + B)'s 1 day's work $= \dfrac{1}{10}$

(B + C)'s 1 day's work $= \dfrac{1}{12}$

(C + A)'s day's work $= \dfrac{1}{15}$

On adding,

$2(A + B + C)$'s 1 day's work $= \dfrac{1}{10} + \dfrac{1}{12} + \dfrac{1}{15} = \dfrac{6+5+4}{60} = \dfrac{1}{4}$

∴ (A + B + C)'s 1 day's work $= \dfrac{1}{8}$

A's 1 day's work $= = \dfrac{1}{8} - \dfrac{1}{12} = \dfrac{3-2}{24} = \dfrac{1}{24}$

∴ A alone will complete the work in 24 days.

Hence option [b] is correct answer.

15. (a) According to question,

$3^{(a+8)} = 27^{(2a+1)} \Rightarrow 3^{(a+8)} = 3^{3(2a+1)}$.

Equating the powers, we get $(a+8) = 3(2a+1)$ or 'a' = 1.

16. (a) Distance $= (44/60) \times 50 = (x/60) \times 55$

∴ $x = 40$ minutes

17. (b) The percentage of reduction in consumption:

$= \dfrac{100 \times 50}{100 + 50} = (100 \times 50)/150 = 33\dfrac{1}{3}\%$

18. (d) Ratio of males and females = 5 : 6

Let the males are 5x and females are 6x

Now,

22 females leave the club

$5x : (6x - 22) = 6 : 5$

$(6x - 22)6 = 5x \times 5$

$36x - 132 = 25x$

$36x - 25x = 132$

$11x = 132$

$\Rightarrow x = 12$

The number of males $= 5x = 5 \times 12 = 60$

19. (a) 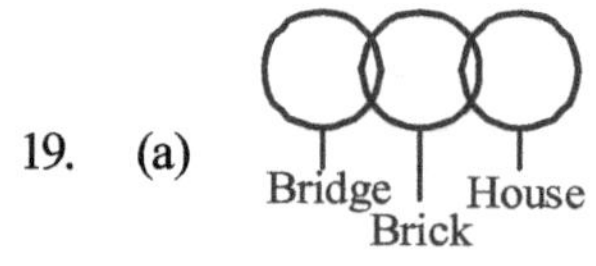

20. (b) 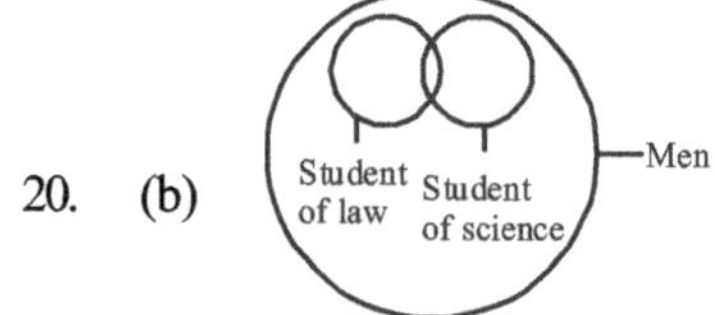

21. (b) 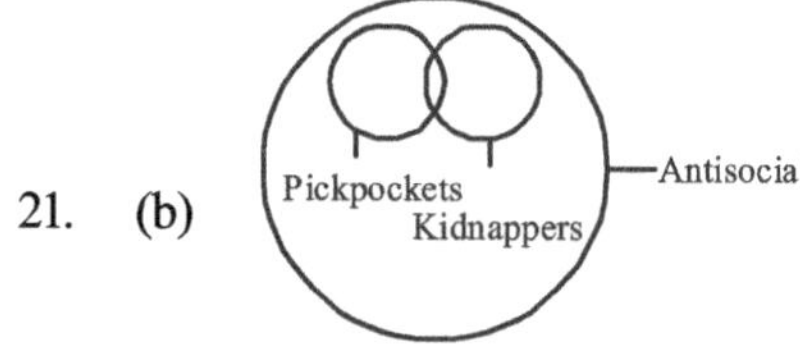

22. (b) According to diagram,

M is poet and singer but not dancer.

23. (b) As, Infant of sheep is lamb. Similarly, Infant of Insect is larva.

24. (a) As, Monk antonyms is Nun. Similarly, Bachelor antonyms is Spinster.

25. (d) Fear comes in Dark same as Trust comes due to Honesty.

26. (c) As, Hungry needs food, Similarly, Weary needs rest.

27. (b) As, Ampere is unit of current. Similarly, Newton is unit of force.

28. (c) Except July, All other month have 30 days.

29. (b) House sparrow is a common type of bird.

30. (b) Except Retina, all others are parts of a flower.

31. (d) In all other pairs, second is prepared by the first.

32. (d) In all other pairs, first is used to hold the second.

33. (c)

34. (b) According to question,

Required Number $= 64 - (17 + 11) + 1 = 37$th

35. (d)

36. (a) In PF(1), top half darkened rectangle turned 900 clockwise, middle half darkened rectangle turned anti-clockwise 900 and bottom half darkened rectangle turned clockwise by 900. So turn the rectangles in PF(C), clockwise, anti-clockwise, and clockwise. So correct Option (a)

37. (c) In each subsequent figure one dot is added and alternatively dots become white. Again, in each subsequent figure one arrow is deleted.

38. (b) 39. (d) 40. (a) 41. (a) 42. (b)

43. (b) 44. (c) 45. (d) 46. (d)

47. (d) 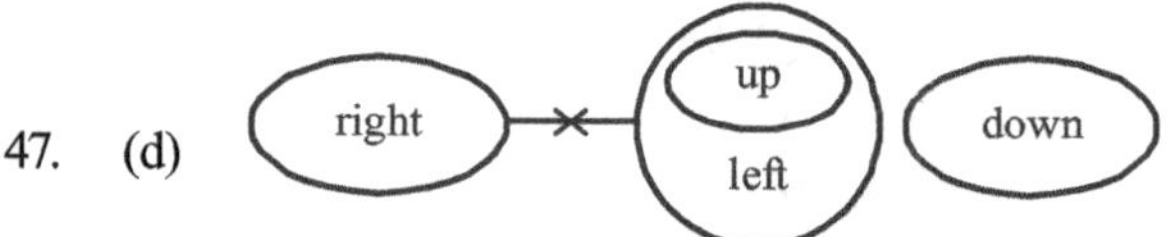

48. (a) 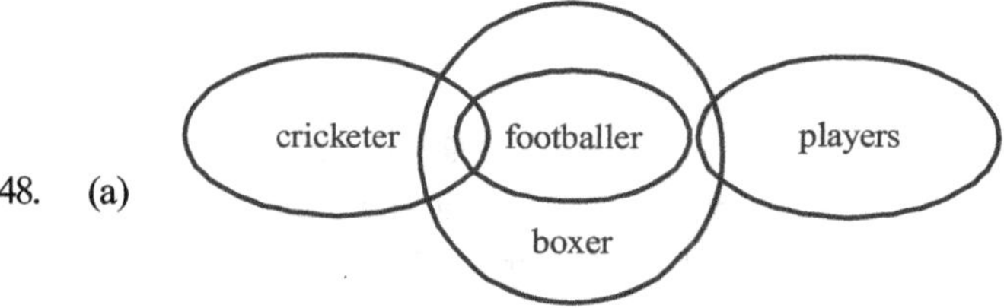

49. (b) 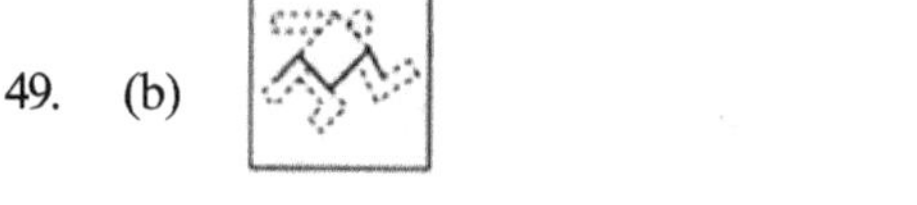

50. (c) 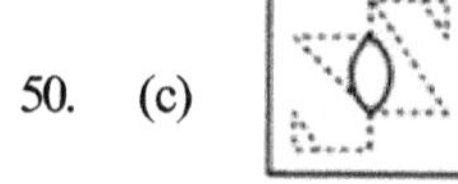

51. (b) 52. (c) 53. (b)

54. (a) The most appropriate word that would fill the blank is 'mistakes' which means an act or judgement that is misguided or wrong. All the other words do not fill the blank appropriately, hence option (a) is the most suitable answer choice. Accuracies means the quality or state of being correct or precise. Obstacles means a thing that blocks one's way or prevents or hinders progress.

55. (c) The most appropriate word that would fill the blank is 'travel' which means journeys, especially abroad. All the other words do not fill the blank appropriately, hence option (c) is the most suitable answer choice. Deportation means the action of deporting a foreigner from a country. Transfer means move from one place to another.

56. (d) The most appropriate word that would fill the blank is 'discretion' which means the freedom to decide what should be done in a particular situation. All the other words do not fill the blank appropriately, hence option (d) is the most suitable answer choice. Omission means someone or something that has been left out or excluded. Affairs means an event or sequence of events of a specified kind or that has previously been referred to.

57. (b) The most appropriate word that would fill the blank is 'opportunity' which means a time or set of circumstances that makes it possible to do something. All the other words do not fill the blank appropriately, hence option (b) is the most suitable answer choice. Negligence means failure to take proper care over something. Surveillance means close observation, especially of a suspected spy or criminal.

58. (d) The most appropriate word that would fill the blank is 'estimation' which means a judgement of the worth or character of someone or something. All the other words do not fill the blank appropriately, hence option (d) is the most suitable answer choice. Consideration means careful thought, typically over a period of time. Guidance means advice or information aimed at resolving a problem or difficulty, especially as given by someone in authority.

59. (b)   60. (a)   61. (c)

62. (a) Replace verb 'relieve' with noun 'relief'. Relief (noun): financial or practical assistance given to those in special need or difficulty.

63. (c) Replace 'in doldrums' with correct idiomatic expression 'in the doldrums' which means 'in a state of stagnation; lacking activity or progress'.

64. (d) No Error.

65. (b) Replace 'come' by 'have come'. As the sentence doesn't imply a regular habit, universal truth or general fact but a time based event hence, Perfect Tense is required.

66. (d)   67. (b)   68. (c)   69. (a)

70. (d) Upend: to achieve a victory over.

71. (a) Turf: force (someone) to leave somewhere.

72. (b) Spleen: bad temper; spite.
Caprice: a sudden and unaccountable change of mood or behaviour.
Sway: rule; control.
Hence 'Cheer' is the correct antonym.

73. (a) Barge: move forcefully or roughly.
Shove: push (someone or something) roughly.
Hence Barge and Shove are synonyms to each other.

74. (c) Cherubic: having the innocence or plump prettiness of a young child.
Adorable: inspiring great affection or delight.
Hence Cherubic and Adorable are synonyms to each other.

75. (d) Hummock: a very small hill or raised part of the ground; hillock.
Knoll: a small hill or mound.
Hummock and Knoll are synonyms to each other.

76. (b) Maximum of 2 time outs per game for a team is allowed. Time out lasts 30 seconds. In official international competitions two 60 seconds technical time-out are used when the leading team reaches the 8 or 16 point mark.

77. (d) Jaipal Singh Munda (3 January 1903 - 20 March 1970) born in a Munda tribal family in Jharkhand, was a politician, prolific writer and sportsman. He captained the Indian field hockey team to clinch gold in the 1928 Summer Olympics in Amsterdam. Lal Shah Bokari , Dhyan Chand and Kishan Lal also became the captain of Indian Hockey Team later.

78. (a) The Radcliffe Line was the boundary demarcation line between the Indian and Pakistani portions of the Punjab and Bengal provinces of British India. It was named after its architect, Sir Cyril Radcliffe, who, as the joint chairman of the two boundary commissions for the two provinces, received the responsibility to equitably divide 175,000 square miles (450,000 km2) of territory with 88 million people.

79. (b)

80. (b) The Annexation of Goa was the process in which the Republic of India annexed the former Portuguese Indian territories of Goa, Daman, and Diu, starting with the "armed action" carried out by the Indian Armed Forces in December 1961.

81. (a) The Baltic Cup is an international football competition contested by the national teams of the Baltic States - Estonia, Latvia and Lithuania. Finland has also participated as a guest twice in this game.

82. (d)

83. (a) Bharata Muni was an ancient Indian theatrologist and musicologist who wrote the Natya Shastra, a theoretical treatise on ancient Indian dramaturgy and histrionics, especially Sanskrit theatre. Bharata is considered the father of Indian theatrical art forms.

84. (a) The Jallianwala Bagh massacre, also known as the Amritsar massacre, took place on 13 April 1919 when a crowd of nonviolent protesters, along with Baishakhi pilgrims, who had gathered in Jallianwala Bagh, Amritsar, Punjab, were fired upon by troops of the British Indian Army under the command of Colonel Reginald Dyer.

85. (c)   86. (a)   87. (b)

88. (a) Indira Point is a village in the Nicobar district at Great Nicobar Island of Andaman and Nicobar Islands, India. It is located in the Great Nicobar tehsil. It is the location of the southernmost point of India's territory.

89. (d)

90. (a) India became a member of the Asian Development Bank (ADB) as a founding member in 1966. The Bank is engaged in promoting economic and social progress of its developing member countries (DMCs) in the Asia Pacific Region.

91. (a) Vitamin K affects the clotting mechanism by being essential for the production of four distinct clotting factors: prothrombin, factors VII, IX and X.

92. (d)   93. (a)   94. (a)   95. (b)   96. (b)

97. (a) Tallinn became the capital of an independent Estonia. After World War II started, Estonia acceded to the Soviet Union (USSR) in 1940, and later occupied by Nazi Germany from 1941 to 1944.

98. (d) Battle of Kannauj (1540 A.D.) - Sher Shah Suri defeated Humayun.

99. (c) The first Indian woman to ever win an Olympic medal was Karnam Malleswari who won a bronze medal at the Sydney Olympics in the Women's 69 kg category in Weightlifting.

100. (a) Colson Whitehead is an American novelist. He is the author of six novels, including his debut work, the 1999 novel The Intuitionist, and The Underground Railroad, for which he won the 2016 National Book Award for Fiction and the 2017 Pulitzer Prize for Fiction.

Instructions for candidates

TIME ALLOTTED – 2 HRS.

1. Total No. of Questions–100. Each Question is of three marks.
2. One mark will be deducted for every wrong answer.

---

1. When was Indian National Congress founded?
   - (a) 18 December, 1885
   - (b) 28, December, 1885
   - (c) 11, September, 1901
   - (d) 11, September, 1903

2. Pugilist is a term used for player of a game. Identify the game.
   - (a) Hockey
   - (b) Badminton
   - (c) Boxing
   - (d) Billiards

3. Theyyam is a tradition of which state?
   - (a) Tamil Nadu
   - (b) Karnataka
   - (c) Andhra Pradesh
   - (d) Kerala

4. How many hurdles are there in 400m race?
   - (a) 6
   - (b) 8
   - (c) 10
   - (d) 12

5. In which two years were Asian games held in India?
   - (a) 1951, 1982
   - (b) 1982, 2011
   - (c) 1951, 1983
   - (d) 1954, 1981

6. Who won 4 back to back titles in badminton?
   - (a) Pankaj Adwani
   - (b) Prannoy Kumar
   - (c) K. Srikanth
   - (d) Mahesh Bhupti

7. When was modern Olympic started?
   - (a) 6th April, 1986
   - (b) 6th April, 1896
   - (c) 11th July, 1807
   - (d) 4th June, 1907

8. How many countries are there in Asia?
   - (a) 26
   - (b) 39
   - (c) 42
   - (d) 48

9. What is the name of first artificial satellite of USA?
   - (a) Explorer 1
   - (b) Discovery
   - (c) Titan
   - (d) Atlantis

10. How many states does tropic of cancer pass through?
    - (a) 6
    - (b) 7
    - (c) 8
    - (d) 9

11. Who is the author of 'India divided'?
    - (a) Jawahar Lal Nehru
    - (b) Shashi Tharoor
    - (c) Rajendra Prasad
    - (d) Kapil Sibbal

12. Speed of wind measured by __________.
    - (a) Speedometer
    - (b) Spectrometer
    - (c) Hydrometer
    - (d) Anemometer

13. Which Indian made the national record in long jump?
    - (a) Ankit Sharma
    - (b) Devendra Jhajharia
    - (c) Anju Bobby George
    - (d) Nayana James

14. Where is NATO headquarter located?
    - (a) Ottawa, Canada
    - (b) Maxico city, Mexico
    - (c) Brussels, Belgium
    - (d) New York, USA

15. Tashkent agreement was signed by ________.
    - (a) Sardar Patel and John Mathai
    - (b) Lal Bahadur Shahstri and Ayub Khan
    - (c) Maulana Abul Kalam Azad and Rajendra Prasad
    - (d) Rajendra Prasad and Jawahar Lal Nehru

16. Who has written Panchtantra?
    - (a) Vaishnu Sharma
    - (b) Munshi Prem Chand
    - (c) Subhadra Kumari Chauhan
    - (d) Maithali Saran Gupt

17. Ruder cup is associated with which sport?
    - (a) Men's golf
    - (b) Soccer
    - (c) Badminton
    - (d) Basketball

18. Salal project is on the river__________.
    - (a) Godavri
    - (b) Ganga
    - (c) Chenab
    - (d) Mahanadi

19. In which city was the first British factory established in India.
    - (a) Kedarpuram
    - (b) Machhilipatnam
    - (c) Agra
    - (d) Panji

20. In which year was the first FIFA world cup held?
    - (a) 1931
    - (b) 1930
    - (c) 1940
    - (d) 1935

21. Guwahati is on the bank of which river?
    - (a) Ganga
    - (b) Barak
    - (c) Brahmaputra
    - (d) Teesta

22. Who was the Governor General of India during formation of Indian National Congress?
    - (a) Lord Dufferin
    - (b) Lord Mountbattern
    - (c) Lord Minto
    - (d) Lord William Bentinck

23. Who is the author of 'Sleeping of Jupiter'?
    - (a) Jhumpa Lahiri
    - (b) Anuradha Roy
    - (c) Shushma Swaraj
    - (d) Vikram Seth

24. Find the odd one out:
    - (a) Plassey
    - (b) Sarnath
    - (c) Haldighati
    - (d) Panipat

25. In 1954 which French settlements joined to India?
    - (a) Pondicherry
    - (b) Dutch
    - (c) Goa
    - (d) Chennai

26. The sum of two numbers is 36 and their H.C.F and L.C.M. are 3 and 105 respectively. The sum of the reciprocals of two numbers is
    - (a) $\dfrac{2}{35}$
    - (b) $\dfrac{3}{25}$
    - (c) $\dfrac{4}{35}$
    - (d) $\dfrac{2}{25}$

27. A teacher wants to arrange his students in an equal number of rows and columns. If there are 1369 students, the number of students in the last row are
    - (a) 37
    - (b) 33
    - (c) 63
    - (d) 47

28. A farmer divides his herd of n cows among his four sons, so that the first son gets one–half the herd, the second one–fourth, the third son $\dfrac{1}{5}$ and the fourth son 7 cows. Then the value of n is
    - (a) 240
    - (b) 100
    - (c) 180
    - (d) 140

29. If $2x - \dfrac{1}{2x} = 6$, then the value of $x^2 + \dfrac{1}{16x^2}$ is
    - (a) $\dfrac{19}{2}$
    - (b) $\dfrac{17}{2}$
    - (c) $\dfrac{18}{3}$
    - (d) $\dfrac{15}{2}$

30. On a journey across Kolkata, a taxi averages 50 km per hour for 50% of the distance. 40 km per hour for 40% of it and 20 km per hour for the remaining. The average speed in km/hour, for the whole journey is :
    (a) 42　　(b) 40　　(c) 35　　(d) 45

31. The average salary of all the workers in a workshop is ₹ 8,000. The average salary of 7 technicians is ₹ 12,000 and the average salary of the rest is ₹ 6,000. The total number of workers in the workshop is
    (a) 20　　(b) 21　　(c) 22　　(d) 23

32. The monthly salaries of A and B together amount to ₹ 40,000. A spends 85% of his salary and B, 95% of his salary. If now their savings are the same, then the salary (in ₹) of A is
    (a) 10,000　(b) 12,000　(c) 16,000　(d) 18,000

33. The price of table depreciates every year by 20%. If the value of the table after 2 years will be ₹ 32000, then what is the present price (in ₹) of the table?
    (a) 48000　(b) 44000　(c) 50000　(d) 51000

34. Krishna purchased a number of articles at ₹10 for each and the same number for ₹ 14 each. He mixed them together and sold them for ₹13 each. Then his gain or loss percent is

    (a) Loss $8\frac{1}{3}\%$　　　　(b) Gain $8\frac{2}{3}\%$

    (c) Loss $8\frac{2}{3}\%$　　　　(d) Gain $8\frac{1}{3}\%$

35. The price of an article is first decreased by 20% and then increased by 30%. if the resulting price is ₹ 416, the original price of the article is.
    (a) ₹ 350　(b) ₹ 405　(c) ₹400　(d) ₹ 450

36. A sum of ₹ 12,000, deposited at compound interest becomes double after 5 years. How much will it be after 20 years ?
    (a) ₹1,44,000　　　　(b) ₹1,20,000
    (c) ₹1,50,000　　　　(d) ₹1,92,000

37. A sum becomes ₹ 2,916 in 2 years at 8% per annum compound interest. The simple interest at 9% per annum for 3 years on the same amount will be
    (a) ₹ 625　(b) ₹ 600　(c) ₹ 675　(d) ₹ 650

38. ₹ 700 is divided among A, B, C in such a way that the ratio of the amount of A and B is 2 : 3 and that of B and C is 4 : 5. Find the amounts in ₹ each received, in the order A, B, C.
    (a) 150, 250, 300　　(b) 160, 240, 300
    (c) 150, 250, 290　　(d) 150, 240, 310

39. A and B can complete a piece of work in 8 days, B and C can do it in 12 days, C and A can do it in 8 days. A, B and C together can complete it in
    (a) 4 days　(b) 5 days　(c) 6 days　(d) 7 days

40. Pipe A alone can fill a tank in 8 hours. Pipe B alone can fill it in 6 hours. If both the pipes are opened and after 2 hours pipe A is closed, then the other pipe will fill the tank in

    (a) 6 hours　　　　(b) $3\frac{1}{2}$ hours

    (c) 4 hours　　　　(d) $2\frac{1}{2}$ hours

41. P is four times as efficient as Q.P can complete a work in 45 days less than Q. If both of them work together, then in how many days the work will be completed?
    (a) 10　　(b) 12　　(c) 15　　(d) 30

42. Two trains 108 m and 112 m in length are running towards each other on the parallel lines at a speed of 45 km/hr and 54 km/hr respectively. To cross each other after they meet, it will take
    (a) 10 sec　(b) 12 sec　(c) 9 sec　(d) 8 sec

43. A boat goes 15 km upstream and $10\frac{1}{2}$ km downstream in 3 hours 15 minutes. It goes 12 km upstream and 14 km downstream in 3 hours. What is the speed of the boat in still water?
    (a) 4　　(b) 6　　(c) 10　　(d) 14

DIRECTIONS (Qs. 44-47): *From the given answer figures, select the one in which the question figure is hidden/embedded.*

44. **Question Figure:**

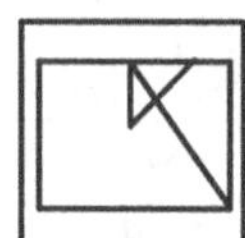

Answer Figures:

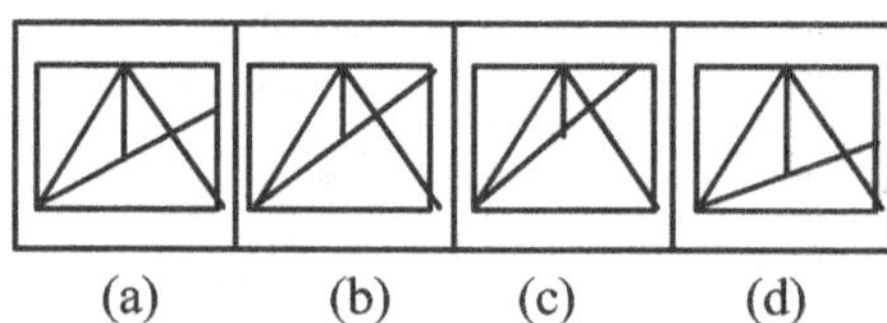

　　(a)　　　(b)　　　(c)　　　(d)

45. **Question Figure**

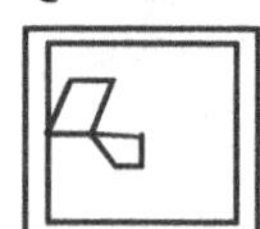

Answer Figures

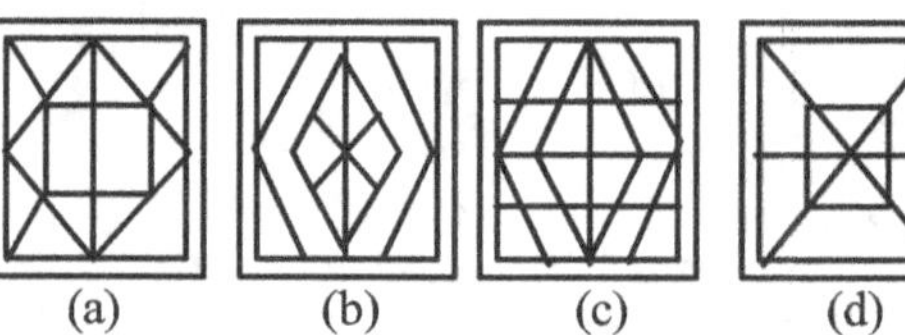

　　(a)　　　(b)　　　(c)　　　(d)

46. **Question Figure**

Answer Figures

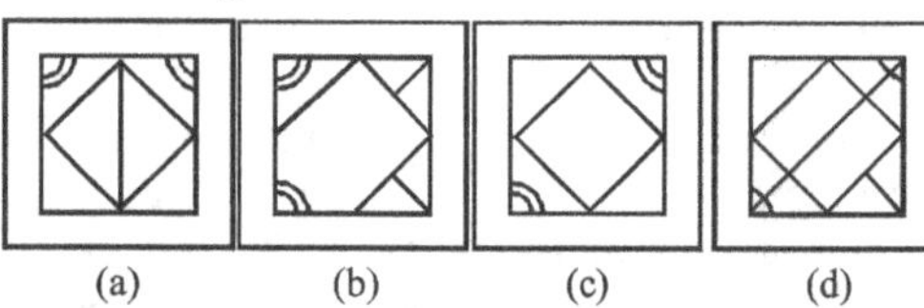

　　(a)　　　(b)　　　(c)　　　(d)

47. **Question Figure:**

Answer Figures :

(a) 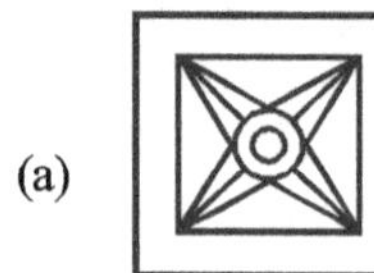　　　(b) 

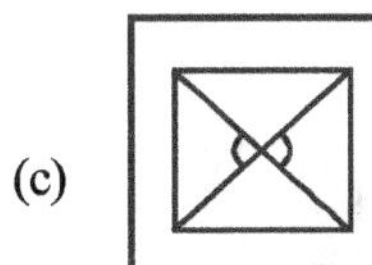 (c)   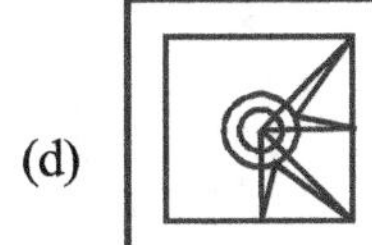 (d)

48. Find out which of the diagrams given in the alternatives correctly represents the relationship stated in the question.
Sharks, Whales, Turtles

(a) 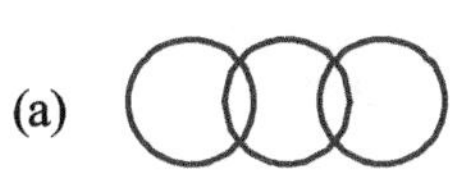   (b) 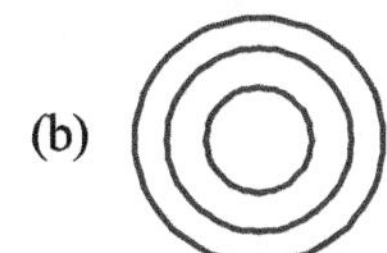

(c) 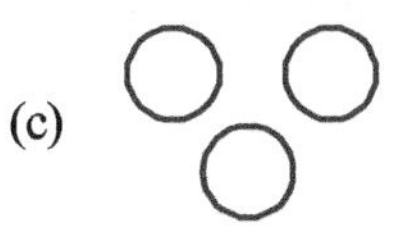   (d) 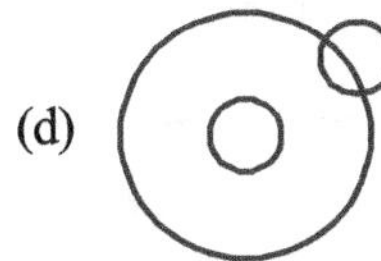

49. Indicate which figure will best represent the relationship amongst the three :
Legumes Seeds, Peas, Kidney Beans

(a)    (b) 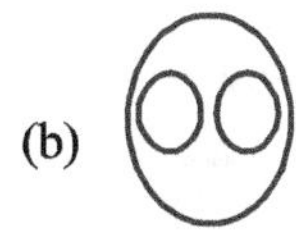

(c) 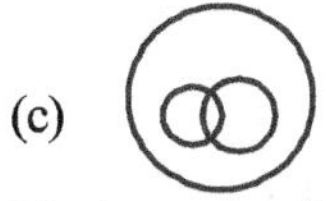   (d) 

50. Find out the figure which best represents the relationship among Garden, Rose and Jasmine.

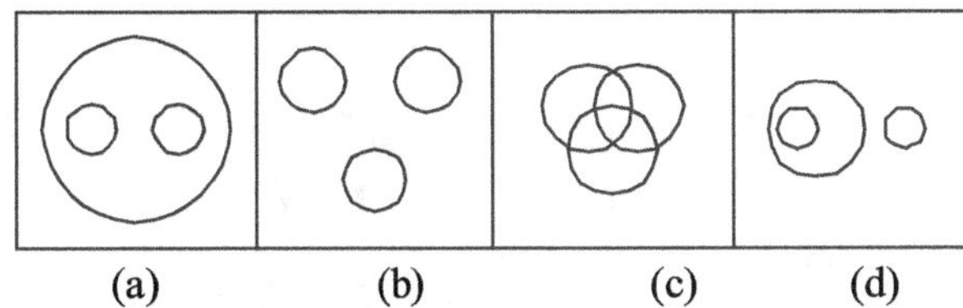

   (a)   (b)   (c)   (d)

51 Identify the diagram that best represents the relationship among classes given below : Christians, Catholics, Pope

51. (a) 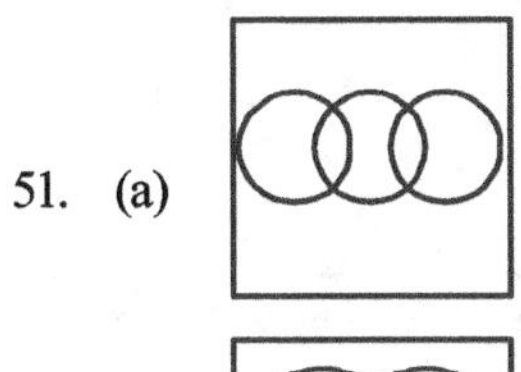   (b) 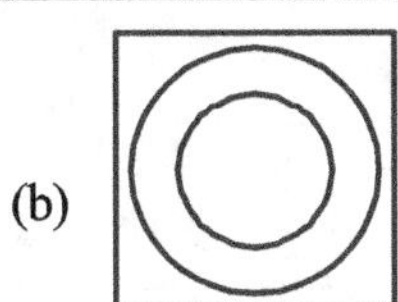

(c) 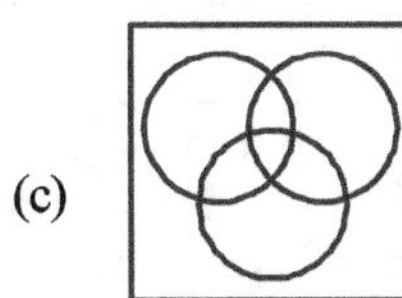   (d) 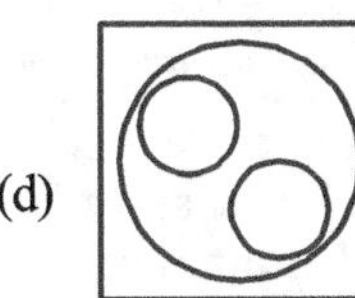

52. Flexible : Rigid : : Confidence : ?
  (a) Diffidence (b) Indifference
  (c) Cowardice (d) Scare
53. Mirage : Desert : : ?
  (a) Sky : Illusion   (b) Rainbow : Sky
  (c) Rain : Rainbow   (d) Image : Mirror

54. Anaemia : Blood : : Anarchy : ?
  (a) Disorder   (b) Monarchy
  (c) Government   (d) Lawlessness
55. Symphony : Composer : : Painter : ?
  (a) Fresco   (b) Colours
  (c) Art   (d) Leonardo
56. Influenza: Virus :: Ringworm: ?
  (a) Bacteria   (b) Fungi
  (c) parasite   (d) Protozoa

57. (a) Annoy   (b) Distress
  (c) Harass   (d) Ravage
58. (a) Hurdle   (b) Disease
  (c) Barrier   (d) Obstacle
59. (a) Rooster   (b) Buck
  (c) Gander   (d) Peahen
60. (a) fastidious   (b) firm
  (c) grave   (d) agreeable
61. (a) Soldier – Barrack   (b) Principal – School
  (c) Artist – Troupe   (d) Singer – Chorous
62. Find the missing figure of the series from the given responses.
Question Figures :

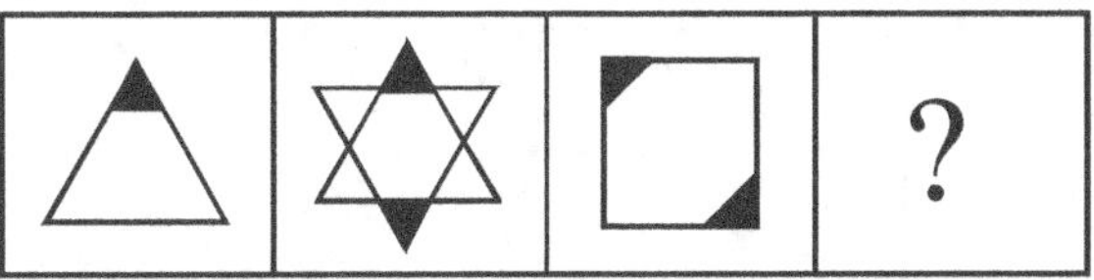

Answer Figures :

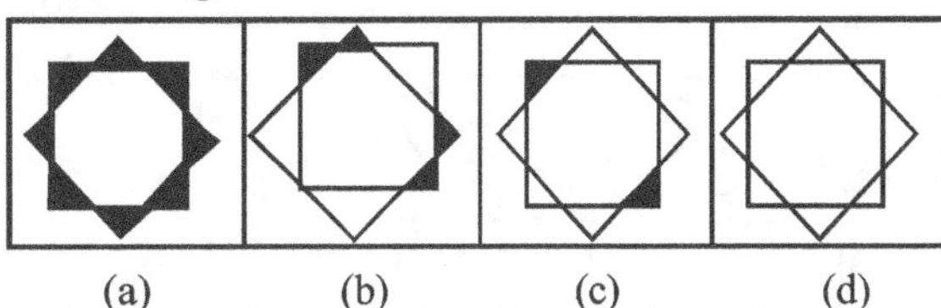

   (a)   (b)   (c)   (d)

63. What comes next in the series?
Question Figures :

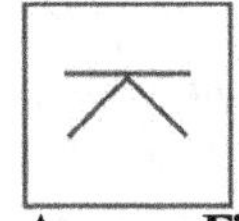 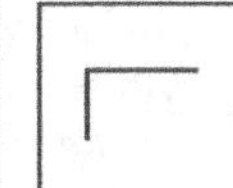 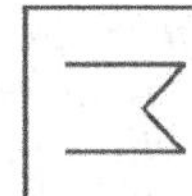 

Answer Figures :

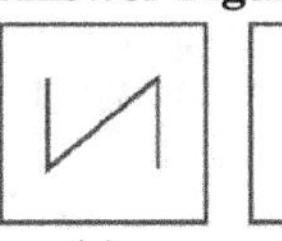 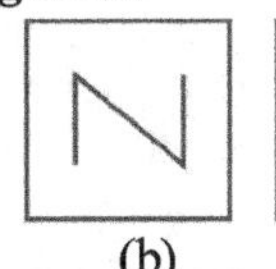  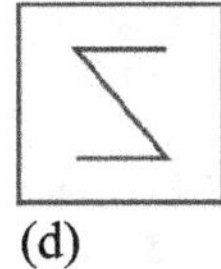

   (a)   (b)   (c)   (d)

64. 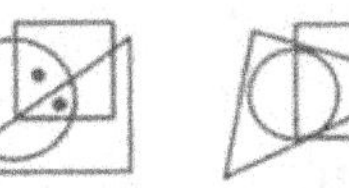  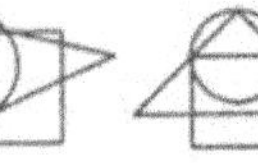 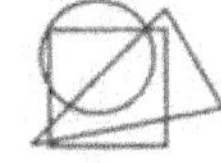 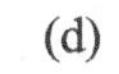

  (X)   (a)   (b)   (c)   (d)

65.  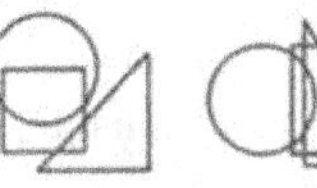 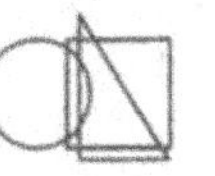 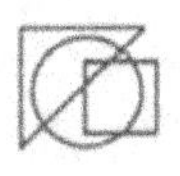 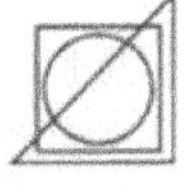

  (X)   (a)   (b)   (c)   (d)

66.

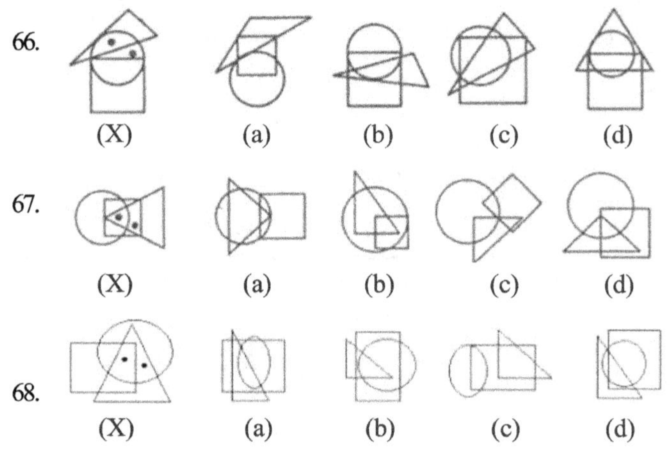

67.

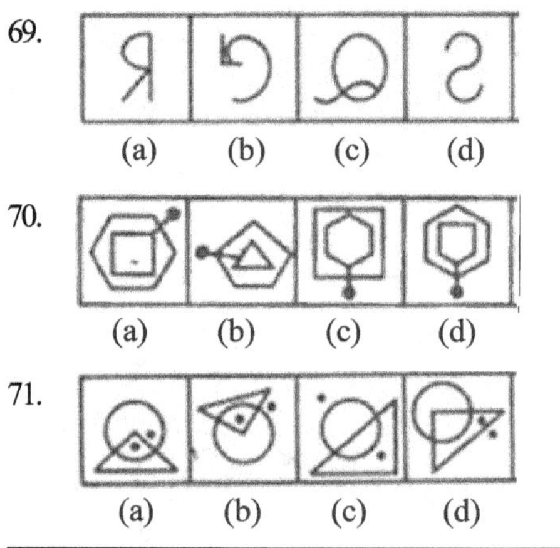

68.

DIRECTIONS (Qs. 69-71): *Each of the questions, out of the four figures marked (a), (b), (c) and (d). three are similar in a certain manner. However, one figure is not like the other three. Choose the figure which is different from the rest:-*

69.

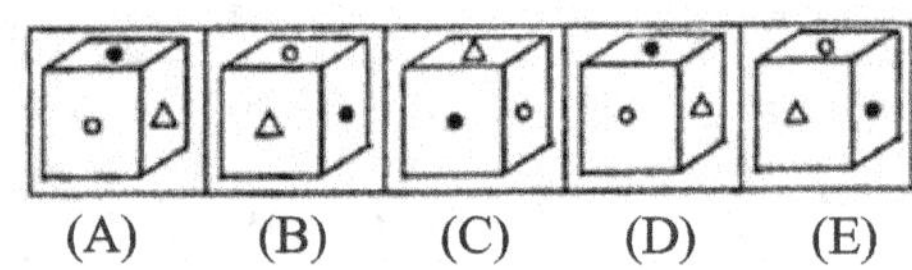

70.

71.

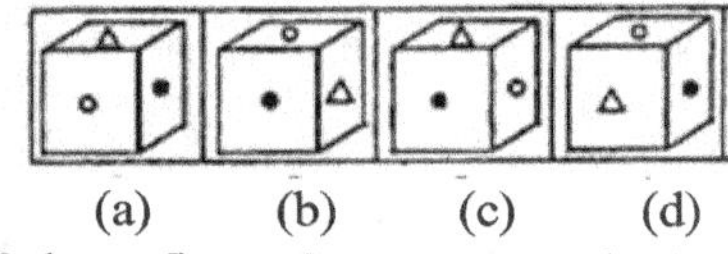

DIRECTIONS (Qs. 72-75): *Each of the following questions consists of five figures marked A, B, C, D and E called the Problem Figures followed by five other figures marked (a), (b), (c), and (d) called the Answer Figures. Select a figure from amongst the Answer Figures which will continue the same series as established by the five Problem Figures.*

72. Select a figure from amongst the Answer Figures which will continue the same series as established by the five Problem Figures.
Problem Figures:

Answer Figures:

73. Select a figure from amongst the Answer Figures which will continue the same series as established by the five Problem Figures.

Problem Figures:

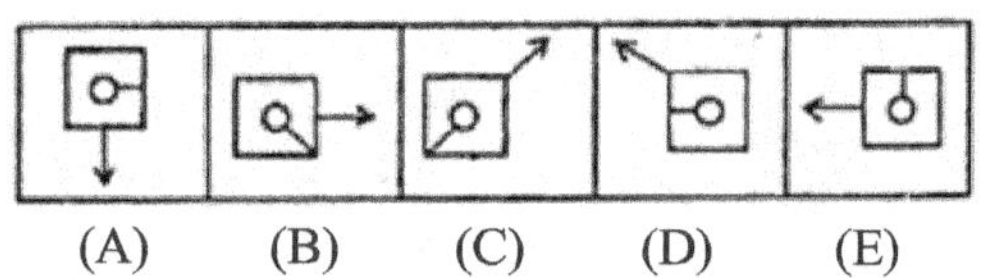

Answer Figures:

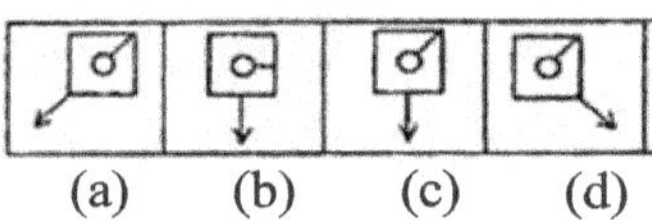

74. Select a figure from amongst the Answer Figures which will continue the same series as established by the five Problem Figures.
Problem Figures:

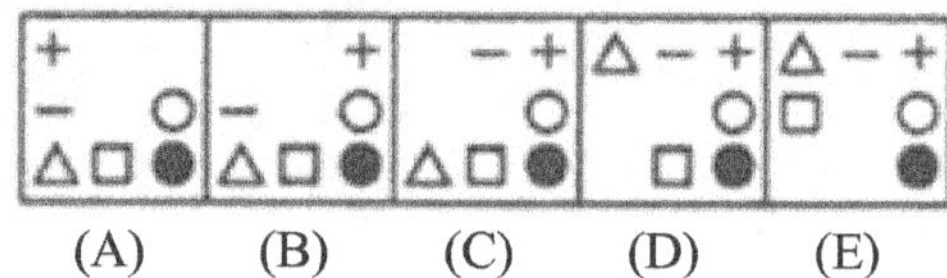

Answer Figures:

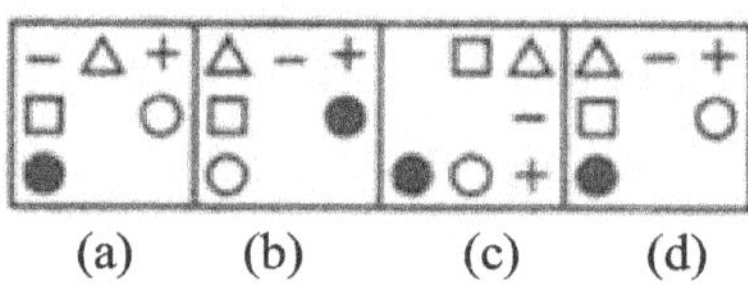

75. Select a figure from amongst the Answer Figures which will continue the same series as established by the five Problem Figures.
Problem Figures:

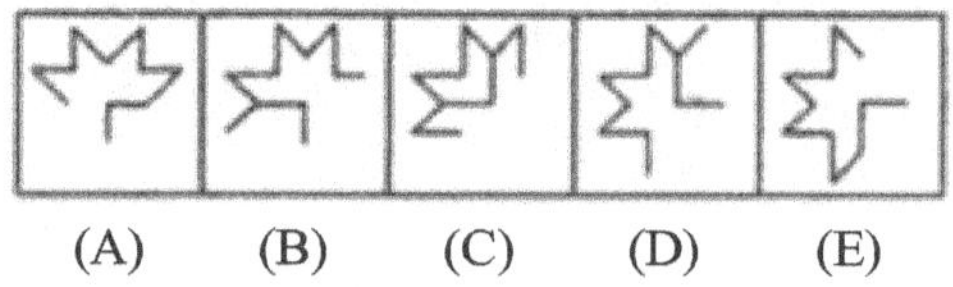

Answer Figures:

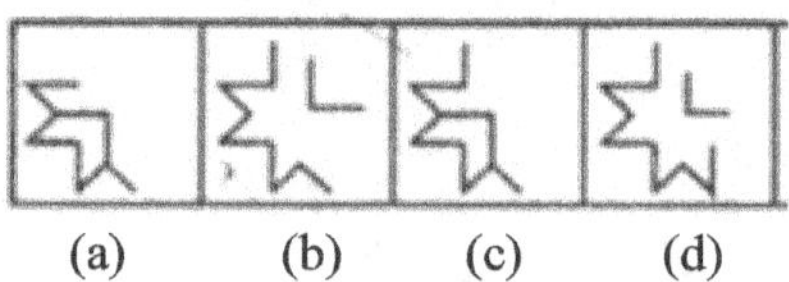

DIRECTIONS (Qs. 76-79) : *Read the following passage and answer the questions given after it.*

Dr. Carver was an American Negro slave, who by dint of his ability became a scientist and educator of world-wide fame. A national monument has now been erected to honour him. This monument has been built at his birth place in the United States of America. Carver's life and achievements prove the American saying: "You can't keep a great man down." From childhood he showed qualities which gave promise of his genius. He would get up before sunrise to study the wonders of nature before the break of dawn in the east. His guardians wanted to educate him, but were too poor to do so. So he left home. He was hardly ten when he began to work at small jobs to earn a little money for his school expenses. He continued to do so even when he was at college. Thus, he passed his M.Sc. examination and became a professor. There he wrote several books on science subjects. His chief desire was to do the greatest good to the greatest number of people. He left all his life's savings to found scholarships for research in Agricultural Chemistry. He know this research, was bound to benefit farmers all over the world. Though world famous, he never felt proud of his discoveries. "I discovered nothing," he once said, "I am God's agent—the instrument through which he works."

76. What can you say about the early life of Dr. Carver?
    (a) He was born with silver spoon in his mouth.
    (b) He was brought up in an orphanage.
    (c) He had to struggle a lot as his parents were poor.
    (d) He was brought up and educated by wealthy parents.

77. Which of the following statements show that he was a great lover of mankind?
    (a) He offered charitable services to the poor.
    (b) He desired to do the greatest good to the greatest number of people.
    (c) He opened several colleges and institutes.
    (d) He donated all his life savings.

78. Find out the statement that he was humble?
    (a) He never felt proud of his discoveries.
    (b) He always respected the women.
    (c) He was very polite in his attitudes.
    (d) He admired his own achievements.

79. What was of Dr. Carver by profession?
    (a) Doctor   (b) Politician
    (c) Scientist   (d) Professor

DIRECTIONS (Qs. 80-84) : *Select the word which means the opposite of the given word.*

80. PROFANE
    (a) Sacred   (b) Artless
    (c) Rigid   (d) Aspersion

81. OBLIGATORY
    (a) Doubtful   (b) Voluntary
    (c) Sincerely   (d) Faithfully

82. OBSCURE
    (a) Suitable   (b) Apt
    (c) Thalamus   (d) Clear

83. MUTUAL
    (a) Reciprocal (b) Agreed
    (c) Common   (d) Conjugal

84. EVIDENT
    (a) Prominent   (b) Seen
    (c) Observed   (d) Quite clear

DIRECTIONS (Q. 85-89) : *In the following passage there are some numbered blanks. Fill in the blanks by selecting the most appropriate word for each blank from the given options.*

In tropical countries, certain crops are grown ....(85)........... the year. These countries have ....(86)........... rainfall for the crops. They also have plenty of sunshine what ....(87)........... the crops. More food than is ....(88)........... can be grown in these places. But there are other countries in the world where it is ....(89)........... to grow crops.

85. (a) Along   (b) Over
    (c) Through out (d) Across

86. (a) Sufficient (b) Little
    (c) Plenty   (d) Inadequate

87. (a) Opens   (b) Gathers
    (c) Destroys   (d) Ripens

88. (a) Cooked   (b) Required
    (c) Planted   (d) Used

89. (a) Difficult   (b) Rough
    (c) Smooth   (d) Impossible

DIRECTIONS (Qs. 90-95) : *Select the meaning of the given phrases/idioms.*

90. man of letters
    (a) a person who writes letters
    (b) a person who receives letters
    (c) an illiterate person
    (d) a learned person

91. All Greek
    (a) totally classical   (b) totally unintelligible
    (c) totally impressive   (d) totally original

92. a live wire
    (a) a person who is full of energy
    (b) an eminent person
    (c) an unruly person
    (d) a critical person

93. writing on the wall
    (a) graffiti
    (b) an event indicating impending danger
    (c) announcement of an event
    (d) a political slogan

94. a fool's paradise
    (a) paradise of idiots
    (b) a state of illusory happiness
    (c) to live in the past
    (d) to have happy dreams

95. nip in the bud
    (a) destroy in the beginning
    (b) extremely good start
    (c) striving from the beginning
    (d) nurture the bud to grow into flower

DIRECTIONS (Qs. 96-100) : *In each of the following questions, choose the correctly spelt word.*

96. (a) Properetry   (b) Propriatory
    (c) Proprietary   (d) Proprietory

97. (a) Reharsal   (b) Rehersal
    (c) Rehearsal   (d) Rehearsel

98. (a) Millionare   (b) Millionaire
    (c) Milionaire   (d) Millunaire

99. (a) Fasist   (b) Facicl
    (c) Facist   (d) Fascist

100. (a) Legendry   (b) Legendary
     (c) Legendery   (d) Legandery

ANSWER KEY

1	(b)	13	(a)	25	(a)	37	(c)	49	(b)	61	(b)	73	(c)	85	(c)	97	(c)
2	(c)	14	(c)	26	(c)	38	(b)	50	(a)	62	(c)	74	(d)	86	(a)	98	(b)
3	(d)	15	(b)	27	(a)	39	(c)	51	(b)	63	(c)	75	(c)	87	(d)	99	(d)
4	(c)	16	(a)	28	(d)	40	(d)	52	(a)	64	(d)	76	(c)	88	(b)	100	(b)
5	(a)	17	(a)	29	(a)	41	(b)	53	(c)	65	(c)	77	(b)	89	(a)		
6	(c)	18	(c)	30	(b)	42	(d)	54	(c)	66	(c)	78	(a)	90	(d)		
7	(b)	19	(b)	31	(b)	43	(c)	55	(a)	67	(d)	79	(c)	91	(b)		
8	(d)	20	(b)	32	(a)	44	(c)	56	(b)	68	(d)	80	(a)	92	(a)		
9	(a)	21	(c)	33	(c)	45	(c)	57	(d)	69	(b)	81	(b)	93	(b)		
10	(c)	22	(a)	34	(a)	46	(b)	58	(b)	70	(d)	82	(d)	94	(b)		
11	(c)	23	(b)	35	(c)	47	(a)	59	(b)	71	(a)	83	(a)	95	(a)		
12	(d)	24	(b)	36	(d)	48	(c)	60	(d)	72	(c)	84	(d)	96	(c)		

HINTS & SOLUTIONS

26. (c) Let the numbers be 3x and 3y.

$\therefore 3x + 3y = 36$

$\Rightarrow x + y = 12$ ...(i)

and $3xy = 105$ ...(ii)

Dividing equation (i) by (ii), we have

$$\frac{x}{3xy} + \frac{y}{3xy} = \frac{12}{105}$$

$$\Rightarrow \frac{1}{3y} + \frac{1}{3x} = \frac{4}{35}$$

> **Shortcut Method:**
>
> $$\frac{1}{x} + \frac{1}{y} = \frac{x+y}{xy}$$

27. (a) If they are equal number of rows and columns then,

$\sqrt{1369} = 37$

28. (d) According to the question,

$$\frac{n}{2} + \frac{n}{4} + \frac{n}{5} + 7 = n$$

$$\Rightarrow \frac{10n + 5n + 4n}{20} + 7 = n$$

$$\Rightarrow \frac{19n}{20} + 7 = n \Rightarrow n - \frac{19n}{20} = 7$$

$$\Rightarrow \frac{n}{20} = 7 \Rightarrow n = 20 \times 7 = 140$$

29. (a) $2x - \dfrac{1}{2x} = 6$

$$\Rightarrow x - \frac{1}{4x} = 3 \quad \text{[on dividing by 2]}$$

$$\Rightarrow x^4 + \frac{1}{16x^2} - 2 \times x \times \frac{1}{4x} = 9$$

[On Squaring]

$$\Rightarrow x^4 + \frac{1}{16x^2} = 9 + \frac{1}{2} = \frac{19}{2}$$

30. (b) Total distance = 100 km.

$$\text{Total time} = \frac{50}{50} + \frac{40}{40} + \frac{10}{20} = 1 + 1 + \frac{1}{2} = \frac{5}{2} \text{ hours}$$

$\therefore$ Average speed $= \dfrac{100 \times 2}{5} = 40 \text{ kmph}$

31. (b) Let total number of workers be n

total salary of all workers = 8000 n

total salary of 7 technicians = 7 × 12000 = 84,000

total salary of remaining workers = (n − 7) × 6000

84000 + (n − 7) × 6000 = 8000 n

84 + 6n − 42 = 8n

42 = 2n

n = 21

32. (a) Let the monthly salary of A be x,,

monthly salary of B is (40000 − x).

Savings of A = (100 − 85)% of x = 0.15x

Savings of B = (100 − 95)% of (40000 − x)

$\qquad\qquad = 0.05 \,(40000 - x)$

0.15 x = 0.05 (40000 − x)

0.15x + 0.05x = 40000 × 0.05

0.2x = 2000

x = 10000

OR

$$A \times \frac{15}{100} = \times \frac{5}{100}$$

$\therefore A : B = 1 : 3$

Salary of A $= 40000 \times \dfrac{1}{4} = 10000$

33. (c) Present price of table $= \dfrac{32000}{\left(1 - \dfrac{20}{100}\right)^2}$

$$= 32000 \times \frac{5}{4} \times \frac{5}{4} = 50000$$

34. (d) Average cost of $= \dfrac{10+14}{2} = 12$

SP $= 13$

$P\% = \dfrac{13-12}{12} \times 100 = 8\dfrac{1}{3}$

35. (c) If the original price of article be ₹ x, then

$x \times \dfrac{80}{100} \times \dfrac{130}{100} = 416$

$\Rightarrow x = \dfrac{416 \times 100 \times 100}{80 \times 130} = ₹\,400$

36. (d) $A = P\left(1 + \dfrac{R}{100}\right)^T$

$\Rightarrow 24000 = 12000\left(1 + \dfrac{R}{100}\right)^5$

$\Rightarrow 2 = \left(1 + \dfrac{R}{100}\right)^5$

$\Rightarrow 2^4 = \left(1 + \dfrac{R}{100}\right)^{20} := 16\text{ times}$

i.e. The sum amounts to ₹192000.

37. (c) $2916 = P\left(1 + \dfrac{8}{100}\right)^2$

$P = \dfrac{2916}{(1.08)^2} = 2500$

$S.I = \dfrac{2500 \times 9 \times 3}{100} = 675$

38. (b) A : B $= 2 : 3 = 8 : 12$
B : C $= 4 : 5 = 12 : 15$
∴ A : B : C $= 8 : 12 : 15$
Sum of ratio $= 35$

∴ A's share $= \dfrac{8}{35} \times 700$

$= ₹\,160$

B's share $= \dfrac{12}{35} \times 700 = ₹\,240$

C's share $= \dfrac{15}{35} \times 700 = ₹\,300$

39. (c) (A + B)'s 1 day's work $= \dfrac{1}{8}$

(B + C)'s 1 day's work $= \dfrac{1}{12}$

(C + A)'s 1 day's work $= \dfrac{1}{8}$

On adding,
2 (A + B + C)'s 1 day's work

$= \dfrac{1}{8} + \dfrac{1}{12} + \dfrac{1}{8} = \dfrac{3+2+3}{24} = \dfrac{8}{24} = \dfrac{1}{3}$

∴ (A + B + C)'s 1 day's work $= \dfrac{1}{6}$

Hence, the work will be compelted in 6 days.

40. (d) Part of the tank filled by both pipes in two hours

$= 2\left(\dfrac{1}{8} + \dfrac{1}{6}\right) = 2\left(\dfrac{3+4}{24}\right) = \dfrac{7}{12}$

Remaining part $= 1 - \dfrac{7}{12} = \dfrac{5}{12}$

Time taken by B in filling the remaining part

$= \dfrac{5}{12} \times 6 = \dfrac{5}{2} = 2\dfrac{1}{2}\text{ hours}$

41. (b) According to question,
If P can complete a work in 1 day, Q can complete the same work in 4 days.
Hence, if the difference is 3 days, Q can complete the work in 4 days
$\Rightarrow$ If the difference is 45 days, Q can complete the work in 60 days

∴ Q's 1 day's work $= \dfrac{1}{60}$

∴ P's 1 day's work $= 4 \times \dfrac{1}{60} = \dfrac{1}{15}$

∴ (P + Q)'s 1 day's work

$= \left(\dfrac{1}{15} + \dfrac{1}{60}\right) = \dfrac{(4+1)}{60} = \dfrac{5}{60} = \dfrac{1}{12}$

∴ P and Q together can do work in 12 days.

42. (d) Relative speed $=$

$(45 + 54) = 99\,km/hr = \dfrac{99 \times 5}{18}\,m/sec$

Distance covered in crossing each other
$= (108 + 112) = 220\text{m}$

Required time $= \dfrac{220}{99} \times \dfrac{18}{5} = 8\text{ sec}$

43. (c) Let speed of the boat in still water be x km/h and speed of current be y km/h.
Then,
upstream speed $= (x - y)$ km/h
and down stream speed $= (x + y)$ km/h
Now,

$\dfrac{15}{(x-y)} + \dfrac{21}{2(x+y)} = 3\dfrac{1}{4}$ ...(i)

$\dfrac{12}{(x-y)} + \dfrac{14}{(x+y)} = 3$ ...(ii)

From Equation (i) and (ii)
x $= 10$ km/hr and y $= 4$ km/hr.

45. (c)

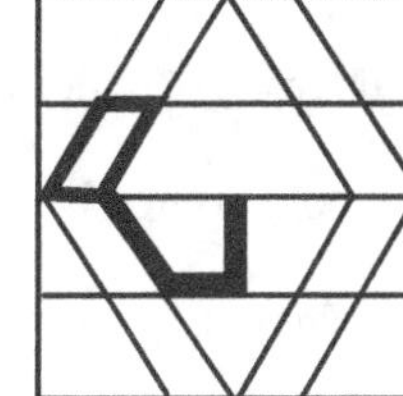

46. (b) Option (b) is the hidden/ embedded figure.
48. (c) Sharks belong to class pisces. Whale is a mammal and Turtle belongs to class reptiles.

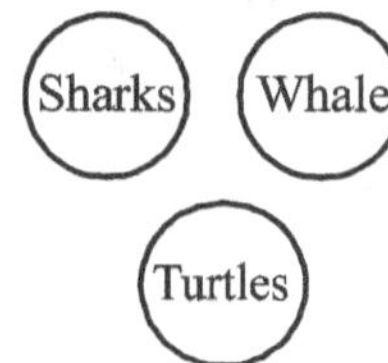

49. (b) Pea is different from kidney bean. But both are Leguminous seeds.

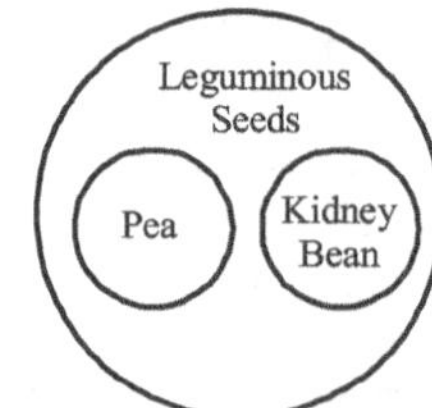

50. (a) Best representation of the relationship is :

51. (b)

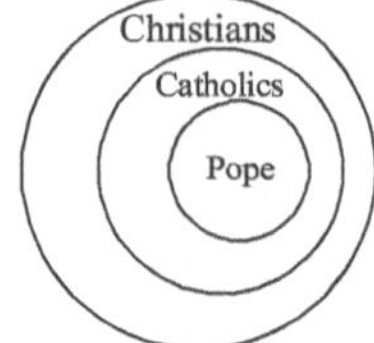

52. (a) Flexible is antonym of Rigid. Similarly, Confidence is antonym of Diffidence.
53. (c) Mirage is an illusion caused by hot air conditions making one see something that is not there, especially the appearance of a sheet of water on a hot road or in a desert. Similarly,
Rainbow is an arch of seven colours formed in the sky when the sun shines through rain.
54. (c) Anaemia is the lack of blood. Similarly, Anarchy is the lack of government.
55. (a) Fresco is an art of painting that is done on freshly spread moist lime plaster.
56. (b) As, Infuenza is caused by virus.
Similarly, Ring worm is caused by Fungi.
57. (d) Ravage is the different from the other words.
58. (b) Except disease, all other terms denote obstruction, hindrance or interruption.
59. (b) Rooster, Gander and Peahen are birds. Buck is an animal.
60. (d) Agreeable is different from the other three words.
Agreeable (Adjective) means 'pleasant', 'giving pleasure', ready to agree'.
61. (b) Barrack is a large building or group of buildings where soldiers live.
Principal is the head of school. Troupe is a group of artists.
Chorous is a large group of singers.

62. (c) 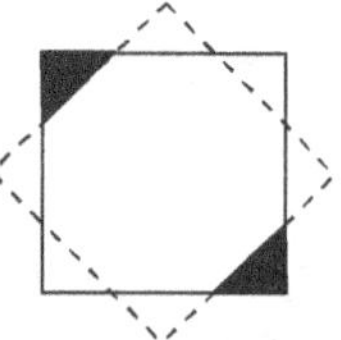

63. (c) The series represents continuous alphabets starting from K. Hence, N is the right answer.
69. (b) Each one of the figures except fig. (b), is obtained by the lateral inversion of an English alphabet.
70. (d) Only in fig. (d), the pin passes through a vertex of each one of the two elements.
71. (a) In all other figures, one of the dots lies outside the triangle as well as the circle.
72. (c) All the three symbols in the dice are rotating clockwise. So option (c)
73. (c) the arrow and small line inside the small square are rotating constantly anti clockwise and clockwise respectively by 90°, 45°, 90°, 45°,... and 45°, 90°, 45°, 90°. So next figure would be option (c).
74. (d) In each step, the CW-end element moves to the ACW-end position.
75. (c) In each step, one line segment is lost from the CW-end of the outer element and a new line segment appears at the ACW-end. Also, the inner 'L' shaped element rotates 90°CW in each step.
76. (c) His guardians wanted to educate him, but were too poor to do so. So he left home. He was hardly ten, when he began to work at small jobs to earn a little money for his school expenses. He continued to do so even when he was at college.
77. (b) His chief desire was to do the greatest good to the greatest number of people.
78. (a) Though world famous, he never felt proud of his discoveries.
79. (c) Dr. Carver was an American Negro slave, who by dint of his ability became a scientist and educator of world-wide fame.
80. (a) Profane means 'unholy, not devoted to holy or religious purposes'. So option 'a' sacred would be the right antonym of this word.
81. (b) The word 'obligatory' means compulsory, mandatory, required whose opposite is optional or voluntary.
82. (d) The word 'obscure' means unclear whose opposite is clear.
83. (a) The word 'mutual' is used to describe feelings that two or more people have for each other equally. Hence, *reciprocal* is similar word in meaning to it.
84. (d) The word 'evident' means obvious, clear, tangible, distinct etc. which is nearest in meaning to 'quite clear'.
90. (d) Man of letters means a person devoted to literary or scholarly activities.
92. (a) A live wire means an energetic and unpredictable person.
93. (b) The writing on the wall means the likelihood that something bad will happen.
94. (b) A fool's paradise means the state of being happy for foolish reasons.
95. (a) Nip in the bud means to end something before it develops into something larger.

1 Vocabulary/One Word Substitution

DIRECTIONS (Qs. 1 - 3) : *In each of the following choose the word most similar in meaning to the word given in capitals.*
[2011-I]

1. CAUSED
   - (a) Brought about
   - (b) Brought forward
   - (c) Brought out
   - (d) Brought over

2. PLACID
   - (a) Plain
   - (b) Clear
   - (c) Poor
   - (d) Calm

3. AUDACIOUS
   - (a) Obvious
   - (b) Daring
   - (c) Ardent
   - (d) Affluent

DIRECTIONS (Qs. 4 - 6) : *Pick out the word that is most nearly the opposite in meaning to the word given in capitals.* *[2011-I]*

4. MONOLOGUE
   - (a) Prologue
   - (b) Epilogue
   - (c) Dialogue
   - (d) Catalogue

5. DELETE
   - (a) Imbibe
   - (b) Improve
   - (c) Insert
   - (d) Inspire

6. AMBIGUITY
   - (a) Certainty
   - (b) Clarity
   - (c) Rationality
   - (d) Laxity

DIRECTIONS (Qs. 7-14) : *This is a test of your ability to understand words. For each question four options are given. There is only one correct answer for each question. Mark the correct answer.* *[2011-I]*

7. INCITE means the same as
   - (a) short
   - (b) delay
   - (c) place
   - (d) provoke

8. SUCCUMB means the same as
   - (a) aid
   - (b) yield
   - (c) check
   - (d) oppose

9. ANOMALOUS means the same as
   - (a) disgraceful
   - (b) formless
   - (c) irregular
   - (d) threatening

10. FORTUITOUS means the same as
   - (a) accidental
   - (b) conclusive
   - (c) courageous
   - (d) prosperous

11. PERMEABLE means the same as
   - (a) flexible
   - (b) variable
   - (c) soluble
   - (d) penetrable

12. CONVOY means the same as
   - (a) carry
   - (b) flock
   - (c) standard
   - (d) escort

13. CITE means the same as
   - (a) illustrate
   - (b) reveal
   - (c) recollect
   - (d) quote

14. VOCATION means the same as
   - (a) hobby
   - (b) occupation
   - (c) post
   - (d) designation

DIRECTIONS (Qs. 15 &16) : *Each of the following questions has an underlined/capitalized word. You are to indicate which one of the four choices most nearly means the same as the underlined/capitalized word.* *[2011-I]*

15. The benefits of the plan are likely to be transitory.
   - (a) significant
   - (b) obvious
   - (c) temporary
   - (d) cumulative

16. The hikers found several crevices in the rocks.
   - (a) cracks
   - (b) minerals
   - (c) canals
   - (d) puddles

DIRECTIONS (Qs. 17-19) : *In each of the following choose the word most similar in meaning to the word given in capitals.*

17. VENERATE
   [2011-II]
   - (a) Reject
   - (b) Remove
   - (c) Love
   - (d) Respect

18. VACILLATE
   - (a) Waver
   - (b) Disintegrate
   - (c) Relegate
   - (d) Salute

19. FELICITY
   - (a) Zeal
   - (b) Excitement
   - (c) Happiness
   - (d) Expertise

DIRECTIONS (Qs. 20-23) : *Pick out the word that is most nearly the opposite in meaning to the word given in capitals.*

20. HYSTERIA
   [2011-II]
   - (a) Disease
   - (b) Ceremony
   - (c) Serenity
   - (d) Frenzy

21. ABSTAIN
   - (a) Indulge
   - (b) Dismiss
   - (c) Repel
   - (d) Acquire

22. SEDENTARY
    (a) Inactive   (b) Sluggish
    (c) Moving   (d) Settled
23. Relaxed means the same as the opposite of   *[2011-II]*
    (a) calm   (b) angry
    (c) tense   (d) sleep

DIRECTIONS (Qs. 24-26) : *In each of the following choose the word most similar in meaning to the word given in capitals.*

24. EMANCIPATE   *[2012-I]*
    (a) Set free   (b) Exist
    (c) Correct morally   (d) Restrain
25. DECEIT
    (a) Simplicity   (b) Gentility
    (c) Sincerity   (d) Dishonesty
26. ADMONITION
    (a) Thrash   (b) Hindrance
    (c) Warning   (d) Exhort

DIRECTIONS (Qs. 27 & 28) : *In each of the following choose the word most nearly opposite in meaning to the word given in capitals.*   *[2012-I]*

27. VOCIFEROUS
    (a) Laudable   (b) Quiet
    (c) Dangerous   (d) Powerful
28. IMPLICATE
    (a) Involve   (b) Exonerate
    (c) Corrupt   (d) Accuse

DIRECTIONS (Qs. 29-31) : *In each of the following choose the word most similar in meaning to the word given in capitals.*

29. OSMOSIS   *[2012-II]*
    (a) Gradual acceptance (b) Slow recovery
    (c) Abrupt ending   (d) Strength
30. OSTRACISE,
    (a) Take away   (b) Cut off
    (c) Include   (d) Expedite
31. ALACRITY
    (a) Hesitatingly   (b) Eagerness
    (c) Unwillingly   (d) Laziness

DIRECTIONS (Qs. 32-35) : *In each of the following choose the word most nearly opposite in meaning to the word given in capitals.*   *[2012-II]*

32. PROFUSION
    (a) Travesty   (b) Validity
    (c) Scarcity   (d) Agitated
33. ESCHEW
    (a) Vicious   (b) Invite
    (c) Use   (d) Emanate
34. ABSTAIN
    (a) Refuse   (b) Oppose
    (c) Run away   (d) Permit
35. INSOLENT
    (a) Affable   (b) Spotted
    (c) Foolish   (d) Mature

DIRECTIONS (Qs. 36 – 38) : *In each of the following, choose the word most similar in meaning to the word given in capitals.*

36. "MEDDLE"   *[2013-I]*
    (a) Disregard   (b) Overlook
    (c) Interfere   (d) Free
37. "ABJURE"
    (a) Renounce   (b) Run off secretly
    (c) Abide   (d) Discuss
38. "ESTRANGE"
    (a) Endanger   (b) To become puzzling
    (c) Miscalculate   (d) Alienate

DIRECTIONS (Qs. 39 & 40) : *In each of the following, choose the word most nearly opposite in meaning to the word given in capitals.*   *[2013-I]*

39. "DEROGATORY"
    (a) Conferred   (b) Immediate
    (c) Praising   (d) Private
40. "WANE"
    (a) Widen   (b) Poor
    (c) Swell   (d) Tight

DIRECTIONS (Qs. 41 & 42) : *Choose the word which is nearest in meaning to the given word :*   *[2014-I]*

41. 'TRANSGRESSOR'
    (a) Passenger   (b) Law-breaker
    (c) Protector   (d) Comrade
42. 'EGREGIOUS'
    (a) Common   (b) Social
    (c) Plain   (d) Atrocious

DIRECTIONS (Qs. 43 – 45) : *Choose the word which is nearly opposite in meaning to the given word:*   *[2014-I]*

43. 'PREDILECTION'
    (a) Oblivion   (b) Objectivity
    (c) Aversion   (d) Defeat
44. 'CACOPHONOUS'
    (a) Tamed   (b) Harmonious
    (c) Domestic   (d) Silent
45. 'CALUMNY'
    (a) Apology   (b) Eulogy
    (c) Enjoyment   (d) Reservation

DIRECTIONS (Qs. 46 – 50) : *Choose the word that best defines the given phrase:*   *[2014-I]*

46. 'Able to use both hands alike'
    (a) Dexterous   (b) Ambidextrous
    (c) Skilful   (d) Expert
47. 'A written account of the life of an individual'
    (a) Autobiography   (b) Epigraph
    (c) Biography   (d) Novel
48. 'The identification of a disease by its symptoms'
    (a) Prescription   (b) Prognosis
    (c) Diagnosis   (d) Biopsy

49. 'Prolonged inability to sleep'
- (a) Amnesia
- (b) Utopia
- (c) Nausea
- (d) Insomnia

50. 'A style in which a writer makes a display of his knowledge'
- (a) Verbose
- (b) Pedantic
- (c) Ornate
- (d) Pompous

DIRECTIONS (Qs. 51–55) : *Choose the correctly spelt word:*
[2014-I]

51. The school alumni gathering put us in a ______ mood.
- (a) Remniscent
- (b) Reminisent
- (c) Reminiscent
- (d) Reminicent

52. 'God is Dead' is a __________ statement.
- (a) Blasphemus
- (b) Blaphemous
- (c) Blasphemous
- (d) Blosphemos

53. The threat of an epidemic caused great alarm and _______ .
- (a) Trepidation
- (b) Terpidation
- (c) Trepidition
- (d) Trepidattion

54. The din caused by the children howling is enough to ____ the dead.
- (a) Ressurect
- (b) Resurrect
- (c) Resurect
- (d) Resurecct

55. Can you ___ the car into that parking spot?
- (a) Manuer
- (b) Manever
- (c) Manoeuvre
- (d) Manuver

DIRECTIONS (Qs. 56 – 59) : *Choose the word which is nearest in meaning to the given word:* *[2014-II]*

56. 'LIBERALISE'
- (a) Resist
- (b) Change
- (c) Function
- (d) Malfunction

57. 'PRAGMATIC'
- (a) Theoretical
- (b) Suitable
- (c) Realistic
- (d) Productive

58. 'PRISTINE'
- (a) Fresh
- (b) Old
- (c) Preserve
- (d) Dirty

59. 'INTREPID'
- (a) Middle
- (b) Tolerant
- (c) Rude
- (d) Fearless

DIRECTIONS (Qs. 60 – 63) : *Choose the word which is nearly opposite in meaning to the given word:* *[2014-II]*

60. 'ANGELICAL'
- (a) Magnanimous
- (b) Benlvolent
- (c) Diabolical
- (d) Critical

61. 'HAUGHTINESS'
- (a) Affability
- (b) Unskilled
- (c) Adduce
- (d) Abject

62. 'Bellow'
- (a) Tout
- (b) Whisper
- (c) Stupour
- (d) Down

63. 'INEQUITY'
- (a) Law
- (b) Illegal
- (c) Slander
- (d) Libel

DIRECTIONS (Qs. 64 – 67) : *Choose the word that best defines the given phrase:*

64. Tickled pink *[2014-II]*
- (a) Greatly pleased
- (b) Coloured
- (c) Deeply upset
- (d) Embarrassed

65. Split one's side
- (a) Intense pain
- (b) To laugh a lot
- (c) To be hurt
- (d) None of these

66. Building castles in the air
- (a) Making impossible plans
- (b) Making tall promises
- (c) Building skyscrapers
- (d) Structures without strong foundation

67. At the drop of a hat
- (a) Willingly and softly
- (b) Willingly and immediately
- (c) Willingly and silently
- (d) Slowly and silently

DIRECTIONS (Qs. 68 – 71) : *Which word or words explains the meaning of the following idioms:-* *[2014-II]*

68. Airy- Fairy
- (a) Most important
- (b) Nervous
- (c) Not practical
- (d) Confident

69. Be given the axe
- (a) To move fast
- (b) Carpenter
- (c) Woodcutter
- (d) To lose job

70. To go like a bomb
- (a) Loud explosion
- (b) To move fast
- (c) Terrorism
- (d) Not practical

71. Bolt from the blue
- (a) Unexpected
- (b) Lighting
- (c) Nervous
- (d) Sudden

DIRECTIONS (Qs. 72 – 75) : *Choose the word which is nearest in meaning to the given word :* *[2015-I]*

72. Sporadic
- (a) Epidemic
- (b) Whirling
- (c) Occasional
- (d) Stagnant

73. Genesis
- (a) Style
- (b) Beginning
- (c) Movement
- (d) Relevant

74. Intransigent
- (a) Authoritative
- (b) Impersonal
- (c) Strenuous
- (d) Unbending

75. Intimidate
- (a) Mislead
- (b) Misplace
- (c) Frighten
- (d) Demoralise

DIRECTIONS (Qs. 76 – 79) : *Choose the word which is nearly opposite in meaning of the given word:* *[2015-I]*

76. Clemency
- (a) Corporal
- (b) Intolerance
- (c) Compromise
- (d) Sensibility

77. Cajole
    (a) Nestle   (b) Secede
    (c) Bully   (d) Moisten
78. Malevolent
    (a) Kindly   (b) Vacuous
    (c) Ambivalent   (d) Primitive
79. Purgatory
    (a) Reward   (b) Celestial
    (c) Flawless   (d) Proximity

DIRECTIONS (Qs. 80 – 83) : *Which word or words explains the meaning of the following idioms :*   *[2015-I]*

80. In a jiffy
    (a) Outstanding   (b) Suddenly
    (c) In a fix   (d) Appropriate
81. Upto the hilt
    (a) Completely   (b) Upto the mark
    (c) Upto the final decision (d) None of these
82. Man of Letters
    (a) Who writes too many letters
    (b) An important person
    (c) A politician
    (d) A literary person
83. Sangfroid
    (a) Composure   (b) Go on leave
    (c) Changed suddenly   (d) Make an attempt

DIRECTIONS (Qs. 84 – 87) : *Choose the word that best defines the given phrases :*   *[2015-I]*

84. A Curtain Lecture
    (a) To speak plainly
    (b) Vulgar ideas
    (c) Private scolding of a husband by his wife
    (d) Hate others

85. Square pegs in round holes
    (a) A genuinely helpful person
    (b) A clever person
    (c) People in the wrong jobs
    (d) To be perplexed
86. In weal and woe
    (a) By hook or crook
    (b) During illness
    (c) In prosperity and adversity
    (d) During the operation
87. Globetrotters
    (a) People against global philosophy
    (b) People indulging in treachery
    (c) Intelligent minds
    (d) Travellers around the world

DIRECTIONS (Qs. 88 – 91) : *Choose the correctly spelt word :*   *[2015-I]*

88. (a) Konnoisseur   (b) Conoisseur
    (c) Connoisseur   (d) Konoisseur
89. (a) Munifisent   (b) Muneficent
    (c) Munificent   (d) Munificient
90. (a) Equanmity   (b) Equannimity
    (c) Equanimmisty   (d) Equinimity
91. (a) Vetarinary   (b) Veterinary
    (c) Vetennary   (d) Vetniary

Hints & Solutions

1. (a)
2. (d) Calm
3. (b) Daring
4. (b) Epilogue
5. (c) Insert
6. (b) Clarity
7. (d) 'INCITE' means to encourage illegal or unpleasant.
8. (b) 'SUCCUMB' means not to be able to fight.
9. (c) 'ANOMALOUS' means different what from is normal or expected.
10. (a) 'FORTUITOUS' and accidental means happening by change.
11. (a) 'PERMEABLE' means allowing something to pass through.
12. (b) 'CONVOY' means a group of vehicles travelling together.
13. (a) 'CITE' means to mention an example in order to support what you are saying.
14. (d) 'VOCATION' and designation mean a type of work that you believe is especially suitable for you.
15. (c) 'TRANSITORY' means continuing for only a short time.
16. (a) 'CREVICES' means cracks in a rock or wall.
17. (d) Venerate means regard with great respect.
18. (a) Vacillate means go back and forth.
19. (c) Felicity means immense happiness.
20. (c) Hysteria means state of extreme upset. Its opposite meaning will be serenity.
21. (a) Abstain means to hold back from doing. Its opposite is indulging in something.
22. (c) Sedentary means motionless or lazy. Its opposite meaning will be moving.
23. (c)
24. (a) Emancipate means free from slavery or servitude; hence, set free is the correct option.
25. (d) The quality of being fraudulent.
26. (c) admonition means cautionary advice about something imminent (especially imminent danger or other unpleasantness).
27. (c) Vociferous may well be replaced with dangerous.
28. (a) Implicate means involve.
29. (a) Osmosis means the process of gradual or unconscious assimilation of ideas, knowledge, etc.
30. (b) Ostracise means avoid speaking to or dealing with and cut off means the same.
31. (b) Alacrity means liveliness and eagerness; hence, option b is right.
32. (c) Profusion means the property of being extremely abundant and its opposite should be scarcity.
33. (c) Eschew means avoid and stay away from deliberately; stay clear of, hence, its opposite should be Use.

34. (c) Abstain means choose not to consume and its opposite should be permit.
35. (a) Insolent means marked by casual disrespect while affable means diffusing warmth and friendliness.
36. (c) Meddle means to interfere in something that is not one's concern.
37. (a) Renounce and abjure means to formally declare one's abandonment.
38. (d) Estrange means to cause someone to be no longer involved or connected with something.
39. (c) Derogatory means showing a critical or disrespectful attitude which is opposite of praising.
40. (c) Wane means to diminish, weaken or lessen which is opposite to swell that means to grow.
41. (b) Transgressor is a person who breaks the law i.e. a law breaker.
42. (d) Egregious means outstandingly bad and atrocious means outrageous.
43. (c) Predilection means preference toward something whereas aversion means opposition.
44. (d) Cacophonous means harsh sounding, whereas quiet is calm and noiseless.
45. (b) Calumny is the making of false statements that damage another's reputation whereas eulogy means praise and acclamation.
46. (b) Ambidextrous means both hands. The ambidextrous person can perform an action with either hand having equal dexterity in the action. Writing is the most striking of these actions.
47. (c) A written account of the life of an individual by himself is called a autobiography. And when it is written by other person, then it is called biography.
48. (c) Diagnosis refers to both the process of attempting to determine or identify a possible disease and to the opinion reached by this process.
49. (d) Insomnia, or sleeplessness, is a sleep disorder in which there is an inability to fall asleep or to stay asleep as long as desired.
50. (b) Pedantic mean overly concerned with minute details or formalisms, especially in teaching.
51. (c) Reminiscent
52. (c) Blasphemous
53. (b) Trepidation
54. (b) Resurrect
55. (c) Manoeuvre.
56. (b) Liberalise - remove or loosen restrictions on something. Hence, option (b) is correct choice.
57. (c) Pragmatic - of or relating to a practical point of view or practical considerations. Hence, option (c) is correct choice.
58. (a) Pristine - in its original condition; unspoilt; clean and fresh as if new; spotless. Hence, option (a) is correct choice.

59. (d) Intrepid means fearless; adventurous. Hence, option (d) is correct choice.

60. (c) Meaning of angelical - having a sweet nature befitting an angel or cherub. Meaning of Diabolical - concerning, or characteristic of the devil; satanic. Hence, antonym of angelical is diabolical.

61. (d) Meaning of haughtiness- the appearance or quality of being arrogantly superior and disdainful.

62. (b) Meaning of bellow - a deep roaring shout or sound. Meaning of whisper - a soft or confidential tone of voice. Hence, antonym of bellow is whisper.

63. (a) Meaning of inequity- lack of fairness or justice. Antonym for inequity is law according to given options.

64. (a) Tickled pink -very much pleased or entertained. So, (a) is the correct choice.

65. (b) Split one's sides or laugh one's head off- be extremely amused, laugh uproariously. So, (b) is the correct choice.

66. (a) Build castles in the air or build castles in Spain- to daydream; to make plans that can never come true. So, (a) is the correct choice.

67. (b) At the drop of a hat - immediately; instantly; on the slightest signal or urging. So, (b) is the correct choice.

68. (c) Airy-fairy means not practical or not useful in real situations. Hence, (c) is the correct choice.

69. (d) Get the axe or also be given the axe means if a person gets the axe, they lose their job. Hence, (d) is the correct choice.

70. (b) Go like a bomb means if a vehicle goes like a bomb, it can move very fast. Hence, (b) is the correct choice.

71. (d) A bolt from the blue or also a bolt out of the blue means something that not expected to happen and that surprises someone very much. Hence, (d) is the correct choice.

72. (c) Sporadic means, occuring at irregular intervals or any in a few places. Ex. A sporadic fighting broke out.

73. (b) Genesis is the origin or mode of formation of something. The nearest meaning is beginning.

74. (d) Intransigent defines unwilling or refusing to change one's views or to agree about something. Therefore unbending is the nearest meaning.

75. (c) Intimidate means frighten or overawe someone, in order to make them do what one wants.

76. (b) The word clemency means mercy or lenience. Here intolerance is the nearly opposite meaning.

77. (c) The word cajole means to persuade someone to do something by sustained coaxing or flattery. Bully is the nearly opposite meaning.

78. (a) Malevolent defines, showing a wish to do evil to others. Kindly is the most appropriate opposite.

79. (b) Purgatory means a place or state of suffering inhabited by the souls of sinners who are expiating their sins before going to heaven. Therefore celestial is the right opposite word.

80. (b) Jiffy means-a very short time, a moment which is used in an informal way in English. Ex. I we'll be back in a jiffy. The other options are not appropriate.

81. (a) Upto the hilt means completely.
Ex. The building was mortgaged up to the hilt.
Other options give different meaning.

82. (d) Literary persons are scholars or male authors known as–man of letters. Ex. He wished to fashion for himself a career as a man of letters.
Other options are not correct as they express different meanings.

83. (a) Sangfroid means composure or coolness shown in danger or under trying circumstances.
Ex. Offering the most welcoming stage for the talented, the city with equal sangfroid accepts the misery of millions who fail to flourish. Other options are simply irrelevat so far the meaning is concerned.

84. (c) The phrase a curtain Lecture means an instance of a wife reprimanding her husband in private.

85. (c) Square pegs in round holes means a misfit. So, people in the wrong jobs is the correct option.

86. (c) The phrase means good and bad day. E.g., Weal and woe comes in everybody's life. Therefore, in prosperity and adversity is the correct option.

87. (d) Globetrotter is a person who travels widely.

88. (c) Connoisseur is an expert judge in matters of taste. E.g., A connoisseur of music.

89. (c) Munificent in its adjective form means characterised by or displaying great generosity.

90. (a) Equanimity means calmness and composure, especially in a difficult situation.

91. (c) Veterinary : Relating to the diseases, injuries and treatment of farm and domestic animals.

2 Error Detection

DIRECTIONS (Qs. 1-5) : *In each of the following questions, find out which part of the sentence has an error. If there is no mistake, the answer is (d) "No error".* **[2011-I]**

1. A person I met (a) / in the theatre (b) /was the playwright himself. (c)/ No error (d)

2. They walked (a) / besides each other (b) / in silence (c) / No error (d)

3. We returned to the guest house (a)/ impressed by (b) / What we had seen (c) / No error (d)

4. The judge was convinced (a)/ that neither (b)/ of the five accused was guilty (c)/ No error (d)

5. The municipality is going (a)/ to built a new school (b)/ near the park (c)/ No error (d)

DIRECTIONS (Qs. 6 - 10) : *In each of the following questions, find out which part of the sentence has an error. If there is no mistake, the answer is (d) "No error".* **[2011-II]**

6. It was a year since (a) / I received any letter (b) / from my sister. (c) / No error. (d)

7. His family members may arrive (a) / any moment (b) / by car. (c)/ No error. (d)

8. He went to office (a) / but returned back (b) / home immediately (c) / No error. (d)

9. The two brothers amicably divided (a) / their parent's property (b) /among them. (c) / No error. (d)

10. To attain a high academic standard (a) / in his college Sunil worked hard (b) / since morning till night (c) /No error.

DIRECTIONS (Qs. 11-15) : *In each of the following questions, find out which part has an error.* **[2012-I]**

11. The boos was irritated (a) / by him neglecting (b) / the duties and (c) / not listening to his advice (d)

12. Each of the three (a) / beggars were (b) / asking for more (c)/ food to eat (d)

13. My brother sent (a) / two pairs (b) / of shoe (c) / from America (d).

14. The young boy said (a) / that he (b) / neither liked me (c)/ nor my wife (d).

15. He was (a) / congratulated for (b) / his success in (c) / the 100 m race (d)

DIRECTIONS (Qs. 16-20) : *In each of the following questions, find out which part has an error.* **[2012-II]**

16. If you will (a) / follow my instructions (b) / you will get (c) / a suitable reward for this (d)

17. Harshad, along with (a) / his brother (b) / Ashwani and six senior officials (c) / were arrested (d)

18. He received timely support (a) / from his elder brother (b) / who is working abroad (c) / for the last six years (d)

19. One of the drawbacks (a) / of modern education are (b) / that it does not encourage original thinking (c) / No error (d)

20. Morphine and other (a) / narcotic drugs are valuable (b)/ medically, if misused (c) / it can cause irreparable damage (d)

DIRECTIONS (Qs. 21 – 25) : *In each of the following questions, find out which part has an error* **[2013-I]**

21. The police has (a)/arrested the thief (b)/who broke into my house (c)/last night. (d)

22. The man who (a)/they thought to be (b)/a gentleman turned out (c)/to be a rogue. (d)

23. I told him on his face (a)/that he could not hope (b)/to pass the stringent (c)/Medical examination of the Services Selection Board. (d)

24. Mohan is one of those boys (a)/who has expressed (b)/ willingness for joining (c)/the education tour. (d)

25. I may spend (a)/ this summer vacations (b)/with one of my friends (c)/ in the back waters of Kerala. (d)

DIRECTIONS (Qs. 26 – 29) : *Choose the correctly spelt word:* **[2014-II]**

26. (a) Parentheses   (b) Parenthsis
    (c) Parentesis   (d) Parenthses

27. (a) Verstile   (b) Versatile
    (c) Versetile   (d) Versatele

28. (a) Hemmorrhage   (b) Hemorrhage
    (c) Haemorrhage   (d) Hemmorrage

29. (a) Vetnerinarian   (b) Veternarian
    (c) Vetrinarian   (d) Veterinarian

Hints & Solutions

1. (a) Here it should be the definite article 'the' person instead of indefinite 'a' person.

2. (b) Beside means next to, at the side of while besides means making an additional point; anyway.

3. (a) The construction of the sentence should be as 'Impressed by what we had seen, we returned to the guest house.

4. (d) The sentence is correct. When neither, a singular form, is followed by a prepositional phrase with a plural object, there is a tendency, esp. in speech and less formal writing, to use a plural verb and pronoun: Neither of the guards were at their stations. In edited writing, however, singular verbs and pronouns are more common: Neither of the guards was at his station. This use of a singular verb and pronoun is usually recommended by usage guides.

5. (b) The infinitive form of the verb is always in the first form and preceded by to (e.g., to run, to dance, to think). Hence here the municipality is going to build a new school' should be correct option.

6. (a) Here 'was a' should be replaced with 'has been'. Thus the sentence should be 'It has been a year since I received any letter from my sister.'

7. (a) Here 'may' should be replaced with 'can'. Thus the sentence should be 'His family members can arrive any moment by car'.

8. (b) Here 'back' should be removed from the sentence. Return means to go backwards to where you have left before.

9. (c) Among should be replaced with between. Between should be used where the relationship is distinctly one-to-one. Whereas Among should be used where the entities are considered as a group.

10. (c) Here 'since' should be replaced with 'from'. From is used to indicate a specified place or time as a starting point.

11. (b) The correct sentence should be the boss was irritated with him for neglecting the duties and not listening to his advice.

12. (c) The correct sentence should be 'each of the three beggars was asking for more food to eat, each is often followed by a prepositional phrase ending in a plural word (Each of the cars), thus confusing the verb choice. Each is always singular and requires a singular verb. Each of the students is responsible for doing his or her work in the library.

13. (c) The correct sentence is 'My brother sent two pairs of shoes from America'.

14. (c) The correct sentence should be 'The young boy said that he liked neither me nor my wife.

15. (b) The preposition for should be replaced with on. Hence, the correct sentence should be he was congratulated on his success in the 100 m race.

16. (a) In the conditional sentence the correct patter should be 'If you follow my instructions........

17. (d) Along with, like in addition to, and together with, is often employed following the subject of a sentence or clause to introduce an addition. The addition, however does not alter the tense of the verb, which is governed by the subject. The king (singular), along with two aides, is expected in an hour. Hence, were is to be replaced with was.

18. (c) Present perfect continuous tense talks of an action or actions that started in the past and continued until recently or that continue into the future. Hence, the correct structure of the sentence should be - who has been working abroad.

19. (b) Here the verb 'are' is to be replaced with is; hence, the correct sequence of the sentence is 'one of the drawbacks of modern education is ....

20. (d) Since morphine and other narcotic drugs is in plural so, the pronoun 'it' should be replaced with 'they'.

21. (a) The police have arrested the thief who broke into my house last night. Here the verb 'has' is to be replaced by 'have' because the subject is a 1st person.

22. (d) Rouge is misspelt as rougue. Rouge means an unprincipled, deceitful, and unreliable person.

23. (b) Here 'could' is to be replaced by 'should'. Could is used in a hypothetical situation, where the speaker wants to express ability instead of willingness. Whereas 'should' expresses advisability.

24. (b) Here 'has' is to be replaced by 'have'.

25. (b) Here vacation is to be used as a singular because the noun 'friend' present after the pronoun is a plural.

26. (a) Parentheses. It's a plural form of parenthesis.

27. (b) Versatile

28. (c) Haemorrhage

29. (d) Veterinarian

3 Sentence Completion/ Cloze Test

1. His actions had ________ pain and suffering on thousands of people.
   - (a) affected
   - (b) imposed
   - (c) inflicted
   - (d) deplored

2. The Government will ______ all resources to fight poverty.
   - (a) collect
   - (b) exploit
   - (c) harness
   - (d) muster

3. The children ______ crackers to celebrate the victory of their team.
   - (a) burst
   - (b) fired
   - (c) shot
   - (d) released

4. I am ______ forward to our picnic scheduled in the next month.
   - (a) seeing
   - (b) looking
   - (c) planning
   - (d) thinking

5. I hope you must have _____ by now that failures are the stepping stones to success.
   - (a) known
   - (b) felt
   - (c) decided
   - (d) realized

6. Mohini is an independent and innovative thinker, it is best to grant her a good deal of __________ with regard to the direction of her research.
   - (a) leverage
   - (b) interest
   - (c) assistance
   - (d) money

7. The __________ of meat in your refrigerator does not necessarily indicate that you are a vegetarian.
   - (a) presence
   - (b) absence
   - (c) amount
   - (d) colour

8. Due to the rise of new media technology, many people predict newspapers will soon be __________ .
   - (a) obsolete
   - (b) ubiquitous
   - (c) commonplace
   - (d) widespread

9. Attention to detail is the __________ of a fine craftsman.
   - (a) hallmark
   - (b) stamp
   - (c) authenticity
   - (d) show

10. Although the two sisters are twins, they look somewhat __________ .
    - (a) alike
    - (b) unique
    - (d) different
    - (d) related

11. Sanjay was______________ with divine vision to see the great battle.
    - (a) demure
    - (b) authorized
    - (c) endowed
    - (d) uttered

12. There was so much__________ material in the essay that it was difficult to get the author's message.
    - (a) variegated
    - (b) superficial
    - (c) extraneous
    - (d) exemplary

13. The world is so constructed that if you wish to enjoy its pleasures, you must also______ its pains.
    - (a) deny
    - (b) neglect
    - (c) ignore
    - (d) endure

14. Indian press did not give ____________ to the British publicity.
    - (a) credence
    - (b) scion
    - (c) augury
    - (d) opportunity

15. Travellers ____________ their reservations well in advance if they want to travel during the Diwali holidays.
    - (a) has better to get
    - (b) had better get
    - (c) had to get better
    - (d) had better got

16. His book was marked by many ______ remarks which made us forget its main theme.
    - (a) irrelevant
    - (b) objective
    - (c) slanted
    - (d) digressive

17. Some people have the capacity for learning foreign languages but they have no ________ to speak.
    - (a) interest
    - (b) ability
    - (c) fondness
    - (d) inclination

18. The dispute among the parties became so _______ that there was every likelihood of a free exchange of blows
    - (a) complicated
    - (b) acrimonious
    - (c) bellicose
    - (d) aggressive

19. The judge decided to resign when he was ________ for promotion to Chief Justice.
    (a) passed by   (b) passed out
    (c) passed off   (d) passed over
20. Questions will be answered by a ________ of experts.
    (a) staff   (b) panel
    (c) bunch   (d) band

DIRECTIONS (Qs. 21-25) : *Pick up the most effective word from the given words to fill in the blanks to make the sentence meaningfully complete.*   *[2013-I]*

21. According to the weather __________ it is going to be cloudy today.
    (a) announcement   (b) indication
    (c) prediction   (d) forecast
22. The villagers __________ the murder of their leader by burning the police van.
    (a) protested   (b) avenged
    (c) mourned   (d) consoled
23. While on the routine fight, the aircraft was hit by a missile and __________ into flames.
    (a) fired (b)   burst
    (c) caught   (d) engulfed
24. Hari got the company car for a __________ price as he was the senior most employee in the company.
    (a) reduced   (b) discounted
    (c) fixed (d)   nominal
25. The unruly behaviour of the soldiers __________ their commander.
    (a) clashed   (b) aggrieved
    (c) incensed   (d) impeached

DIRECTIONS (Qs. 26-31) : *Select the most appropriate word from the options against each number :*

Those living in the slums are **26** and tough because they are totally **27** to the vagaries and hardships of life. The rising sun **28** the day and the setting sun closes the day for them. It is like a drama where the curtain **29** up in the morning and comes down in the evening. They don't **30** hypertension and heart attacks because there is, after all **31** to worry about.   *[2014-I]*

26. (a) Poor   (b) Sick
    (c) Hardy   (d) Weak
27. (a) Dependent   (b) Independent
    (c) Exposed   (d) Tried
28. (a) Heralds   (b) Herald
    (c) Bring   (d) Brings
29. (a) Hangs   (b) Hand
    (c) Goes   (d) Shines
30. (a) Know   (b) Get
    (c) Think   (d) Have
31. (a) Everything   (b) Something
    (c) Somewhere   (d) Nothing

DIRECTIONS (Qs. 32-37) : *Select the most appropriate word from the options against each number:*   *[2014-II]*

Science has made an _**32**_ contribution to the relief of human suffering and humanity _**33**_ a deep _**34**_ of gratitude to scientists whose _**35**_ and sacrifices have led to many _**36**_ discoveries and inventions which have done so much to _**37**_ human pain and misery.

32. (a) excessive   (b) enormous
    (c) intensive   (d) active
33. (a) feels   (b) offers
    (c) owes   (d) acknowledges
34. (a) amount   (b) fund
    (c) loan   (d) debt
35. (a) labours   (b) discoveries
    (c) achievements   (d) successes
36. (a) strange   (b) useful
    (c) advantageous   (d) profitable
37. (a) decrease   (b) disappears
    (c) alleviate   (d) belittle

DIRECTIONS (Qs. 38-43) : *Select the most appropriate word from the options against each number :*   *[2015-I]*

As home entertainment, television is rapidly becoming more **(38)** than any other form. A news broadcast becomes more immediate when people **(39)** actually see the scene **(40)** question and the movement of the figures. Films could be viewed in the **(41)** of the home and a variety of shows are also available. One of the advantages of travel programmes is the **(42)** of faraway places which many viewers would not **(43)** see.

38. (a) interesting   (b) popular
    (c) powerful   (d) purposeful
39. (a) could   (b) would
    (c) might   (d) shall
40. (a) of   (b) with
    (c) as   (d) in
41. (a) surroundings   (b) assistance
    (c) comfort   (d) privilege
42. (a) glimpses   (b) image
    (c) portrait   (d) picture
43. (a) possible   (b) rather
    (c) else   (d) otherwise

Hints & Solutions

1. **(c)** Inflicted which means make (someone) do something unpleasant; e.g. "The teacher inflicted his rage on the students. Other options do not correspond.

2. **(c)** Harness means exploit the power of.

3. **(a)** Burst. If you are bursting crackers then you are setting off fireworks.

4. **(b)** The correct phrase is look forward to.

5. **(d)** Realize means perceive (an idea or situation) mentally which is correct filler.

6. **(a)** Leverage means to use (something) to maximum advantage.

7. **(b)** Absence is the most appropriate word because a contrast is made here.

8. **(a)** Obsolete means no longer in use.

9. **(b)** Here stamp is being used as a trademark or a signature style.

10. **(c)** Although is used to show a contrast. Twins are usually considered similar looking but using although makes the sentence contrasting.

11. **(c)** The correct option is endowed which means provided or supplied or equipped with (especially as by inheritance or nature).

12. **(c)** Extraneous means not pertinent to the matter under consideration.

13. **(d)** Endure means put up with something or somebody unpleasant.

14. **(a)** Credence means the mental attitude that something is believable and should be accepted as true.

15. **(b)** The correct filler is 'had better get'. Hence, the correct sentence should be the travellers had better get their reservations well in advance if they want to travel during the Diwali holidays.

16. **(d)** The correct filler here should be digressive.

17. **(d)** Here the right option should be 'inclination'.

18. **(b)** Acrimonious is the most effective word among the given options.

19. **(d)** Pass over means to leave out, disregard.

20. **(b)** Panel rightly corresponds with the experts.

21. **(d)** Forecast is used to predict or estimate a future event.

22. **(b)** Avenged means to inflict harm in return for an injury or wrong done to oneself or another.

23. **(b)** Burst means to break open or apart suddenly and violently, especially as a result of an impact (here the impact is hit by a missile).

24. **(b)** Being the senior most employee, Hari got a discount on the company car. The discount was proportional to his long service for the company.

25. **(c)** Incensed means extremely angry. Thus the unruly behaviour of the soldiers made their commander extremely angry.

26. **(c)** Hardy. In the sentence, hardy is used along with the word tough to describe the people living in slums.

27. **(c)** Exposed. In the sentence, the author tells how slum people are subject to uncertainties and hardships of life.

28. **(d)** Brings. Using the third person singular present form of bring instead of infinitive form.

29. **(c)** goes. In the sentence, comes is used with evening. And goes is the opposite of come which will thus come along morning.

30. **(d)** have. It is the most appropriate word from the given options.

31. **(d)** nothing. The sentence begins with don't, which means negation.

32. **(b)** enormous

33. **(c)** owes

34. **(d)** debt

35. **(a)** labours

36. **(b)** useful

37. **(c)** alleviate

38. **(b)** The word rapidly can match popular, not with other options.

39. **(a)** Could shows the ability.

40. **(d)** In question' means being discussed or considered ex. On the days in question there were several serious questions.

41. **(c)** In the comfort of home' defines in the home atmosphere without going out for the purpose of entertainment.

42. **(a)**

43. **(d)** Otherwise television this would not have possible.

4

Reading Comprehension

DIRECTIONS (Qs. 1- 5) : *Read the following passage carefully and answer the questions given below it.*

We stand poised precariously and challengingly on the razor's edge of destiny. We are now at the mercy of atom bombs and the like which would destroy us completely if we fail to control them wisely. And wisdom in this crisis means sensitiveness to the basic values of life; it means a vivid realization that we are literally living in one world where we must either swim together or sink together. We cannot afford to tamper with man's single minded loyalty to peace and international understanding. Anyone, who does it is a traitor not only to man's past and present, but also to his future, because he is mortgaging the destiny of unborn generations.

1. From the tone and style of the passage it appears that the writer is **[2011-I]**
   (a) a prose writer with a fascination for images and metaphors.
   (b) a humanist with a clear foresight.
   (c) a traitor who wishes to mortgage the destiny of future generations.
   (d) unaware of the global power situation.

2. The best way to escape complete annihilation in an atomic war is to **[2011-I]**
   (a) work for international understanding and harmony.
   (b) invent more powerful weapons.
   (c) turn to religion.
   (d) ban nuclear weapons.

3. The phrase 'razor's edge of destiny' means a/an **[2011-I]**
   (a) enigma that cuts through the pattern of life like the edge of a razor.
   (b) critical situation that foreordains the future.
   (c) sharp line of division that marks the alternative courses of action in the future.
   (d) destiny with sharp edges.

4. According to the writer, 'wisdom' on the razor's edge of destiny means **[2011-I]**
   (a) awareness that we stand poised precariously on the razor's edge of destiny.
   (b) determination to ban nuclear weapons.
   (c) responsibility to the 'unborn generations'.
   (d) awareness of the basic values of life.

5. The author is concerned about the threat of nuclear weapons because he feels that **[2011-I]**
   (a) a nuclear war will destroy human civilization.
   (b) all countries are interlinked and one cannot escape the consequences of what happens to another country.
   (c) the world is on the brink of disaster.
   (d) his country is threatened by a nuclear war.

DIRECTIONS (Qs. 6-9) : *Read the following passage carefully and answer the questions given below it.*

Educational planning should aim at meeting the educational needs of the entire population of all age groups. While the traditional structure of education as a three layer hierarchy from the primary stage to the university represents the core, we should not overlook the periphery which is equally important. Under modern conditions, workers need to rewind, or renew their enthusiasm, or strike out in a new direction, or improve their skills as much as any university professor. The retired and aged have their needs as well. Educational planning, in other words, should take care of the needs of everyone.

Our structures of educational have been built up on the assumption that there is a terminal point of education. This basic defect has become all the more harmful today. A UNESCO report entitled 'Learning to Be' prepared by Edgar Faure and other in 1973 asserts that the education of children must prepare the future adult for various forms of self-learning. A viable education system of the future should consist of modules with different kind of functions serving a diversity of constituents. And performance, not the period of study, should be the basis for credentials. The writing is already on the wall.

In view of the fact that the significance of a commitment of lifelong learning and lifetime education is being discussed only in recent years even in educationally advanced countries, the possibility of the idea becoming an integral part of educational thinking seems to be a far cry. For, to move in that direction means so much more than some simple rearrangement of the present organisation of education. But a good beginning can be made by developing Open University programmes for older learners of different categories and introducing extension services in the conventional colleges and schools. Also, these institutions should learn to cooperate with numerous community organisations such as libraries, museums, municipal recreational programmes, health services etc. **[2011-II]**

6. What is the main thrust of the author?

(a) Traditional systems should be strengthened.

(b) Formal education is more important than non-formal.

(c) One should never cease to learn.

(d) It is impossible to meet the needs of everyone.

7. What should be the major characteristic of the future educational system?

(a) Different modules with same function.

(b) Same module for different groups.

(c) No modules but standard compulsory programme for all.

(d) None of the above

8. According to the author, what measures should open university adopt to meet modern conditions?

(a) Develop various programmes for adult learners.

(b) Open more colleges in traditional lines.

(c) Cater to the needs of those who represent 'cone'.

(d) Primary education should be under the control of open universities.

9. In the context of the passage, what is the meaning of the sentence "The writing is already on the wall"?

(a) Everything is uncertain now-a-days.

(b) Changes have already taken place.

(c) The signs of change are already visible.

(c) You cannot change the future.

DIRECTIONS (Qs. 10-14) : *Read the following passage carefully and answer the questions given below:*

Pablo Picasso showed his truly exceptional talent from a very young age. His first word was lapiz (Spanish for pencil) and he learnt to draw before he could talk. He was the only son in the family and very good-looking, so he was thoroughly spoilt. He hated school and often refused to go unless his doting parents allowed him to take one of his father's pet pigeons with him.

Apart from pigeons, his great love was art and when in 1891 his father, who was an amateur artist, got a job as a drawing teacher at a college, Pablo went with him to the college. He often watched his father paint and sometimes was allowed to help. One evening his father was painting a picture of their pigeons when he had to leave the room. He returned to find that Pablo had completed the picture, and it was so amazingly beautiful and lifelike that he gave his son his own palette and brushes and never painted again. Pablo was just thirteen.   *[2012-I]*

10. As a boy Pablo Picasso was

(a) ordinary looking but talented.

(b) handsome and talented.

(c) handsome and studious.

(d) handsome and hardworking.

11. He was spoilt mostly because he was

(a) a smart boy.

(b) loved by one and all.

(c) the only son in the family.

(d) always surrounded by notorious boys.

12. Picasso went to school only when

(a) his friends accompanied him.

(b) his father went with him.

(c) he was allowed to paint at school.

(d) he was allowed to carry a pet with him.

13. When his father painted in the college, Pablo

(a) occasionally helped him. (b) rarely helped him.

(c) always helped him.   (d) invariably helped him.

14. Pablo's father gave up painting because he

(a) did not like the job.

(b) retired from the college.

(c) was impressed by his son's talent.

(d) lost interest in painting.

DIRECTIONS (Qs. 15- 17) : *Read the following passage carefully and answer the questions given below:*

The development and widespread use of computer technology and the internet have transformed how we communicate, how business is conducted, how information is dispersed, and how society is organised. Prior to 1980, in-depth information about any one subject matter was attained through laborious research involving countless visits to libraries and via repeated interviews with persons of known reputation and reputable expertise. Now, a great deal of information is available at the click of a mouse button, all attainable from within the confines of one's own home or from the use of a computer in an office. Previous labour-intensive support Jobs. such as loading and unpacking of trucks', luggage handling at airports, and food manufacturing, once performed by a large middle-class workforce, are now performed routinely by robots which are monitored by computer-controlled systems. Our lives have been simplified but these benefits which have been ushered in by the technology revolution have had an adverse effect on the core of our interpersonal-relationships. Mere communication is no longer via postal mail or face-to-face contact, but rather via electronic email, personal internet message boards and by virtue of hand-held personal electronic assistants. Although computer technology has brought us to within a mouse-click of any sought-after piece of information, this technology boom has sequestered us to the confines of our computer desks and homes and has removed us away from those traditional settings where personal and communication skills are developed.   *[2012-II]*

15. The author's attitude the advent of computer technology can be best summarised as

(a) optimistic and thankful

(b) appreciative but reserved

(c) candid and reverent.

(d) understanding and obsessive

16. The author would agree with which of the following statements?

(a) The advent of computer technology has decreased access to libraries

(b) Because of advancements in robotics, labour-intensive jobs are more plentiful

(c) Although heralded as a great leap forward, the widespread use of computer technology is not without its setbacks

(d) Of all the benefits ushered in by the use the internet. electronic email is the most beneficial

17. The author's primary purpose in writing this passage is most likely which of the following?

(a) To downplay the need for the internet

(b) To explain how robotics and the internet have had both a positive and negative influence on how we live

(c) To pave way for the next great technology revolution

(d) To showcase the wonders of recent technology advancements

DIRECTIONS (Qs. 18-22) : *Read the following passage carefully and answer the questions given below:*

We shall go on the end, we shall fight in France, we shall fight on the seas and oceans, we shall fight with the growing confidence and strength in the air, we shall defend our island, whatever the cost may be, we shall fight on the beaches, we shall fight on the landing grounds, we shall fight in the fields and in the streets, we shall fight in the hills. We shall never surrender, and even if this island or a large part of it was subjugated and starving, then our empire beyond the seas would carry on the struggle, until the New World steps forth to the rescue and the liberation of the Old.

[2013-I]

18. On the basis of the passage which of the following statements may be said to be correct?

(a) The speaker is encouraging his men for the conquest of France

(b) The speaker is an aggressive and maniacal war-monger

(c) The speaker is not satisfied with the conquest of the island

(d) The speaker is a patriot urging the defence of his motherland

19. The speaker in the passage wants to go on fighting because

(a) he is a raving lunatic

(b) he is in a state of utter despair

(c) he expects help from other quarters

(d) he is the leader of a suicide squad

20. Which of the following pair of the phrases helps best to bring out the intension of the speaker?

(a) "Go on to the end", "shall never surrender"

(b) "Growing confidence", "subjugated and starving"

(c) "Subjugated and starving", "fighting and landing around"

(d) "Fighting in the streets", "subjugated and starving"

21. The passage consists of repetitive patterns in syntax and vocabulary. The effect of this style is that it

(a) reveals the speaker's defects in giving a speech

(b) produces the impression of bad poetry

(c) conveys the speaker's helpless situation

(d) reinforces the speaker's basic intention

22. The tone of the speaker is

(a) pleading and urging

(b) inspiring and encouraging

(c) discouraging and gloomy

(d) menacing and bullying

DIRECTIONS (Qs. 23–26) : *Read the following passage carefully and answer the questions given below it:*

And then Gandhi came. He was like a powerful current of fresh air that made us stretch ourselves and take deep breaths, like a beam of light that pierced the darkness and removed the scales from our eyes, like a whirlwind that upset many things but most of all the working of people's minds. He did not descend from the top; he seemed to emerge from the millions of India, speaking their language and incessantly drawing attention to them and their appalling condition. Get off the backs of these peasants and workers, he told us, all of you who live by their exploitation; get rid of the system that produces this poverty and misery. *[2014-I]*

23. Gandhi came like a powerful current of fresh air and

(a) awakened us to the plight of the masses in the grip of oppressors

(b) made us patriotic

(c) emboldened us to attack and destroy the oppressors

(d) praised our culture

24. The rise of Gandhi

(a) shocked people

(b) made India powerful

(c) made the condemnation of the exploiter final

(d) made women feel secure

25. Gandhi fought the

(a) rich   (b) oppressor

(c) apathetic masses   (d) unjust system

26. The conspicuous role of Gandhi is that of a

(a) father   (b) reformer

(c) teacher   (d) liberator

DIRECTIONS (Qs. 27–29) : *Read the following passage carefully and answer the questions given below it:*

Language is often used for one of the following three purposes, namely, to inform, to convince and to persuade. The first requiring talent of telling what we know, is a matter of little difficulty. The second demands reasoning. The third, besides reasoning, demands all the aid that we can obtain from the use of figures of speech or figures of rhetoric, which means the power of persuasion.

[2014-II]

27. Rhetoric is the

(a) art of reasoning

(b) use of figure of speech

(c) power of persuasion

(d) means of communicating information

28. The art of persuasion requires the use of
(a) information and talent feels
(b) reasoning and information
(c) figure of speech
(d) reasoning and figure of speech

29. The above passage is
(a) informative   (b) persuasive
(c) convincing   (d) rhetorical

DIRECTIONS (Qs. 30–32) : *Read the following passage carefully and answer the questions given below it :*

In spring, polar bear mothers emerge from dens with three months old cubs. The mother bear has fasted for as long as eight months but that does not stop the young from demanding full access to her remaining reserves. If there are triplets, the most persistent stands to gain an extra meal at the expense of others. The smallest of the cubs forfeits many meals to stronger siblings. Females are protective of their cubs but tend to ignore family rivalry over food. In 21 years of photographing polar bears. I have only once seen the smallest of triplets survive till autumn.   *[2015-I]*

30. With reference to the passage, the following assumptions have been made :
I. Polar bears fast as long as eight months due to non availability of prey.
II. Polar bears always give birth to triplets.
Which of the assumptions given above is/are true?
(a) I only   (b) II only
(c) Both I and II   (d) Neither I nor II

31. Female polar bears give birth during
(a) Spring   (b) Summer
(c) Autumn   (d) Winter

32. Mother bear
(a) Takes sides over cubs
(b) Lets the cubs fend for themselves
(c) Feeds only their favourites
(d) Sees that all cubs get an equal share

Hints & Solutions

1. (b) The writer appears to be a humanist with a clear foresight according to the passage.
2. (d) The best option to escape complete annihilation in an atomic war is to ban nuclear weapons.
3. (b) The phrase 'razor's edge of destiny' implies here the critical situation that foreordains the future.
4. (d) 'Wisdom' on the razor's edge of destiny in the chapter signifies awareness of the basic values of life.
5. (a) The author is concerned about the threat of nuclear weapons because he feels that a nuclear war will destroy human civilization.
6. (c) The author highlights the importance and need of lifelong learning for everyone from different spheres of life and age groups.
7. (d) The major characteristic of the future educational system includes modules with different kind of functions serving a diversity of constituents.
8. (a) Developing different programmes for adult learners in conjunction with cooperation from various community organisation like libraries, museums etc.
9. (b) the meaning of the idiom "The writing is already on the wall" is to know that something is about to happen.
10. (b) As a boy Pablo Picasso was handsome and talented.
11. (c) Picasso was spoilt mostly because he was the only son in the family.
12. (d) Picasso went to school only when he was allowed to carry a pet with him.
13. (a) When his father painted in the college, Pablo occasionally helped him.
14. (c) Pablo's father gave up painting because he was impressed by his son's talent.
15. (b) The author's attitude the advent of computer technology can be best summarised as the appreciative but reserved.
16. (c) The sentence '....but these benefits which have been ushered in by the technology revolution have had an adverse effect on the core of our interpersonal-relationships' affirms that the author would agree with the widespread use of computer technology is not without its setbacks.
17. (b) The author's primary purpose in writing this passage is to explain how robotics and the internet have had both a positive and negative influence on how we live.
18. (d) The speaker is a patriot who is urging to fight against France for saving his motherland at any cost.
19. (c) The speaker wants a change, for which he is expecting his people (countrymen) and people from other quarters to come forth and fight for it.
20. (a) The phrase "Go on to the end, shall never surrender" means turning all odds to save his motherland from France.
21. (d) Repetition of something means putting pressure and highlighting it. In this paragraph, speaker is highlighting his intentions of fighting for the country till the very end.
22. (b) Speaker is encouraging his countrymen to fight for their island and his words are inspiring.
23. (a) The author states how Gandhi showed the mirror to the masses on how the cruel system is deteriorating the country and urged them to stand up for themselves.
24. (b) The rise of Gandhi empowered the people which thus made the country strong.
25. (c) Gandhi fought the unjust system that was exploiting the peasants and workers.
26. (d) As seen in the paragraph, Gandhi is seen as a liberator. A liberator is a person who liberates a person or place from imprisonment or oppression.
27. (c) Rhetoric is the power of persuasion.
28. (d) The art of persuasion requires the use of reasoning and figure of speech.
29. (d)
30. (a)
31. (d)
32. (b) The sentence means, Mother Bear never interfers in the food sharing of her cubs.

1 Number System/ Simplification

1. In a 225 meter long yard 26 trees are planted at equal distance, one tree being at each end of the yard. What is the distance between two consecutive trees ? *[2011-I]*

   (a) 10 meters   (b) 8 meters
   (c) 12 meters   (d) 9 meters

2. A bonus of ₹ 1000 is divided among three employees. Rohit gets twice the amount Sachin gets. Sachin gets one fifth of what Gagan gets. How much amount does Gagan get ? *[2011-I]*

   (a) ₹ 500   (b) ₹ 625
   (c) ₹ 750   (d) ₹ 120

3. A boy was asked to multiply a number by 25. Instead, he multiplied the number by 52 and got the answer 324 more than the correct answer. The number to be multiplied was *[2011-I]*

   (a) 12   (b) 15
   (c) 25   (d) 32

4. The value of (?) in the equation $365.089 - ? + 89.72 = 302.35$ is *[2011-I]*

   (a) 152.456   (b) 152.459
   (c) 153.456   (d) 153.459

5. A sum of ₹ 312 is divided among 60 boys and some girls in such a way that each boy gets ₹ 3.60 and each girl gets ₹ 2.40. The number of girls are- *[2011-I]*

   (a) 35   (b) 60
   (c) 40   (d) 65

6. The number of girls in a class in five times the number of boys. Which of the following cannot be the total number of children in the class ? *[2011-II]*

   (a) 24   (b) 30
   (c) 35   (d) 54

7. Ram went to a shop to buy 50 kg of rice. He bought two varieties of rice which cost him ₹ 4.50 per kg and ₹ 5 per kg. He spent a total of ₹ 240. What was the quantity of the cheaper rice purchased by him ? *[2011-II]*

   (a) 20 Kg   (b) 25 Kg
   (c) 30 Kg   (d) None of these

8. A man has ₹ 640 in the denominations of one rupee, five rupee and ten rupee notes. The number of each type of notes are equal. What is the total number of notes he has ? *[2011-II]*

   (a) 60   (b) 150
   (c) 90   (d) 120

9. A man has few hens and cows. If the total number of heads are 48 and the total number of feet are 140, then the number of hens are *[2011-II]*

   (a) 22   (b) 23
   (c) 24   (d) 26

10. A student was asked to divide a number by 3. But, instead of dividing it he multiplied it by 3 and got 29.7 as the answer. What was the correct answer had he not made the mistake ? *[2011-II]*

   (a) 3.3   (b) 9.3
   (c) 9.8   (d) 9.9

11. Which of the following fraction is the smallest ? *[2011-II]*

   (a) 9/13   (b) 17/26
   (c) 28/39   (d) 33/52

12. Which of the following fractions are in ascending order ? *[2012-I]*

   (a) 2/3, 3/5,7/9,9/11,8/9   (b) 3/5, 2/3, 9/11, 7/9, 8/9
   (c) 3/5, 2/3, 7/9, 9/11, 8/9   (d) 8/9, 9/11, 7/9, 2/3, 3/5

13. Find the sum of : $337.62 + 8.591 + 34.4 = ?$ *[2012-I]*

   (a) 370.611   (b) 380.511
   (c) 380.611   (d) 426.97

14. Find the sum of :- $1/9+1/6+1/12+1/72$ *[2012-I]*

   (a) 3/5   (b) 3/2
   (c) 3/8   (d) 4/7

15. Find the value of : $?\% \text{ of } 932 + 30 = 309.6$ *[2012-I]*

   (a) 25   (b) 30
   (c) 35   (d) 40

16. The difference between a number and its two-fifth is 510. What is 10% of that number ? *[2012-I]*

   (a) 12.75   (b) 85
   (c) 204   (d) None

17. If $4/5^{th}$ of an estate is worth ₹ 16,800, then the value of $3/7^{th}$ of the estate is *[2012-I]*

   (a) ₹ 9000   (b) ₹ 21000
   (c) ₹ 72000   (d) ₹ 90000

18. If $a/b = 3/4$ and $8a + 5b = 22$, then the value of 'a' is *[2012-I]*

   (a) 1   (b)   1/2
   (c) 3/2   (d)   3/4

19. If $(a - b)$ is 6 more than $(c + d)$ and $(a + b)$ is 3 less than $(c - d)$, then the value of $(a - c)$ is *[2012-I]*

   (a) 0.5   (b) 1.0
   (c) 1.5   (d) 2.0

20. The number whose square is equal to the difference of the squares of 40 and 32 is *[2012-II]*
- (a) 45.09
- (b) 24
- (c) 25
- (d) 28

21. 15 buckets of water fill a tank when the capacity of each bucket is 7 litres How many buckets will be needed to fill the same tank, if the capacity of the bucket is 5 litres ? *[2012-II]*
- (a) 12
- (b) 24
- (c) 21
- (d) 30

22. A vessel, full of water, weighs 27.5 kg. when the vessel is 1/4 full, it weighs 12.26 kg. Find the weight of empty vessel ? *[2012-II]*
- (a) 7.18 kg
- (b) 6.54 kg
- (c) 2.75 kg
- (d) 2 5 kg

23. If $a+b = 10$ and $ab = 21$, find the value of a^3+b^3 *[2012-II]*
- (a) 370
- (b) 210
- (c) 730
- (d) 598

24. If $a/(a+b)=17/23$, what is $(a+b)/(a-b)$ equal to ? *[2012-II]*
- (a) 13/7
- (b) 23/11
- (c) 14/5
- (d) 25/9

25. Find the value of : $\dfrac{(598+479)^2-(598-479)^2}{(598\times479)}$
- (a) 2
- (b) 6
- (c) 4
- (d) 8

26. A jar contains black and white marbles. If there are ten marbles in the jar, then which of the following could not be the ratio of black to white marbles ? *[2012-III]*
- (a) 9:1
- (b) 7:3
- (c) 1:10
- (d) 6:4

27. The number whose square is equal to the difference of the squares of 37 and 23 is *[2013-I]*
- (a) 45.09
- (b) 28.98
- (c) 47.09
- (d) 28

28. A vessel, full of water, weights 24 kg. When the vessel is 1/4 full, it weighs 9 kg. Find the weight of empty vessel. *[2013-I]*
- (a) 4 kg
- (b) 5 kg
- (c) 8 kg
- (d) 3 kg

29. If $a-b = 4$ and $ab = 45$ find the value of a^3-b^3. *[2013-I]*
- (a) 604
- (b) 370
- (c) 253
- (d) 199

30. If $a/(a+b) = 15/21$, what is $(a+b)/(a-b)$ equal to ? *[2013-I]*
- (a) 13/9
- (b) 23/11
- (c) 14/5
- (d) 21/9

31. Find the value of : $\dfrac{(798+579)^2-(798-579)^2}{(798\times579)} = ?$

[2013-I]
- (a) 2
- (b) 6
- (c) 4
- (d) 8

32. 18 buckets of water fill a tank when the capacity of each bucket is 8 litres. How many buckets will be needed to fill the same tank, if the capacity of the bucket is 12 litres ? *[2013-I]*
- (a) 12
- (b) 13.5
- (c) 24
- (d) can not be determined due to insufficient data

33. Find two natural numbers whose sum is 85 and the least common multiple is 102. *[2014-I]*
- (a) 30 and 55
- (b) 17 and 68
- (c) 35 and 55
- (d) 51 and 34

34. In a fort there was sufficient food for 200 soldiers for 31 days. After 27 days, 120 soldiers left the fort. For how many extra days will the rest of the food last for the remaining soldiers ? *[2014-I]*
- (a) 12 days
- (b) 10 days
- (c) 8 days
- (d) 6 days

35. 10 is added to a certain number, the sum is multiplied by 7, the product is divided by 5 and 5 is subtracted from the quotient. The remainder left is half of 88. What is the number ? *[2014-I]*
- (a) 21
- (b) 20
- (c) 25
- (d) 30

36. A bag contains 25 paise, 50 paise and 1 ₹ coins. There are 220 coins in all and the total amount in the bag is ₹ 160. If there are thrice as many 1 ₹ coins as there are 25 paise coins, then what is the number of 50 paise coins ? *[2014-I]*
- (a) 60
- (b) 40
- (c) 120
- (d) 80

37. The sum of two numbers is equal to thrice their difference. If the smaller of the numbers is 10 find the other number. *[2014-I]*
- (a) 15
- (b) 30
- (c) 40
- (d) None of these.

38. Simplify: $\dfrac{69\times69\times69-65\times65\times65}{69\times69+69\times65+65\times65}$ *[2014-I]*
- (a) 1
- (b) 4
- (c) 0.216
- (d) 0.164

39. 7 is added to a certain number, the sum is multiplied by 5; the product is divided by 9 and 3 is subtracted from the quotient. The remainder left is 12. What is the number ? *[2014-II]*
- (a) 20
- (b) 30
- (c) 40
- (d) 5

40. In Arun's opinion his weight is greater than 65 kg but less than 72 kg. His brother does not agree with Arun and he thinks that Arun's weight is greater than 60 kg but less than 70 kg. His mother's view is that his weight cannot be greater than 68 kg. If all of them are correct in their estimation, what is the average of different probable weights of Arun ? *[2014-II]*
- (a) 71 kg
- (b) 66 kg
- (c) 66.5 kg
- (d) 68 kg

41. How many digits will be there to the right of the decimal point in the product of 95.75 and 0.02554 ? *[2014-II]*
- (a) 5
- (b) 6
- (c) 7
- (d) Insufficient data

Hints & Solutions

1. (d) Distance between two consecutive trees $= \dfrac{222}{25} =$ meters.

2. (b) According to question

$R = 2S$

$S = \dfrac{1}{5}G$

$R + S + G = 1000$

$2S + S + 5S$ ₹ 1000

$8S = 1000$

$S = 125$

Hence, Gagan's get ₹ 625.

3. (a) Let the number be x.

$25x + 324 = 52x$

$52x - 25x = 324$

$27x = 324$

$x = 12$

4. (b) $365.089 - ? + 89.72 = 302.35$

$? = 365.089 + 89.72 - 302.35$

$? = 152.459$

5. (c) Let the number of girls be x.

$60 \times 3.60 + x \times 2.40 = 312$

$x = 40$

6. (c) Let the number of boys in class be x.

Therefore the number of girls in class be 5x.

Total number of children in class $= x + 5x = 6x$.

Hence, 35 cannot be the total number of children as it's not the multiple of 6.

7. (a) Let one variety of rice be x kg.

Another quantity $= (50 - x)$ kg

According to question $x \times 4.50 + (50 - x)\, 5 = 240$

$4.5x + 250 - 5x = 240$

$0.5x = 10$

$x = 20$

Hence, the quantity of cheaper rice was 20 kg.

8. (d) Let the number of each type of notes be x. According to question $1 \times x + 5 \times x + 10 \times x = 640$

$16x = 640$

$x = 40$

Total number of notes $= 40 + 40 + 40 = 120$

9. (d) Let hens and cows are x and y respectively

$x + y = 48$ ....(1)

$2x + 4y = 140$

$x + 2y = 70$ ....(2)

After solving eq. (1) & (2)

$y = 22$

$\therefore\ x = 26$

10. (a) Let the number $= x$

According to question

$3x = 29.7$

$x = 9.9$

Correct answer $= \dfrac{9.9}{3} = 3.3$

11. (d) $\dfrac{9}{13} = 0.692;\quad \dfrac{17}{26} = 0.654$

$\dfrac{28}{39} = 0.717;\quad \dfrac{33}{52} = 0.634$

Hence, $\dfrac{33}{52}$ is the smallest fraction.

12. (c) $\dfrac{2}{3} = 0.67$

$\dfrac{3}{5} = 0.6$

$\dfrac{7}{9} = 0.7$

$\dfrac{9}{11} = 0.81$

$\dfrac{8}{9} = 0.88$

Correct ascending order

$= \dfrac{3}{5} < \dfrac{2}{3} < \dfrac{7}{9} < \dfrac{9}{11} < \dfrac{8}{9}$

13. (c) $337.62 + 8.591 + 34.4 = 380.611$

14. (c) $\dfrac{1}{9} + \dfrac{1}{6} + \dfrac{1}{12} + \dfrac{1}{72}$

$\Rightarrow \dfrac{8 + 12 + 6 + 1}{72}$

$\Rightarrow \dfrac{27}{72} = \dfrac{3}{8}$

15. (b) ?% of $932 + 30 = 309.6$

?% of $932 = 309.6 - 30$

$\dfrac{?}{100} \times 932 = 279.6$

$? = 30.$

16. (b) Let the number $= x$

According to question

$x - \dfrac{2}{5}x = 510$

$\dfrac{3x}{5} = 510$

$x = \dfrac{510 \times 5}{3}$

$x = 850$

10% of $x = \dfrac{10}{100} \times 850 = 85$

17. **(a)** Let the value of estate be x.

$$\frac{4}{5}x = 16800 \Rightarrow x = 16800 \times \frac{5}{4} = 21000$$

Then, $\frac{3}{7} \times 21000 = 9000$

18. $\dfrac{a}{b} = \dfrac{3}{4} \Rightarrow b = \dfrac{3}{4}a$

$8a + 5b = 22$

$\Rightarrow 8a + 5 \times \dfrac{4}{3} \times a = 22$

$$a = \frac{3}{2}$$

19. $a - b = (c + d) + 6$ ...(1)

$a + b = (c - d) - 3$ ...(2)

adding eq. (1) and (2)

$a - c = \dfrac{3}{2} = 1.5$

20. **(b)** $(40)^2 - (32)^2 = 1600 - 1024 = 576$

Hence, 24 is the required number.

21. **(c)** Less capacity, more buckets. (Indirect proportion)

$\therefore 5 : 15 :: 7 : x$

$$\frac{5}{15} = \frac{7}{x}$$

$x = 21$

Hence, 21 buckets will be needed to fill the same tank.

22. **(a)** Let 'x' be the weight of empty vessel and 'y' be the weight of full vessel.

$x + y = 27.5$ ...(1)

$x + \dfrac{y}{4} = 12.26$

$4x + y = 4 \times 12.26$ ...(2)

Subtracting equation (1) from (2)

$4x - x = 49.04 - 27.5$

$3x = 21.54$

$x = 7.18$ kg

23. **(a)** Given, $a + b = 10$

Squaring on both sides

$a^2 + b^2 + 2ab = 100$

$a^2 + b^2 = 100 - 2 \times 21$

$a^2 + b^2 = 58$

Now, $a^3 + b^3 = (a + b)(a^2 + b^2 - ab)$

$= (10)(58 - 21)$

$= 10 \times 37 = 370$

24. **(b)** $\dfrac{a}{a + b} = \dfrac{17}{23}$

$23a = 17a + 17b$

$6a = 17b$

$a = \dfrac{17}{6}b$

$$\frac{a + b}{a - b} = \frac{\dfrac{17}{6}b + b}{\dfrac{17}{6}b - b} = \frac{\dfrac{17}{6} + 1}{\dfrac{17}{6} - 1}$$

$$\Rightarrow \frac{a + b}{a - b} = \frac{23}{11}$$

25. **(c)** $\dfrac{(598 + 479)^2 - (598 - 479)^2}{598 \times 479}$

$$\frac{(598)^2 + (479)^2 + 2 \times 598 \times 479 - (598)^2 - (478)^2 + 2 \times 598 \times 479}{598 \times 479}$$

$$\Rightarrow \frac{4 \times 598 \times 479}{598 \times 479}$$

$$\Rightarrow 4$$

26. **(c)** $1 : 10$ could not be the ratio of black to white marbles.

27. **(b)** Let the number $= x$

$x^2 = (37)^2 - (23)^2$

$x^2 = 1369 - 529$

$x = 28.98$

28. **(a)** Let 'x' be the weight of empty vessel and 'y' be the weight of full vessel.

$x + y = 24$ ....(1)

$x + \dfrac{y}{4} = 9$ ....(2)

Solving eq. (1) and (2)

$x = 4$ kg.

29. **(a)** $a - b = 4$

$ab = 45$

$(a - b)^2 = a^2 + b^2 - 2ab$

$(4)^2 = a^2 + b^2 - 2 \times 45$

$16 + 90 = a^2 + b^2$

$a^2 + b^2 = 106$

$a^3 - b^3 = (a - b)(a^2 + b^2 + ab)$

$= (4)(106 + 45)$

$= 604$

30. **(d)** $\dfrac{a}{a + b} = \dfrac{15}{21}$

$21a = 15a + 15b$

$6a = 15b$

$2a = 5b$

$a = \dfrac{5}{2}b$

$$\frac{a + b}{a - b} = \frac{\dfrac{5}{2}b + b}{\dfrac{5}{2}b - b} = \frac{5b + 2b}{5b - 2b} = \frac{7}{3} \times \frac{3}{3} = \frac{21}{9}$$

31. (c) $\dfrac{(798+579)^2-(798-579)^2}{(798+579)}$

$\Rightarrow \dfrac{(798)^2+(579)^2+2\times798\times579-(798)^2-(579)^2+2\times798\times579}{798\times579}$

$\Rightarrow \dfrac{4\times798\times579}{798\times579}=4$

32. (a) More capacity, less buckets (Indirect proportion)

$12:18::8:x$

$\dfrac{12}{18}=\dfrac{8}{x}\Rightarrow x=\dfrac{18\times8}{12}=12$

33. (d) By using option (d) is
correct answer in which
$51+34=85$
and LCM of 51 & 34 is 102.

34. (b) Let rest of the food last for the x days.

$\therefore\quad 200\times4=(200-120)\times x$

$200\times4=80\times x$

$x=\dfrac{800}{80}=10$ days.

35. (c) Let the number be $=x$

$\therefore\quad \dfrac{(x+10)\times7}{5}-5=\dfrac{88}{2}$

$7x+70-25=220$

$7x=220-45$

$7x=175$

$x=25$

$\therefore$　Number is 25.

36. (a) Let 25 paise coins $=x$

$1\ ₹:50\ P:25\ P$

$3x:220-4x:x$ Ratio in number of coins

$3x:\dfrac{220-4x}{2}:\dfrac{x}{4}$ Ratio in amount

$\therefore\quad 3x+110-2x+\dfrac{x}{4}=160$

$x+110+\dfrac{x}{4}=160$

$4x+440+x=640$

$5x=200$

$x=40$

$\therefore 50$ paise coins $=220-4x=220-160=60$

37. (d) Let largest no. $=x$

$\therefore\quad x+10=3\,(x-10)$

$10+30=3x-x$

$40=2x$

$x=20$

$\therefore$　other number $=20$

38. (b) $\dfrac{69\times69\times69-65\times65\times65}{69\times69+69\times65+65\times65}$

Using $\dfrac{a^3-b^3}{a^2+ab+b^2}=a-b$

$\therefore\quad 69-65=4$

39. (a) Let the number be x

$\dfrac{5(7+x)}{9}-3=12$

$\dfrac{5(7+x)}{9}=15$

$7+x=\dfrac{15\times9}{5}=27$

$x=27-7=20$

40. (c) Let Arun's weight be x kg
According to Arun, $65<x<72$
According to Arun's brother, $60<x<70$
According to Arun's mothers, $x<68$
The value satisfying all the above Conditions are 66
and 67

$\therefore$　Required average $=\left(\dfrac{66+67}{2}\right)=66.5$kg

41. (b) $95.75\times0.02554=2.445455$
There are 6 digits to the right of the decimal point in
the product of 95.75 and 0.02554.

2 Arithmetic

1. The average age of 35 students in a class is 16 years. Out of these students the average age of 21 students is 14 years. The average age of remaining students is **[2011-I]**
   (a) 15 years
   (b) 17 years
   (c) 20 years
   (d) 19 years

2. After replacing an old member by a new member, it was found that the average age of five members of a club is the same as it was 3 years ago. What is the difference between the age of replaced member and new member? **[2011-I]**
   (a) 2 years
   (b) 8 years
   (c) 15 years
   (d) 25 years

3. The average salary of all the workers in a workshop is Rs. 8000. The average salary of seven technicians is ₹12000 and average salary of others is ₹ 6000. The total number of workers in the workshop are- **[2011-I]**
   (a) 20
   (b) 21
   (c) 22
   (d) 23

4. The price of a scooter and a TV are in the ratio of 7 : 5. If the scooter costs ₹8000 more than a TV set, then the price of TV set is- **[2011-I]**
   (a) ₹ 20000
   (b) ₹ 24000
   (c) ₹ 32000
   (d) ₹ 28000

5. The speed of three cars is in the ratio of 5 : 4 : 6. The ratio between the time taken by them to travel the same distance is **[2011-I]**
   (a) 5 : 4 : 6
   (b) 6 : 4 : 5
   (c) 10 : 12 : 15
   (d) 12 : 15 : 10

6. The ratio between two numbers is 3 : 4. If each number is increased by 6 the ratio becomes 4 : 5. The difference between the numbers is **[2011-I]**
   (a) 1
   (b) 3
   (c) 6
   (d) 8

7. The average of five consecutive odd number is 61. What is the difference between the highest and lowest number? **[2011-II]**
   (a) 2
   (b) 5
   (c) 8
   (d) 12

8. Jayesh is twice as old as Vijay and half as old as Suresh. If the sum of Vijay's age and Suresh's age is 85 years what is the age of Jayesh? **[2011-II]**
   (a) 34 years
   (b) 36 years
   (c) 68 years
   (d) 24 years

9. A cricketer has an average of 30 runs in 14 innings. How many runs should he score in his next innings to achieve an average of 32 runs? **[2011-II]**
   (a) 65
   (b) 60
   (c) 55
   (d) 50

10. The ratio of three numbers is 3 : 4 : 5 and the sum of their squares is 1250. The sum of the three numbers is **[2011-II]**
    (a) 30
    (b) 50
    (c) 60
    (d) 90

11. The average age of three boys is 25 years and their ages are in the proportion 3 : 5 : 7. What is the age of the youngest boy? **[2011-II]**
    (a) 15 years
    (b) 18 years
    (c) 21 years
    (d) 13 years

12. Find the average of all the numbers between 6 and 34 which are divisible by 5. **[2012-I]**
    (a) 18
    (b) 20
    (c) 24
    (d) 30

13. The average of first 80 natural numbers is **[2012-I]**
    (a) 40
    (b) 41
    (c) 40.5
    (d) 142

14. If the sum of a few numbers is 450 and their mean is 50 and if another number 100 is included, the mean would become **[2012-I]**
    (a) 55
    (b) 60
    (c) 75
    (d) 150

15. Two numbers are in the ratio 7 : 8. If 3 is added to each of them their ratio becomes 8:9. The numbers are **[2012-I]**
    (a) 14, 16
    (b) 24, 27
    (c) 21, 24
    (d) 16, 18

16. The sum of three numbers is 98. If the ratio of the first to the second is 2 : 3 and that of the second to the third is 5 : 8, then the second number is **[2012-I]**
    (a) 20
    (b) 30
    (c) 48
    (d) 58

17. A certain amount was divided between Sita and Gita in the ratio 9 : 8. If Sita's share was ₹ 4500 then the amount is **[2012-I]**
    (a) ₹ 9000
    (b) ₹ 8500
    (c) ₹ 6750
    (d) ₹ 9025

18. A man's average monthly expenditure for the first four months of the year was ₹ 225.25. For the next five months, the average monthly expenditure was ₹ 20.75 more than what it was during the first four months. If the person spent ₹ 700 in all during the remaining three months of the year, find what percntage of his annual income of ₹ 3500 he saved in the year ?   *[2012-II]*

    (a) 10%   (b) 15%

    (c) 19.11%   (d) 25%

19. The ratio of the present age of P and Q is 2.3. The ratio of their age after 18 years will be 4.5. What is the present age of Q ?   *[2012-II]*

    (a) 26 years   (b) 25 years

    (c) 24 years   (d) 27 years

20. The mean temperature of Monday to Wednesday was 37°C and of Tuesday to Thursday was 34°C. If the temperature on Thursday was $4/5^{th}$ that of Monday, the temperature on Thursday' was   *[2012-II]*

    (a) 36.5°C   (b) 36°C

    (c) 35.5°C   (d) 34°C

21. A sum of money is to be distributed among P, Q and R in the ratio of 6:19:7. If R gives ₹ 200 from his share to Q, the ratio of P, Q and R becomes 3:10:3, what is the total sum ?   *[2012-II]*

    (a) ₹ 3200   (b) ₹ 12800

    (c) ₹ 6400   (d) data inadequate

22. In what ratio should tea worth ₹ 10 per kg be mixed with tea worth ₹ 14 per kg so that the average price of the mixture may be ₹ 11 per kg ?   *[2012-II]*

    (a) 2:1   (b) 3:1

    (c) 3:2   (d) 4:3

23. The average age of 8 men is increased by 4 years when one of them whose age is 30 years is replaced by a new man. What is the age of new man ?   *[2013-I]*

    (a) 55 years   (b) 62 years

    (c) 42 years   (d) 69 years

24. A man's average monthly expenditure for the first four months of the year was ₹ 231.25. For the next five months, the average monthly expenditure was ₹ 22.75 more than what it was during the first four months. If the person spent ₹ 605 in all during the remaining three months of the year, find what percentage of his annual income of ₹ 3500 did he save in the year ?   *[2013-I]*

    (a) 10%   (b) 15%

    (c) 20%   (d) 25%

25. The average age of students of a class is 15.8 years. The average age of boys in the class is 16.4 years and that of the girls is 15.4 years. The ratio of the number of boys to the number of girls in the class is   *[2013-I]*

    (a) 1 : 2   (b) 2 : 3

    (c) 3 : 4   (d) 3 : 5

26. Divide ₹ 80 in the production of 3 : 6 : 7.   *[2013-I]*

    (a) ₹ 10, ₹ 35, ₹ 40   (b) ₹ 15, ₹ 30, ₹ 35

    (c) ₹ 15, ₹ 35, ₹ 30   (b) ₹ 10, ₹ 40, ₹ 35

27. In a mixture of 60 litres, the ratio of milk and water is 2 : 1. What amount of water must be added to make the ratio of milk and water as 1 : 2 ?   *[2013-I]*

    (a) 42 Litres   (b) 56 Litres

    (c) 60 Litres   (d) 77 Litres

28. There were 35 students in a hostel. If the number of students be increased by 7, the expenditure on food increases by ₹ 42 per day while the average expenditure of students is reduced by ₹ 1. What was the initial expenditure on food per day ?   *[2014-I]*

    (a) ₹ 432   (b) ₹ 442

    (c) ₹ 420   (d) ₹ 400

29. There were 24 students in a class. One of them, who was 18 years old, left the class and his place was filled up by a new comer. If the average of the class was thereby lowered by 1 month, the age of new comer is   *[2014-I]*

    (a) 14 years   (b) 15 years

    (c) 16 years   (d) 17 years

30. 19 persons went to a hotel for a combined dinner party. 13 of them spent ₹ 79 each on their dinner and the rest spent ₹ 4 more than the average expenditure of all the 19. What was the total money spent by them ?   *[2014-I]*

    (a) 1628.4   (b) 1534

    (c) 1492   (d) None of these

31. A factory employs skilled workers, unskilled workers and clerks in the proportion 8: 5 : 1 and the wages of a skilled worker as unskilled worker and a clerk are in the ratio 5 : 2 : 3. When 20 unskilled workers are employed, the total daily wages of all, amount to ₹ 318. What is the daily wages in ₹ paid to each category of employees ?   *[2014-II]*

    (a) 240,57,19   (b) 210,70,13

    (c) 230,65,12   (d) 240,60,18

32. A cat takes 5 leaps for every 4 leaps of a dog, but 3 leaps of the dog are equal to 4 leaps of the cat. What is the ratio of the speed of the cat to that of the dog ?   *[2014-II]*

    (a) 13 : 14   (b) 15 : 11

    (c) 17 : 15   (d) 15 : 16

33. Ram Shiv and Ganesh assemble for a contributory party. Ram brings 3 apples while Shiv brings 5. Since Ganesh did not bring any, he contributed ₹ 8/-. How many rupees should Ram and Shiv respectively get, assuming each of the three consumes an equal portion of the apples ?   *[2014-II]*

    (a) 1, 7 (b)   2, 5

    (c) 5, 3 (d)   2, 6

34. The average weight of 5 men is increased by 2 Kg when one of the men whose weight is 60 Kg is replaced by a new man. The weight of the new man is   *[2015-I]*

    (a) 50 Kg   (b) 65 Kg

    (c) 68 Kg   (d) 70 Kg

Hints & Solutions

1. (d) Total sum of ages of 35 students = 35×16
Total sum of ages of 21 students = 21×14

The average of remaining students $= \dfrac{35 \times 16 - 21 \times 14}{14}$

= 19 years

2. (c) Age decreased $= (5 \times 3)$ years $= 15$ years
So, the required difference $= 15$ years

3. (b) Let the total number of workers be x. Then,
$8000x = (12000 \times 7) + 6000\,(x - 7)$
$8000\,x = 84000 + 6000\,x - 42000$
$2000x = 42000 \quad \therefore \ x = 21$

4. (a) Let the price of a scooter and a TV be 7x and 5x respectively.
According to question
$7x = 5x + 8000$
$2x = 8000$
$x = 4000$
Hence, the price of TV = ₹ 20,000

5. (d) Speed of cars is $5 : 4 : 6$

Time ratio $= \dfrac{1}{5} : \dfrac{1}{4} : \dfrac{1}{6} = \dfrac{12 : 15 : 10}{60}$

The ratio between the time taken by them to travel the same distance is $12 : 15 : 10$

6. (c) Let the number are 3x and 4x.

$\dfrac{3x + 6}{4x + 6} = \dfrac{4}{5}$

$15x + 30 = 16\,x + 24$

$x = 6$

Number are 18 and 24.

Hence, required difference is 6.

7. (c) Let the numbers are
x, x +2, x + 4, x + 6 and x + 8.

Average $= \dfrac{x + x + 2 + x + 4 + x + 6 + x + 8}{5}$

$61 \times 5 = 5x + 20$
$5x = 305 - 20$
$5x = 285$
$x = 57$
First number = 57
Last number = 65
Required difference = $65 - 57 = 8$

8. (a) Let the age of Jayesh = x yr.

Therefore age of Vijay $= \dfrac{x}{2}$ yr.

And, age of Suresh = 2x yr.
According the question

$\dfrac{x}{2} + 2x = 85$
$5x = 85 \times 2$
$x = 34$ yr.

9. (b) New Average $= \dfrac{30 \times 14 + \text{required run}}{15}$

$32 \times 15 - 30 \times 14 = \text{Required run}$
Required run = 60

10. (c) Let the numbers are 3x, 4x and 5x respectively.
According to question $(3x)^2 + (4x)^2 + (5x)^2 = 1250$
$9x^2 + 16x^2 + 25x^2 = 1250$
$50x^2 = 1250$
$x^2 = 25$
$x = 5$
Numbers are 15,20 and 25.
Sum $= 15 + 20 + 25 = 60$

11. (a) Let the ages of three boys are 3x, 5x and 7x.

Average age $= \dfrac{3x + 5x + 7x}{3}$

$25 \times 3 = 15x$
$x = 5$
The age of youngest boy = 15 yr.

12. (b) Numbers are 10, 15, 20, 25 and 30.

Required average $= \dfrac{10 + 15 + 20 + 25 + 30}{5}$

$= \dfrac{100}{5} = 20$

13. (c) Average $= \dfrac{(n)\,(n + 1)}{(2) \times n}$
Where 'n' be the natural number

Therefore, average $= \dfrac{80 \times (80 + 1)}{2 \times 80}$

$= \dfrac{81}{2} = 40.5$

14. (a) $50 = \dfrac{\text{Sum of all numbers}}{\text{number of observations}}$

$50 = \dfrac{450}{\text{Number of observations}}$

Number of observations $= \dfrac{450}{50} = 9$

New mean $= \dfrac{450 + 100}{10} = \dfrac{550}{10} = 55$

15. (c) Let the numbers are 7x and 8x

$\dfrac{7x + 3}{8x + 3} = \dfrac{8}{9}$

$63x + 27 = 64x + 24$
$x = 3$
Numbers are 21 and 24

16. (b) Let the numbers are a, b and c

$a : b = 2 : 3$

$b : c = 5 : 8$

$a : b : c$

$2 : 3$

$5 : 8$

$10 : 15 : 24$

$10x + 15x + 24x = 98$

$49x = 98$

$x = 2$

Second number $= 15 \times 2 = 30$

17. (b) Sita's share $= \dfrac{9}{17} \times$ Amount

$\therefore$ Amount $= \dfrac{17 \times 4500}{9} = ₹\, 8500$

18. (c) Total expenditure spent on four months

$= 4 \times 225.25 = ₹\, 901$

Total expenditure spent on next five months

$= 5 \times (225.25 + 20.75)$

$= 5 \times 246 = ₹\, 1230$

Total expenditure for 12 months

$= ₹\, [901 + 1230 + 700] = 2831$

Required % $= \dfrac{669}{3500} \times 100 = 19.11\%$

19. (d) Let the present age of P and Q be 2x and 3x.

According to question

$\dfrac{2x + 18}{3x + 18} = \dfrac{4}{5}$

$10x + 90 = 12x + 72$

$2x = 18$

$x = 9$

Present age of Q $= 9 \times 3 = 27$ years

20. (b) $\dfrac{\text{Mon} + \text{Tues} + \text{Wed}}{3} = 37°C$ ...(1)

$\dfrac{\text{Tues} + \text{Wed} + \text{Thur}}{3} = 34°C$ ...(2)

Subtracting equation (2) from (1)

Mon $-$ Thurs $= 37 \times 3 - 34 \times 3$

$\dfrac{5}{4}$ Thus $-$ Thurs $= 9$

Thurs $= 36°C$

21. (c) Going by options,

If the total sum is 6400 then distribution among P, Q and R was 1200, 3800 and 1400.

After giving 200 to Q by R.

New sum would be 1200, 4000 and 1200.

Or, $1200 : 4000 : 1200 = 3 : 10 : 3$

22. (b)

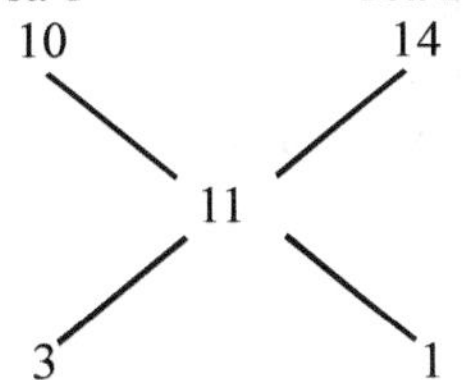

Hence, the ratio should be 3 : 1.

23. (b) Total age increased $= (8 \times 4) = 32$ years

Age of new man $= 30 + 32 = 62$ years

24. (c) Total expenditure spent on first four months

$= 4 \times 231.25 = ₹\, 925$

Total expenditure spent on next five months

$= 5 \times (231.25 + 22.75)$

$= 5 \times 254 = ₹\, 1270$

Total expenditure for 12 months

$= 925 + 1270 + 605 = ₹\, 2800$

Required % $= \dfrac{3500 - 2800}{3500} \times 100 = 20\%$

25. (b)

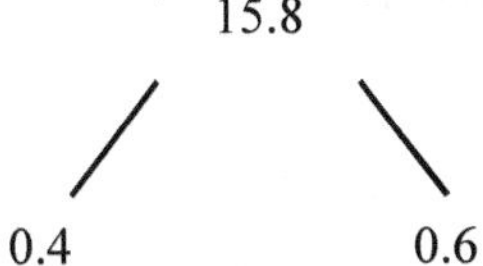

Boys to girls ratio $= 0.4 : 0.6$ or $2 : 3$

26. (b) $3x + 6x + 7x = 80$

$16x = 80$

$x = 5$

Numbers are 15, 30, 35

27. (c) Milk $= \dfrac{2}{3} \times 60 = 40l$

Water $= \dfrac{1}{3} \times 60 = 20l$

Let 'x' be the amount to be added to milk and water.

$\dfrac{40 + x}{20 + x} = \dfrac{1}{2}$

$80 + 2x = 20 + x$

$60 = x$

28. (c) Let expenditure per day $= x$

$\therefore \quad \dfrac{x}{35} = \dfrac{x + 42}{42} + 1$

$\therefore \quad x = 420$

Hence, the initial expenditure on food per day $= ₹\, 420$

29. (c)   Age of new comer $= 18 - 24 \times \dfrac{1}{12} = 16$ years.

30. (d)   Let average of all persons $= x$

$\therefore \quad (13 \times 79) + 6(x + 4) = 19 \times x$

$\qquad 13 \times 79 + 6x + 24 = 19x$

$\qquad 13 \times 79 + 24 = 13x$

$$x = \frac{13 \times 79 + 24}{13} = 80.25$$

Total money spent $= 1536$

31. (d)   Skilled workers : Unskilled workers : Clerks $= 8:5:1$

Ratio of the respective wages $= 5:2:3$

Hence, the amount must be paid in the ratio

$8 \times 5 : 5 \times 2 : 1 \times 3 = 40 : 10 : 3$

Sum of the ratios $= 40 + 10 + 3 = 53$

If the total amount is ₹ 53, the skilled workers get ₹ 40.

If the total amount is ₹ 318, the skilled worker will get

$$= \frac{40}{53} \times 318 = ₹ \, 240$$

Unskilled workers get $= \dfrac{10}{53} \times 318 = ₹ \, 60$

and clerk get $= \dfrac{3}{53} \times 318 = ₹ \, 18$

32. (d)   3 leaps of dog $= 4$ leaps of Cat

$\therefore$ 4 leaps of dog $= \dfrac{16}{3}$ leaps of Cat

$\therefore$ the rate of dog : rate of cat $= \dfrac{16}{3} : 5 = 16 : 15$

rate of cat : rate of dog $= 15 : 16$

33. (a)   Each one receive $\dfrac{8}{3}$ apple

Ram gave $= 3 - \dfrac{8}{3} = \dfrac{1}{3}$ apple

Shiv gave $= 5 - \dfrac{8}{3} = \dfrac{7}{3}$ apples

$\therefore$ Ram : Shiv $= \dfrac{1}{3} : \dfrac{7}{3} = 1 : 7$

Ram got $= 8 \times \dfrac{1}{8} = ₹ \, 1$

Shiv got $= 80 \times \dfrac{7}{8} = ₹ \, 7$

34. (d)   Let total weight of 5 men be x kg and weight of new man y kg.

$$\frac{x - 60y + y}{5} = \frac{x}{5} + 2$$

$$\Rightarrow \frac{x}{5} - 12 + \frac{y}{5} = \frac{x}{5} + 2$$

$$\Rightarrow y = 70 \text{ kg}$$

weight of new man $= 70$ kg

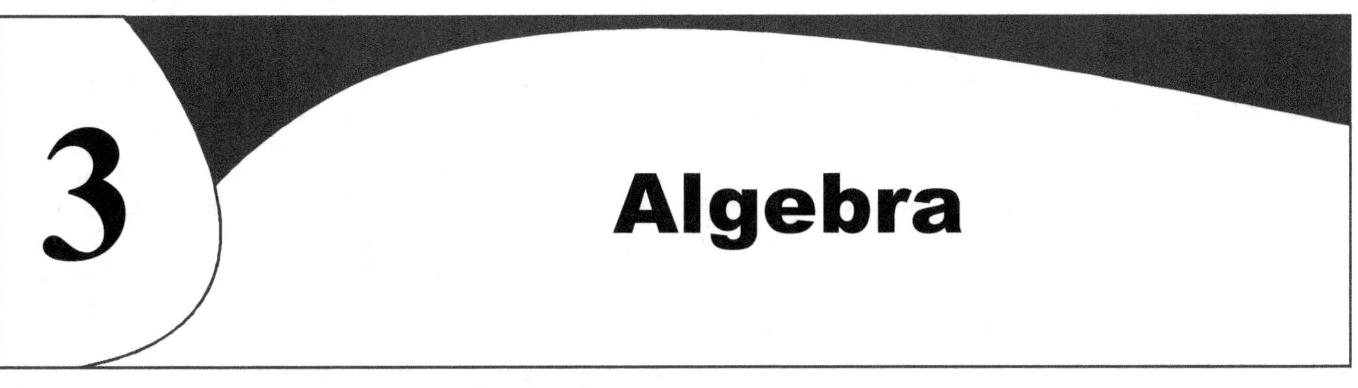

3 Algebra

1. In an examination a candidate has to get 35% of total marks to pass. In one paper he gets 62 out of 150 and in the second 35 out of 150. How many marks should he get out of 200 marks in the third paper to pass ? *[2011-I]*
   (a) 61   (b) 68
   (c) 70   (d) 78

2. The salary of A & B together amounts to ₹ 2000. A spends 95% of his salary and B 85% of his salary. If their savings are same what is the salary of A ? *[2011-I]*
   (a) ₹ 750   (b) ₹ 1250
   (c) ₹ 1500   (d) ₹ 1600

3. Out of the 1000 inhabitants of a town, 60% are male of whom 20% are literate. If, amongst all the inhabitants, 25% are literate, then what percentage of the females of the town are literate ? *[2011-I]*
   (a) 22.5   (b) 32.5
   (c) 27.5   (d) 37.5

4. A trader mixes 26 kg of rice at ₹ 20 per kg with 30 kg rice of another variety costing ₹ 36 per kg. If he sells the mixture at ₹ 30 per kg his profit will be- *[2011-I]*
   (a) −7%   (b) 5%
   (c) 8%   (d) 10%

5. The difference between the cost price and sale price is ₹ 240. If the profit is 20%, the selling price is *[2011-I]*
   (a) ₹ 1200   (b) ₹ 1440
   (c) ₹ 1800   (d) ₹ 2440

6. Samant bought a microwave oven and paid 10% less than Maximum Retail Price(MRP). He sold it with 30% profit on his purchase cost. What percentage of profit did he earn on MRP ? *[2011-I]*
   (a) 17%   (b) 20%
   (c) 27%   (d) 32%

7. ₹ 800 becomes ₹ 956 in 3 years at a certain rate of interest. If the rate of interest is increased by 4% what amount will ₹ 800 become in 3 years ? *[2011-I]*
   (a) ₹ 1020   (b) ₹ 1052
   (c) ₹ 1282   (d) ₹ 1080

8. How much time will it take for an amount of ₹ 450 to gain ₹ 81 as interest, if rate of interest is 4.5% p.a on simple interest ? *[2011-I]*
   (a) 4.5 years   (b) 3.5 years
   (c) 5 years   (d) 4 years

9. At what rate of annual simple interest will ₹10000 double in 15 years ? *[2011-I]*
   (a) 5.5%   (b) 8%
   (c) 6.67%   (d) 7.25%

10. What percentage of profit should be added in the cost price of an item so as to gain a profit of 33% after allowing 5% discount to the customer ? *[2011-II]*
    (a) 45   (b) 40
    (c) 52   (d) 48

11. If the manufacturer gains 10%, the wholesale dealer gains 15% and the retailer gains 25%, find the cost of production of a table. The retail price of table is ₹ 1265 *[2011-II]*
    (a) ₹ 800   (b) ₹ 1000
    (c) ₹ 950   (d) ₹ 1180

12. A loss of 19% on a shirt gets converted into a profit of 17% when the selling price is increased by ₹ 162. What is the cost price of the shirt ? *[2011-II]*
    (a) ₹ 540   (b) ₹ 450
    (c) ₹ 600   (d) ₹ 360

13. In an examination 75% of the total students passed in English and 65% passed in Mathematics, while 15% failed in English as well as Mathematics. If a total of 495 candidates who passed in both exams. Find the total number of students who appeared in the exam. *[2011-II]*
    (a) 850   (b) 900
    (c) 1000   (d) 1050

14. When the price of a product was increased by 15%, the number of items sold was decreased by 20%. What was the net effect ? *[2011-II]*
    (a) 10% gain   (b) 6% loss
    (c) 8% loss   (d) 4% gain

15. A mixture of 40 litres of milk and water contains 10% water. How much water should be added to this mixture so that the new mixture contains 20% water ? *[2011-II]*
    (a) 4 litres   (b) 5 litres
    (c) 6.5 litres   (d) 7.5 litres

16. A certain sum of money becomes three times of itself in 20 years at simple interest. In how many years will the initial sum become double at the same rate of simple interest ? *[2011-II]*
    (a) 8   (b) 10
    (c) 12   (d) 14

17. Ram borrows ₹ 8000 at 12% p.a. simple interest and Mohan borrows ₹ 9100 at 10% p.a. simple interest. In how many years will their borrowed amounts (debt) be equal ? *[2011-II]*
    (a) 18   (b) 20
    (c) 22   (d) 24

18. Reena took a loan of ₹ 1200 with simple interest for a certain numbers of years. The number years are same as the interest rate. If she has paid ₹ 432 as interest at the end of the loan period, what was the rate of interest ? *[2011-II]*
    (a) 3.6
    (b) 6
    (c) 12
    (d) None of these

19. Hari's income is 20% more than Madhu's income. Madhu's income is less than Hari's income by *[2012-I]*
    (a) 15%
    (b) 16.66 %
    (c) 20%
    (d) 22.25%

20. A sum of money lent out at simple interest doubled itself in 20 years. In how many years will it triple itself ? *[2012-I]*
    (a) 28 yrs
    (b) 30 yrs
    (c) 40 yrs
    (d) 35 yrs

21. One litre of water is evaporated from 6 litres of a solution containing 5% salt. The percentage of salt in the remaining solution is *[2012-I]*
    (a) 16%
    (b) 5%
    (c) 4%
    (d) 6%

22. A shopkeeper professes to sell all things at a discount of 10% but increases the selling price of each article by 20%. His gain on each article is *[2012-I]*
    (a) 6%
    (b) 8%
    (c) 10%
    (d) 12%

23. If the selling price of an article is $4/3^{rd}$ of its cost price, the profit in transaction is *[2012-I]*
    (a) 16.75%
    (b) 20.50%
    (c) 25.50%
    (d) 33.33%

24. If selling price is doubled, the profit triples. Find the profit percent. *[2012-I]*
    (a) 66.66
    (b) 100
    (c) 105.33
    (d) 120

25. Srinivasan invests two equal amounts in two banks giving 10% and 12% rate of interest respectively. At the end of year the interest earned is ₹ 1650. Find the sum invested in each. *[2012-II]*
    (a) ₹ 8500
    (b) ₹ 15000
    (c) ₹ 7500
    (d) ₹ 17,000

26. The simple interest on sum of money is 1/9 of the sum. The number of years is numerically equal to the rate percent per annum. The rate percent per annum is *[2012-II]*
    (a) 3.33
    (b) 5
    (c) 6.66
    (d) 10

27. A sum of ₹ 10.000 is lent partly at 8% and the remaining at 10% per annum, If the yearly interest on the average is 9.2%. the money lent at 10% is *[2012-II]*
    (a) ₹ 6000
    (b) ₹ 5500
    (c) ₹ 5000
    (d) ₹ 4500

28. In an election between two candidates, 60% of the voters cast their votes, out of which 4% of the votes were declared invalid. A candidate got 7344 votes which were 75% of the total valid votes. Find the total number of votes enrolled in that election. *[2012-II]*
    (a) 1700
    (b) 17590
    (c) 17000
    (d) 7344

29. If the price of kerosene be raised by 9%, find how much percent a house holder must reduce his consumption of kerosene so that not to increase his expenditure *[2012-II]*
    (a) 9%
    (b) 8.25%
    (c) 9%
    (d) 9.25%

30. Sixty five pupils from a school entered for an examination and 80% of them passed. Another school entered 10 more pupils than the first school and four more pupils passed. The % of pass in the second school was *[2012-II]*
    (a) 75%
    (b) 84%
    (c) 72%
    (d) 74.6%

31. Calculate the amount on ₹ 1250 for 2 years at 4% per annum. compounded yearly. *[2012-II]*
    (a) ₹ 676
    (b) ₹ 1352
    (c) ₹ 1778
    (d) ₹ 255

32. A sum of ₹ 3200 is lent out into two parts, one at 6% and another at 4%. If the total annual income is ₹ 176, find the money lent at 6%. *[2012-II]*
    (a) ₹ 2400
    (b) ₹ 800
    (c) ₹ 1600
    (d) ₹ 3200

33. Srinivasan invests two equal amounts in two banks giving 8% and 12% rate of interest respectively. At the end of year the interest earned is ₹ 1500. Find the sum invested in each. *[2013-I]*
    (a) ₹ 8500
    (b) ₹ 15000
    (c) ₹ 7500
    (d) ₹ 17000

34. The simple interest accrued on a sum of money at the end of four years is $1/5^{th}$ of its principal. What is the rate of interest per annum ? *[2013-I]*
    (a) 4%
    (b) 5%
    (c) 6%
    (d) Inadequate data

35. A sum of ₹ 2600 is lent out into two parts, one at 9% and another at 7%. If the total annual income is ₹ 206, find the money lent at 7%. *[2013-I]*
    (a) ₹ 1400
    (b) ₹ 900
    (c) ₹ 1600
    (d) ₹ 1200

36. In an election between two candidates, 70% of the voters cast their votes, out of which 2% of the votes were declared invalid. A candidate got 7203 votes which was 60% of the total valid votes. Find the total number of voters enrolled in that election. *[2013-I]*
    (a) 18050
    (b) 17500
    (c) 17000
    (d) 7203

37. If the price of kerosene be raised by 11%, find by how much percent a house holder must reduce his consumption of kerosene so as not to increase his expenditure ? *[2013-I]*
    (a) 11%
    (b) 9.9%
    (c) 11.09%
    (c) 8.25%

38. 75 pupils from a school appeared for an examination and 80% of them passed. Another school entered 10 more pupils than the first school and five pupils less than the first school passed. The pass % of in the second school was *[2013-I]*
    (a) 75%
    (b) 84%
    (c) 72%
    (d) 64.7%

39. Calculate the amount on ₹ 1875 for 2 years at 4% per annum, compounded yearly. *[2013-I]*
    (a) ₹ 676
    (b) ₹ 776
    (c) ₹ 1778
    (d) ₹ 2028

40. If x varies as y and x = 8 when y = 15 then the values of x when y = 10 is *[2013-I]*
(a) 5
(b) 15/8
(c) 8/15
(d) 16/3

41. A sum of ₹ 10,000 is lent partly at 6% and the remaining at 10% p.a. If the yearly interest on the average is 9.2%, the money lent at 10% is *[2013-I]*
(a) ₹ 2000
(b) ₹ 8500
(c) ₹ 5000
(d) ₹ 8000

42. An article costs ₹ 50 presently. The rate of inflation is 300%. What will be cost of this article after two years ? *[2014-I]*
(a) ₹ 200
(b) ₹ 600
(c) ₹ 800
(d) ₹ 1000

43. A dishonest shopkeeper professes to sell his groceries at his cost price, but uses a false weight of 900 grams for each kilogram. Find his gain percentage. *[2014-I]*
(a) 91/9 %
(b) 100/9%
(c) 100/11%
(d) 95/9%

44. A man purchased a bullock and a cart for ₹ 1800. He sold the bullock at a profit of 20% and the cart at a profit of 30%. His total profit was 155/6 %. Find the cost price of bullock. *[2014-I]*
(a) ₹ 650
(b) ₹ 750
(c) ₹ 900
(d) ₹ 800

45. If a person repaid ₹ 22500 after 10 years of borrowing a loan, at 10% per annum simple interest find out what amount did he take as a loan ? *[2014-I]*
(a) 11,225
(b) 11,250
(c) 10,000
(d) 7,500

46. A sum of money invested at simple interest triples itself in 8 years. How many times will it become in 20 years time ? *[2014-I]*
(a) 8 times
(b) 7 times
(c) 6 times
(d) 9 times.

47. Two-third of a consignment was sold at a profit of 5% and the remainder at a loss of 2% if the total profit was ₹400, what was the value of the consignment ? *[2014-II]*
(a) ₹13,000/-
(b) ₹17,000/-
(c) ₹15,000/-
(d) ₹40,000/-

48. In three annual examinations' of which the aggregate marks of each was 500, a student secured average marks 45% and 55% in the first and the second yearly examinations respectively. To secure 60% average total marks, it is necessary for him in third yearly examination to secure ___ marks. *[2014-II]*
(a) 300
(b) 350
(c) 355
(d) 400

49. A towel was 50 cm broad and 100 cm long. When bleached, it was found to have lost 20% of its length and 10% of its breadth. Find the percentage of decrease in area ? *[2014-II]*
(a) 32%
(b) 28%
(c) 33%
(d) 24%

50. A man deposited a total sum of ₹ 88400/- in the name of his two sons aged 19 and 17 years so that at the age of 21, both will get equal amounts. If the money is invested at the rate of 10% compound interest per annum what are the shares of his two sons ? *[2014-II]*
(a) ₹48200/-
(b) ₹48400
(c) ₹42600/-
(d) ₹44200

51. The sum of the number of boys and girls in a school is 150. If the number of boys is x, then the number of girls becomes x% of the total number of students. How many boys are there in the school ? *[2014-II]*
(a) 51
(b) 65
(c) 60
(d) 95

52. 'A' scored 30% marks and failed by 15 marks. 'B' scored 40% marks and obtained 35 marks more than those required to pass what is the pass percentage ? *[2014-II]*
(a) 33%
(b) 40%
(c) 34%
(d) 48%

53. A banker lent ₹6000/- at 10% and ₹5000/- at 12% at the same time and for same period of time. The banker received ₹2400 as total interest on both loans. Find the period for which the banker had lent the amount. *[2014-II]*
(a) 3 years 6 months
(b) 3 years
(c) 2 years 6 months
(d) 2 years

54. If a sum becomes double in 16 years, how many times will it be in 8 years? *[2015-I]*
(a) $1\frac{1}{2}$ times
(b) $1\frac{1}{3}$ times
(c) $1\frac{3}{4}$ items
(d) $1\frac{1}{4}$ times

55. In how many years will a sum of ₹ 800 at 10% per annum compounded semi-annually become ₹ 926.10? *[2015-I]*
(a) $1\frac{1}{3}$
(b) $1\frac{1}{2}$
(c) $2\frac{1}{3}$
(d) $2\frac{1}{2}$

56. A sell 2 TV sets, one at a loss of 15% and another at a profit of 15%. Find the loss/gain percentage in the overall transaction? *[2015-I]*
(a) 2.25%
(b) 3%
(c) 4%
(d) No profit, no loss

57. The price of sugar increases by 20% due to the festive season. by what percentage should a family reduce the consumption of sugar so that there is no change in the expenditure ? *[2015-I]*
(a) 20%
(b) $18\frac{1}{3}\%$
(c) $16\frac{2}{3}\%$
(d) $16\frac{1}{3}\%$

58. A's salary is 20% lower than B's salary, which is 15% lower than C's salary. By how much percent is C's salary more than A's salary? *[2015-I]*
(a) 44.05%
(b) 45.05%
(c) 46.05%
(d) 47.05%

Hints & Solutions

1. (d) Total marks $= 150 + 150 + 200 = 500$
35% of 500 = 175
$175 = 62 + 35 + x$
$x = 78$

2. (c) Let the salary of A and B are x and (2000 – x) resp.
According to question
$x - 95\%$ of $x = [(2000 - x - 85\%$ of $(2000 - x)]$

$$x\left[1 - \frac{95}{100}\right] = (2000 - x)\left[1 - \frac{85}{100}\right]$$

$5x = (2000 - x)\,15$
$20x = 30000$
$x = 1500$
Hence, the salary of A is ₹ 1500.

3. (b) Total number of males those are literate $= 60\%$ of 20% of 1000

$$= \frac{60}{100} \times \frac{20}{100} \times 1000 = 120$$

Total number of males in the town = 600
Total number of females in the town = 400
Total number of all inhabitants those are literate = 25% of 1000 = 250
Remaining females those are literates $= 250 - 120 = 130$

$$\therefore \quad \text{Required } \% = \frac{130}{400} \times 100$$

$$= 32.5\%$$

4. (b) C. P. of 56 kg rice
$= (26 \times 20 + 30 \times 36)$
$= ₹ (520 + 1080) = ₹ 1600$
S. P. of 56 kg rice $= 56 \times 30 = ₹ 1680$

$$\text{Profit } \% = \frac{80}{1600} \times 100 = 5\%$$

5. (a) Profit = S. P – C. P
Profit = 240

$$\text{Profit } \% = \frac{\text{Profit}}{\text{C.P.}} \times 100$$

$$20 = \frac{240}{\text{C.P.}} \times 100 \Rightarrow \text{C.P.} = 1200$$

Therefore, S.P $= 1200 + 240 = ₹ 1440$

6. (a) Let the original price $= ₹100$
Then, C.P. $= ₹ 90$

$$\text{S. P.} = 130\% \text{ of } 90 = ₹ \left(\frac{130}{100} \times 90\right)$$

$$= ₹ 117$$

$\therefore$ Required percentage $= (117 - 100)$
$= 17\%$

7. (b) S.I. $= ₹ (956 - 800) = ₹ 156$;
P = 800, T = 3 yrs.

$$\therefore \ R = \left(\frac{100 \times 156}{800 \times 3}\right)\% = 6.5\%$$

New rate $= (6.5 + 4) = 10.5\%$

$$\text{New, S.I} = ₹ \left(\frac{800 \times 10.5 \times 3}{100}\right) = ₹ 252$$

$\therefore$ New amount $= 800 + 252 = 1052$

8. (d) $\text{SI} = \dfrac{P \times R \times T}{100}$

$$81 = \frac{450 \times 4.5 \times T}{100}$$

$$T = \frac{100 \times 81}{450 \times 4.5} = 4 \text{ years}$$

9. (c) S.I $= 2P - P = P$

$$P = \frac{P \times R \times 15}{100}$$

$$R = \frac{100}{15} = 6.67\%$$

10. (b) Let the C.P $= ₹ 100$
The, S.P $= ₹133$
Let the marked price ₹ x
Then, 95% of $x = 133$

$$x = \frac{133 \times 100}{95} = 140$$

Marked price = 40% above C.P.

11. (a) Let the cost of production of a table $= ₹$ x.

$$x \times \frac{110}{100} \times \frac{115}{100} \times \frac{125}{100} = 1265$$

$$x = \frac{1265 \times 1000000}{110 \times 115 \times 125} = ₹ 800$$

12. (b) Let C. P. = x
Loss = 19%

then S.P. is $\dfrac{119}{100} x$

If profit = 17% then S. P. $= \dfrac{83}{100} x$

According to question

$$\frac{119x}{100} - 162 = \frac{83x}{100}$$

$\therefore \quad x = 450$

13. **(b)** Let A and B represent the sets of students who passed in English and Mathematics respectively.

If 15% of candidates failed in both, then 85% passed at least one of the exams.

Then, the total number of students passed in one or both subjects

$$= (A \cup B) = n(A) + n(B) = n(A \cap B)$$

$$0.85 = 0.75 + 0.65 - n(A \cap B)$$

$$n(A \cap B) = 1.40 - 0.85 = 0.55$$

0.55% of number of students = 495

$$\therefore \quad \text{Number of students} = \frac{495}{55} \times 100 = 900$$

14. **(c)** Net effect $= x + y + \dfrac{xy}{100}$

$$= 15 - 20 + \frac{(15 \times -20)}{100} = -5 - 3 = -8$$

Negative sign indicates that there is a loss of 8%.

15. **(b)** Milk contains in mixture = 36 liters.

Water contains in mixture = 4 liters

Let 'x' be the water added to the mixture.

$$\frac{36}{4+x} = \frac{80}{20}$$

$$36 = 16 + 4x$$

$$20 = 4x$$

$$\therefore \ x = 5 \text{ litres}$$

16. **(b)** Let Principal = x

Amount = 3x

Simple interest = 2x

$$\text{Rate} = \frac{2x \times 100}{x \times 20} = 10\%$$

Now, required time $= \dfrac{x \times 100}{x \times 10} = 10$ years

17. **(c)** Simple interest for Ram $= \dfrac{8000 \times 12 \times 1}{100} = 960$

Simple interest for Mohan $= \dfrac{9100 \times 10 \times 1}{100} = 910$

Let 'x' be the years when borrowed amount be equal.

$$8000 + 960 \, x = 9100 + 910 \, x$$

$$50x = 9100 - 8000$$

$$50x = 1100$$

$$x = 22 \text{ years}$$

18. **(b)** Let Time = T years and Rate = T%

Then, $\dfrac{1200 \times T \times R}{100} = 432$

$$T^2 = \frac{432 \times 100}{1200} = 36$$

$$T = 6$$

19. **(b)** If Hari's income is 20% more than Madhu, then Madhu's income is less than Hari by

$$= \left(\frac{20}{20 + 100} \times 10 \right) \% = 16.66\%$$

20. **(c)** Let P = x, S. I = x

$$\text{Rate} = \frac{\text{SI} \times 100}{\text{P} \times \text{T}} = \frac{x \times 100}{x \times 20} = 5\%$$

Now, P = x, S.I = $2x$, Rate = 5%

$$\text{Time} = \frac{\text{SI} \times 100}{\text{P} \times \text{R}} = \frac{2x \times 100}{x \times 5} = 40 \text{ yrs}$$

21. **(d)** Amount of salt in the solution = 5% of 6 l = 0.3 l

Percentage of salt in the remaining solution $= \dfrac{0.3}{5} \times 100$

$$= 6\%$$

22. **(b)** Let C. P. = ₹ 100

Then M.P. = ₹ 120

$$\therefore \quad \text{S.P.} = \frac{90}{100} \times 120 = 108$$

$$\therefore \quad \text{Gain \% } = 8\%$$

23. **(d)** Let C. P. = ₹ x, then S.P. = ₹ $\dfrac{4x}{3}$

$$\text{Gain} = ₹ \left(\frac{4x}{3} - x \right) = ₹ \frac{x}{3}$$

$$\therefore \quad \text{Gain \%} \left(\frac{x}{3} \times \frac{1}{x} \times 100 \right) = 33.33\%$$

24. **(b)** Let C.P. = ₹ x, S.P. = ₹ y

Profit = $y - x$

According to question

Profit = S.P. – C.P.

$$3(y - x) = 2y - x$$

$$3y - 3x = 2y - x$$

$$\Rightarrow \quad y = 2x$$

Profit = $2x - x = x$

$$\text{Profit \%} = \left(\frac{x}{x} \times 100 \right) \% = 100\%$$

25. **(c)** Let 'x' be the sum invested in the bank.

According to question

$$\frac{x \times 10 \times 1}{100} + \frac{x \times 12 \times 1}{100} = 1650$$

$$10x + 12x = 165000$$

$$22x = 165000$$

$$x = ₹ 7500$$

26. (a) Let sum = ₹ x, S.I. = $\dfrac{1}{9}$ x

Rate = R%

Time = R yrs.

$$\frac{1}{9}x = \frac{x \times R \times R}{100}$$

$$R^2 = \frac{100}{9}$$

R = 3.33%

27. (a)

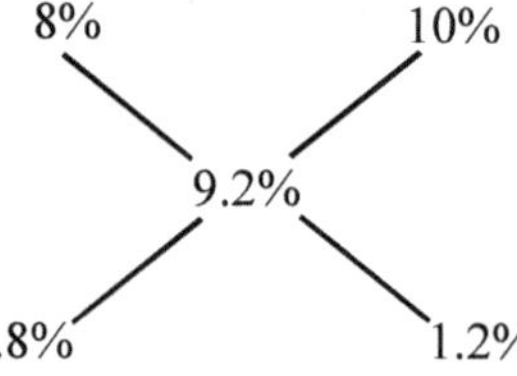

The ratio in which money lent is 0.8 : 1.2 or 2 : 3

Therefore, money lent at 10%

$$= \frac{3}{5} \times 10000 = 6000$$

28. (c) Let the total number of votes enrolled be x.

Then, number of votes cast = 60% of x

Valid votes = 96% of (60% of x)

75% of [96% of (60% of x)] = 7344

$$\frac{75}{100} \times \frac{96}{100} \times \frac{60}{100} \times x = 7344$$

$$x = \frac{7344 \times 100 \times 100 \times 100}{75 \times 96 \times 60}$$

x = 17000

29. (b) If the price of a commodity increases by R%, then the reduction in consumption. So as not to increase the expenditure is

$$\left[\frac{R}{100+R} \times 100\right]\% = \frac{9}{100+9} \times 100$$

$$= 8.25\%$$

30. (d) Pupils from first school appeared for an examination

= 80% of 65 = 52

Pupils from second school appeared for an examination

= 52 + 4 = 56

Total pupils in second school = 65 + 10 = 75

Pass % of second school = $\dfrac{56}{75} \times 100$ = 74.6%

31. (b) Amount = Principal $\left(1 + \dfrac{\text{Rate}}{100}\right)^{\text{Time}}$

$$= 1250\left(1 + \frac{4}{100}\right)^2$$

$$= 1250 \times \frac{26}{25} \times \frac{26}{25}$$

$$= ₹\ 1352$$

32. (a) Let the sum lent at 6% be ₹ x and that lent at 4% be ₹ (3200 – x). Then,

$$\frac{x \times 6 \times 1}{100} + \frac{(3200 - x)4 \times 1}{100} = 176$$

6x + 4 × 3200 – 4x = 17600

2x = 17600 – 4 × 3200

2x = 17600 – 12800 = 4800

x = ₹ 2400

33. (c) Let the sum invested be ₹ x.

$$\frac{x \times 8 \times 10}{100} + \frac{x \times 12 \times 1}{100} = 1500$$

8x + 12x = 150000

20x = 150000

x = 7500

34. (b) Let sum = ₹ x, S.I = $\dfrac{1}{5}$ x

Time = 4 years, Rate = ?

$$S.I. = \frac{P \times R \times T}{100}$$

$$\Rightarrow \quad \frac{1}{5}x = \frac{x \times R \times 4}{100}$$

$$R = \frac{100}{5 \times 4} = 5\%$$

35. (a) Let the sum lent at 7% be ₹ x and that lent at 9% be ₹ (2600 – x).

Then,

$$\frac{x \times 7 \times 1}{100} + \frac{(2600 - x) \times 9 \times 1}{100} = 206$$

7x + 9 × 2600 – 9x = 20600

– 2x = 20600 – 9 × 2600

$$\Rightarrow \quad x = 1400$$

36. (b) Let the total number of votes enrolled be x. Then, number of votes cast = 70% of valid votes = 98% of (70% of x)

60% of [98% of 70% of x] = 7203

$$\frac{70}{100} \times \frac{98}{100} \times \frac{60}{100} \times x = 7203$$

$$x = \frac{7203 \times 100 \times 100 \times 100}{70 \times 98 \times 60}$$

x = 17500

37. (b) If the price of a commodity increases by R%, then the reduction in consumption so as not to increase the expenditure is

$$\left[\dfrac{R}{100+R}\times 100\right]\% = \dfrac{11}{100+11}\times 100 = 9.9\%$$

38. (d) Pupils from first school appeared for an examination
$$= 80\% \text{ of } 75 = 60$$
Pupils from second school appeared for an examination = 55
Total pupils in second school = 75 + 10 = 85

Pass % of second school $= \dfrac{55}{85}\times 100 = 64.7\%$

39. (d) $A = P\left(1+\dfrac{R}{100}\right)^{T}$

Where A = Amount, P = Principal, R = Rate % per annum
T = Time in years

$$A = 1875\times\dfrac{26}{25}\times\dfrac{26}{25}$$

$$A = ₹\,2028.$$

40. (d) $x = ky$
$$8 = 4\,k\times 15$$

$$k = \dfrac{8}{15}$$

$$x = ky$$

$$x = \dfrac{8}{15}\times 10$$

$$x = \dfrac{16}{3}$$

41. (d) Let x be the money lent at 10%

$$920 = \dfrac{(10000-x)\times 6 + x\times 10}{100}$$

$$92000 = 60000 - 6x + 10x$$
$$32000 = 4x$$
$$x = ₹\,8000$$

42. (c) Cost of article = ₹ 50
Inflation = 300%

After 2 years cost $= 50\left(1+\dfrac{300}{100}\right)^{2} = 50\times 16 = ₹\,800$

43. (b) Gain % $= \dfrac{1000-900}{900}\times 100 = \dfrac{100}{900}\times 100 = \dfrac{100}{9}\%$

44. (b) Let CP of bullock = ₹ x

$$SP = \dfrac{x\times 120}{100}$$

CP of cart = (1800 − x)
P = 30%

$$SP = \dfrac{(1800-x)\times 130}{100}$$

$$\text{Total SP} = \dfrac{1800\times\left(100+\dfrac{155}{6}\right)}{100} = ₹\,226500$$

$$\therefore\quad \dfrac{120}{100} + \dfrac{(1800-x)\times 130}{100} = 226500$$

$$\therefore\quad x = 750$$
Reset sequence property
Hence, cost price of bullock = ₹ 750

45. (b) Let P = ₹ x

$$SI = \dfrac{x\times 10\times 10}{100} = x$$

$$A = P + SI$$
$$22500 = x + x$$
$$2x = 22500$$
$$x = 11250$$
$\therefore$ He took 11,250 as a lone.

46. (c) Let P = x
$$A = 3x$$
$$SI = 2x$$
$$T = 8 \text{ years}$$

$$R = \dfrac{2x\times 100}{x\times 8} = 25\%$$

$$\text{Now SI} = \dfrac{x\times 25\times 20}{100} = 5x$$

$$A = 5x + x = 6x$$
$\therefore$ In 6 years it becomes 6 times

47. (c) Let value of consignment was ₹ x

$\left(\dfrac{2}{3}\right)^{rd}$ consignment costs $\dfrac{2x}{3}$

Selling price of $\left(\dfrac{2}{3}\right)^{rd}$ consignment

$$= \dfrac{2x}{3} + \dfrac{5}{100}\times\dfrac{2x}{3} = \dfrac{7}{10}x$$

S.P of $\left(\dfrac{1}{3}\right)^{rd}$ consignment $= \dfrac{x}{3} - \dfrac{2}{100}\times\dfrac{x}{3} = \dfrac{49}{150}x$

$$\text{Total S.P} = \dfrac{49x}{150} + \dfrac{7x}{10} = \dfrac{49x+105x}{150} = \dfrac{154x}{150}$$

Profit = S.P − C.P

$$400 = \dfrac{154x}{150} - x = \dfrac{4x}{150}$$

$$x = \dfrac{400\times 150}{4} = 15000$$

Value of consignment was ₹ 15,000

48. (d) Let in third yearly examination he Secure x %

Then, $\dfrac{45+55+x}{3} = 60$

$100 + x = 180$

$x = 80$

To secure 60% average, he has to get 80%

80% of 500 = $\dfrac{80}{100} \times 500 = 400$ marks

49. (b) Area of towel = $l \times b$ =100 cm × 50cm = 5000 cm²

Now, length decreased by 20% and breadth decreased by 10%

$l' = 100 - 20\%$ of $100 = 80$cm

$b' = 50 - 10\%$ of $50 = 45$cm

New area = $l' \times b' = 80$cm × 45cm = 3600cm²

Change in area = (5000 – 3600) cm² = 1400 cm²

% change in area = $\dfrac{1400}{5000} \times 100 = 28\%$

50. (b) Let son aged 19 years getting ₹x and son aged 17 years getting $(88400 - x)$.

At the age of 21, both will get equal amount

$$x\left(1 + \dfrac{10}{100}\right)^2 = (88400 - x)\left(1 + \dfrac{10}{100}\right)^4$$

$$\Rightarrow \dfrac{121x}{100} = (88400 - x) \times \dfrac{121}{100} \times \dfrac{121}{100}$$

$$\Rightarrow 100x = 88400 \times 121 - 121x$$

$$\Rightarrow 221x = 88400 \times 121$$

$$\Rightarrow x = \dfrac{88400 \times 121}{221} = 48400$$

$$x = ₹\,48400$$

51. (c) If number of boys is x, then number of girls is (150–x)

$(150 - x) = x$ % of 150

$$150 - x = \dfrac{x}{100} \times 150 = \dfrac{3x}{2}$$

$$\Rightarrow \dfrac{5x}{2} = 150$$

$$\Rightarrow x = \dfrac{150 \times 2}{5} = 60$$

Number of boys is 60

52. (a) Difference in percentage of A and B = (40–30) = 10%

Difference in marks = 50

Let maximum marks be x

10% of x = 50 x $= \dfrac{50 \times 100}{10} = 500$

A scored 30% of 500 means 150 marks

minimum marks required to pass = 150 + 15 = 165

Pass % = $\dfrac{165}{500} \times 100 = 33\%$

53. (d) Let time Period be x years

$$\dfrac{6000 \times 10 \times t}{100} + \dfrac{5000 \times 12 \times t}{100} = 2400$$

$\Rightarrow 600t + 600t = 2400$

$\Rightarrow t = \dfrac{2400}{1200} = 2$

Time period is 2 years

54. (a) S.I. = 2P – P = P

$$P = \dfrac{P \times R \times 16}{100}$$

$$R = \dfrac{25}{4}\%$$

(S.I) For 8 years = $\dfrac{P \times \dfrac{25}{4} \times 8}{100} = \dfrac{P}{2}$

Amount = $P + \dfrac{P}{2} = \dfrac{3P}{2}$

Amount increased by 1½ times.

55. (b) $926.1 = 800\left(1 + \dfrac{\dfrac{10}{2}}{100}\right)^{2t}$

$$\dfrac{9261}{8000} = \left(\dfrac{21}{20}\right)^{2t}$$

$$\left(\dfrac{21}{20}\right)^3 = \left(\dfrac{21}{20}\right)^{2t} \Rightarrow t = \dfrac{3}{2} \text{ years or } 1\dfrac{1}{2} \text{ years.}$$

56. (d) Let x be the cost price of T.V.

loss = 15%

then, $S.P_1 = x - 15\%$ of x = 0.85x

Profit = 15%

then, $S.P_2 = x + 15\%$ of x = 1.15x

total S.P = 0.85 x + 1.15x = 2x

Profit = 2x – 2x = 0

No profit, no loss

57. (c) Let x and y be the rate of sugar per Kg and quantity of sugar.

$$xy = \left(x + \dfrac{20}{100} \times x\right)y'$$

$$xy = \dfrac{6x}{5}y'$$

$$y' = \dfrac{5}{6}y = y - \dfrac{y}{6}$$

Reduction in consumption $= \dfrac{100}{6} = 16\dfrac{2}{3}\%$

58. (d) A = B – 20% of B = 0.8 B

B = C – 15% of C = 0.85 C

A = 0.8 × 0.85 C = 0.68 C

$$\dfrac{C - A}{A} \times 100 = \dfrac{C - 0.68C}{0.68C} \times 100 = \dfrac{32}{68} \times 100 = 47.05\%$$

4 — Time, Speed and Distance

1. Two typists of varying skills can do a typing job in 6 minutes if they work together. If the first typist typed alone for 4 minutes and then the second typist typed alone for 6 minutes, they would be left with 1/5 of the whole work. How many minutes would it take the slower typist to complete the typing job working alone ?   *[2014-I]*
   (a) 10 minutes
   (b) 15 minutes
   (c) 12 minutes
   (d) 20 minutes

2. A train covers a distance of 10 km in 12 minutes. If its speed is decreased by 5 kmph, what is the time taken train to cover the same distance ?   *[2014-II]*
   (a) 14 min. 33 sec
   (b) 13 min. 33 sec
   (c) 13 min. 20 sec
   (d) 15 min. 20 sec

3. 'A' is thrice as good a workman as 'B' and takes 10 days less to do a piece of work than 'B' takes. How many days will 'B' take to complete if he works alone ?   *[2014-II]*
   (a) 21 days
   (b) 15 days
   (c) 18 days
   (d) 24 days

4. 'A' and 'B' can do a piece of work in 30 days while 'B' and 'C' can do the same work in 24 days and 'C' and 'A' in 20 days. They all work for 10 days and 'B' and 'C' leave. How many days more will 'A' take to finish the work ?   *[2014-II]*
   (a) 12 days
   (b) 18 days
   (c) 20 days
   (d) 22 days

5. A train is moving at a speed of 132 kmph. If the length of the train is 110 meters, how long will it take to cross a railway platform 165 m long ?   *[2014-II]*
   (a) 6.0 secs
   (b) 7.5 secs
   (c) 7.0 secs
   (d) 8.5 secs

6. Two pipes 'A' and 'B' can fill a tank in 20 and 30 minutes respectively. If both the pipes are used together, then how long are will it take to fill the tank ?   *[2014-II]*
   (a) 12 Min
   (b) 15 Min
   (c) 25 Min
   (d) 50 Min

7. Speed of a boat in still water is 9 kmph and the speed of the stream is 1.5 kmph. A man rows to a place at a distance of 105 kms and comes back to the starting point. What will be the total time taken by him ?   *[2014-II]*
   (a) 16 Hrs
   (b) 18 Hrs
   (c) 24 Hrs
   (d) 28 Hrs

8. A man can row $9\dfrac{1}{3}$ Kmph in still water and finds that it takes him thrice as much time to row up than as to row down the same distance in the river. The speed of the current is   *[2015-I]*
   (a) $3\dfrac{1}{3}$ Kmph
   (b) $3\dfrac{1}{9}$ Kmph
   (c) $4\dfrac{2}{3}$ Kmph
   (d) $4\dfrac{1}{3}$ Kmph

9. The speed of a boat in still water is 10 Kmph. If it can travel 26 Km downstream and 14 Km upstream in the same time, the speed of the stream is   *[2015-I]*
   (a) 2 Kmph
   (b) 2.5 Kmph
   (c) 3 Kmph
   (d) 4 Kmph

10. A man travelled from a point A to B at the rate of 25 Kmph and walked back at the rate of 4 Kmph. If the whole journey took 5 hrs 48 minutes, the distance between A and B is   *[2015-I]*
    (a) 30 km
    (b) 24 km
    (c) 20 km
    (d) 51.6 km

11. A train travelling at a uniform speed clears a platform 200 m long in 10 seconds and passes a telegraph post in 5 seconds. The speed of the train is   *[2015-I]*
    (a) 36 km/h
    (b) 39 km/h
    (c) 72 km/h
    (d) 78 km/h

12. A and B can do a piece of work in 18 days; B and C can do it in 24 days, A and C can do it in 36 days. In how many days B alone can finish the work?   *[2015-I]*
    (a) 48 days
    (b) 45 days
    (c) $28\dfrac{4}{5}$ days
    (d) 144 days

Hints & Solutions

1. (b) Let first complete the job in = x minutes
   Second complete the job in = y minutes

   $$\therefore \quad \frac{1}{x}+\frac{1}{y}=\frac{1}{6} \qquad \qquad ...(1)$$

   $$\text{and } \frac{4}{x}+\frac{6}{y}=1-\frac{1}{5}=\frac{4}{5} \qquad ...(2)$$

   By (1) and (2)
   x = 10, y = 15
   Hence slower typist complete the jobs in 15 minutes.

2. (c) Speed of train $=\dfrac{10\,\text{km}}{12/60\,\text{h}}=50\,\text{km/h}$

   Speed is decreased by 5 kmph then new Speed of the train will be 45 kmph

   Time taken to cover 10 km, $t=\dfrac{10}{45}=\dfrac{2}{9}\text{h}$

   Time taken = 13min. 20 sec

3. (b) Let A finish the work in x days
B finish same work in $3x$ days
$3x - x = 10 \Rightarrow x = 5$ days
B finish the work in $3 \times 5 = 15$ days

4. (b) Let A,B and C individualy complete the work in x,y and z days respectively.

$$\frac{1}{x} + \frac{1}{y} = \frac{1}{30} \qquad ...(1)$$

$$\frac{1}{y} + \frac{1}{z} = \frac{1}{24} \qquad ...(2)$$

$$\frac{1}{z} + \frac{1}{x} = \frac{1}{20} \qquad ...(3)$$

adding equ (1) , (2) and (3)

$$2\left(\frac{1}{x} + \frac{1}{y} + \frac{1}{z}\right) = \frac{1}{8} \Rightarrow \frac{1}{x} + \frac{1}{y} + \frac{1}{z} = \frac{1}{16} \qquad ...(4)$$

A,B and C together complete the work in 16 days.

In 10 days they completed $\frac{10}{16} = \frac{5}{8}$ Part

Remaining work = $1 - \frac{5}{8} = \frac{3}{8}$

Subtracting equ (2) from (4)

we get, $\frac{1}{x} = \frac{1}{48}$ or x = 48

A alone can finish the Remaining work in

$\frac{3}{8} \times 48 = 18$ days

5. (b) Speed of train = 132 kmph = $132 \times \frac{5}{18}$ m/s = $\frac{110}{3}$ m/s

Total distance = 110m + 165m = 275m

Time taken to cover the distance = $\frac{275\text{ms}}{110\text{m}}$ = 7.5s.

6. (a) In one minute A can fill $\left(\frac{1}{20}\right)^{th}$ Part

In one minute B can fill $\left(\frac{1}{30}\right)^{th}$ Part

In one minute A and B together can fill

$\frac{1}{20} + \frac{1}{30} = \left(\frac{1}{12}\right)^{th}$ Parts

A and B together can fill the tank in 12 minutes

7. (c) Speed of upstream = 9 – 1.5 = 7.5 Kmph
Speed of down stream = 9 + 1.5 = 10.5 Kmph

Time taken for up stream = $\frac{105}{7.5} = 14$h

Time taken for down stream = $\frac{105}{7.5} = 10$h

Total time taken = 10 + 14 = 24 hours

8. (c) Distance covered by man = D Km
Speed of Man in still water = x Kmph

Speed of current = $\frac{28}{3}$ Kmph

According to question,

$$\frac{D}{\frac{28}{3} - x} = 3\left(\frac{D}{\frac{28}{3} + x}\right)$$

$$\Rightarrow \frac{28}{3} + x = 3\left(\frac{28}{3} - x\right) \quad \Rightarrow 4x = 2 \times \frac{28}{3}$$

$$\Rightarrow x = \frac{14}{3} \text{ or } 4\frac{2}{3} \text{ Kmph}$$

9. (c) Let speed of steam be x Kmph.
Then,

$$\frac{26}{10 + x} = \frac{14}{10 - x}$$
$$260 - 26x = 140 + 14x$$
$$40x = 120$$
$$x = 3$$

Speed of steam 3 Kmph.

10. (c) Let D Km be the distance between A and B.

$$\frac{D}{25} + \frac{D}{4} = 5\frac{48}{60}$$

$$\frac{4D + 25D}{100} - \frac{29}{5}$$

$$\frac{29D}{100} = \frac{29}{5}$$

$$D = 20 \text{ Km}$$

11. (*) Let 'x' be the length of the train.
Let 's' be the speed of train.
Distance travelled by train to cross the platform
= (x + 200)m
According to question
(x + 200) = s × 10 sec.   ...(1)
Distance travelled by train to cross he telegraph post
= x m
According to question
x = s × 5 sec.   ...(2)
Puting 'x' value in (1) from (2)
(5s + 200) = 105
200 = 10s – 5s = 5s
s = 40 m/s

$$s = \frac{\overset{8}{\cancel{40}} \times 18}{\cancel{5}} = 144 \text{ km/h}$$

None of the option is matching.

12. (c)

$$\frac{1}{A} + \frac{1}{B} = \frac{1}{18} \qquad ...(1)$$

$$\frac{1}{B} + \frac{1}{C} = \frac{1}{24} \qquad ...(2)$$

$$\frac{1}{C} + \frac{1}{A} = \frac{1}{36} \qquad ...(3)$$

Adding eqn. (1), (2) and (3)

$$2\left(\frac{1}{A} + \frac{1}{B} + \frac{1}{C}\right) = \frac{1}{18} + \frac{1}{24} + \frac{1}{36}$$

$$\frac{1}{A} + \frac{1}{B} + \frac{1}{C} = \frac{1}{16} \qquad ...(4)$$

Subtract eqn. (3) from (4)

$$\frac{1}{B} = \frac{1}{16} - \frac{1}{36} = \frac{5}{144}$$

B alone can finish work in $\frac{144}{5} = 28\frac{4}{5}$ days

VERBAL REASONING

1

Analogy & Odd One Out

1. BOOK is to CHAPTER as BUILDING is to *[2011-I]*
   (a) ELEVATOR   (b) LOBBY
   (c) ROOF   (d) STOREY

2. CARROT is to VEGETABLE as *[2011-I]*
   (a) DOGWOOD is to OAK   (b) FOOT is to PAW
   (c) PEPPER is to SPICE   (d) SHEEP is to LAMB

3. CONCAVE is to CONVEX as *[2011-I]*
   (a) CAVITY is to MOUND   (b) HILL is to HOLE
   (c) OVAL is to OBLONG   (d) ROUND is to POINTED

4. GOWN is to GARMENT as GASOLINE is to *[2011-I]*
   (a) COOLANT   (b) FUEL
   (c) OIL   (d) LUBRICANT

5. HYPER- is to HYPO- as *[2011-I]*
   (a) DIASTOLIC is to SYSTOLIC
   (b) OVER is to UNDER
   (c) SMALL is to LARGE
   (d) STALE is to FRESH

6. IMMIGRATION is to EMIGRATION as *[2011-I]*
   (a) ARRIVAL is to DEPARTURE
   (b) FLIGHT is to VOYAGE
   (c) LEGAL is to ILLEGAL
   (d) MIGRATION is to TRAVEL

7. OCTAGON is to SQUARE as HEXAGON is to *[2011-I]*
   (a) POLYGON   (b) PYRAMID
   (c) RECTANGLE   (d) TRIANGLE

8. TELL is to TOLD as
   (a) RIDE is to RODE   (b) SINK is to SANK
   (c) WEAVE is to WOVE   (d) WEEP is to WEPT

9. SHEEP is to LAMB as HORSE is to *[2011-I]*
   (a) COLT   (b) DOE
   (c) FAWN   (d) MARE

10. IGNORE is to OVERLOOK as *[2011-I]*
    (a) AGREE is to CONSENT
    (b) CLIMB is to WALK
    (c) DULL is to SHARPEN
    (d) LEARN is to REMEMBER

11. FREQUENTLY is to SELDOM as *[2011-I]*
    (a) ALWAYS is to NEVER
    (b) EVERYBODY is to EVERYONE
    (c) GENERALLY is to USUALLY
    (d) OCCASIONALLY is to CONSTANTLY

DIRECTIONS (Qs. 12-31) : *Each question consists of two words which have a certain relationship to each other, followed by four pairs of related words. Select the pair which has the same relationship.*

12. STORY : NOVEL *[2011-II]*
    (a) Sea : Ocean   (b) School : University
    (c) Book : Dictionary   (d) Poetry : Drama

13. GRAIN : SALT *[2011-II]*
    (a) Shard : Pottery   (b) Shred : Wood
    (c) Blades : Grass   (d) Chips : Glass

14. WAITER : TIP *[2011-II]*
    (a) Student : Marks   (b) Worker : Bonus
    (c) Employee : Wages   (d) Clerk : Bribe

15. PAIN : SEDATIVE *[2011-II]*
    (a) Comfort : Stimulant   (b) Grief : Consolation
    (c) Trance : Narcotic   (d) Ache : Extraction

16. SILENCE : NOISE *[2011-II]*
    (a) Quiet : Peace   (b) Baldness : Hair
    (c) Talk : Whisper   (d) Singer : Dance

17. WAN : COLOUR *[2011-II]*
    (a) Corpulent : Weight   (b) Insipid : Flavour
    (c) Pallid : Complexion   (d) Enigmatic : Puzzle

18. PORK : PIG *[2011-II]*
    (a) Rooster : Chicken   (b) Mutton : Sheep
    (c) Steer : Beef   (d) Lobster : Crustacean

19. AFTER : BEFORE *[2011-II]*
    (a) First : Second   (b) Present : Past
    (c) Contemporary : Historic   (d) Successor : Predecessor

20. EAST : ORIENT *[2011-II]*
    (a) North : Polar   (b) South : Capricorn
    (c) West : Indian   (d) West : Occident

21. DISTANCE : MILE *[2011-II]*
    (a) Liquid : Litre   (b) Bushel : Corn
    (c) Weight : Scale   (d) Fame : Television

22. TEN : DECIMAL *[2011-II]*
    (a) Seven : Seplet   (b) Four : Quartet
    (c) Two : Binary   (d) Five : Quince

23. MUNDANE : SPIRITUAL   *[2011-II]*
   (a) Common : Ghostly   (b) Worldly : Unworldly
   (c) Routine : Novel   (d) Secular : Clerical

24. LAWYER : COURT   *[2011-II]*
   (a) Businessman : Market   (b) Chemist : Laboratory
   (c) Labourer : Factory   (d) Athelete : Olympics

25. ARMY : LOGISTICS   *[2011-II]*
   (a) Business : Strategy   (b) Soldier : Students
   (c) War : Logic   (d) Team : individual

26. GRAVITY : PULL   *[2011-II]*
   (a) Iron : Metal   (b) North pole : Directions
   (c) Magnetism : Attraction (d) Dust : Desert

27. FILTER : WATER   *[2011-II]*
   (a) Curtail : Activity   (b) Expunge : Book
   (c) Edit : Text   (d) Censor : Play

28. HOPE : ASPIRES   *[2011-II]*
   (a) Love : Elevates   (b) Film : Flam
   (c) Fib : Lie   (d) Fake : Ordinary

29. SADIEST : PAIN   *[2011-II]*
   (a) Killer : Death   (b) Teacher : Pupil
   (c) Injury : Bandage   (d) Alcohol : Dipsomaniac

30. SYMPHONY : COMPOSER   *[2011-II]*
   (a) Leonardo : Music   (b) Fersco : Painter
   (c) Colours : Pallet   (d) Art : Appreciation

31. CURATOR : MUSEUM   *[2011-II]*
   (a) Wit : Wisdom   (b) Bank : Teller
   (c) Manager : Office   (d) Doctor : Patient

32. Which word in each set of four is the odd one out ? *[2011-II]*
   (a) Look   (b) See
   (c) Watch   (d) Face

33. This test requires you to identify the relationship between
   two words. Shoe is to foot as sock is to   *[2011-II]*
   (a) wind   (b) hand
   (c) foot   (d) leg

DIRECTIONS (Qs. 34-38) : *Find the odd one out.* *[2012-I]*

34. (a) Advice   (b) Counsel
   (c) Direct   (d) Suggest

35. (a) Tumble   (b) Topple
   (c) Crumble   (d) Sprain

36. (a) Sobriquet   (b) Alias
   (c) Pseudonym   (d) Anonymous

37. (a) Mumbai   (b) Goa
   (c) Visakhapatnam   (d) Thiruvananthapuram

38. (a) Petrol   (b) Acetone
   (c) Mercury   (d) Kerosene

DIRECTIONS (Qs. 39-48) : *In the following questions the words
given bear a certain relationship. Your task is to find out from the
choices the words with the same relationship.* *[2012-I]*

39. Hope : Despair
   (a) Work : Failure   (b) Worship : Adore
   (c) Cow : Milk   (d) Encourage : Dishearten

40. Army : Logistics
   (a) War : Logic   (b) Soldiers : Students
   (c) Business : Strategy   (d) Team : Individual

41. Bouquet : Flower
   (a) Skin : Body   (b) Chain : Link
   (c) Product : Factory   (d) Page : Book

42. Revenge : Vendetta
   (a) Sleep : Dream   (b) Sun : Moon
   (c) Envy : Jealousy   (d) Heaven : God

43. Refine : Style
   (a) Retouch : Photograph   (b) Paint : Wall
   (c) Compose : Song   (d) Author : Book

44. Fear : Tremble
   (a) Hand : Shake   (b) Heat : Perspire
   (c) Distance : Walk   (d) Evening : Star

45. Condone : Offence
   (a) Punish : Criminal   (b) Mitigate : Penitence
   (c) Overlook : Aberration   (d) Ignore : Loyalty

46. Plant : Flower
   (a) Face : Eye   (b) Stem : Tree
   (c) Chair : Sofa   (d) Blades : Grass

47. Protoplasm : Cell
   (a) Fibre : Plastic   (b) Coin : Money
   (c) Chemistry : Elements   (d) Chain : Link

48. Nalanda : Takshshila
   (a) Venus : Mars   (b) University : College
   (c) Office : Department   (d) Ship : Cargo

DIRECTIONS (Qs. 49-53) : *In the following questions (Q56-
60) the first word is related to the second in the same way as the
third word is related to the fourth. In the given problems either
the third or the fourth word is missing and is left blank. You have
to choose the correct word to fill in the blank.* *[2012-I]*

49. Foot is to Man as Hoof is to ________.
   (a) Dog   (b) Cow
   (c) Cat   (d) Rabbit

50. Broad is to Narrow as ________ is to Lane.
   (a) Footpath   (b) Field
   (c) Pavement   (d) Road

51. Back is to Backbone as Belly is to ________.
   (a) Throat   (b) Ribs
   (c) Heart   (d) Navel

52. Ankle is to Knee as Wrist is to ____________.
   (a) Elbow   (b) Finger
   (c) Hand   (d) Foot

53. Sting is to Bee as ______ is to Snake.
   (a) Slithering   (b) Rats
   (c) Poison   (d) Fangs

DIRECTIONS (Qs 54-63) : *In the following questions the words
given bear a certain relationship. Find out from the choices the
words with the same relationship.* *[2012-II]*

54. Surgeon : Scalpet
   (a) Musician : Instrument   (b) Sculptor : Chisel
   (c) Carpenter : Cabinet   (d) Baker : Oven

55. Creche : Infants
   (a) School : Pupils   (b) Deck : Sailors
   (c) Cottage : Guests   (d) Aircraft : Crew

56. Pesticide : Plant
   (a) Injection : Disease   (b) Teacher : Student
   (c) Medicine : Cure   (d) Vaccination : Body

57. Stare : Glance
   (a) Gulp : Sip   (b) Story : tell
   (c) Hunt : Stalk   (d) Step : Walk

58. Fish : Aquarium
   (a) Student : Hostel   (b) Bird : Forest
   (c) Goods : Consignment   (d) Bee : Apiary

59. Ecstasy : Pleasure
   (a) Hatred : Affection   (b) Rage : Anger
   (c) Joy : Grief   (d) Mumble : Speak

60. Necromancy : Ghosts
   (a) Romance : Stories   (b) Magic : Amulets
   (c) Alchemy : Gold   (d) Sorcery : Spirit

61. Coin : Mint
   (a) Grain : Field   (b) Hay : Stable
   (c) Wine : Brewery   (d) Book : Publisher

62. Oak : Coniferous
   (a) Chimpanzee : Ape   (b) Animals : Carnivore
   (c) Fish : Sea   (d) Tree : Grove

63. Onam : Kerala
   (a) Christmas : Christians (b) Bhangra : Punjab
   (c) Kathak : Uttar Pradesh (d) Bihu : Assam

DIRECTIONS (Qs 64-68) : *In each of the following questions, a group of three inter related words is given. Choose a word from the given alternatives, that belongs to the same group.* **[2012-II]**

64. Calendar : Dates : : Dictionary : ?
   (a) Vocabulary   (b) Language
   (c) Words   (d) Book

65. Heed : Neglect : : Pacify : ?
   (a) Incite   (b) Allay
   (c) War   (d) Victory

66. Malaria : Disease : : Sword : ?
   (a) Wound   (b) Spear
   (c) Weapon   (d) Rifle

67. Eye : Wink : : Heart : ?
   (a) Move   (b) Throb
   (c) Pump   (d) Quiver

68. Earth : Sun : : Moon : ?
   (a) Orbit   (b) Sky
   (c) Star   (d) Earth

DIRECTIONS (Qs 69-73) : *Choose the word which is least like the other words in the group.* **[2012-II]**

69. (a) Rose   (b) Lotus
   (c) Marigold   (d) Tulip

70. (a) Book   (b) Sharpener
   (c) Pencil   (d) Paper

71. (a) Copper   (b) Tin
   (c) Brass   (d) Zinc

72. (a) Kiwi   (b) Eagle
   (c) Emu   (d) Penguin

73. (a) Raniganj   (b) Jharia
   (c) Bokaro   (d) Baroda

DIRECTIONS (Qs. 74 – 78) : *Choose the word which is least like the other words in the group* **[2013-I]**

74. (a) Garo   (b) Khasi
   (c) Kangra   (d) Jayantia

75. (a) Virgo   (b) Pisces
   (c) Cancer   (d) Orion

76. (a) Shoulder   (b) Foot
   (b) Finger   (d) Elbow

77. (a) Canoe   (b) Dingy
   (c) Yatch   (d) Igloo

78. (a) Inn   (b) Club
   (c) Motel   (d) Hostel

DIRECTIONS (Qs. 79 – 83) : *The following questions consist of two words that have a certain relationship to each other, followed by four alternatives. Select the best alternative that has the same relationship as the original pair of words* **[2013-I]**

79. Liquor : Drink
   (a) Bread : Butter   (b) Tea : Beverage
   (c) Sniff : Inhale   (d) Water : Sip

80. Evaporation : Cloud
   (a) Mountain : Snow   (b) Book : Pages
   (c) Pressure : Atmosphere (d) Tension : Breakdown

81. Barrel : Vial
   (a) Book : Pamphlet   (b) Book : Reader
   (c) Brochure : Complier (d) Length : Height

82. Cream : Cosmetics
   (a) Tiger : Forest   (b) Mountain : Valley
   (c) Magazine : Editor   (d) Teak : Wood

83. Carnivore : Herbivore
   (a) Flesh : Plant   (b) Horse : Lion
   (c) Camel : Giraffe   (d) Animal : Bird

DIRECTIONS (Qs. 84 – 93) : *Three words in bold letters are given in each question, which have something in common among themselves. Out of the four given alternatives, choose the most appropriate description about these three words.* **[2013-I]**

84. **Hamlet : Macbeth : Faustus**
   (a) They are princes
   (b) They are plays by Shakespear
   (c) They are characters from various dramas
   (d) They were romantic hereoes.

85. **Vesuvius : Etna : Kilimanjaro**
   (a) These are sites of volcanoes
   (b) These are island countries.
   (c) These are hills of Italy.
   (d) These lie in polar region.

86. Knot : Watt : Fathorn
(a) The terms are used by sailors
(b) The terms are used for installing electricity
(c) The terms are connected with rope
(d) They are units of measurement.

87. Barauni : Digboi : Ankleshwar
(a) They are famous for oil fields.
(b) They are famous for religious places.
(c) They are tourist places of South India.
(d) They are famous for handlooms.

88. Knight : Rook : Bishop
(a) These are missionaries
(b) They are churchmen.
(c) These are chessmen.
(d) These are ranks of military.

89. Abhi Bhattacharya : Utpal Dutt : Satyajit Ray
(a) They are character actors.
(b) They are directors of Bengali movies.
(c) They are famous poets and writers.
(d) These personalities belong to Bengali

90. Voodoo : Sorcery : Necromancy
(a) They are ancient arts found in sculptures.
(b) They are terms connected with black magic.
(c) They are ancient scripts.
(d) They are means of communication of pre-historic age.

91. Rourkela : Bokaro : Durgapur
(a) They are steel plants.
(b) They have coal mines.
(c) They have atomic plants
(d) They are on the sea coast.

92. Spinach : Fenugreek : Celery
(a) These are cactus plants
(b) These are wild plants
(c) These are wild flowers.
(d) These are leafy vegetables.

93. Yeats : Ghalib : Kabir
(a) They were social reformers.
(b) They were famous poets.
(c) They were saints.
(d) They were yoga instructors

Direction

DIRECTIONS (Qs.94–96). *Choose the most appropriate word:*
[2014-I]

94. 'RUSTLE' is to 'LEAVES' as 'PATTER' is to________
(a) Snow   (b) Wind
(c) Rain (d)   Storm

95. 'INDISCREET' is to 'IMPRUDENT' as 'INDISPOSED' is to ______
(a) Concerned   (b) Reluctant
(c) Crucial   (d) Clear

96. 'ACCIDENT' is to 'CAREFULNESS' as 'DISEASE' is to ________
(a) Sanitation   (b) Treatment
(c) Medicine   (d) Doctor

DIRECTIONS (Qs. 97 & 98) : *Choose the word which is least like the other words in the group.*   *[2014-I]*

97. (a) Tsangpo   (b) Hazaribagh
(c) Kanha   (d) Bandipur

98. (a) Wheat   (b) Rice
(c) Mustard   (d) Gram

DIRECTIONS (Qs. 99 - 103) : *The following questions consist of two words that have a certain relationship to each other, followed by four alternatives. Select the best alternative that has same relationship as the original pair of words*   *[2014-I]*

99. Crèche : Infants
(a) School : Pupils   (b) Deck : Sailors
(c) Cottage : Guests   (d) Aircraft : Crew

100. Pesticide : Plant
(a) Injection : Disease   (b) Vaccination : Body
(c) Medicine : Cure   (d) Teacher : Student

101. Stare : Glance
(a) Gulp : Sip   (b) Confide : tell
(c) Hunt : Stalk   (d) Step : Walk

102. Ecstasy : Pleasure
(a) Hatred : Affection   (b) Rage : Anger
(c) Joy : Grief   (d) Mumble : Speak

103. Necromancy : Ghosts
(a) Romance : Stories   (b) Magic : Amulets
(c) Alchemy : Gold   (d) Sorcery : Spirit

DIRECTIONS (Qs.104–106). *There is certain relationship between two given words on one side of : : and one word is given on another side of : : while another word is to be found from the given alternatives, having the same relation with this word as the given pair has. Select the best alternatives/ relationship.*   *[2014-I]*

104. Firm : Flabby : : Piquant : ?
(a) Salty   (b) Pleasant
(c) Bland   (d) Smell

105. Funk : Vitamins : : Curie : ?
(a) Uranium   (b) Radioactivity
(c) Photography   (d) Radium

106. Contamination : Food : : Infection : ?
(a) Diseases   (b) Body
(c) Germs   (d) Microbes

DIRECTIONS (Qs.107–111) : *In each of the following questions find out the alternative which will replace the question mark.*

107. Carbon: Diamond   Corundum: ...... ? .....
(a) Garnet   (b) Ruby
(c) Pukhraj   (d) Pearl

108. Architect Building   Sculptor: ...... ? .....
(a) Museum   (b) Stone
(c) Chisel   (d) Statue

109. Eye: Myopia   Teeth ..... ?.......
     (a) Pyorrhoea   (b) Cataract
     (c) Trachoma   (d) Eczema

110. Conference: Chairman   Newspaper: ..... ?......
     (a) Reporter   (b) Distributor
     (c) Printer   (d) Editor

111. Safe: Secure   Protect ..... ?......
     (a) Lock   (b) Sure
     (c) Guard   (d) Conserve

DIRECTION (Qs. 112-116) : *In each of the following questions, five words have been given out of which four are alike in some manner, while the different fifth one is Choose the word which is different from the rest.*   *[2014-II]*

112. (a) Potassium   (b) Silicon
     (c) Zirconium   (d) Gallium

113. (a) Tea   (b) Cinchona
     (c) Rubber   (d) Chalk

114. (a) Hanger   (b) Platform
     (c) Dock   (d) Park

115. (a) Deck   (b) Quay
     (c) Stern   (d) Bow

116. (a) Tall   (b) Huge
     (c) Thin   (d) Sharp

DIRECTIONS (Qs.117 - 121) : *In each of the following questions find out the alternative which will replace the question mark.*   *[2015-I]*

117. East : Orient ::?:?
     (a) North : Polar   (b) North : Tropic
     (c) South : Capricorn   (d) West : Occident

118. ignominy : Disloyalty ::?:?
     (a) Dealth : Victory   (b) Martyr : Man
     (c) Fame : Heroism   (d) Destruction : Victory

119. Loath : Coercion :: ? : ?
     (a) Detest : Caressing   (b) Irritate : Caressing
     (c) Irate : Antagonism   (d) Reluctant : Persuasion

120. Trilogy : Novel :: ? : ?
     (a) Rice : Husk   (b) Milk : Cream
     (c) Serial : Episode   (d) Gun : Cartridge

121. Wife : Marriage :: ? : ?
     (a) Bank : Money
     (b) Nationality : Citizenship
     (c) Service : Qualification
     (d) Attendance : Register

DIRECTIONS (Qs.122 - 126) : *86-90. In each of the following questions, four words have been given out of which three are alike in some manner, while the fourth one is different. Choose the word which is different from the rest.*   *[2015-I]*

122. (a) Othello   (b) King Lear
     (c) Oliver Twist   (d) Macbeth

123. (a) Nimitz   (b) Yamamoto
     (c) Nelson   (d) Montgomery

124. (a) Blaze   (b) Glint
     (c) Simmer   (d) Shimmer

125. (a) Aravalli hills   (b) Shivalik hills
     (c) Mole hills   (d) Satpura hills

126. (a) Beaver   (b) Alpaca
     (c) Walrus   (d) Koala

Hints & Solutions

1. (d) Chapter is a part of book, in the same way storey is a level of building.

2. (c) As carrot is a vegetable, in the same way pepper is a spice.

3. (a) 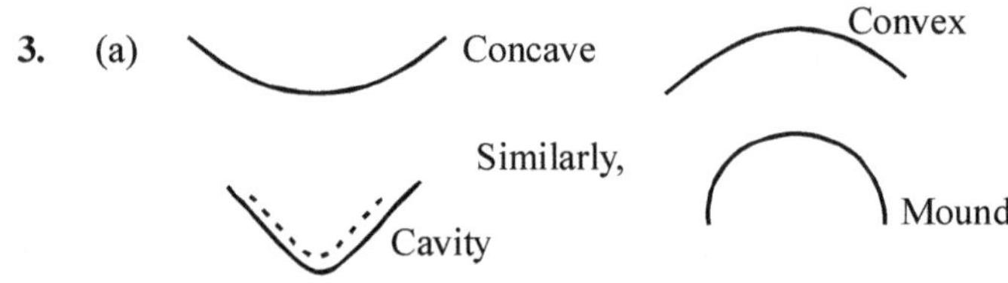

4. (b) Gown is type of garment. Similarly, Gasoline is a type of fuel.

5. (b) Hayper is the antonym of hype. Similarly, over is the antonym of under.

6. (a) Immigration (arrival) is the antonym of emigration (departure).

7. (d) Square is a four sided figure while octagon is a eight sided figure, i.e., four side more. Similarly hexagon has three more sides than triangle.

8. (d) Told is the third form of the verb tell, similarly, wept is the third form of weep.

9. (a) Lamb is young sheep. Similarly colt is a young horse.

10. (c) Ignore is the antonym of overlook. Similarly, dull is the antonym of sharpen.

11. (a) Frequently is the antonym of seldom.
Similarly always is the antonym of never.

12. (a) First is the shorter form of the second.

13. (d) First is the splitted parts of the second.

14. (b) Second is the additional money given for good service to first.

15. (b) Second is the relieve of first.

16. (b) As silence is opposite to noise, Similary Baldness is opposite to Hair.

17. (c) Pallid refers to pale complexion as wan refers to pale colour.

18. (b) First is a kind of meat of second.

19. (d) First one refers to later on stage and second one previous stage.

20. (d) First and second have similar meaning.

21. (a) First is the quantity and second is its unit.

22. (c) Decimal has base 10 and binary has base 2.

23. (b)

24. (b) As Lawyer practices in court similarly chemist practices in laboratory.

25. (a) Second is required for first to be successful.

26. (c) Second is the property of the first.

27. (d) Filter is used to remove impurities from water similarly censor removes objectionable scenes from play.

28. (c) Both words have nearly same meaning.

29. (b) Sadist is the one who enjoys giving pain to others while teacher pupil relation is the one where teacher enjoys white teaching to pupil.

30. (b) Fresco is prepared by painter similarly symphony is prepared by composer.

31. (c) First one manages the second one.

32. (d)

33. (d)

34. (c) Direct is different from the other three words. Direct means 'to give a formal order or command.'

35. (d) **Sprain** means 'to injure a joint in the body, especially a wrist or an ankle by suddenly twisting it so that there is pain and usually swelling.'
Crumble means to break into very small pieces, 'to begin to fail or lose strength', "to come slowly to an end.'
Topple means 'to move from side to side and fail, 'to cause somebody to lose their position of power and authority.
Trimble means 'to make fall,' to move or rush in the specified direction.

36. (a) **Anonymous** means : with a name that is not known or not made public; written or given by somebody whose name is not known or revealed; having no outsanding or unusual features; not particularly noticeable.
Alias and pseudonym refer to a name by which a person is called at other times or in other places.
Sobriquet refers to other name of a place.

37. (d) Except Thiruvananthapuram, all others are ports.

38. (c) Except Mercury all others are organic compounds. Mercury is a metal.

39. (d) Hope is Antonym of Despair. Similarly, Encourage is Antonym of Dishearten.

40. (c) The second is necessary for the first to be successful.

41. (b) The second is the unit of the first.

42. (c) Revenge and Vendetta are synonymous. Similarly. Envy and Jealousy are synonymous.

43. (a) Style can be refined to make it more beautiful and attractive. Similarly, photograph is made beautiful by retouching it.

44. (b) **Tremble** means 'to shake from fear, cold, weakness', Perspire means 'to give out sweat through the skin'.

45. (c) **Condone** means 'to accept wrong behaviour or to treat it as if it were not serious', 'to ignore something'.
The first is the act of neglecting the second.

46. (a) The second is a part of the first.

47. (b) The first is a vital part of the second.

48. (a) Nalanda ad Taxila are ancient seats of learning. Similarly, Venus and Mars are planets.

49. (b) Foot is the lower part of human's leg. Similarly, hoof is the lower part of cow's leg.

50. (d) Broad refers to spacious thing. Similarly, road is wider than lane.

51. (b) Back of a human being rests on backbone. Similarly, belly rests on ribs.

52. (a) Ankle is analogous to wrist (hand) knee is analogous to elbow.

53. (d) The first is used by the second to bite.

54. (b) Second is the tool used to first.

55. (b) Infants are kept in Creche like wise sailors.

56. (d) Plant is given pesticide for cure and body is given vaccination.

57. (a) First is bigger than the second.

58. (d) Second is the place where first lives.

59. (b) First is more intense form of second.

60. (d) Necromancy is the practice to deal with ghosts similarly Sorcery deals with spirits.

61. (c) Second is the place where first is manufactured.

62. (a) First is a kind or type of second.

63. (d) Onam is a festival of Kerala and Bihu is of Assam.

64. (c) Calendar consists of dates and dictionary consists of words.

65. (a) The words in pair are opposite to each other.

66. (c) Second is the class to which first belongs.

67. (b) Second is the activity done by first.

68. (d) First revolves around the second.

69. (b) Lotus grow in water and rest grow on land.

70. (b) All except sharpener are used in writing.

71. (c) Brass is an alloy and rest are metals.

72. (b) All except eagle are flightless birds.

73. (d) All except Baroda are famous for coal fields.

74. (c) Garo, Khasi, Jainti are hills and Kangra is a valley.

75. (d) All expect orion are Zodiac signs while orion is a cosntellaiton.

76. (b) Expect foot all are parts of hand.

77. (d) Igloo is a type of house whereas rest are type of boats.

78. (b) Club is the place of entertainment and rest are places of living.

79. (b) Liquor is a drink. Similarly tea is a beverage.

80. (d) Tension causes the breakdown as evaporation forms the cloud.

81. (a) Second one is the bigger form of first.

82. (d) First is a kind of second.

83. (a) Carnivore are flesh eating animals and herbivores are plant eating animals.

84. (c) They were characters from various dramas.

85. (a) These are sites of volcanoes.

86. (d) They are units of measurement.

87. (a) They are famous for oil fields.

88. (c) These are chessmen.

89. (d) These personalities belong to Bengal.

90. (b) These are terms connected with black magic.

91. (a) These are places having steel plants.

92. (d) These are the leafy vegetables.

93. (b) They were the famous poets.

94. (c) Rustle is sound of leaves and Patter is the sound of rain.

95. (b) The words in each pair are synonyms of each other.

96. (a) Lack of carefulness causes accident similarly lack of sanitation causes disease.

97. (a) All expect Tsangpo are national parks.

98. (b) All except rice are rabi crops.

99. (d)

100. (b) Plant is given pesticide for cure and body is given vaccination.

101. (a) First is of higher intensity than the second.

102. (b) First is more intense form of second.

103. (d) Necromancy deals with ghosts. Similarly sorcery deals with spirits.

104. (c) Words in each pair are antonym to each other.

105. (d) Funk discovered vitamins and curie discoverd radium.

106. (b) Food is contained by germs and body is infected by germs.

107. (b) Carbon is a chemical element found in diamond. Similarly, corundum is a form of alumina found in ruby.

108. (d) An archietect is a person whose job is designing building similarly,

sculptor is a person whose job is creating statue.

109. (a) Myopia is a disease of eye. Similary, Pyorrhoea is a disase of teeth.

110. (d) A chairman is a person who is in charge of a conference. Similarly, an editor is a person who is in charge of a Newspaper.

111. (d)

112. (a) All except potassium are metal used in semiconductor devices.

113. (d) All except chalk are abtained from crops.

114. (d) All others, except park are halting places where aeroplanes, ships and trains are kept.

115. (b) All except quay are parts of a ship.

116. (d) All except sharp are related to dimension

117. (d) Second is another name for the first.

118. (a) Ignominy is the result of disloyalty. Fame is the result of heroism.

119. (d) Loath and Reluctant are synonyms. Coercion and Persuasion are synonyms.

120. (c) Second is the past of first.

121. (b)

122. (c) All except Oliver Twist are works of Shakespeare, while Oliver Twist is a work of Charles Dickens.

123. (d) All except Montgomery were Admirals. Nimitz was U.S. Admiral, Yamamoto was Japanese Admiral and Nelson was British Admiral, while British Admiral, while Montgomery was British Field Marshal.

124. (c) All except Simmer are connected with light, while simmer is a way of cooking.

125. (c) All others are hills located in India.

126. (c) All except Walrus are fur-bearing animals.

2

Series / Coding-Decoding

1. Which number comes next in this series ? *[2011-II]*
   1 4 7 10 13 16
   (a) 17
   (b) 19
   (c) 21
   (d) None of these

2. Which number comes next in this series ? *[2011-II]*
   0 1 3 6 10 15
   (a) 19
   (b) 21
   (c) 26
   (d) 32

3. Look at the series 36, 34, 30, 28, 24, ... what number should come next ? *[2011-II]*
   (a) 20
   (b) 22
   (c) 23
   (d) 26

4. Look at the series 22, 21, 23, 22, 24, 23 ..... what number should come next ? *[2011-II]*
   (a) 22
   (b) 24
   (c) 25
   (d) 26

5. Look at the series 53, 53, 40, 40, 27, 27 ..... what number should come next ? *[2011-II]*
   (a) 12
   (b) 14
   (c) 27
   (d) 53

6. Look at the series 8, 22, 8, 28, 8 ..... what number should come next ? *[2011-II]*
   (a) 9
   (b) 34
   (c) 29
   (d) 32

7. Look at the series 31, 29, 24, 22, 17 ..... what number should come next ? *[2011-II]*
   (a) 15
   (b) 14
   (c) 13
   (d) 12

DIRECTIONS (Qs. 8 – 10) : *Complete the series* *[2014-I]*

8. A, B, D, G, ?, P
   (a) I
   (b) J
   (c) K
   (d) L

9. Z , S , W, O ,T ,K, Q, G, ?, ?
   (a) N,D
   (b) N,C
   (c) O,C
   (d) O,D

10. BCD , RQP , LMN, TS?
    (a) U
    (b) V
    (c) R
    (d) T

DIRECTIONS (Qs. 11) : *If A = C , B = D , C = E and so on, code the following:* *[2014-I]*

11. 'STUDENT'
    (a) VWVFGPV
    (b) UUWFGPV
    (c) UVWFGPV
    (d) UVVFGPV

DIRECTIONS (Qs. 12) : *If A = Z, B = Y and so on , code the following:* *[2014-I]*

12. 'EDITOR'
    (a) VWRGLI
    (b) VWRGVI
    (c) VWVGLI
    (d) VWRLLI

Hints & Solutions

1. (b)

$$+3 \quad +3 \quad +3 \quad +3 \quad +3 \quad +3$$
$$1 \quad 4 \quad 7 \quad 10 \quad 13 \quad 16 \quad 19$$

2. (b) $0 + 1 = 1, 1 + 2 = 3, 3 + = 6, 6 + 4 = 10, 10 + 5 = 15, 15 + 6 = 21$

3. (b) $36 - 2 = 34, 34 - 4 = 30, 30 - 2 = 28, 28 - 4 = 24, 24 - 2 = 22$

4. (c) $22 - 1 = 21, 21 + 2 = 23, 23 - 1 = 22, 22 + 2 = 24,$
$24 - 1 = 23, 23 + 2 = 25$

5. (b) $53, 53 - 13 = 40, 40, 40 - 13 = 27, 27, 27 - 13 = 14, 14$

6. (b)

$$8 \quad 22 \quad 8 \quad 28 \quad 8 \quad 34$$

with $+6$ links

7. (a) $31 - 2 = 29, 29 - 5 = 22, 22 - 5 = 17, 17 - 2 = 15$

8. (c)

A, B, D, G, $\boxed{K}$, P
$$+1 \quad +2 \quad +3 \quad +4 \quad +5$$

9. (b)

$$-4 \quad -4 \quad -4 \quad -4$$
Z S W O T K Q G $\boxed{N}$ $\boxed{C}$
$$-3 \quad -3 \quad -3 \quad -3$$

10. (c)

B C D, R Q P, L M N, T S $\boxed{R}$
$$+1 \quad +1 \quad +1 \quad +1 \quad +1 \quad +1 \quad +1 \quad +1$$

11. (c)

S	T	U	D	E	N	T
↓	↓	↓	↓	↓	↓	↓
U	V	W	F	G	P	V

12. (a)

E	D	I	T	O	R
↓	↓	↓	↓	↓	↓
V	W	R	G	L	I

3 Logical Deduction / Statement & Assumption

DIRECTIONS (Qs.1 - 2) : *Each of the following questions has four statements. Three are logically correct. Some of which may look factually absurd. Ignore this absurdity and look to the logical corrections. Choose the statement which is wrong or doubtful:* ***[2014-I]***

1. (a) Birds fly in the air. Trees are birds. Therefore, trees fly in the air.
(b) Some boys steal. All who steal are naughty. All naughty are honest. Therefore, some boys are honest
(c) All girls like dance. Some girls are Indian. All Indians are artists. Therefore, some artists like dance.
(d) All liars are not thieves. All thieves are criminals. Therefore, all liars are criminals.

2. (a) Ramesh is tall. Ramesh is a boy. Therefore, boys are tall.
(b) All who can fly are animals. Some birds can fly. Therefore, some birds are animals.
(c) Men live in houses. Houses grow on trees. Trees float in water. Therefore, men float in water.
(d) All living things are mobile. Some non- living things are mobile. Therefore, some mobile are living and some non-living.

3. (a) All books can read. Some pencils are books. All pencils are clever. Therefore, all clever cannot read.
(b) Some who fail are stupid. Some criminals are stupid. Therefore, all criminals fail.
(c) Some liar are thieves. All thieves are criminals. Therefore, some liars are criminals.
(d) All that is given is black. Trees are green. Therefore, trees are black.

DIRECTIONS (Qs.4 - 5) : *Consider the statement and assumptions that follow. Which of these assumptions is/are implicit in the statement:* ***[2014-I]***

4.. **Statement:** "You won't get sweets at any cost. I will not let you eat things that are not good for your teeth" — a mother tells her child

Assumption:
(i) The mother cares for her child.
(ii) Sweets are not good for her child.
(iii) The mother has the authority to decide what her child is to eat.

(a) (i) & (ii) are implicit (b) (ii) & (iii) are implicit
(c) (i) & (iii) are implicit (d) All are implicit

5. **Statement:** "Clearly, the judiciary cannot provide all answers. But it seems the public, weary of an inactive Executive, is turning to the Supreme Court as a last resort"—an article.

Assumption :
(i) The Supreme Court is above the Executive.
(ii) The Supreme Court is more active than the Executive.
(iii) The Executive does not have sufficient powers.

(a) (i) & (ii) are implicit (b) (ii) & (iii) are implicit
(c) (i) & (iii) are implicit (d) Only (ii) is implicit

DIRECTION (Qs. 6 - 10) : *Each of these questions given below contains three elements. These elements may or may not have some inter- linkage. Each group of elements may fit into one of these diagrams at (a), (b), (c) or (d). You have to indicate the group of elements which correctly fits into the diagrams.* ***[2014-II]***

6. Which of the following diagrams indicates the best relation between Judge, Thieves and Criminals ?

(a) 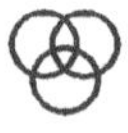 (b) 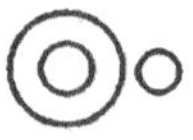
(c) 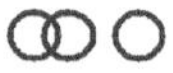 (d) 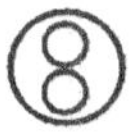

7. Which of the following diagrams indicates the best relation between India, Haryana and World ?

(a) 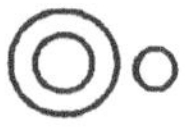 (b) 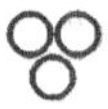
(c) 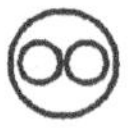 (d) 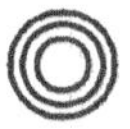

8. Which of the following diagrams indicates the best relation between Pigeon, Bird and Dog ?

(a) 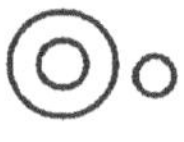 (b) 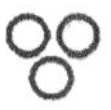
(c) 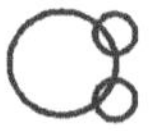 (d) 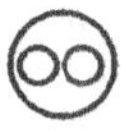

9. Which of the following diagrams indicates the best relation between Earth, Sea and Sun ?

(a) 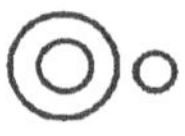 (b) 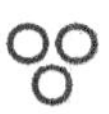
(c) 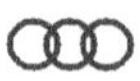 (d) 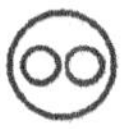

10. Which of the following diagrams indicates the best relation between Hockey, Football and Cricket ?

(a)　　(b)

(c)　　(d)

DIRECTION (Qs. 11 - 15) : *Choose the most appropriate answer.*

[2014-II]

11. Which one of the following is always with 'Bargain'?

(a) Exchange (b) Sumptuousness

(c) Triviality (d) Eloquence

12. Which one of the following a 'Drama' must have?

(a) Actors (b) Story

(c) Sets (d) Director

13. A boy is sitting at the back seat of a car. When the driver suddenly start moving the car (in forward direction) the boy experiences a backward force ?

(a) Always (b) Never

(c) Often (d) Sometimes

14. Which one of the following is always found in 'Wonder'?

(a) Crowd (b) Lumber

(c) Astonishment (d) Rustic

15. 'Disclosure' always involves

(a) Agents (b) Display

(c) Exposition (d) Secrets

DIRECTION (Qs. 16 - 20) : *Each of these questions given below contains three elements. These elements may or may not have some inter-linkage. Each group of elements may fit into one of these diagrams at (a), (b), (c) or (d). You have to indicate the group of elements which correctly fits into the diagrams.*

16. Which of the following diagrams indicates the best relation between Doctors. Human Beings and Married People?

17. Which of the following diagrams indicates the best relation Children, Naughty and Studious?

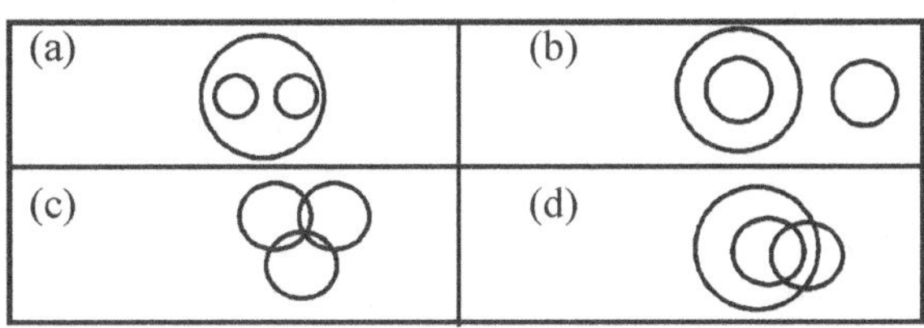

18. Which of the following diagrams indicates the best relation between Thief, Criminal and Police ?

19. Which of the following diagrams indicates the best relation between Man, Worker and Garden?

20. Which of the following diagrams indicates the best relation between Males, Cousins and Nephews?

Hints & Solutions

1. (d)
2. (a)
3. (b)
4. (d)
5. (d)

6. (b) 

7. (d) 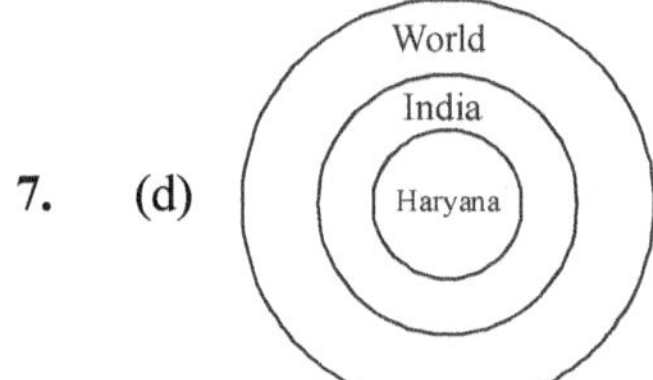

8. (a) 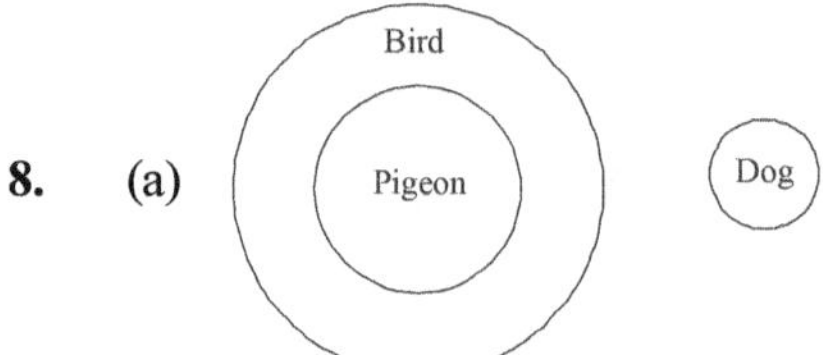

9. (a) 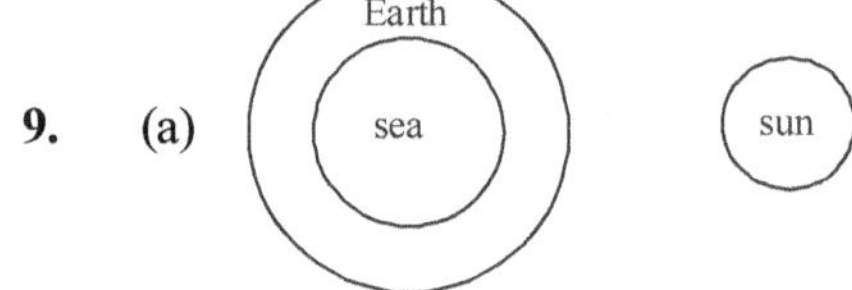

10. (b) 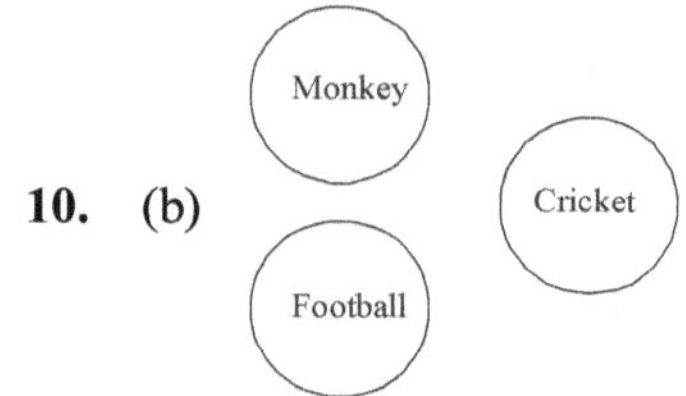

11. (a) Bargain is a thing bought for less than the usual price.
12. (b) A drama can not be performed without a story.
13. (a) It occurs due to inertia of rest. When a car suddenly starts the lower part of the boy's body will be in the motion while his upper will be at rest.
14. (c) Astonishment is a feeling of very great surprise.
15. (d) A disclosure always has secrets.
16. (d) Some doctors may be married people. All doctor, married people are human being.
17. (a)
18. (a) All thiefs are criminal. No criminal is police.
19. (d) Some workers are man. No man is garden.

20. (a) 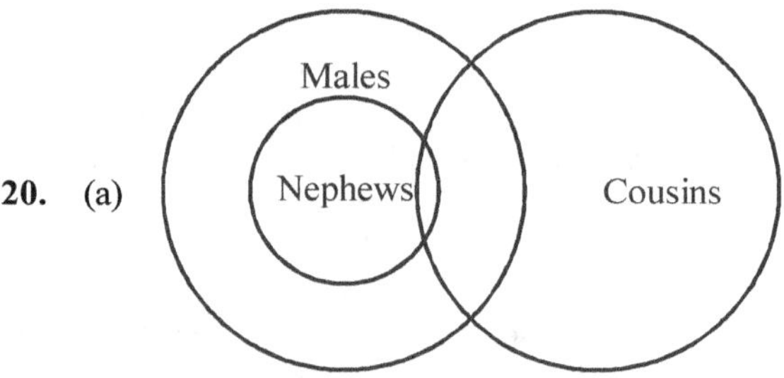

4

Analogy /
Odd One Out / Series

DIRECTIONS (Qs. 1 to 4) : *This set of questions is based upon the continuation of figures in a logical manner. There is a sequence of figures depicting a change step by step. Select one of the figure from the four choices shows as (a), (b), (c) & (d) which will continue the sequence.* **[2011-II]**

1. Problem Figure

Answer Figure

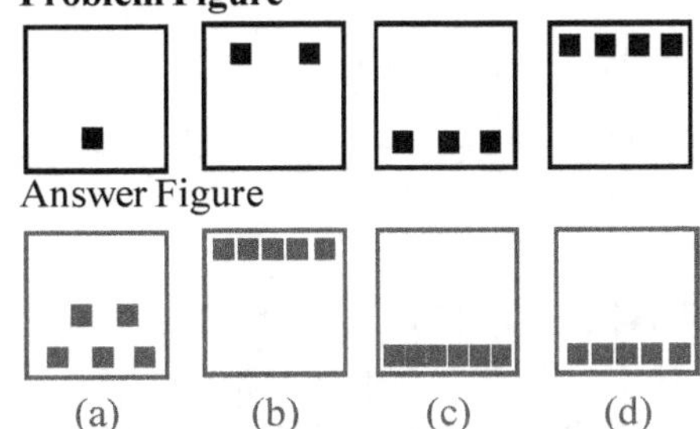

(a)   (b)   (c)   (d)

2. Problem Figure

Answer Figure

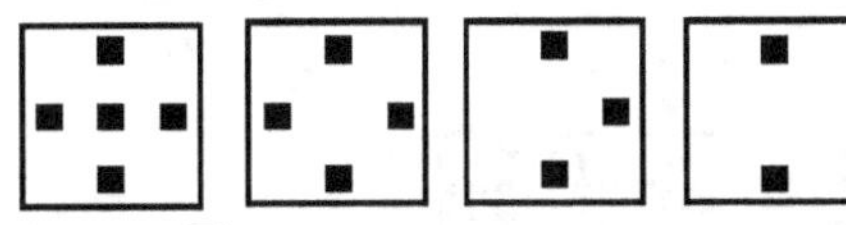

(a)   (b)   (c)   (d)

3. Problem Figure

Answer Figure

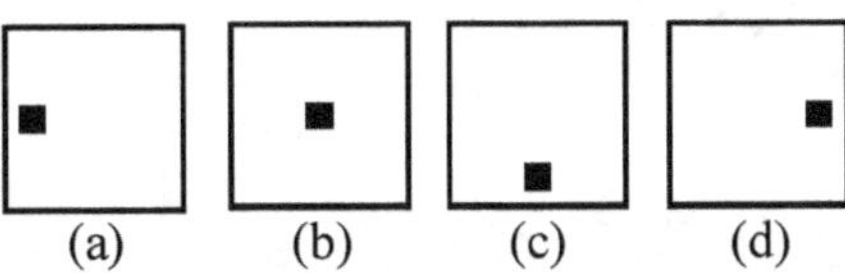

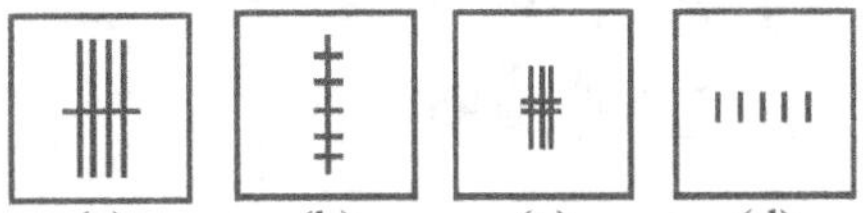

(a)   (b)   (c)   (d)

4. Problem Figure

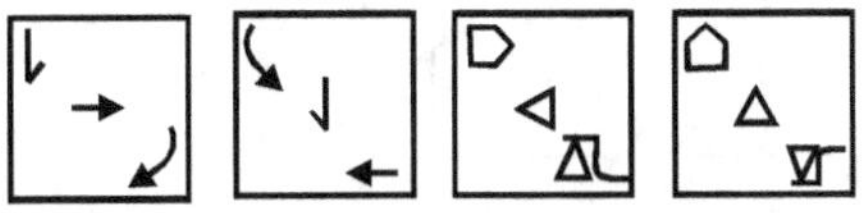

Answer Figure

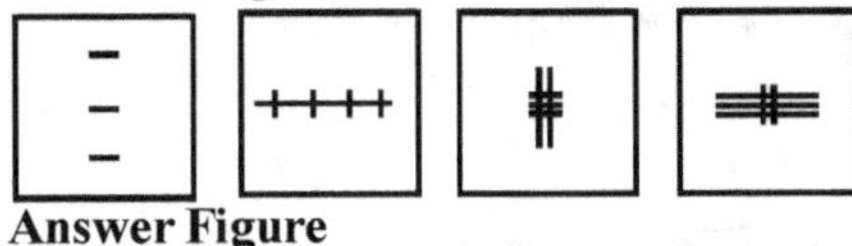

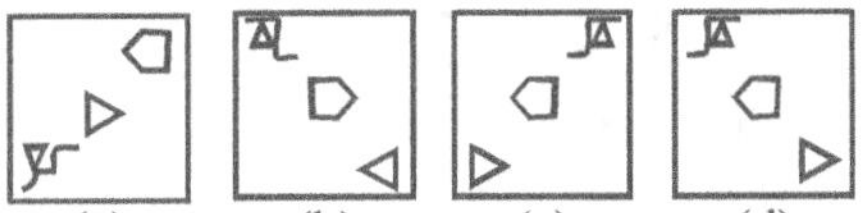

(a)   (b)   (c)   (d)

DIRECTIONS (Q. 5) : *Which symbol in the Answer Figure completes the sequence in the problem figure:* **[2011-II]**

5.

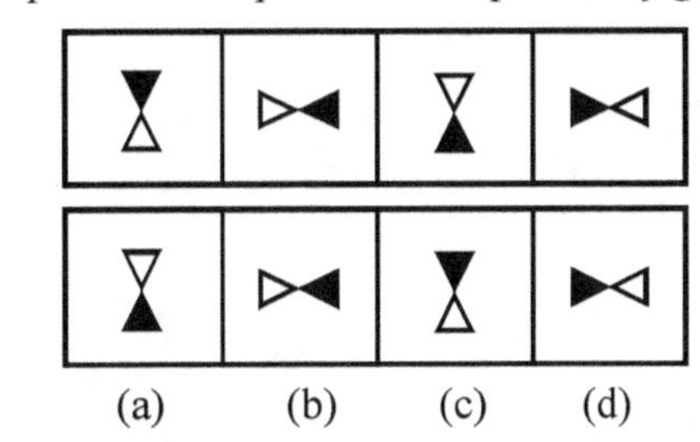

(a)   (b)   (c)   (d)

DIRECTIONS (Q. 6) : *There are certain common characteristics/ properties between the two problem figures. Select the figure from amongst the Answer Figures which shows similar characteristics/ properties as shown by the problem figures.* **[2011-II]**

6.

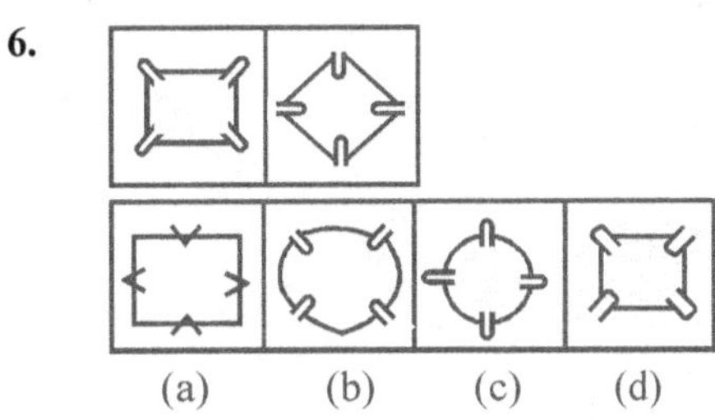

(a)   (b)   (c)   (d)

DIRECTIONS (Q. 7) : *Your task here is to look at the series of four figures and work out the rule which links them all. Choose which of the three following figures obey that rule and identify the one which does not.* **[2011-II]**

7.

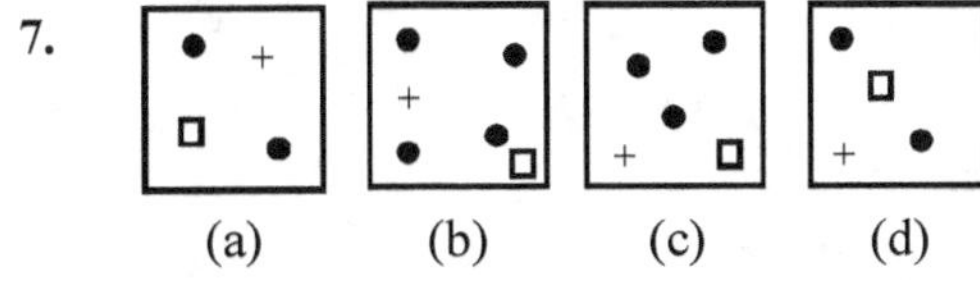

(a)   (b)   (c)   (d)

DIRECTIONS (Qs. 8 - 12) : *In each of the following questions find out which of the answer figures (1), (2), (3) and (4) completes the figure matrix* **[2012-I]**

8.

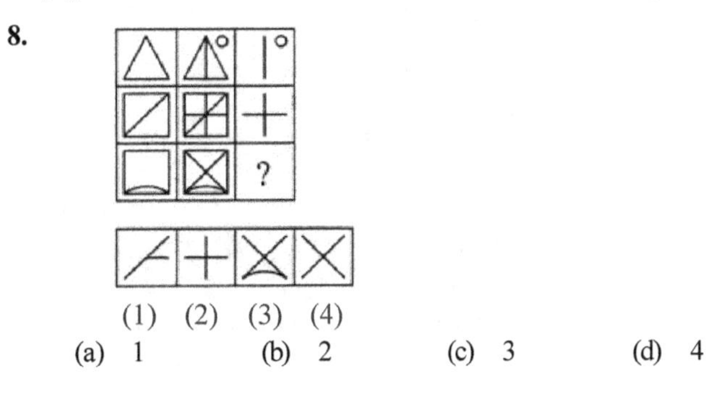

(1)   (2)   (3)   (4)

(a)   1   (b)   2   (c)   3   (d)   4

9.

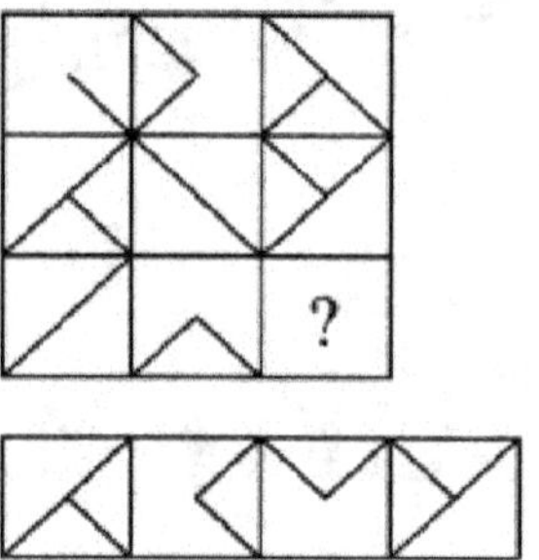

(1) (2) (3) (4)

(a) 1   (b) 2   (c) 3   (d) 4

10.

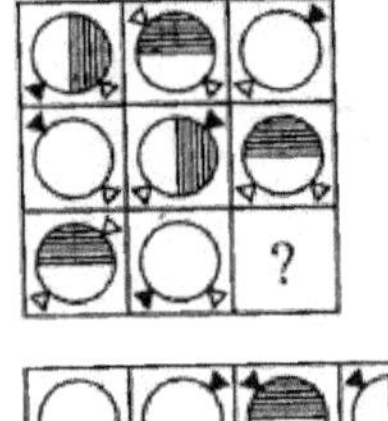

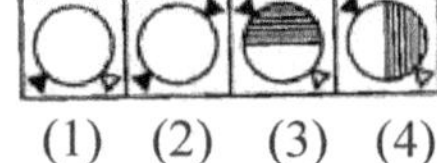

(1) (2) (3) (4)

(a) 1   (b) 2   (c) 3   (d) 4

11.

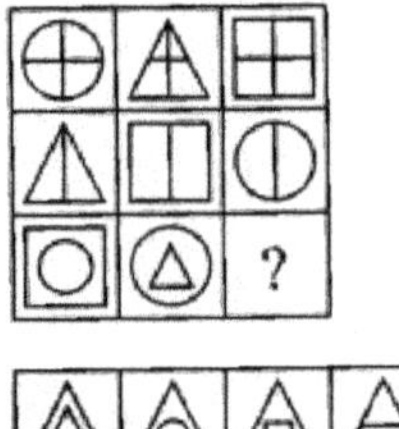

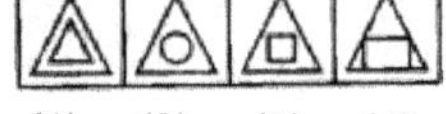

(1) (2) (3) (4)

(a) 1   (b) 2   (c) 3   (d) 4

12.

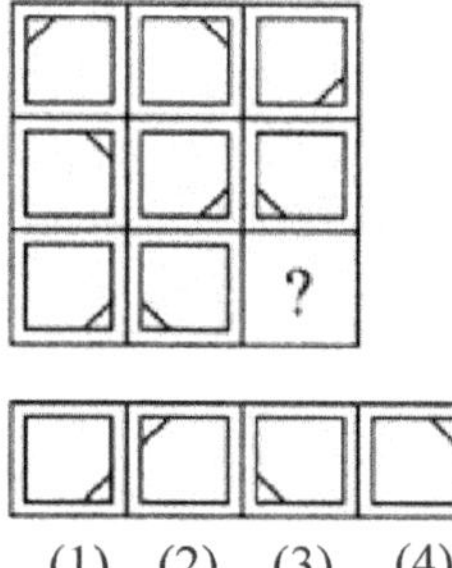

(1) (2) (3) (4)

(a) 1   (b) 2   (c) 3   (d) 4

DIRECTIONS (Qs 13 - 17): *There are two sets of figures namely the Problem figures containing five figures 1, 2, 3, 4, 5 and Answer figures (a), (b), (c), (d). Select one figure from the Answer figures which will continue the same series as given in the Problem figures.*   *[2012-II]*

13.

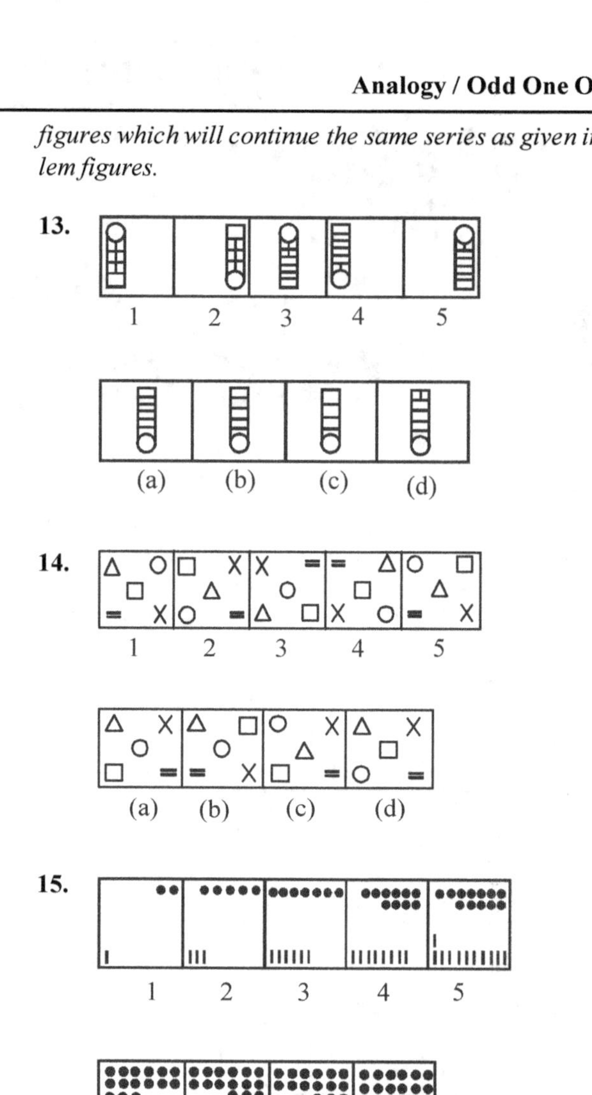

14.

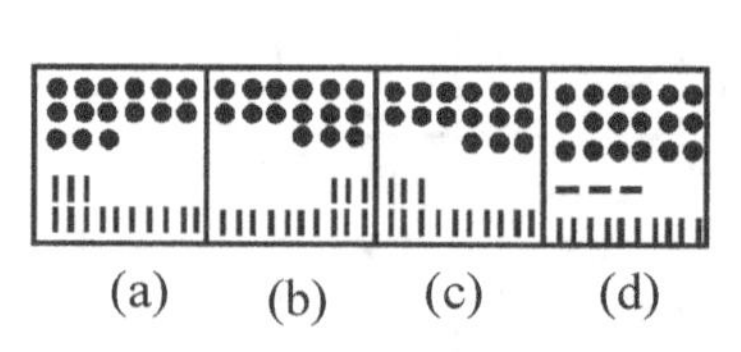

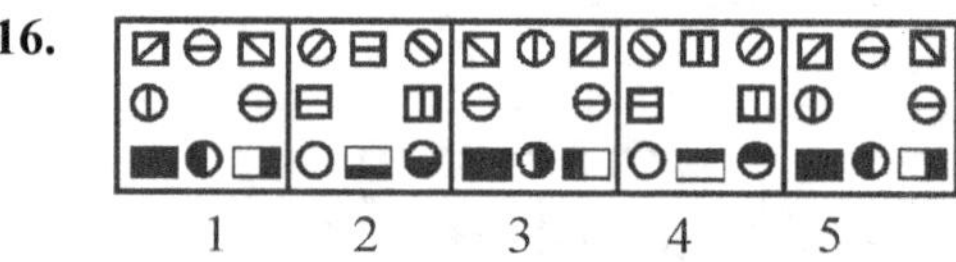

15.

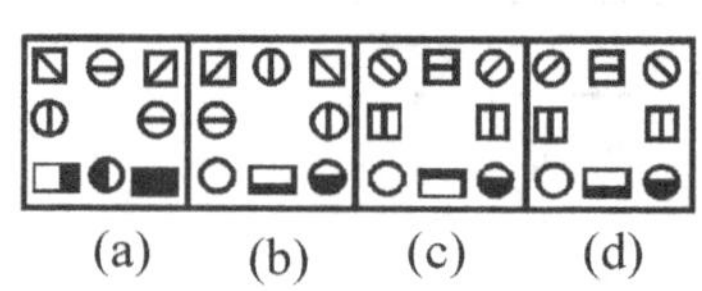

16.

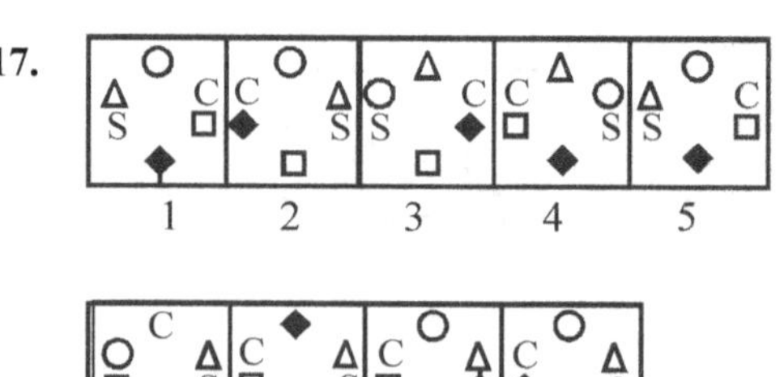

17.

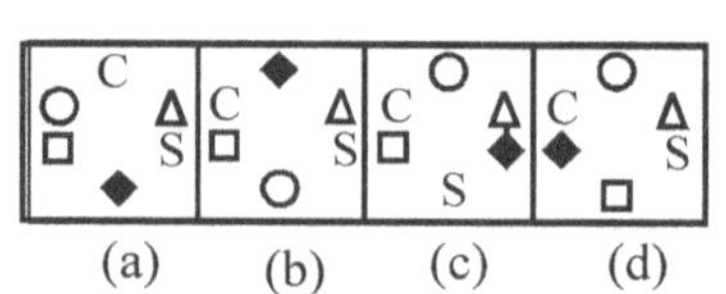

DIRECTIONS (Qs. 18 – 22) : *There are two sets of figures namely the Problem figures containing five figures 1, 2, 3, 4, 5 and answer figures (a), (b), (c), (d). You have to select one figure from the Answer figures which will continue the same series as given in the Problem figures.* *[2013-I]*

DIRECTIONS (Qs. 23 - 26) : *In these tests find the odd figure out:* *[2014-I]*

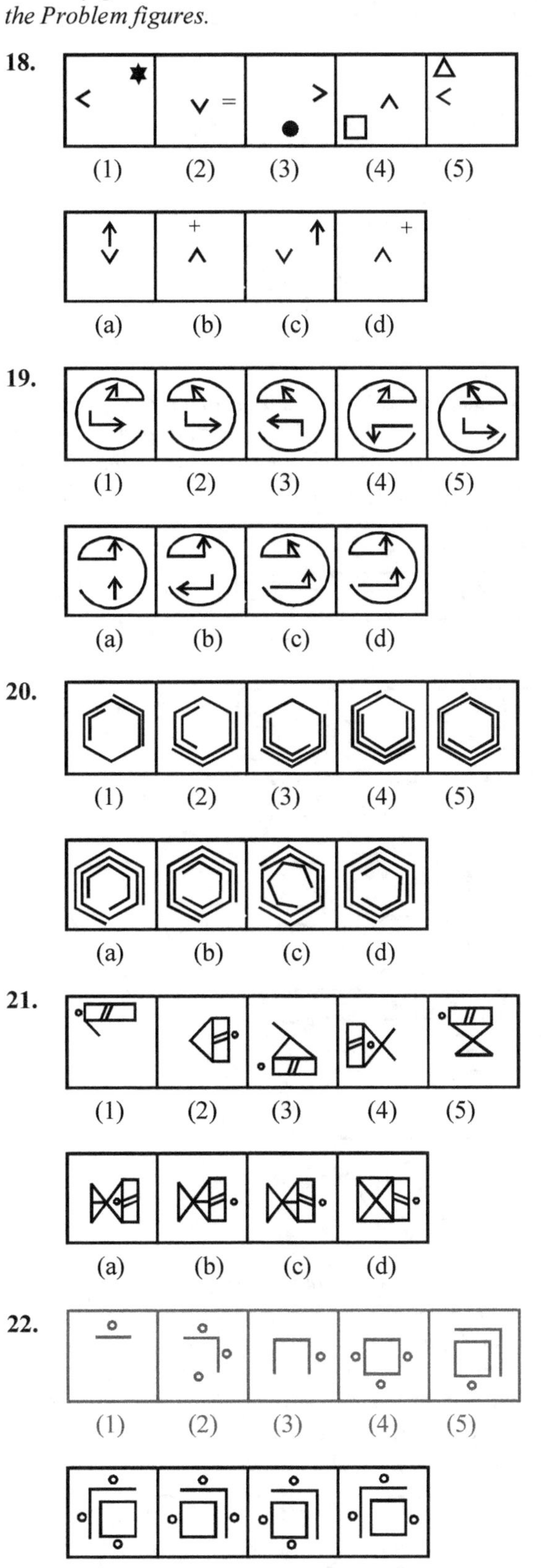

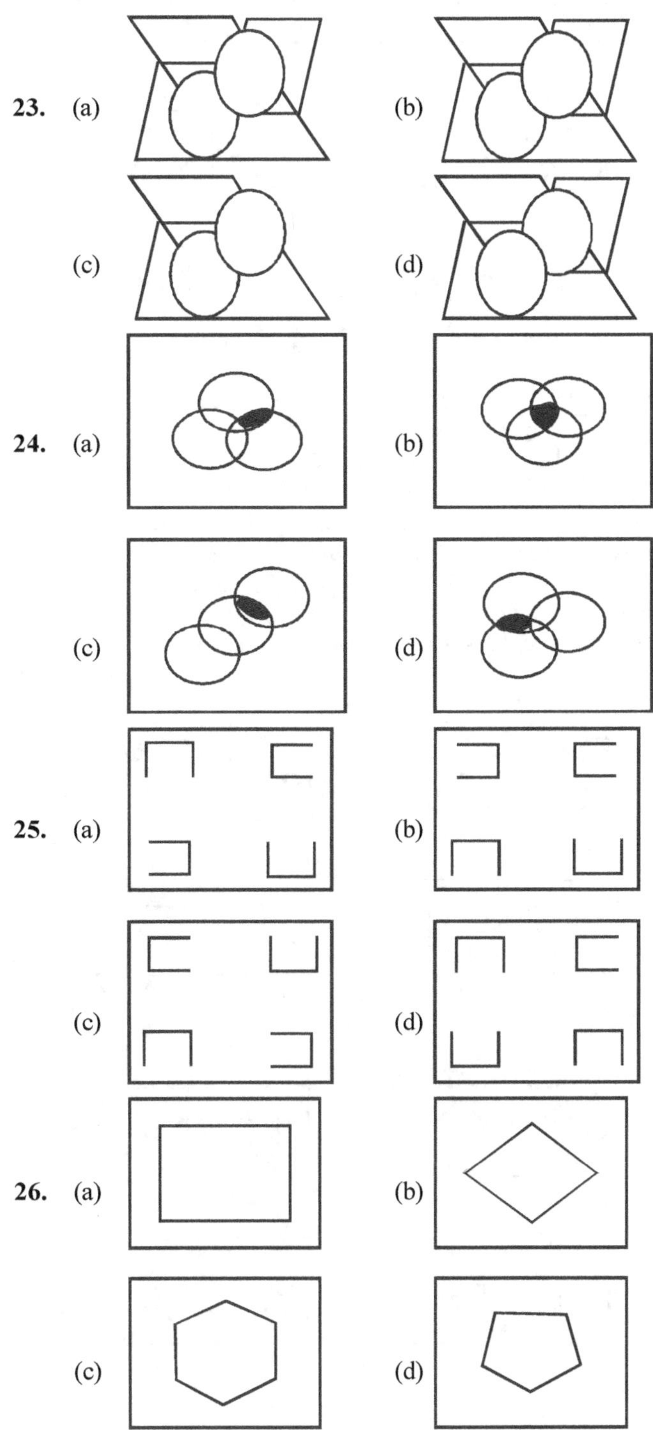

DIRECTION (Qs. 27 - 30) : *Each of the following questions consists of five figures marked 1, 2, 3, 4 and 5 called the Problem Figures followed by four other figures marked a, b, c and d called the Answer Figures. select a figure from amongst the answer Figures which will continue the same series as established by the five Problem Figures.* *[2014-II]*

27. Problem Figures: Answer Figures:

28. Problem Figures: Answer Figures:

29. Problem Figures: Answer Figures:

30. Problem Figures: Answer Figures:

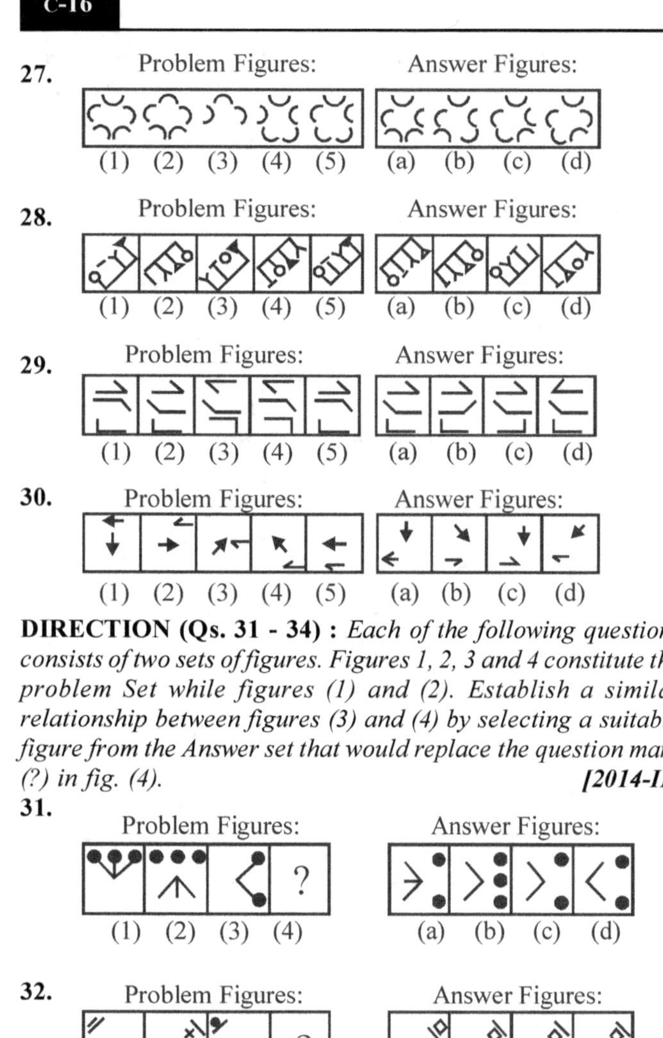

DIRECTION (Qs. 31 - 34) : *Each of the following questions consists of two sets of figures. Figures 1, 2, 3 and 4 constitute the problem Set while figures (1) and (2). Establish a similar relationship between figures (3) and (4) by selecting a suitable figure from the Answer set that would replace the question mark (?) in fig. (4).*   *[2014-II]*

31. Problem Figures: Answer Figures:

32. Problem Figures: Answer Figures:

33. Problem Figures: Answer Figures:

34. Problem Figures: Answer Figures:

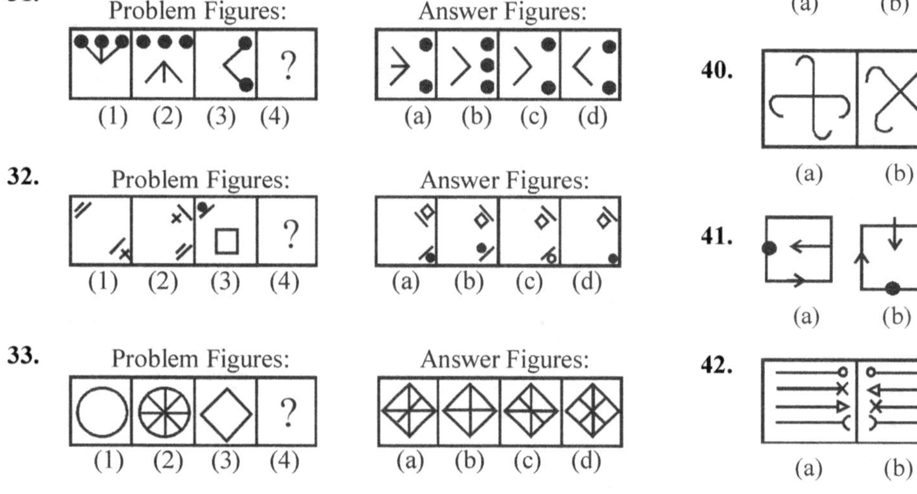

DIRECTION (Qs. 35 - 38) : *In each problem, out of the four figures marked (a) (b) (c) (d) three are similar in a certain manner. However, one figure is not like the other three. Choose the figure which is different from the rest.*   *[2014-II]*

35.

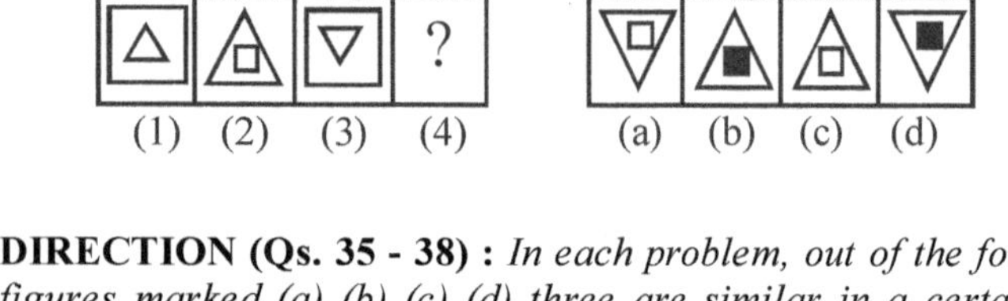

36.

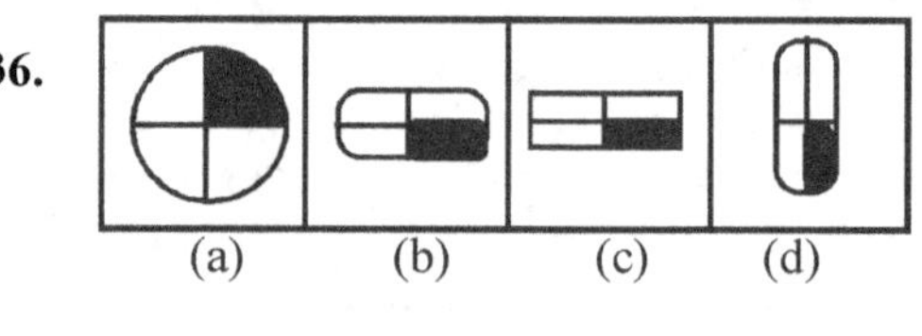

37.

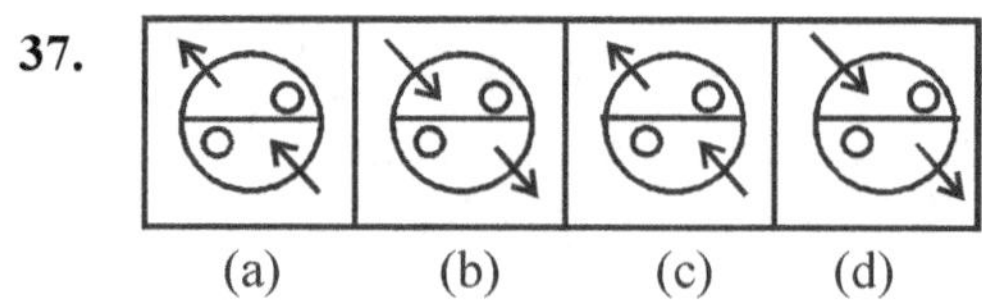

38.

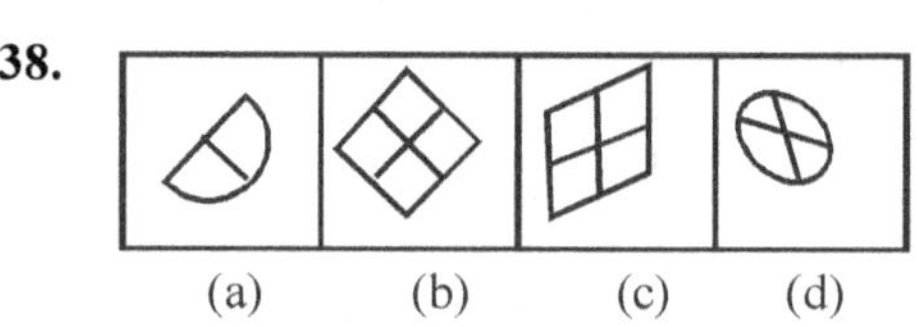

DIRECTION (Qs. 39 - 43) : *In each problem, out of the four figures marked (a) (b) (c) and (d) three are smililar in a certain manner. However, one figure is not like the other three. Choose the figure which is different from the rest.*   *[2015-I]*

39.

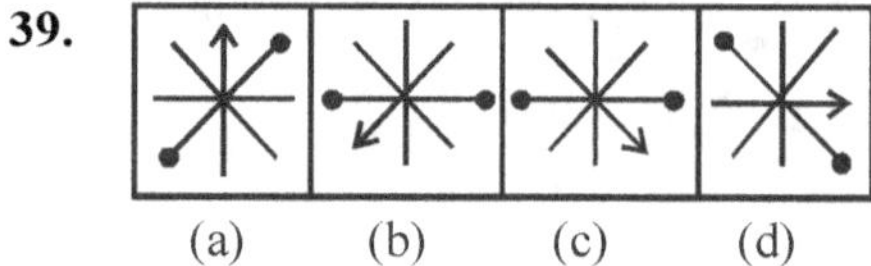

40.

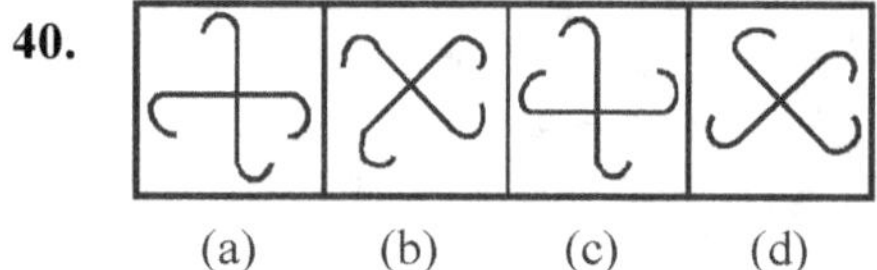

41.

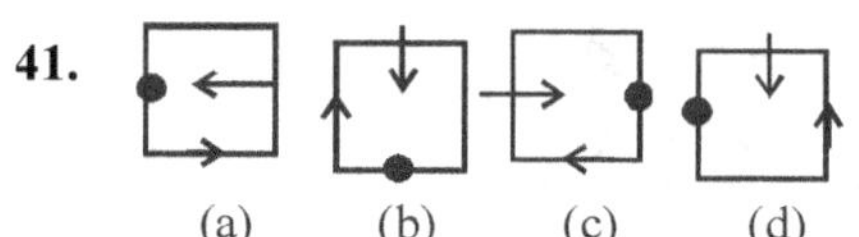

42.

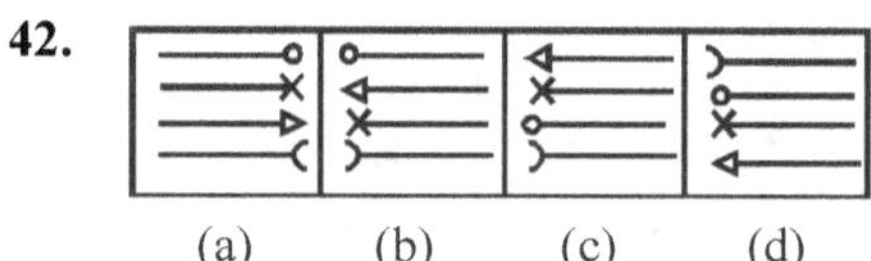

43.

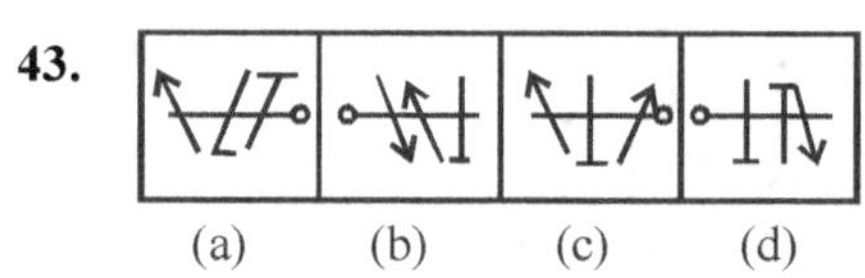

DIRECTION (Qs. 44 - 48) : *Each of the following questions consists of two sets of figures. Figures 1, 2, 3 and 4 constitute the Problem Set while figures a, b, c and d constitute the Answer Set. There is a definite relationship between figures (1) and (2). Establish a similar relationship between figures (3) and (4) by selecting a suitable figure from the Answer set that would replace the question mark (?) in fig. (4).*   *[2015-I]*

44.

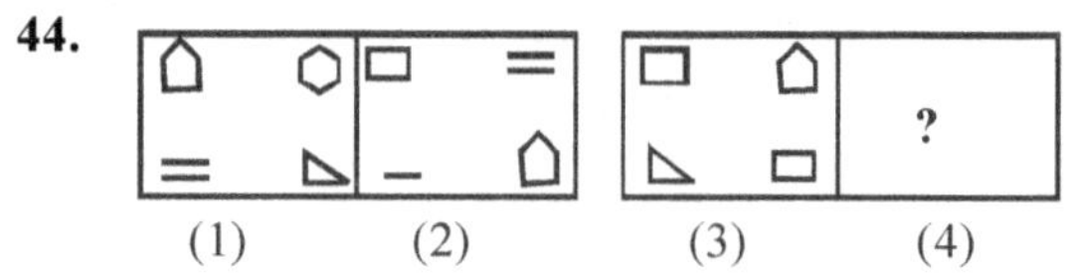

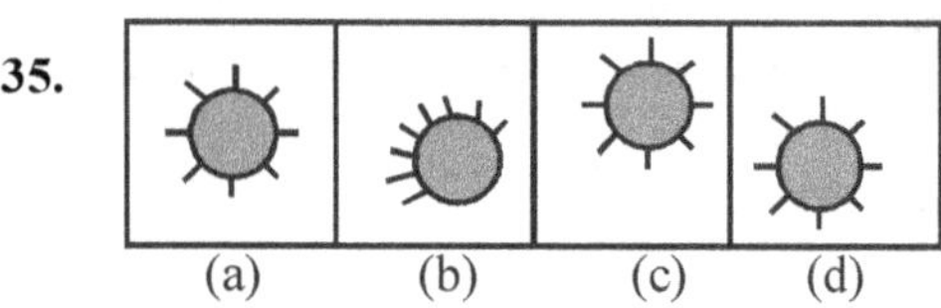

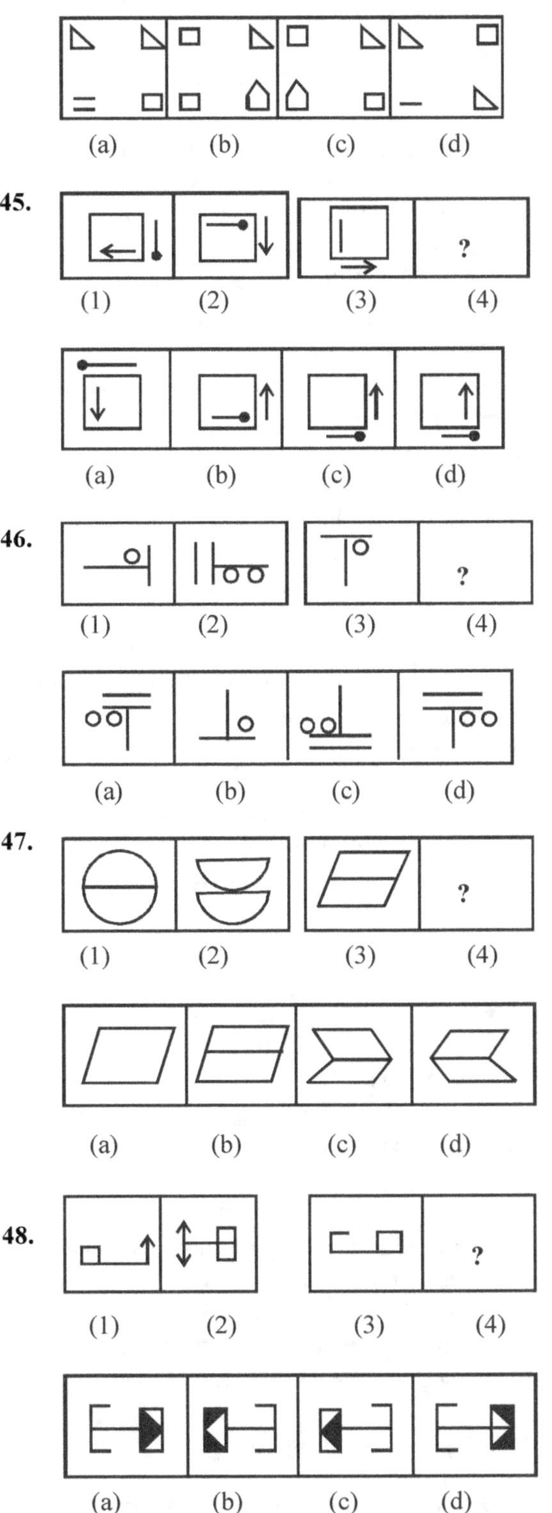

45.

46.

47.

48.

DIRECTION (Qs. 49 - 53) : *Each of the following questions consists of five figures marked 1, 2, 3, 4 and 5 called the Problem Figures followed by four other figures marked a, b, c and d called the Answer Figurs. Select a figure from amongst the Answer Figures which will continue the same series as established by the Five Problem Figures.* *[2015-I]*

49. Problem Figures :

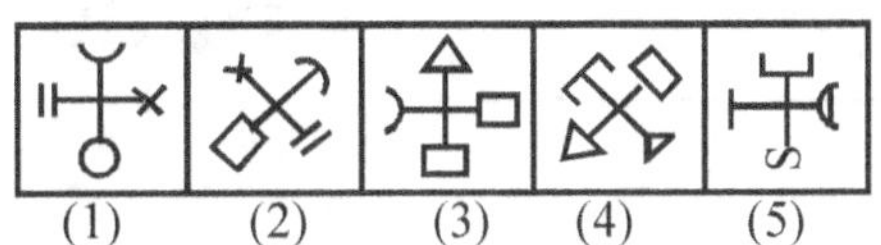

Answer Figures :

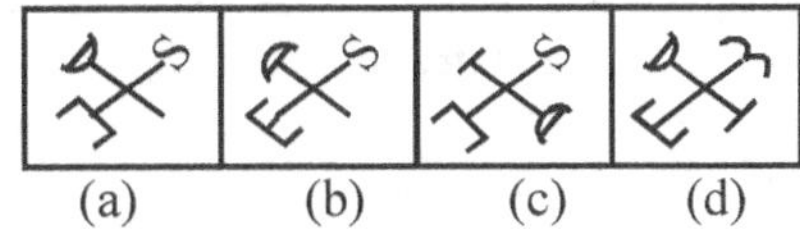

50. Problem Figures :

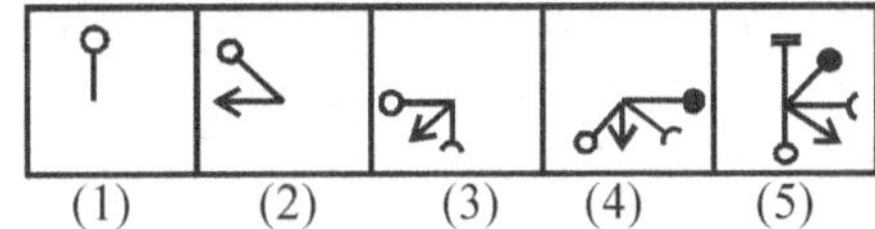

Answer Figures :

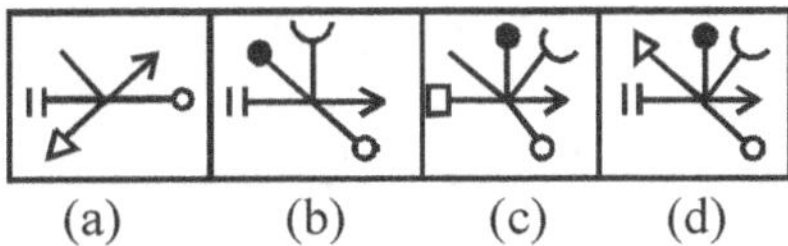

51. Problem Figures :

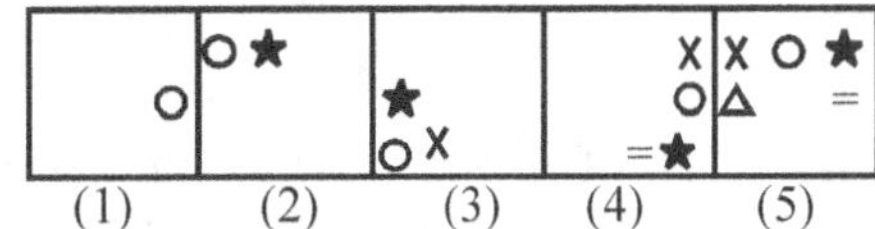

Answer Figures :

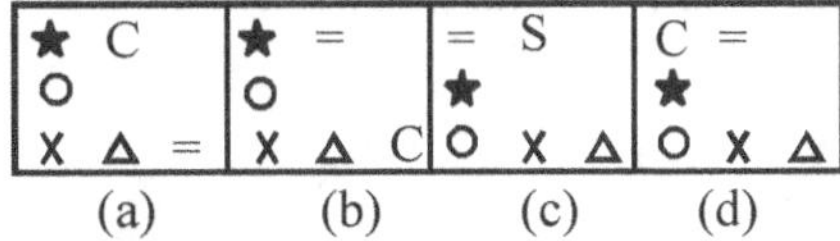

52. Problem Figures :

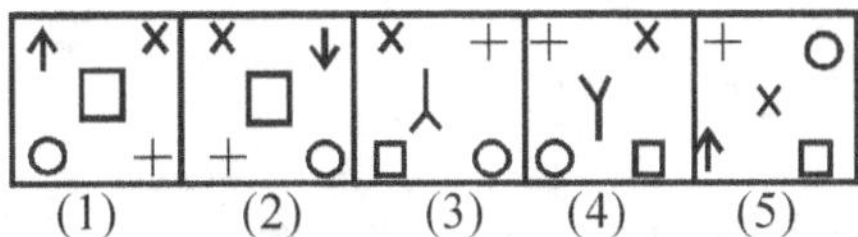

Answer Figures :

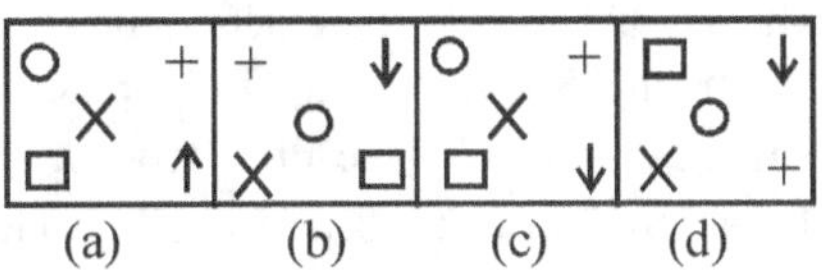

53. Problem Figures:

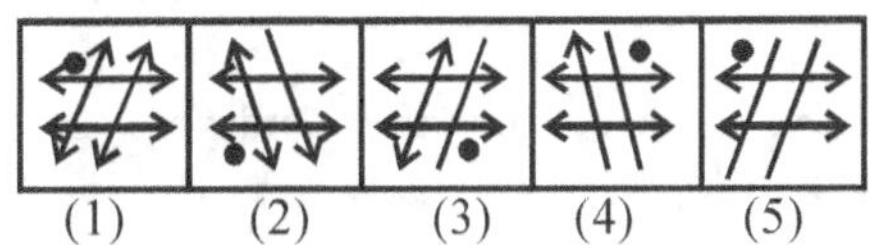

Answer Figures :

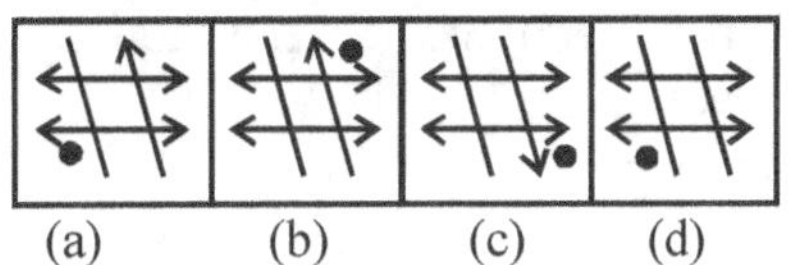

Hints & Solutions

1. (d)

2. (c)

3. (a) Each step, horizontal lines gets rotated and increased by 1 and vertical lines rotated as well decreased by 1.

4. (c)

5. (c) Figure is rotated by 90° every time.

6. (d)

7. (c)

8. (d) In each row, the first unit is deleted in the third unit.

9. (d) Answer figure (d) will complete the matrix.

10. (d) Answer figure (d) will complete matrix.

11. (d) Answer figure (d) will complete matrix.

12. (b) Answer figure (b) will complete matrix.

13. (a)

14. (a)

15. (c)

16. (d)

17. (d)

18. (a) 'V' shifts by half and rotate by 45° and another figure shift alternatively by 45° and 90° and figure also changes.

19. (c)

20. (d) In all even number of figures outer most line increases by one shift by 60° and innermost line increases by one in even figures and shift by 60° in odd figures.

21. (b) Figure rotates by 90° and everytime one extra line is added to figure.

22. (a)

23. (c)

24. (b) In this figure shaded regions covers all the three circles and in rest figures only two circles.

25. (d)

26. (d)

27. (d)

28. (b) The whole figures inverts alternatively upside and downside

- ♀ figure which is 4th position in problem figure 1 change its position 1st, 2nd, 3rd, 4th and again 1st places.

- T figure shifts 1st and 2nd place alternatively.

- Y figure goes from 2nd to 3rd, 3rd to 4th, 4th to 1st and 1st to 2nd

- T figurer shifts 3rd and 4th place alternatively.

29. (a)

- change its directions after 2nd step, so (d) is eliminated.

- changes its direction after 1st step and then 2nd step so, (b) is eliminated.

- changs its direction after 2nd step so (c) is eliminated.

Hence, (a) is the answer.

30. (a) Upper arrow becomes half and rotates clockwise by 45° middle arrow rotates anticlockwise by 45°.

31. (c) Dots remain on the same place, the rest figures becomes invert.

32. (b) Upper figure (=) shifts diagnally opposite direction. Bottom figure (∓) shifts 90° antinclockwise and becomes invert.

33. (a) The whole figure is devided into eight sections.

34. (d) The inner figure becomes outer and outer becomes inner and got shading.

35. (c)

36. (a) In all other figures bottom right corners have been shaded.

37. (b) Arrows are not in the same direction.

38. (a) All others have four parts.

39. (c) In all other options line with arrow is shifting three steps forward clockwise, while in option (c) it is shifting two steps forward clockwise.

40. (d) In option (d) curves in vertical line are not following pattern.

41. (a) In all other options arrow cuts on the line and dot is shifting 90° anti clockwise.

42. (a) Designs are not following the pattern.

43. (d)

44. (a) 

Pattern follows (1) to (2)

and after they change the diagonal of the respective image have one less than shapes.

45. (d)

46. (c)

47. (d) Lower portion of the figure (1) remains same while upper portion gets inverted in the figure (2).

48. (c) Figure (1) gets inverted by 180° then its mirror image is formed in 2nd figure. Hence (c) is the correct choice.

49. (d) • (Ⅱ⟶✕) line is rotating 135° anticlockwise.

• ( ) line is rotating 45° clockwise.

• (Ⅱ⟶✕) line is changing its design at third and fifth step.

50. (c) Each branch is rotating 45° anticlock-wise and new branch is added in each step.

51. (c) Form (1) to (2)

Small circle shifts three steps anticlockwise. New image gets added behind small circle.

from (2) to (3).

Small circle and star shifts two steps anticlockwise. New image gets added ahead of small circle.

From (3) to (4)

Small circle, star and cross shifts three steps anticlockwise and new image added behind of small circle.

From (4) to (5)

Small circle, star, cross and eual to shifts two steps anticlockwise and new image added ahead of small circle.

From (5) to answer will be

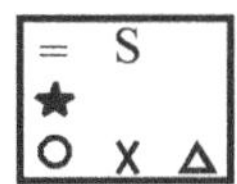

52. **(c)** From (1) to (2), all images change their position as well as gets inverted.

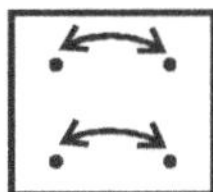

From fig. (2) to (3), pattern follows Image gets inverted as well as change their position.

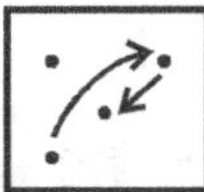

Same pattern follows till (5).

Now, from figure (5) to Answer figure. Pattern follows.

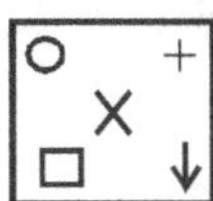

53. **(d)** Dots shifts two steps clockwise in each step, everytime one arrow gets reduced in Horizontally and lines changes its position also.

5 Completion Of Figure/ Embedded Figure

DIRECTIONS (Qs. 1-9) : *The hidden figures test is designed to perceive simple figures in complex drawings. At the top of each section are five figures lettered* a, b, c, d, *and* e. *Below these are several numbered drawings. You must determine which lettered figure is embedded in each of the numbered drawings.*

[2011-I]

a   b   c   d   e

1.

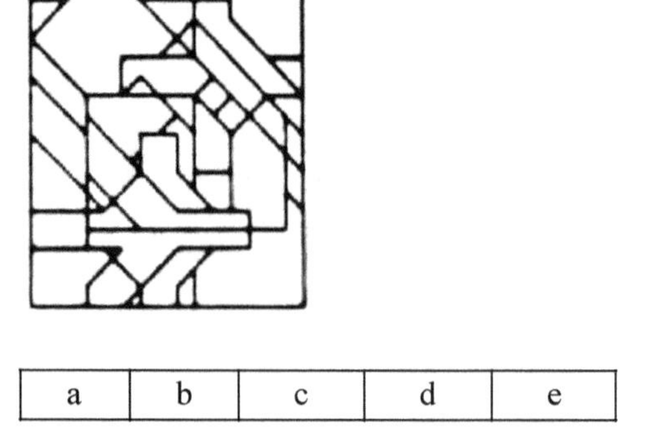

a	b	c	d	e

2.

3.

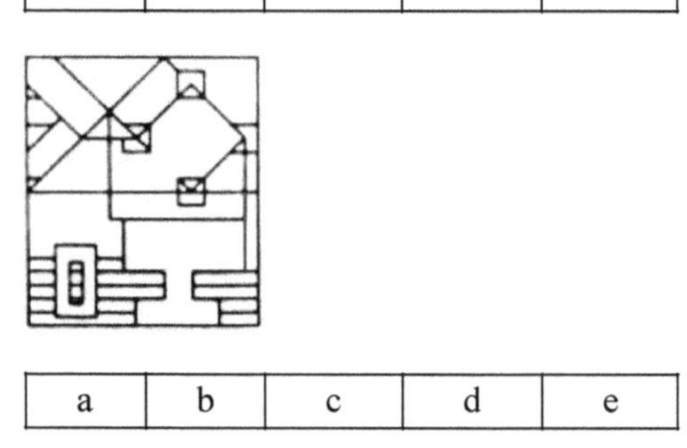

a	b	c	d	e

4.

a	b	c	d	e

5.

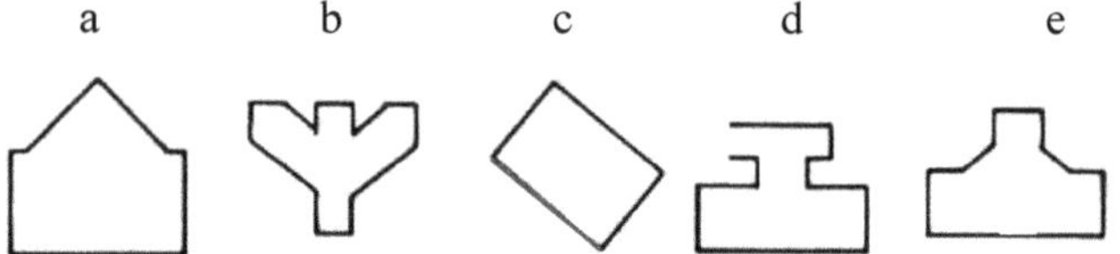

a	b	c	d	e

a   b   c   d   e

6.

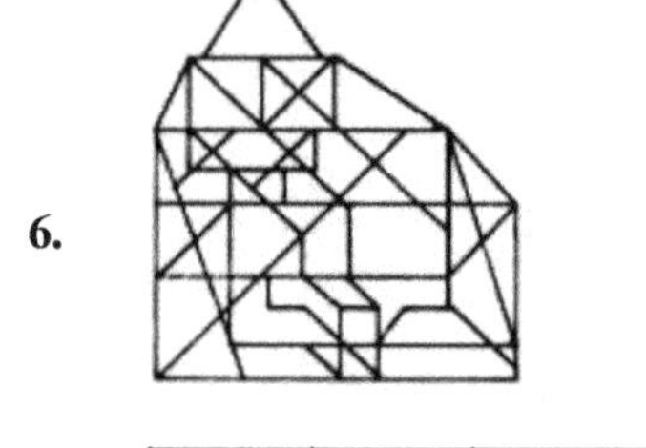

a	b	c	d	e

7.

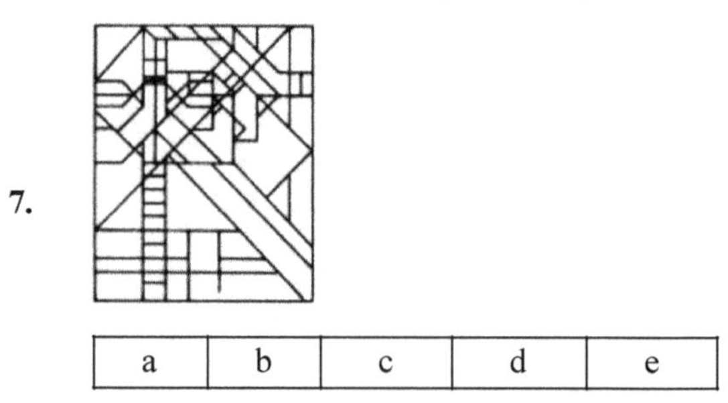

a	b	c	d	e

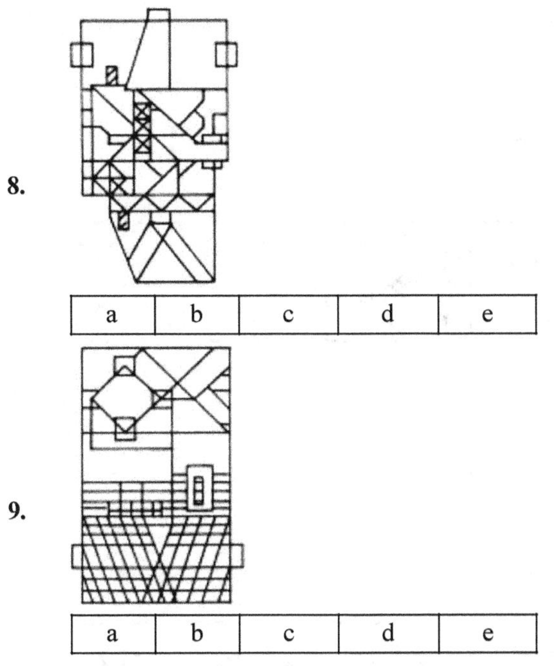

8.

| a | b | c | d | e |

9.

| a | b | c | d | e |

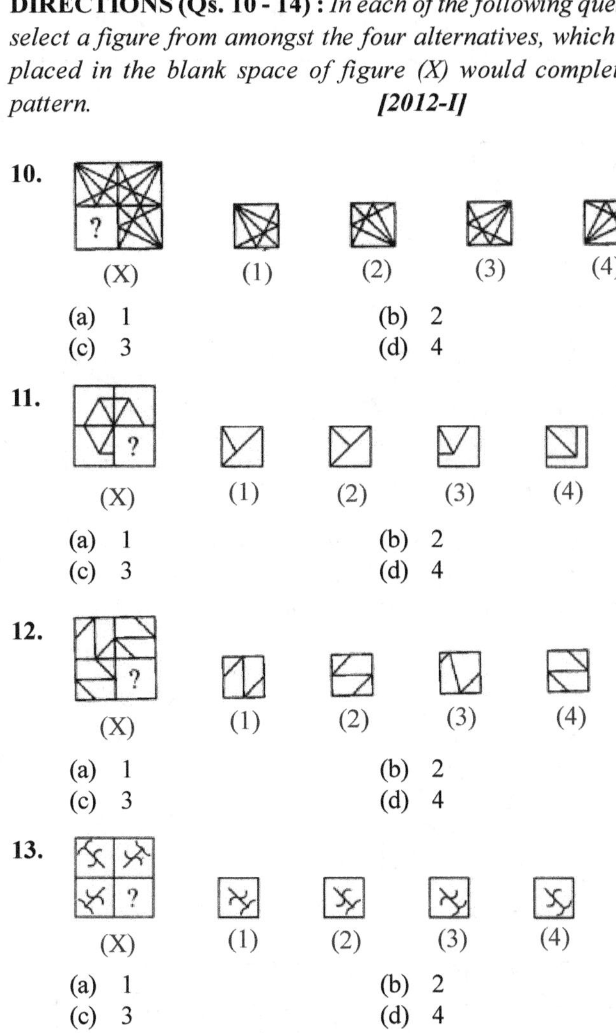

DIRECTIONS (Qs. 10 - 14) : *In each of the following questions select a figure from amongst the four alternatives, which when placed in the blank space of figure (X) would complete the pattern.*   *[2012-I]*

10.

(X)   (1)   (2)   (3)   (4)

(a) 1   (b) 2
(c) 3   (d) 4

11.

(X)   (1)   (2)   (3)   (4)

(a) 1   (b) 2
(c) 3   (d) 4

12.

(X)   (1)   (2)   (3)   (4)

(a) 1   (b) 2
(c) 3   (d) 4

13.

(X)   (1)   (2)   (3)   (4)

(a) 1   (b) 2
(c) 3   (d) 4

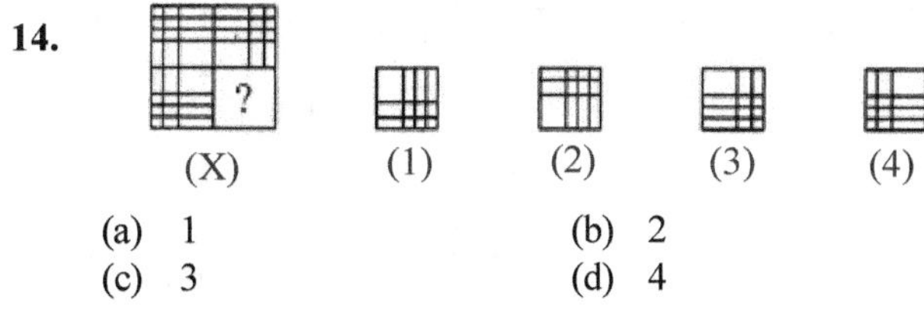

14.

(X)   (1)   (2)   (3)   (4)

(a) 1   (b) 2
(c) 3   (d) 4

DIRECTIONS (Qs. 15-19) : *In each of the following questions you are given a figure (X) followed by four alternative figures (1), (2), (3) and (4) such that figure (X) is embedded in one of them. Trace out the alternative figure which contains fig. (X) as its part.*   *[2012-I]*

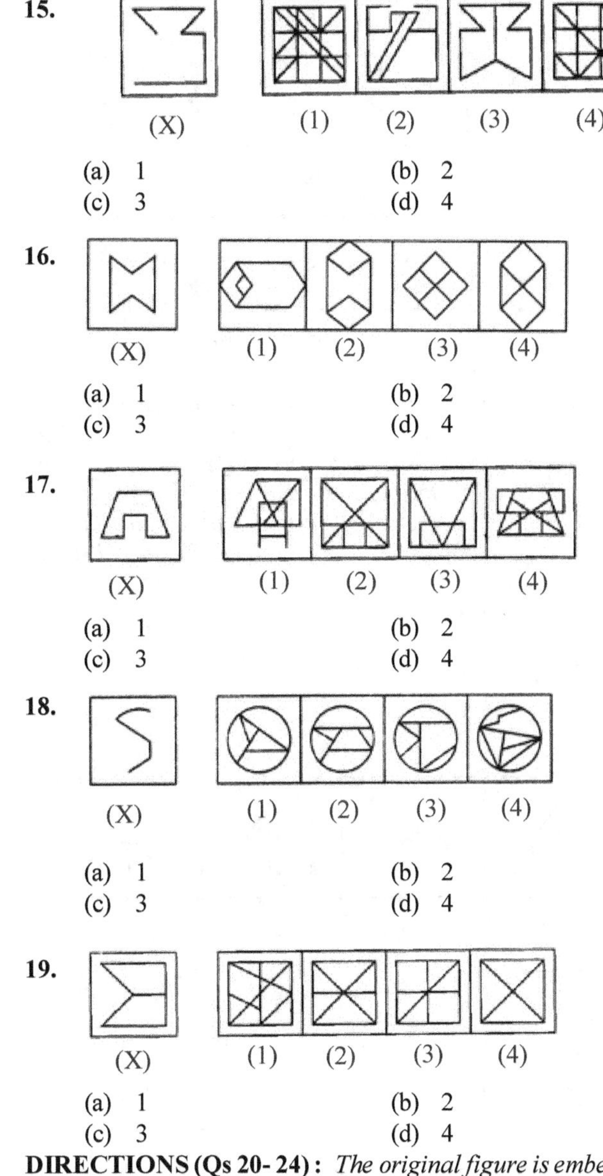

15.

(X)   (1)   (2)   (3)   (4)

(a) 1   (b) 2
(c) 3   (d) 4

16.

(X)   (1)   (2)   (3)   (4)

(a) 1   (b) 2
(c) 3   (d) 4

17.

(X)   (1)   (2)   (3)   (4)

(a) 1   (b) 2
(c) 3   (d) 4

18.

(X)   (1)   (2)   (3)   (4)

(a) 1   (b) 2
(c) 3   (d) 4

19.

(X)   (1)   (2)   (3)   (4)

(a) 1   (b) 2
(c) 3   (d) 4

DIRECTIONS (Qs 20- 24) : *The original figure is embedded or hidden in one of the answer figures (a), (b), (c) and (d). Select the alternative that carries the correct figure which clearly shows the embedded portion of the original figure.*

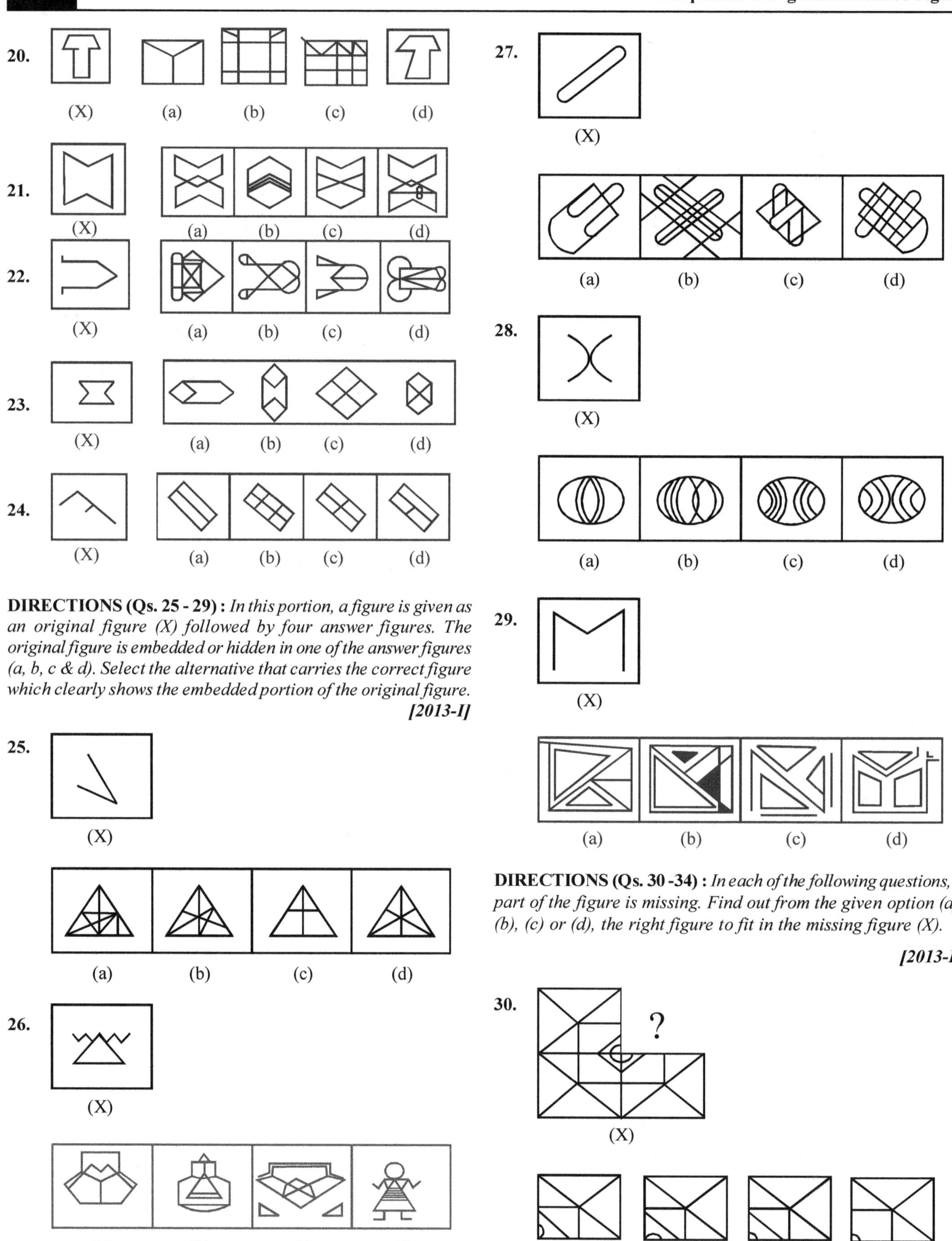

20. (X) (a) (b) (c) (d)

21. (X) (a) (b) (c) (d)

22. (X) (a) (b) (c) (d)

23. (X) (a) (b) (c) (d)

24. (X) (a) (b) (c) (d)

DIRECTIONS (Qs. 25 - 29) : *In this portion, a figure is given as an original figure (X) followed by four answer figures. The original figure is embedded or hidden in one of the answer figures (a, b, c & d). Select the alternative that carries the correct figure which clearly shows the embedded portion of the original figure.*

[2013-I]

25. (X) (a) (b) (c) (d)

26. (X) (a) (b) (c) (d)

27. (X) (a) (b) (c) (d)

28. (X) (a) (b) (c) (d)

29. (X) (a) (b) (c) (d)

DIRECTIONS (Qs. 30 -34) : *In each of the following questions, a part of the figure is missing. Find out from the given option (a), (b), (c) or (d), the right figure to fit in the missing figure (X).*

[2013-I]

30. (X) (a) (b) (c) (d)

31.

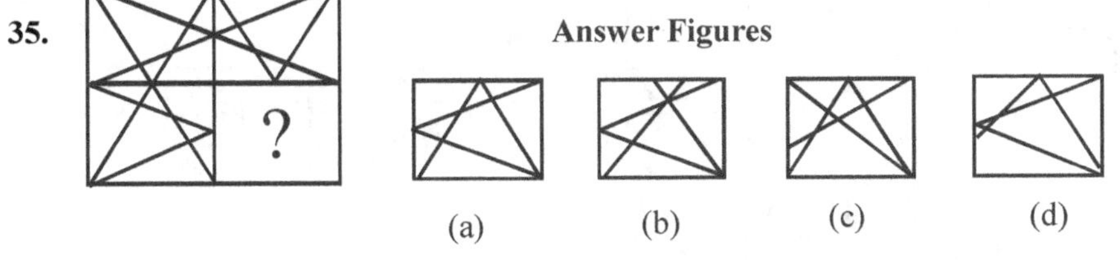

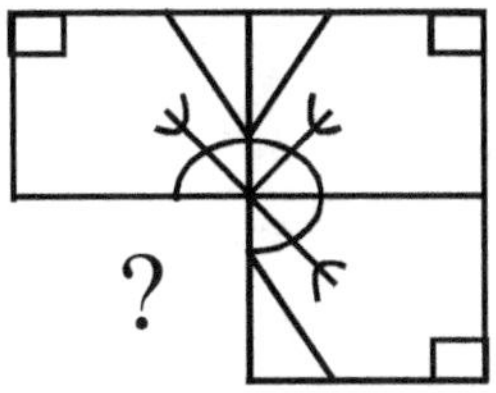

(X)

(a) (b) (c) (d)

33.

(X)

(a) (b) (c) (d)

32.

(X)

(a) (b) (c) (d)

34.

(X)

(a) (b) (c) (d)

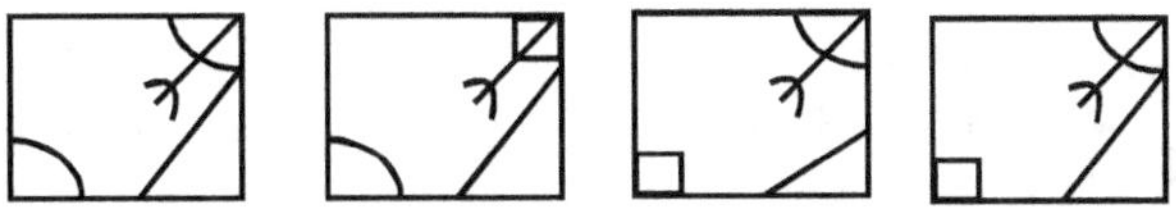

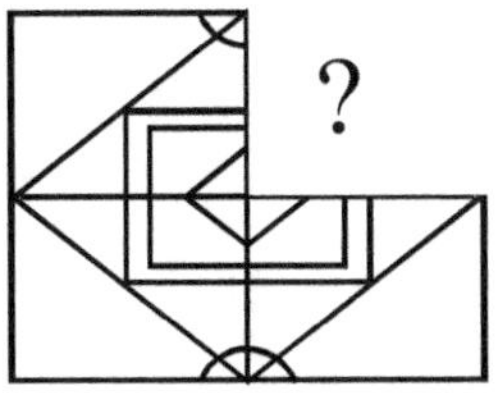

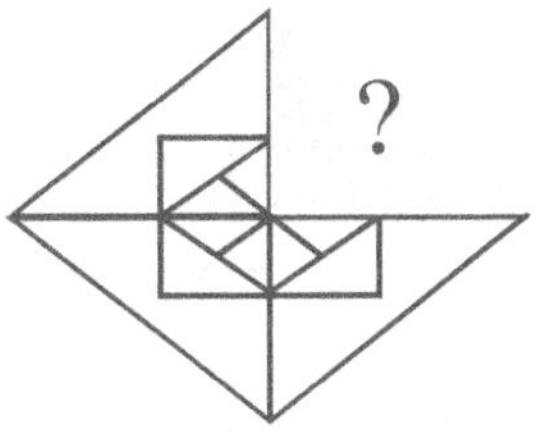

DIRECTIONS (Q35-38): *In these tests you will find an Incomplete Figure and four Answer Figures. You have to select one diagram from the Answer Figures which fits into the blank column in Incomplete Figure in order to complete it:* ***[2014-I]***

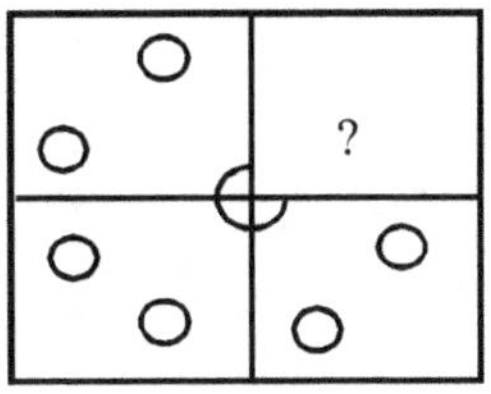

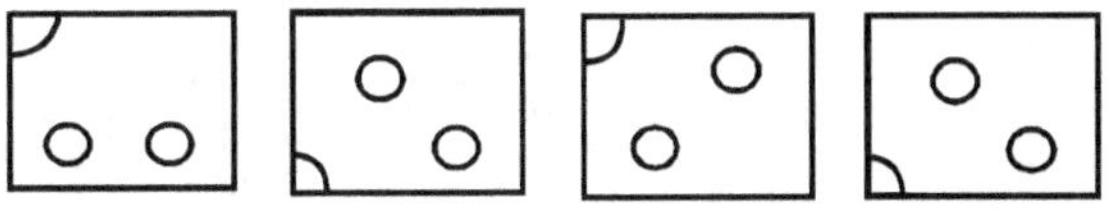

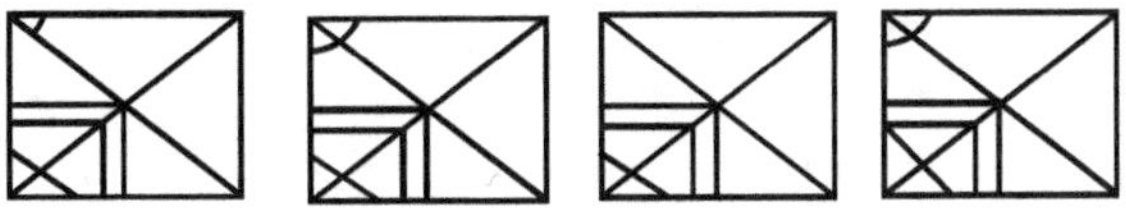

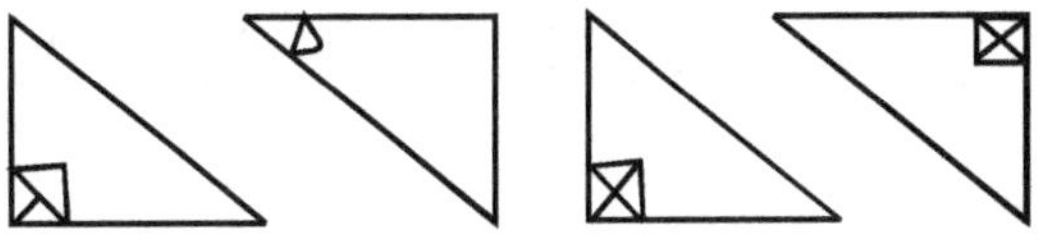

35. **Incomplete Figure**

Answer Figures

(a) (b) (c) (d)

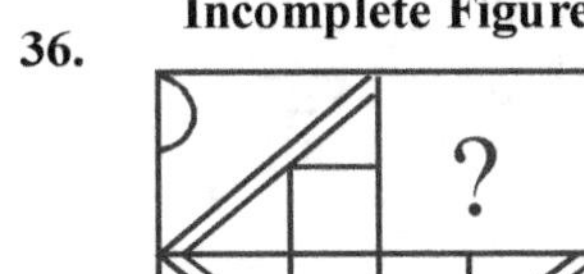

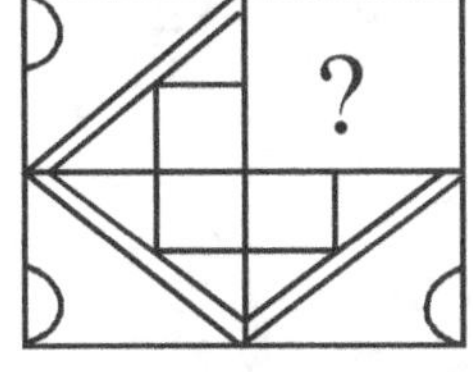

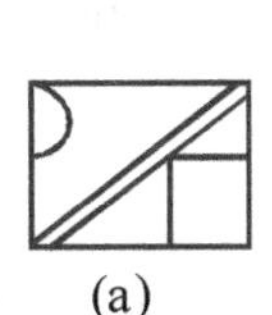

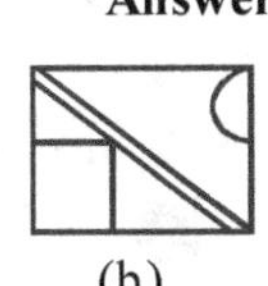

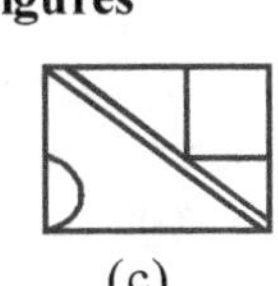

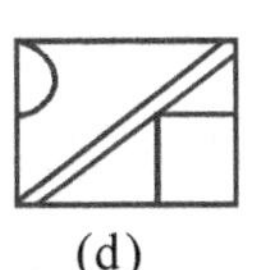

36. **Incomplete Figure**

Answer Figures

(a) (b) (c) (d)

37. **Incomplete Figure**

Answer Figure

(a) (b) (c) (d)

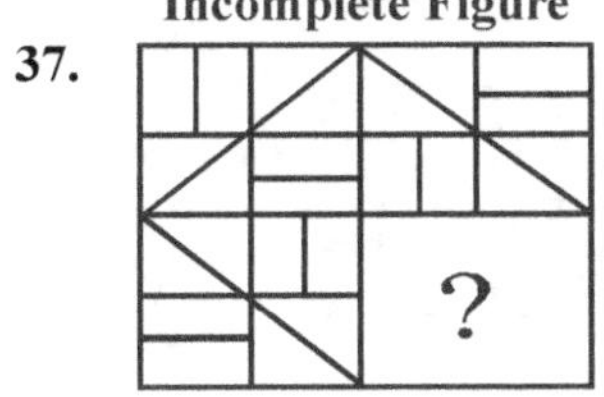

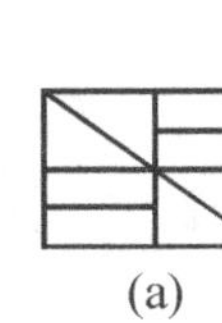

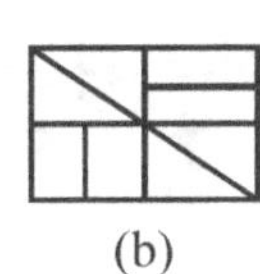

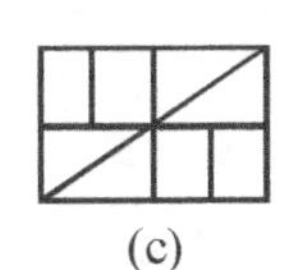

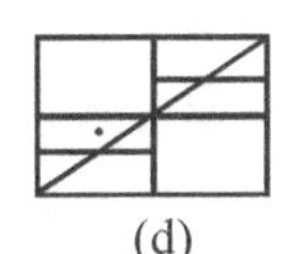

38. **Incomplete Figure**   **Answer Figures**

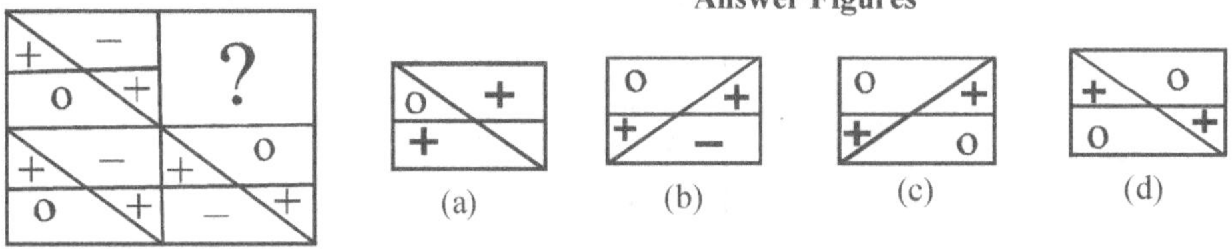

(a)   (b)   (c)   (d)

DIRECTIONS (Q.39-41) : *In these tests Figure X is Hidden in the option figures. Find the correct option.*

39.

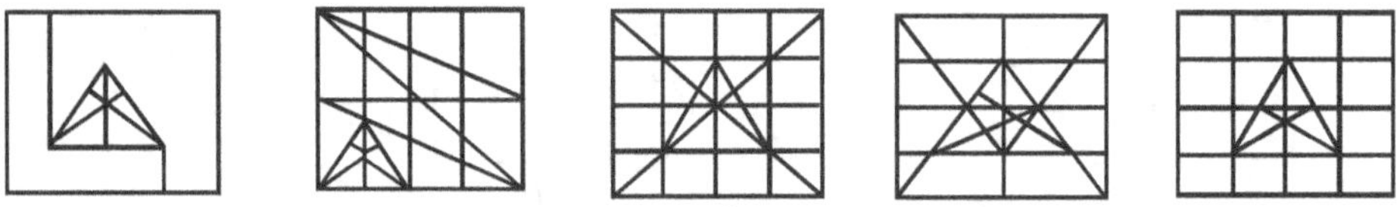

X   (a)   (b)   (c)   (d)

40.

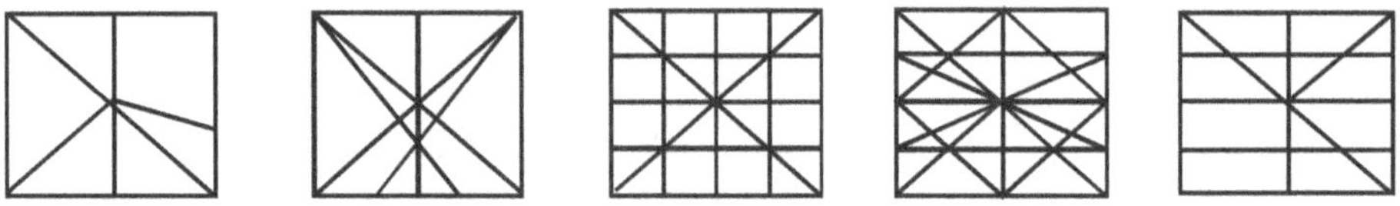

X   (a)   (b)   (c)   (d)

41.

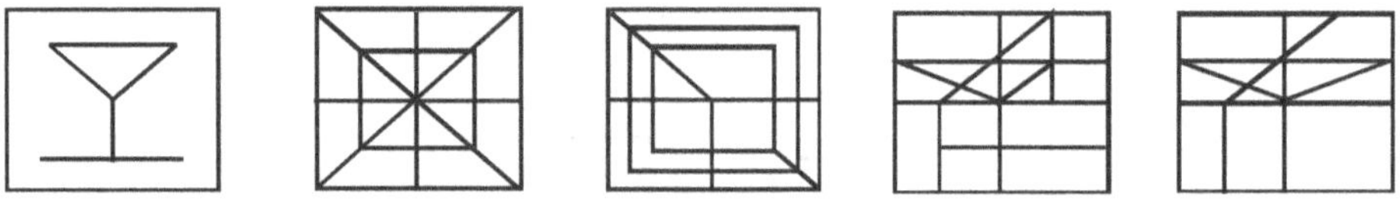

X   (a)   (b)   (c)   (d)

DIRECTION (Qs. 42 - 44) : *In each of the following quesions, select a figure from amongst the four alternatives which when placed in the blank space of figure (X) would complete The pattern.*   *[2014-II]*

42.

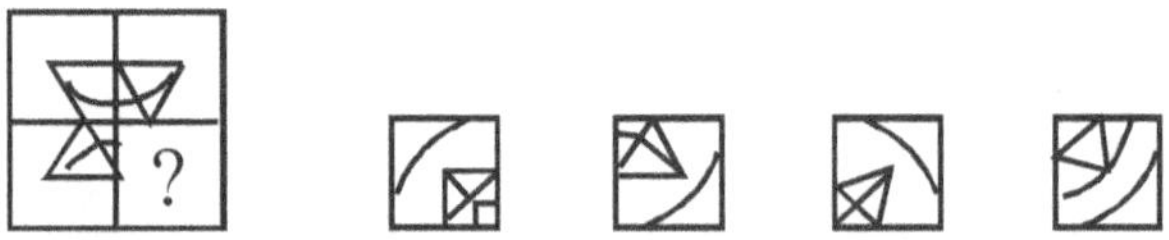

(X)   (a)   (b)   (c)   (d)

43.

(X)   (a)   (b)   (c)   (d)

44.

(X)   (a)   (b)   (c)   (d)

DIRECTION (Qs. 45 - 49) : *In each of the following questions, select a figure from amongst the four alternatives, which when placed in the blank space of figure (X) would complete the pattern.*

45.

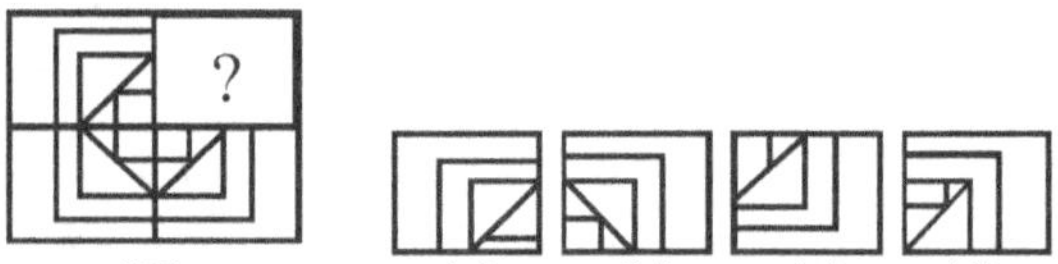

(X)   (a)   (b)   (c)   (d)

46.

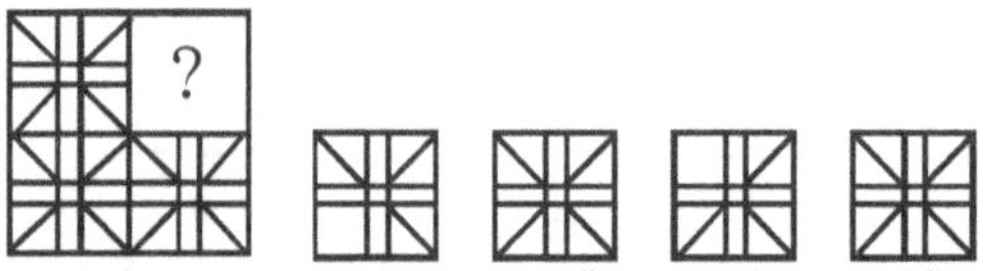

(X)   (a)   (b)   (c)   (d)

47..

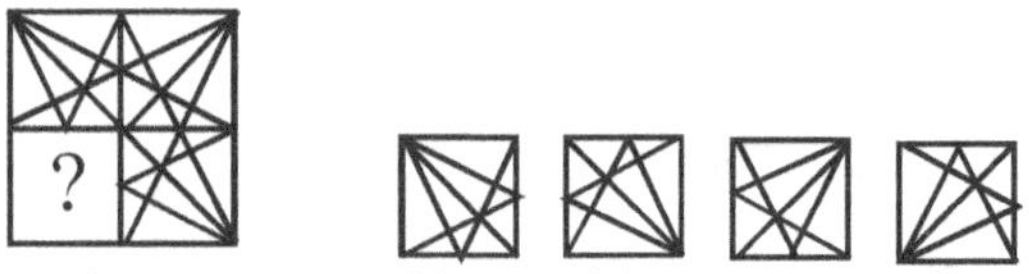

(X)   (a)   (b)   (c)   (d)

48.

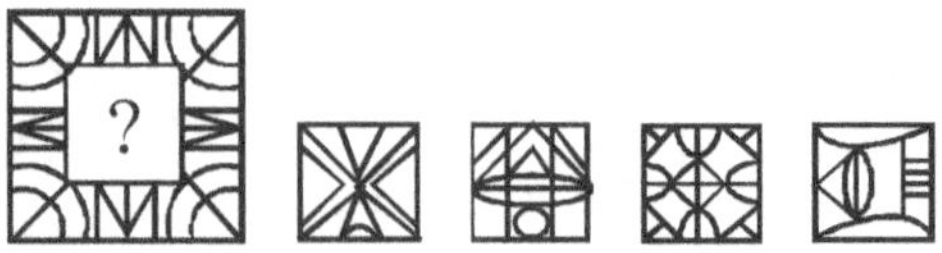

(X)   (a)   (b)   (c)   (d)

49.

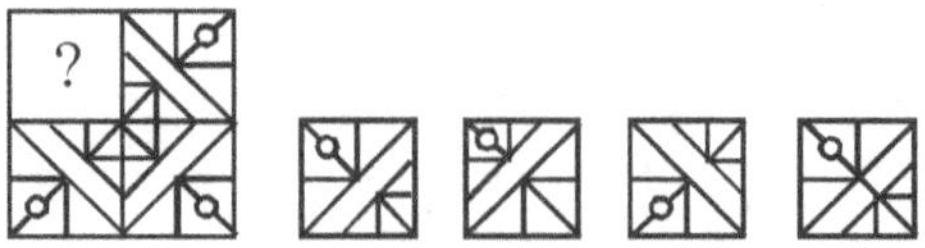

(X)   (a)   (b)   (c)   (d)

Answer Key

1.	(e)	10.	(d)	19.	(b)	28.	(d)	37.	(c)	46.	(d)
2.	(a)	11.	(c)	20.	(d)	29.	(a)	38.	(d)	47.	(d)
3.	(c)	12.	(b)	21.	(c)	30.	(b)	39.	(d)	48.	(c)
4.	(d)	13.	(c)	22.	(b)	31.	(d)	40.	(c)	49.	(a)
5.	(d)	14.	(c)	23.	(b)	32.	(b)	41.	(a)		
6.	(a)	15.	(a)	24.	(c)	33.	(b)	42.	(b)		
7.	(c)	16.	(b)	25.	(b)	34.	(a)	43.	(b)		
8.	(a)	17.	(d)	26.	(d)	35.	(a)	44.	(d)		
9.	(e)	18.	(b)	27.	(b)	36.	(b)	45.	(b)		

6 Spatial Ability/Image Analysis/Rotated Figure

DIRECTIONS (Qs. 1-9) : *This test is designed to test your ability to visualize and manipulate objects in space. In each question, you are shown a picture of a block. To the right of the pictured block, there are five choices shown as a, b, c, d and e. Select the choice containing a block that is just like the pictured block at the left although turned in a different position.* **[2011-I]**

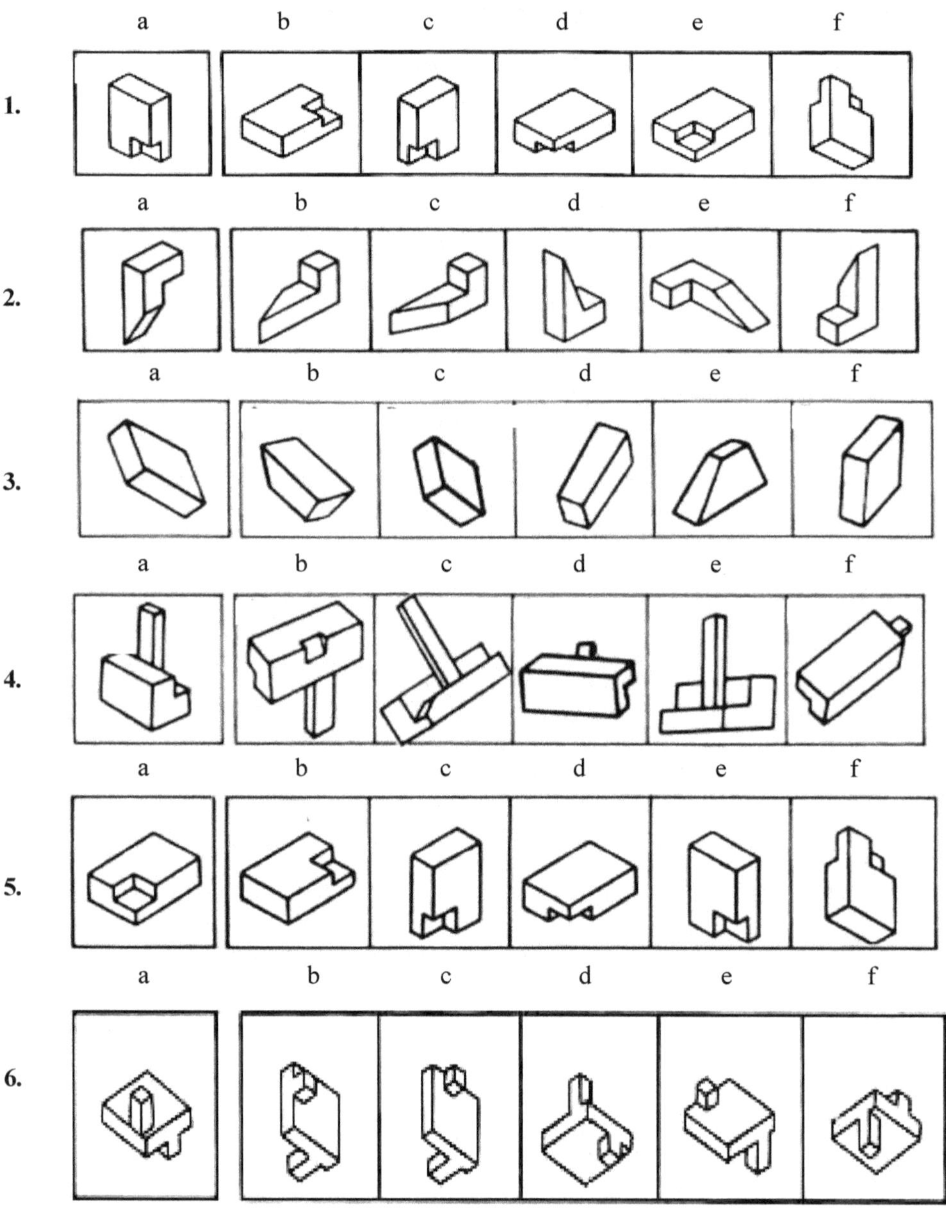

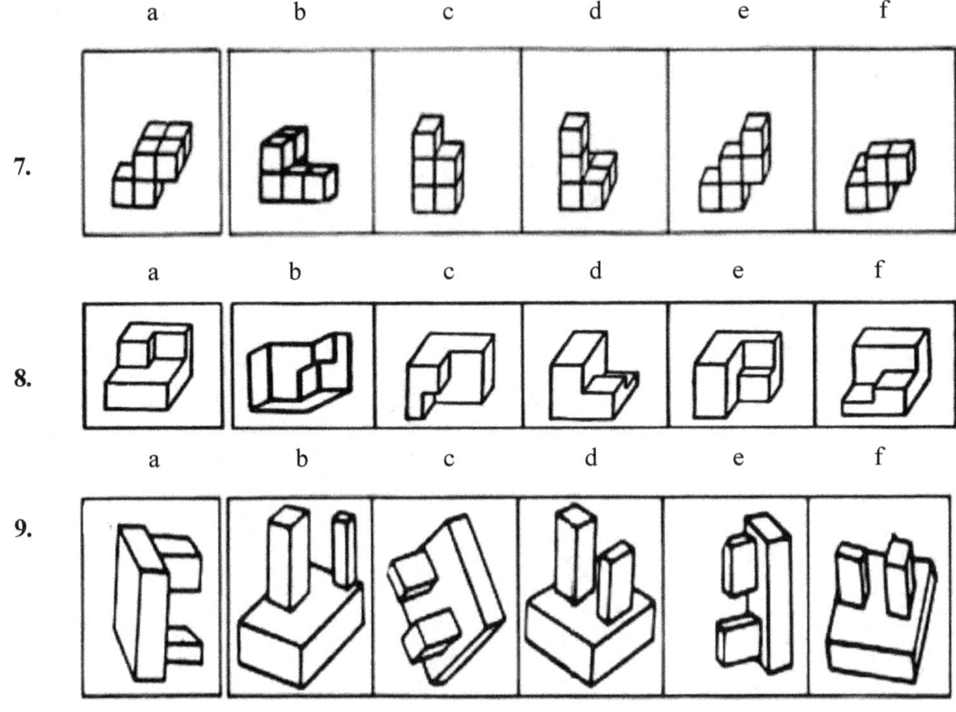

7. a   b   c   d   e   f

8. a   b   c   d   e   f

9. a   b   c   d   e   f

DIRECTIONS (Qs. 10-12) : *Your task here is to look at the target figure and decide which of the rotated figures below is identical to it. If you do not think any of the figures is same as the target shape then choose the answer option (d) 'none of these'.*

[2011-II]

10. 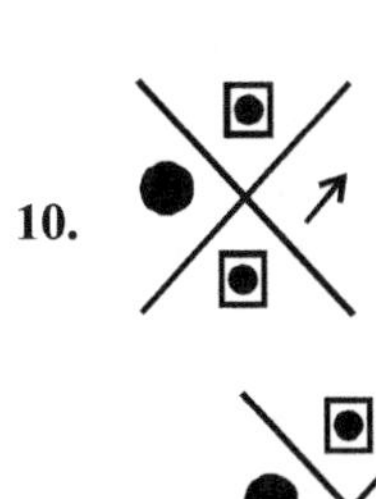

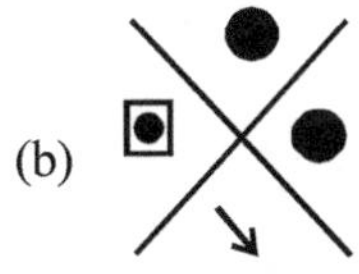

(a)   (b)

(c)   (d) None of these

11. 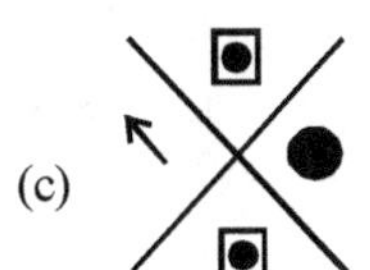

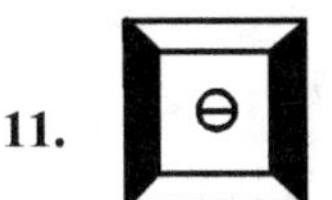

(a)   (b)

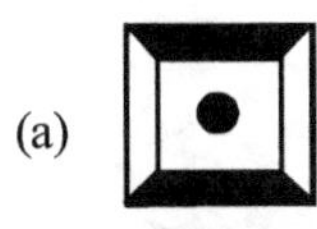

(c)   (d) None of these

12. 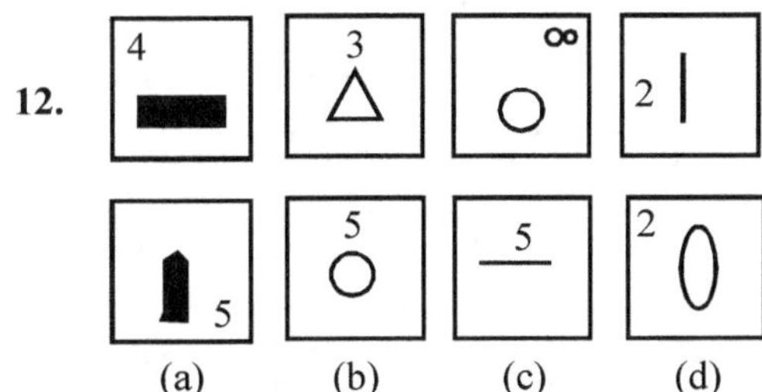

(a)   (b)   (c)   (d)

DIRECTIONS (Qs 13-17) : *Find out which of the figures (1), (2), (3) and (4) can be formed from the pieces given in figure (X). [2012-I]*

13. 

(X)   (1) (2) (3) (4)

(a) 1   (b) 2
(c) 3   (d) 4

14. 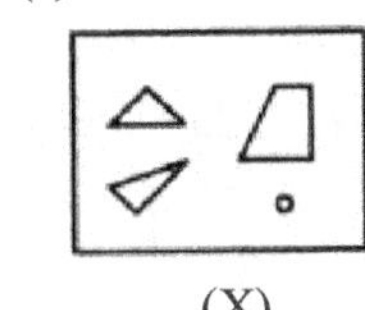

(X)   (1) (2) (3) (4)

(a) 1   (b) 2
(c) 3   (d) 4

15. 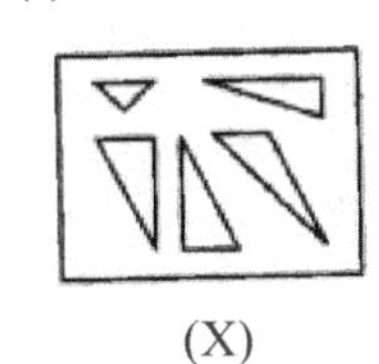

(X)   (1) (2) (3) (4)

(a) 1   (b) 2
(c) 3   (d) 4

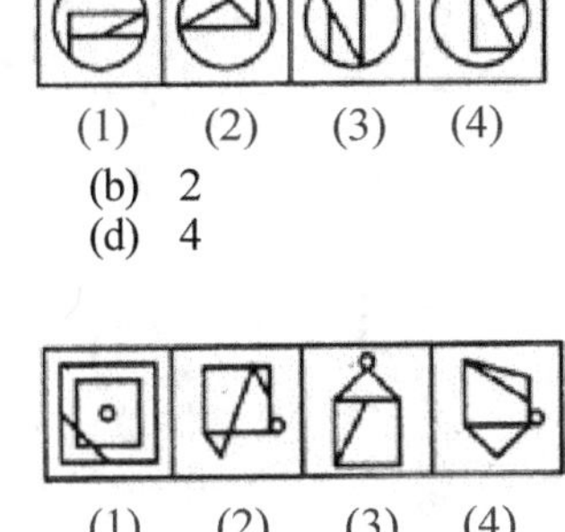

16.

(a) 1   **(b)** 2
(c) 3   **(d)** 4

17. Find out how the key figure (X) will look like after rotation.

(a) 1   **(b)** 2
(c) 3   **(d)** 4

DIRECTIONS (Qs 18-22) : *From amongst the figures marked (a), (b), (c) and (d), select the figure which satisfies the same conditions of placement of the dot as in fig. (X)*   *[2012-II]*

18.

19.

20.

21.

22.

DIRECTIONS (Qs. 23-26) : *The following situations involve a cluster of three or more geometrical figures, having one or more dots placed at any point inside the cluster. This cluster is followed by a set of four alternative figures each composed of a cluster of the same type of figures. Now, for each dot we have to observe the region in which it is enclosed i.e. in which of the geometrical figure this region is common.*

From amongst the figures marked (a), (b), (c) and (d), select the figures which satisfies the same conditions of placement of the dot as in fig. (X).   *[2013-I]*

23.

24.

25.

26.

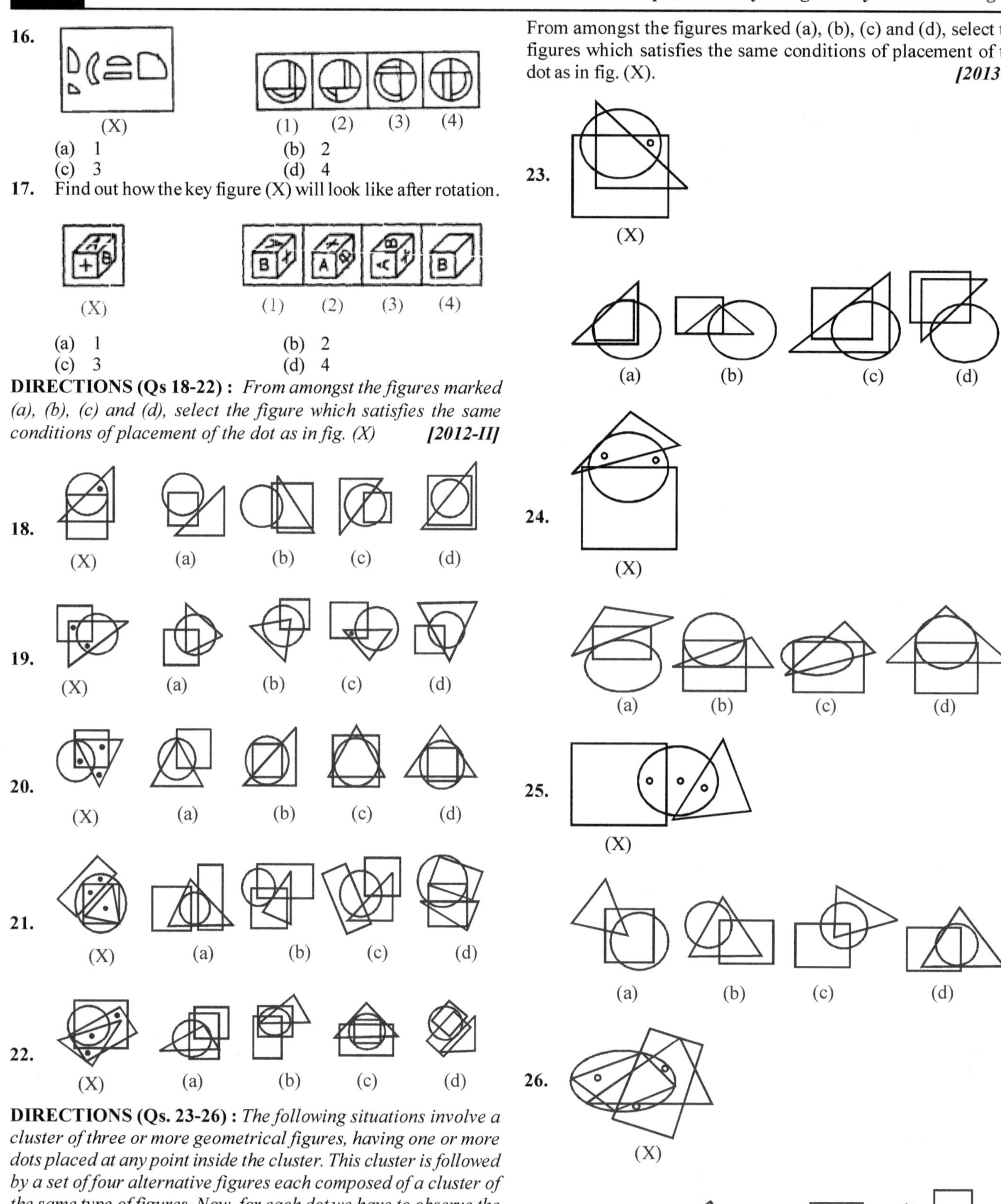

27.　　　　　　　　　　　　　　　　　　　　　　　　　　*[2013-I]*

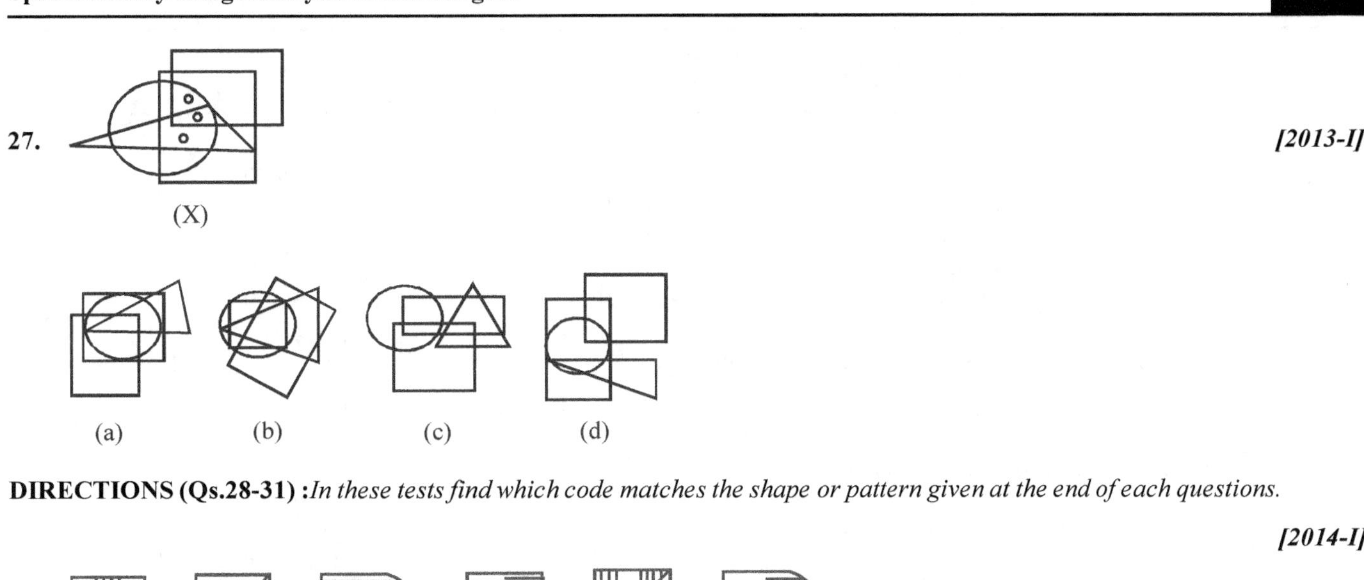

(X)

(a)　　　　(b)　　　　(c)　　　　(d)

DIRECTIONS (Qs.28-31) : *In these tests find which code matches the shape or pattern given at the end of each questions.*

[2014-I]

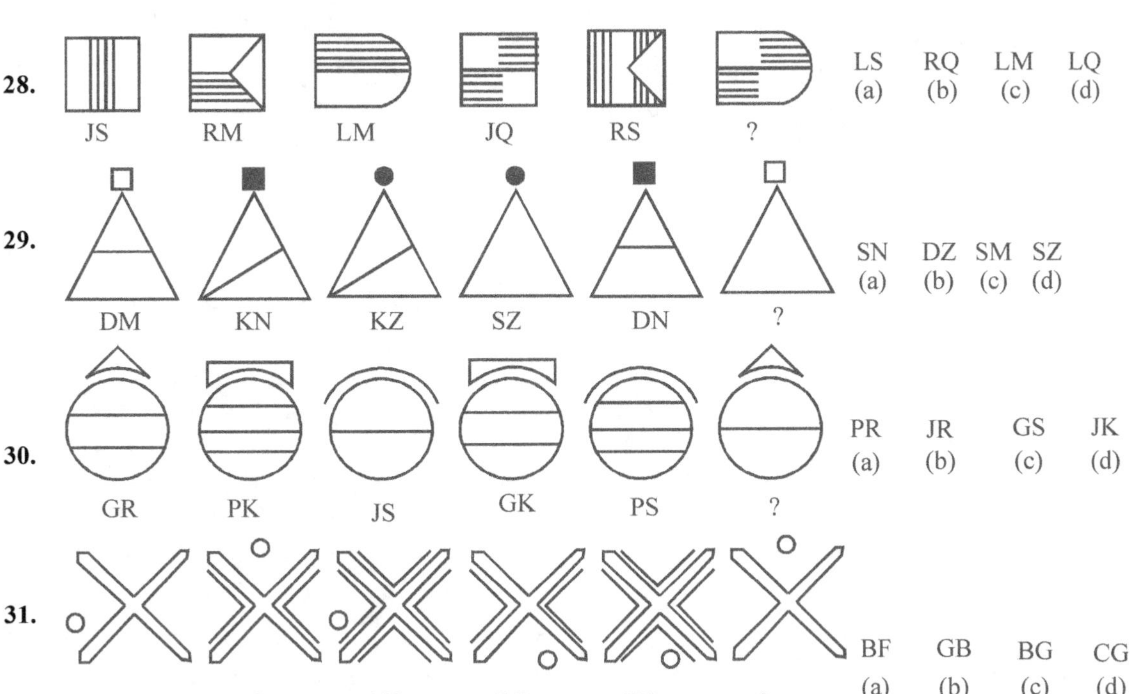

28.　JS　RM　LM　JQ　RS　?

	LS	RQ	LM	LQ
	(a)	(b)	(c)	(d)

29.　DM　KN　KZ　SZ　DN　?

	SN	DZ	SM	SZ
	(a)	(b)	(c)	(d)

30.　GR　PK　JS　GK　PS　?

	PR	JR	GS	JK
	(a)	(b)	(c)	(d)

31.　AF　BG　AH　CG　CH　?

	BF	GB	BG	CG
	(a)	(b)	(c)	(d)

Hints & Solutions

1. (d)   2. (b)
3. (e)   4. (a)
5. (d)   6. (c)
7. (d)   8. (e)
9. (b)   10. (c)
11. (c)   12. (d)
13. (c) All of the components of figure (X) are present in the figure (3)
14. (c) All of the components of figure (X) are present in the figure (3)
15. (c) All of the components of figure (X) are present in the figure (3)
16. (a) All of the components of figure (X) are present in the figure (1)
17. (c) When the key figure (X) will be rotated it will look like figure (3). The three faces are in the following manner in clock wise direction.

     A → B → X

18. (c)   19. (c)
20. (c)   21. (d)
22. (a)   23. (d)
24. (c)   25. (c)
26. (d)   27. (b)

28. (d) 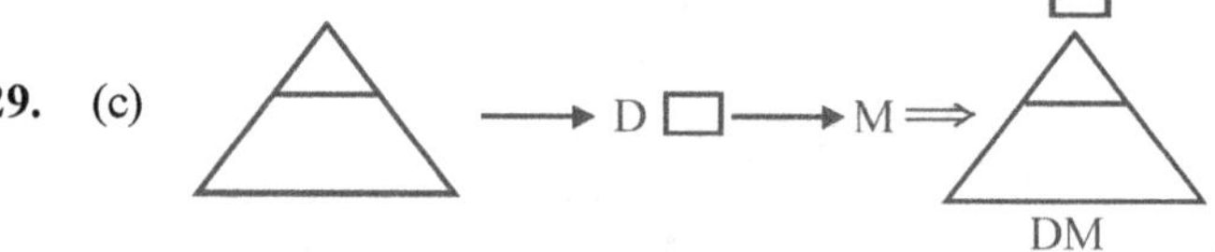

29. (c)

30. (b)   31. (a)

1 History/Civics & Polity

1. The First Battle of Panipat was fought between *[2011-I]*
   - (a) Akbar & Hemu
   - (b) Babur and Ibrahim Lodhi
   - (c) Akbar & Rana Sanga
   - (d) Ahmad Shah Abdali & Marathas
2. Fa-hien visited India during the reign of *[2011-I]*
   - (a) Chandra Gupta Maurya
   - (b) Bindusara
   - (c) Chandra Gupta II
   - (d) Bimbisara
3. Gandhiji's first experience with Satyagraha came up in *[2011-I]*
   - (a) Dandi
   - (b) Champaran
   - (c) Bengal
   - (d) Natal
4. During whose tenure as the viceroy of India were the great Martyrs Bhagat Singh, Sukhdev and Rajguru hanged ? *[2011-I]*
   - (a) Lord Curzon
   - (b) Lord Irwin
   - (c) Lord Minto
   - (d) Lord Chelmford
5. The boundary between China and India is known as
   - (a) Mc Mohan Line
   - (b) Radcliffe Line
   - (c) Hindenberg Line
   - (d) Line of Control
6. The famous Grand Trunk (GT) Road from Peshawar to Kolkata was built by
   - (a) Akbar
   - (b) Ashok
   - (c) Sher Shah Suri
   - (d) Chandragupta
7. The Ashoka Pillar whose Lion Capitol (Carving) was adopted by the Government of India as National Emblem is situated at *[2011-II]*
   - (a) Varanasi
   - (b) Puri
   - (c) Prayag
   - (d) Sarnath
8. The Preamble of the Constitution of India was prepared by *[2011-II]*
   - (a) Member of Constituent Assembly
   - (b) BR Ambedkar
   - (c) Jawaharlal Nehru
   - (d) Dr. Radhakrishna
9. The two great revolutionaries who threw a bomb in Legislative Assembly were *[2011-II]*
   - (a) Bhagat Singh & BK Dutt
   - (b) Bhagat Singh & Chandrashekhar Azad
   - (c) Chandrashekar Azad & Bismil
   - (d) Bhagat Singh & Ashfak Ullah Khan
10. Which one of the following is the exclusive power of the Lok Sabha ? *[2011-II]*
    - (a) To introduce Money Bill.
    - (b) To ratify declaration of Emergency.
    - (c) To impeach the President.
    - (d) To pass No Confidence Motion against Council of Ministers.
11. The person who is regarded as the greatest law giver of ancient India is *[2012-I]*
    - (a) Panini
    - (b) Kautilya
    - (c) Manu
    - (d) Patanjali
12. The immortal fame of Ashoka largely rests upon *[2012-I]*
    - (a) his conversion to Buddhism and its propagation.
    - (b) his policy for the welfare of his subjects.
    - (c) his work in the sphere of politics and moral teaching.
    - (d) his extensive conquests.
13. Gandhiji started Dandi March *[2012-I]*
    - (a) to demonstrate against the British Empire.
    - (b) to break the salt law.
    - (c) to boycott foreign goods.
    - (d) None of the above.
14. The first war of Indian Independence began on 10 May 1857 at *[2012-I]*
    - (a) Meerut
    - (b) Jhansi
    - (c) Barrackpore
    - (d) Delhi
15. Who among the following had discovered the Bramhi Script in 1838 ? *[2012-II]*
    - (a) Sir William Jones
    - (b) Dr. Rajendra Lal Mitra
    - (c) Dr. Bhaw Dagi
    - (d) Jones Prinsep
16. Who was known as father of administration in medieval India ? *[2012-II]*
    - (a) Akbar
    - (b) Sher Shah Suri
    - (c) Humayun
    - (d) Aurangzeb
17. Brahma Samaj was founded by *[2012-II]*
    - (a) Raja Rammohan Roy
    - (b) Jawaharlal Nehru
    - (c) William Carey
    - (d) Jonathan Duncan
18. Who discharges the function of the President when vacancy occur In the office of President & Vice President simultaneously, owing to removal, death, resignation or th incumbent or otherwise ? *[2012-II]*
    - (a) Chief Justice of High Court
    - (b) Chief Justice of India
    - (c) Speaker of Lok Sabha
    - (d) Chairman of Rajya Sabha
19. Who accorded the title 'Mahatma" to MK Gandhi ? *[2013-I]*
    - (a) Sardar Patel
    - (b) Nehru
    - (c) Sarojini Naidu
    - (d) Rabindranath Tagore

20. The Non co-operation Movement started in which year ?
[2013-I]
(a) 1900 (b) 1921
(c) 1940 (d) 1935

21. During the Middle Ages education was confined only to
(a) Kshatriyas (b) Brahmins
(c) Peasants (d) Shudras

22. Who among the following was responsible for the spread of Buddhism in Sri Lanka ? *[2013-I]*
(a) Ashoka (b) Mahavira
(c) Parsavanth (d) Chandra Gupta Maurya

23. Who was the Governor-General of India during the 'Sepoy Mutiny'? *[2014-I]*
(a) Lord Dalhousie (b) Lord Harding
(c) Lord Canning (d) Lord Lytton.

24. Which of the following statements is incorrect ? *[2014-I]*
(a) Goa attained full statehood in 1987
(b) Diu is an island in the Gulf of Khambhat
(c) Daman & Diu were separated from Goa by the 56th Amendment of the Constitution of India
(d) Dadar & Nagar Haveli were under French colonial rule till 1954.

25. Who among the following has been called the 'Napoleon of India'? *[2014-I]*
(a) Ashoka (b) Samudragupta
(c) Chandragupta (d) Harshavardhana

26. Who is known as the 'Grand Old Man of India'? *[2014-I]*
(a) Dadabhai Naoroji (b) Gopal Krishna Gokhale
(c) Bal Gangadhar Tilak (d) A.O. Hume

27. Which amongst the following has the power to regulate the right of citizenship in India ? *[2014-I]*
(a) Union Cabinet (b) Parliament
(c) Supreme Court (d) Law Commission

28. Kalhana's 'Rajatarangini' is a history of *[2014-I]*
(a) Kashmir (b) Harsha's reign
(c) Rajasthan (d) Chandragupta's reign

29. The Constitution of India was promulgated on January 26, 1950 because *[2014-I]*
(a) This day was being celebrated as the Independence Day since 1929
(b) This was desired by the farmers of India
(c) The British did not want to leave India earlier than this date
(d) It was an auspicious day

30. Which of the following rulers had the title 'Kaviraja'
[2014-II]
(a) Kumaragupta (b) Chandragupta
(c) Skandagupta (d) Samudragupta

31. The Viceroy who divided Bengal by following the divide and rule policy was:- *[2014-II]*
(a) Lord Curzon (b) Lord Ripon
(c) Lord Lytton (d) Lord Mayo

32. The right to vote in the national elections in India is based on the principle of *[2014-II]*
(a) Restricted franchise (b) Hereditary privileges
(c) Property qualifications (d) Universal adult suffrage

33. In which respect have the Centre-State relations been specifically termed as municipal relations ? *[2014-II]*
(a) Centre's control of the State in the legislative sphare
(b) Centre's control of the State in Financial matter
(c) Centre's control of the State in the administrative sector
(d) Centre's control of the State in the planning process

34. 'Satyameva Jayate' is borrowed from which of the following ?
[2014-II]
(a) Mundaka Upanishad (b) Mahabharat
(c) Ramayana (d) Arthshashtra

35. The opposition part status is accorded to a political party in the Lok Sabha only if it captures at least *[2015-I]*
(a) 5% Seats (b) 10% Seats
(c) 15% Seats (d) 20% Seats

36. How many Vice Presidents are elected at the start of its each regular session of UN General Assembly? *[2015-I]*
(a) Nine (b) Fifteen
(c) Two (d) Twenty one

37. Who among the following was the Congress President at Madras Session of 1927 when it boycotted the Simon Commission? *[2015-I]*
(a) Maulana Abul Kalam Azad
(b) MA Ansari
(c) Lala Lajpat Rai
(d) Subhash Chandra Bose

38. Why did Kalinga prove to be a turning point in the life of Ashoka? *[2015-I]*
(a) Ashoka annexed Kalinga
(b) It was the starting point of the expansion of his empire
(c) Ashoka became a zealous Buddhist
(d) It enabled Mauryan Empire to reach its climax.

39. Which of the following wings was not part of the espionage system described by Kautilya? *[2015-I]*
(a) Crime Branch (b) Special Branch
(c) Political Branch (d) None of these

40. Alauddin Khilji did not build *[2015-I]*
(a) Siri Fort (b) Tomb of Jalaluddin
(c) Hauz-i-Alai (d) Jamaat Khana Masjid

41. Which of the following dynasties was ruling over North India at the time of Alexander's invasion? *[2015-I]*
(a) Nanda (b) Maurya
(c) Sunga (d) Kanva

Hints & Solutions

1. **(b)** The First Battle of Panipat, on 21 April 1526, was fought between the invading forces of Babur and the Lodi Empire. It took place in north India and marked the beginning of the Mughal Empire. This was one of the earliest battles involving gunpowder firearms and field artillery. Ibrahim Lodi died on the field of battle along with 15,000 of his troops.

2. **(c)** Fahien visited India in the early fifth century AD. He is said to have walked all the way from China across icy desert and rugged mountain passes. Fahien's visit to India occurred during the reign of Chandragupta II.

3. **(b)** The first Satyagraha revolutions inspired by Mahatma Gandhi in the Indian Independence Movement occurred in Champaran district of Bihar on 1916.

4. **(b)**

5. **(a)** The McMahon Line is a line agreed to by Britain and Tibet as part of the Simla Accord, a treaty signed in 1914. It is the effective boundary between China and India, although its legal status is disputed by the Chinese government. The line is named after Sir Henry McMahon, foreign secretary of the British-run Government of India and the chief negotiator of the convention at Simla. It extends for 550 miles (890 km) from Bhutan in the west to 160 miles (260 km) east of the great bend of the Brahmaputra River in the east, largely along the crest of the Himalayas.

6. **(c)** The Grand Trunk Road is one of Asia's oldest and longest major roads. For more than two millennia, it has linked the eastern and western regions of the Indian subcontinent, connecting South Asia with Central Asia. It runs from Chittagong, Bangladesh west to Howrah, West Bengal in India, across north India into Peshawar, up to Kabul, Afghanistan. The predecessor of the modern road was rebuilt by Sher Shah Suri, who renovated and extended the ancient Mauryan route in the 16th century.

7. **(d)** The Lion Capital of Ashoka is a sculpture of four Indian lions standing back to back, on an elaborate base that includes other animals. A graphic representation of it was adopted as the official Emblem of India in 1950. It was originally placed atop the Ashoka pillar at the important Buddhist site of Sarnath by the Emperor Ashoka, in about 250 BCE.

8. **(b)** The preamble of the Constitution of India was prepared by B R Ambedkar.

9. **(a)** Seeking revenge for the death of Lala Lajpat Rai at the hands of the police, Bhagat Singh was involved in the murder of British police officer John Saunders. He eluded efforts by the police to capture him. Soon after, together with Batukeshwar Dutt, he undertook a successful effort to throw two bombs and leaflets inside the Central Legislative Assembly while shouting the slogan of revolution.

10. **(a)** Money Bills can be introduced only in Lok Sabha (the directly elected 'people's house' of the Indian Parliament).

11. **(c)**

12. **(a)** Ashoka converted gradually to Buddhism beginning about 263 BCE at the latest. He was later dedicated to the propagation of Buddhism across Asia, and established monuments marking several significant sites in the life of Gautama Buddha.

13. **(b)** The Salt March, also mainly known as the Salt Satyagraha, began with the Dandi March on 12 March 1930. It was a direct action campaign of tax resistance and nonviolent protest against the British salt monopoly in colonial India, and triggered the wider Civil Disobedience Movement.

14. **(a)** The Indian Rebellion of 1857 began as a mutiny of sepoys of the East India Company's army on 10 May 1857, in the cantonment of the town of Meerut, Utar Pradesh.

15. **(d)** The script was deciphered in 1837 by Jones Prinsep, an archaeologist, philologist, and official of the British East India Company.

16. **(a)**

17. **(a)** Brahma Samaj is the societal component of Brahmoism, a monotheistic reformist and renaissance movement of Hindu religion. It was started at Calcutta on 20 August 1828 by Raja Ram Mohan Roy and Debendranath Tagore.

18. **(b)** When President Zakir Hussain died in office, the Vice President VV Giri, acted as the President. However, Mr. Giri resigned as the Vice President. Then the Chief Justice Hidayatullah became the acting President of India. The most senior judge of the Supreme Court became the acting Chief Justice of India. When the newly elected President took office a month later, Justice Hidayatullah again became the Chief Justice of India.

19. **(d)** Rabindranath Tagore bestowed the title 'mahatma' to M.K.Gandhi.

20. **(b)** The Non-cooperation movement was a significant phase of the Indian struggle for freedom from British rule. It was led by Mohandas Gandhi and was supported by the Indian National Congress.

21. **(b)** In ancient India, during the Vedic period from about 1500 BC to 600 BC, most education was based on the Veda (hymns, formulas, and incantations, recited or chanted by priests of a pre-Hindu tradition) and later Hindu texts and scriptures.Education, at first freely available in Vedic society, became over time more discriminatory as the caste system, originally based on occupation, evolved, with the brahman (priests) being the most privileged of the castes.

22. **(a)** Ashoka sent his only daughter Sanghamitra and son Mahindra to spread Buddhism in Sri Lanka (then known as Tamraparni).As a Buddhist emperor, Ashoka believed that Buddhism is beneficial for all human beings as well as animals and plants, so he built a number of stupas, Sangharama, viharas, chaitya, and residences for Buddhist monks all over South Asia and Central Asia.

23. **(c)** A major cause of resentment that arose ten months prior to the outbreak of the Rebellion was the General

Service Enlistment Act of 25 July 1856. As noted above, men of the Bengal Army had been exempted from overseas service. Specifically they were enlisted only for service in territories to which they could march. Governor-General Lord Dalhousie saw this as an anomaly, since all sepoys of the Madras and Bombay Armies and the six "General Service" battalions of the Bengal Army had accepted an obligation to serve overseas if required. As signed into effect by Lord Canning, Dalhousie's successor as Governor-General, the Act required only new recruits to the Bengal Army to accept a commitment for general service. However, serving high-caste sepoys were fearful that it would be eventually extended to them, as well as preventing sons following fathers into an Army with a strong tradition of family service.

24. **(d)** To keep the British at bay and to enlist their support against the Moghuls, the Marathas, who had founded their own empire/kingdom made friends with the Portuguese and signed with them a treaty in 1779. Under this, the Maratha-Peshwa agreed that the Portuguese would be allowed to collect revenues from Dadra and Nagar Haveli which consisted of 72 villages (then known as parganas, now referred to as district places). It was annexed by India from Portugal on 2 August 1954. The people of the territory established free administration of Dadra and Nagar Haveli, which was finally merged into the Union of India in 1961.

25. **(b)** Samudragupta, ruler of the Gupta Empire (c. 335 - c. 375 CE), and successor to Chandragupta I, is considered to be one of the greatest military geniuses in Indian history. He was the third ruler of the Gupta Dynasty, who ushered in the Golden Age of India. He was perhaps the greatest king of Gupta dynasty. He was a benevolent ruler, a great warrior and a patron of arts. His name appears in the Javanese text `Tantrikamandaka'.

26. **(a)** Dadabhai Naoroji (4 September 1825 - 30 June 1917), known as the Grand Old Man of India, was a Parsi intellectual, educator, cotton trader, and an early Indian political and social leader. He was a Member of Parliament (MP) in the United Kingdom House of Commons between 1892 and 1895, and the first Asian to be a British MP. Naoroji is also credited with the founding of the Indian National Congress, along with A.O. Hume and Dinshaw Edulji Wacha. His book Poverty and Un-British Rule in India brought attention to the draining of India's wealth into Britain.

27. **(b)** Nothing in the foregoing provisions of this Part shall derogate from the power of Parliament to make any provision with respect to the acquisition and termination of citizenship and all other matters relating to citizenship.

28. **(a)** Rajatarangini is a metrical historical chronicle of northwestern Indian subcontinent, particularly the kings of Kashmir, written in Sanskrit by Kashmiri Brahman Kalhana in 12th century CE. The work generally records the heritage of Kashmir, but 120 verses of Rajatarangini describe the misrule prevailing in Kashmir during the reign of King Kalash, son of King Ananta Deva of Kashmir. Although the earlier books are inaccurate in their chronology, they still provide an invaluable source of information about early Kashmir and its neighbors in the north western parts of the Indian subcontinent, and are widely referenced by later historians and ethnographers.

29. **(a)** This day was being celebrated as the Independence Day since 1929

30. **(d)** Samudragupta, ruler of the Gupta Empire (c. 335 - c. 375 CE), and successor to Chandragupta I, is considered to be one of the greatest military geniuses in Indian history. He was the third ruler of the Gupta Dynasty, who ushered in the Golden Age of India. His title of Kaviraja (King of poets) is justified by various poetical compositions.

31. **(a)** The decision to effect the Partition of Bengal was announced in July 1905 by the Viceroy of India, Lord Curzon. The partition took place in October 1905 and separated the largely Muslim eastern areas from the largely Hindu western areas.

32. **(d)** The democratic system in India is based on the principle of Universal Adult Suffrage. All citizens of India who are 18 years of age as on 1st January of the year for which the electoral roll is prepared are entitled to be registered as a voter in the constituency where he or she ordinarily resides. Only persons who are of unsound mind and have been declared so by a competent court or disqualified due to 'Corrupt Practices' or offences relating to elections are not entitled to be registered in the electoral rolls. The right to vote is irrespective of caste, creed, religion or gender.

33. **(d)** Centres control of the State in the planning process.

34. **(a)** Satyameva Jayate is a mantra from the ancient Indian scripture Mundaka Upanishad. Upon independence of India, it was adopted as the national motto of India. It is inscribed in Devanagari script at the base of the national emblem. The emblem and the words "Satyameva Jayate" are inscribed on one side of all Indian currency. The emblem is an adaptation of the Lion Capital of Ashoka which was erected around 250 BC at Sarnath, near Varanasi in the north Indian state of Uttar Pradesh.

35. **(b)** A political party is officially accorded the status of an opposition party in Lok Sabha, only if it secures at least 10 percent of the seats.

36. **(d)** Twenty one Vice Presidents are elected at the start of each regular session of General Assembly.

37. **(b)** M. A. Ansari was the Congress President at the Madras session of 1927, when it boycotted the Simon Commission.

38. **(c)** Ashoka invaded Kalinga in 261 B. C. In this war more than 2 lakh people died, wounded and made prisoners in war. Such a huge carnage and massacre of human lives and the sufferings of the wounded made a deep impression on Ashoka's mind. So he decided to spare his life to the spread of Buddhism around the world.

39. **(c)**

40. **(d)** The Jama 'at-Khana-Masjid or Khilji mosque was built in 1325 by Khizr Khan, son of Alauddin Khilji while all the other monuments were built by Allauddin Khilji.

41. **(a)** During the invasion Alexander, Nanda dynasty was ruling the North India in the Magadha empire.

Geography/General Science

1. Which one of the following soils is most suitable for cotton cultivation *[2011-I]*
   (a) Red soil (b) Black soil
   (c) Loamy soil (d) Laterite soil

2. Equinox means two days in a year when day and night are almost equal. If March 21 is an equinox which is the next ? *[2011-I]*
   (a) 09 October (b) 31 August
   (c) 23 September (d) 03 November

3. Vitamin necessary to prevent prolonged bleeding is *[2011-I]*
   (a) Vitamin A (b) Vitamin E
   (c) Vitamin D (d) Vitamin K

4. The term 'Carbon Credit' is associated with *[2011-I]*
   (a) Coal reserve of a nation
   (b) Reduction of Green House Gas emissions
   (c) Fossil Fuel reserve
   (d) Amount of CO_2 an individual emits in a year

5. India tops the world in production of *[2011-II]*
   (a) Aluminium (b) Copper
   (c) Chromite (d) Mica

6. DPT vaccine does not give protection to a child from *[2011-II]*
   (a) Tetanus (b) Polio
   (c) Diphtheria (d) Whooping Cough

7. What will be the colour of a red rose when it is seen through green glass ? *[2011-II]*
   (a) White (b) Black
   (c) Pink (d) Brown

8. Which one of the following crops enriches nitrogen content in the soil ? *[2011-II]*
   (a) Pea (b) Sunflower
   (c) Potato (d) Wheat

9. Which of the following periodical winds blowing from sea to land cause summer monsoon in India ? *[2011-II]*
   (a) East West (b) North East
   (c) South West (d) South East

10. India's permanent research station 'Dakshin Gangotri" is situated in the *[2011-II]*
    (a) Great Himalayas (b) Indian Ocean
    (c) Arabian Sea (d) Antarctica

11. Which one of the following is the busiest ocean route in the world ? *[2011-II]*
    (a) Indian Ocean (b) Pacific Ocean
    (c) North Atlantic Ocean (d) South Atlantic Ocean

12. The sun rises in Arunachal Pradesh two hours before it does in Dwaraka in Gujarat. This is because the former is *[2012-I]*
    (a) higher in elevation than Dwaraka and the earth rotates from West to East.
    (b) situated further North than Dwaraka and the earth rotates from West to East.
    (c) situated further East (about 30° Longitude) than dwaraka and the earth rotates from West to East.
    (d) situated about 30° East of Dwaraka and the earth rotates from West to East.

13. Srinagar is situated on the banks of the river *[2012-I]*
    (a) Ravi (b) Sutlej
    (c) Jhelum (d) Chenab

14. The areas in India that receive approximately an average of more than 200 cms of rainfall annually are *[2012-I]*
    (a) Meghalaya, Assam, Nagaland, Arunachal Pradesh.
    (b) Odisha, Madhya Pradesh, Gujarat, Maharashtra.
    (c) Meghalaya, Assam, Rajasthan, Jammu & Kashmir.
    (d) Meghalaya, Delhi, Punjab, Rajasthan.

15. Isotherms are imaginary lines drawn on a map which connect places of equal *[2012-I]*
    (a) Atmospheric pressure (b) Humidity
    (c) Rainfall (d) Temperature

16. Jim Corbett National Park is situated in which state ? *[2012-I]*
    (a) Arunachal Pradesh (b) Himachal Pradesh
    (c) Andhra Pradesh (d) Uttaranchal

17. Which one of the following statement regarding the sun is correct ? *[2012-I]*
    (a) The sun is composed mainly of hydrogen.
    (b) Its energy is generated by nuclear collision in its interior.
    (c) It is calculated that the sun consumes about a trillion pounds of hydrogen every second.
    (d) All of the above.

18. Supersonic speed is speed greater than the speed of sound (in air at sea level) that is to say around______ miles/hour. *[2012-I]*
    (a) 760 (b) 860
    (c) 960 (d) 1060

19. An aeroplane rises because   *[2012-I]*
   (a) of upward reaction of air.
   (b) the density of air above the plane is less than below it.
   (c) the pressure above its wings is less than the pressure below them.
   (d) its nose points upwards.

20. Rocks formed on the solidification of molten matter are called   *[2012-I]*
   (a) Metamorphic   (b) Sedimentary rocks
   (c) Volcanic rocks   (d) Igneous rocks

21. River Jhelum emerges from   *[2012-II]*
   (a) Northern slopes of the Kailash range
   (b) Spring at Verinarg
   (c) Rakas Lake
   (d) Amarkantak plateau

22. Haematite ores is the ore of which metal ?   *[2012-II]*
   (a) Iron   (b) Aluminium
   (c) Zink-   (d) Cobalt

23. Green revolution relates to which of the following ?   *[2012-II]*
   (a) Self-dependence in foodgrains production
   (b) Self-dependence in milk production
   (c) Self-dependence in petroleum crude oil production
   (d) None of the above

24. Vertebrates have two endocrine glands associated with the brain, namely   *[2012-II]*
   (a) Thyroid, Thymus   (b) Pituitary, Pancreas
   (c) Pituitary, Pineal (d) Pancreas, Pineal

25. The layer common to two adjacent plant cells called Middle Lamella is composed of   *[2012-II]*
   (a) Calcium Phosphate (b) Calcium Sulphate
   (c) Calcium Carbonate (d) Calcium Pectate

26. With the increase of the effective nuclear charge, the size of the atom or ion   *[2012-II]*
   (a) increases
   (b) decreases
   (c) remain the same, since it has no bearing on size
   (d) it will depend on period to period and group to group

27. On which of the following statements, is the kinetic theory of matter base ?   *[2012-II]*
   (a) Matter is made up of molecules
   (b) Molecules are in rapid motion
   (c) Molecules experience forces of attraction between one another
   (d) All of the above

28. When heated with chloroform, secondary amines and tertiary amines   *[2012-II]*
   (a) gives isocyanides
   (b) gives cyanides
   (c) do not give isocyanides
   (d) Both (a) and (b)

29. The elements which have low value of ionization potential are strong   *[2013-I]*
   (a) oxidising agents
   (b) reducing agents
   (c) oxidising and Reducing agents depending upon the reactants
   (d) none of these

30. Term 'Visible Horizon' in astronomy is defined as   *[2013-I]*
   (a) The circle of contact of the earth and the cone of visual rays passing through the meridian of the place
   (b) The circle of contact of the earth and the cone of visual rays not passing through the meridian of the place
   (c) The circle of contact of the earth and the cone of visual rays passing through the point of observation
   (d) The circle of contact of the earth and the cone of visual rays not passing through the point of observation

31. River Satluj originates from   *[2013-I]*
   (a) Northern slopes of the Kailash range
   (b) Spring at Verinag
   (c) Rakas Lake
   (d) Amarkantak plateau

32. Limonitic ore is the ore of which metal ?   *[2013-I]*
   (a) Iron (b)   Aluminium
   (c) Zinc (d)   Cobalt

33. Black revolution relates to which of the following ?   *[2013-I]*
   (a) Self-dependence in foodgrains production
   (b) Self-dependence in milk production
   (c) Self-dependence in petroleum/crude oil
   (d) None of these

34. ___________ is a thyroid hormone which controls the balance of calcium in the body   *[2013-I]*
   (a) Calcitonin   (b) Thyroxine
   (c) Calmodulin   (d) All of these

35. The cell wall in plants is interrupted by narrow pores carrying fine strands of cytoplasm which interlink the contents of the cells. These strands are called:-   *[2013-I]*
   (a) Plasmohole   (b) Microvilli
   (c) Plasmodesmata   (d) Plasmalemma

36. The transport phenomenon occurs only in __________ state of a gas and is __________.   *[2013-I]*
   (a) non-equilibrium, irreversible
   (b) non-equilibrium, reversible
   (c) equilibrium, irreversible
   (d) equilibrium, reversible

37. Which of the following compounds form nitrites with nitrous acid ?   *[2013-I]*
   (a) Primary amines   (b) Secondary amines
   (c) Tertiary amines   (d) All of these

38. On which river is Washington DC situated ?   *[2014-I]*
   (a) Potomac   (b) Irrawaddy
   (c) Mississippi   (d) Hudson

39. When body is accelerated: *[2014-I]*
   (a) Its velocity never changes
   (b) Its speed will always changes
   (c) Its direction always changes

(d) Its speed may or may not change

40. Which of the following is not a unit of energy ? *[2014-I]*
   (a) Calorie   (b) Joule
   (c) Electron volt   (d) Watt

41. The Baglihar Hydroelectric power project in J & K is built across the river. *[2014-I]*
   (a) Beas   (b) Chenab
   (c) Jhelum   (d) Sutlej

42. Which is the longest bone in the human body ? *[2014-I]*
   (a) Fibula   (b) Radius
   (c) Stapes   (d) Femur

43. A US team of scientists has found that the mechanism responsible for the ageing process is located *[2014-I]*
   (a) inside the face   (b) inside the skin
   (c) inside the brain   (d) inside the heart

44. The outer most layer of the Sun is known as *[2014-I]*
   (a) Corona   (b) Photosphere
   (c) Chromosphere   (d) Granule

45. Which one of the following pairs of water bodies are connected by the Suez Canal ? *[2014-I]*
   (a) Indian Ocean- Pacific Ocean
   (b) Mediterranean sea- Black Sea
   (c) Mediterranean Sea-Red Sea
   (d) Atlantic Ocean- Pacific Ocean

46. Which of the following is not correctly matched ? *[2014-I]*
   (a) Indonesia - Jakarta   (b) Maldives - Male
   (c) North Korea - Seoul   (d) Zimbabwe - Harare

47. Algae often float on surface of water during day but sink during night due to:- *[2014-II]*
   (a) evolution and trapping of oxygen bubbles during the day in their photosynthesis process
   (b) Becoming light as they consume most of their food in the night
   (c) warming action of sun during the day
   (d) Release of absorbed air by warming of water

48. On which river is Berlin city situated ? *[2014-II]*
   (a) Potomac   (b) Irrawaddy
   (c) Rhine   (d) Spree

49. What is the splash and burn agriculture' in Indonesia called as ? *[2014-II]*
   (a) Jhoom cultivation   (b) Roke cultivation
   (c) Milpa cultivation   (d) Ladang cultivation

50. Which theory gave birth to the French Revolution and the Revolution in America ? *[2014-II]*
   (a) Legal theory of rights
   (b) Theory of natural rights
   (c) Social welfare theory
   (d) Historical theory of rights

51. 38th parallel is a boundary line between _______ *[2014-II]*
   (a) United States and Canada
   (b) Pakistan and India
   (c) Turkey and Cyprus
   (d) South and North Korea

52. The branch of science that studies cells is called *[2015-I]*
   (a) Cytology   (b) Entomology
   (c) Homoplastic   (d) Hormonolgy

53. Kaziranga National Park is famous for *[2015-I]*
   (a) One-horned Rhinos
   (b) Tigers
   (c) Swamp Dears (Barasingha)
   (d) Elephants

Hints & Solutions

1. **(b)** Black soil is most suitable for cotton cultivation, locally called regard or black cotton soils, and internationally known as 'tropical black earths' or 'tropical chernozems' have been developed by the weathering of the Deccan lava in majorparts of Maharashtra, western MadhyaPrades, Gujarat, Andhra Pradesh, Karnataka, Rajasthan, Tamil Nadu and Uttar Pradesh.

2. **(c)** An equinox occurs twice a year, around 20 March and 22 September. If march 21 is an equinox then next equinox will be 23 september.

3. **(d)** Vitamin K is a group of structurally similar, fat-soluble vitamins that the human body needs for modification of certain proteins that are required for blood coagulation, and in bone and other tissue.

4. **(c)** The term Carbon Credit is associated with Reduction of Green House Gas emissions in the atmosphere.

5. **(d)** The British Geological Survey reported that as of 2005, Koderma district in Jharkhand state in India had the largest deposits of mica in the world.

6. **(b)** DPT (also DTP and DTwP) refers to a class of combination vaccines against three infectious diseases in humans: diphtheria, pertussis (whooping cough), and tetanus.

7. **(b)** Black, because red and green are two primary colours which when mixed together gives black colour in terms of light and wavelength.

8. **(a)** Many legumes (alfalfa, clover, peas, beans, lentils, soybeans, peanuts and others) contain symbiotic bacteria called Rhizobia within root nodules of their root systems.These bacteria have the special ability of fixing nitrogen from atmospheric, molecular nitrogen (N_2) into ammonia (NH_3).

9. **(c)** The southwestern summer monsoons occur from June through September. The moisture-laden winds from the Indian Ocean rush in to the subcontinent. These winds, rich in moisture, are drawn towards the Himalayas. The Himalayas act like a high wall, blocking the winds from passing into Central Asia, and forcing them to rise. As the clouds rise their temperature drops and precipitation occurs.

10. **(d)** Dakshin Gangotri was the first scientific base station of India situated in Antarctica, part of the Indian Antarctic Program. It is located at a distance of 2,500 kilometres from the South Pole.

11. **(c)** The North Atlantic sea route, linking the US and Canada to Europe, is very busy as well.

12. **(c)** Situated further East (about 30o Longitude) than Dwaraka and the earth rotates from West to East.

13. **(c)** Srinagar is the summer capital of the Indian State of Jammu and Kashmir. It is situated in the Kashmir Valley and lies on the banks of the Jhelum River, a tributary of the Indus. The city is famous for its gardens, lakes and houseboats. It is also known for traditional Kashmiri handicrafts and dry fruits.

14. **(a)** Meghalaya, Assam, Nagaland, Arunachal Pradesh. Mawsynram, the wettest place on earth (annual rainfall of 1,141 cm approx), is a small village in Meghalaya's Khasi Hills near Shillong. Cherrapunji, now the second wettest place on earth, is located 10 km from Mawsynram and has the distinction of having just one season the year round - monsoon. It receives about 1,087 cm of rain annually.

15. **(d)** Isotherm, line drawn on a map or chart joining points with the same temperature.

16. **(d)** Jim Corbett National Park is the oldest national park in India and was established in 1936 as Hailey National Park to protect the endangered Bengal tiger. It is located in Nainital district of Uttarakhand(Earlier Uttaranchal) and was named after Jim Corbett who played a key role in its establishment. The park was the first to come under the Project Tiger initiative.

17. **(d)**

18. **(a)** Supersonic speed speed is approximately 343.2 m/s, 1,125 ft/s, 768 mph, 667 knots, or 1,235 km/h.

19. **(c)**

20. **(d)** Igneous rock is formed through the cooling and solidification of magma or lava.

21. **(b)** Verinag is approximately 80 km from Srinagar, by road, at an elevation of 1,876 m. It is believed that the eponymous Verinag spring is the chief source of the river Jhelum. There is an octagonal base at the spring, surrounded by a covered passage.

22. **(a)** Hematite, also spelled as haematite, is the mineral form of iron oxide, one of several iron oxides. Hematite crystallizes in the rhombohedral lattice system, and it has the same crystal structure as ilmenite and corundum.

23. **(a)**

24. **(c)** The endocrine system refers to the collection of glands of an organism that secrete hormones directly into the circulatory system to be carried toward a distant target organ. The major endocrine glands include the pineal gland, pituitary gland, pancreas, ovaries, testes, thyroid gland, parathyroid gland, hypothalamus, gastrointestinal tract and adrenal glands.

25. **(d)** The middle lamella is a pectin layer which cements the cell walls of two adjoining cells together. Plants need this to give them stability and so that they can form plasmodesmata between the cells. It is the first formed layer which is deposited at the time of cytokinesis. The cell plate that is formed during cell division itself develops into middle lamella or lamellum. The middle lamella is made up of calcium and magnesium pectates. In plants, the pectins form an unified and continuous layer between adjacent cells.

26. (d) The effective nuclear charge is the net positive charge experienced by an electron in a multi-electron atom. The term "effective" is used because the shielding effect of negatively charged electrons prevents higher orbital electrons from experiencing the full nuclear charge by the repelling effect of inner-layer electrons. The effective nuclear charge experienced by the outer shell electron is also called the core charge. It is possible to determine the strength of the nuclear charge by looking at the oxidation number of the atom.

27. (c)

28. (b)

29. (b) Elements with a low ionization energy tend to be reducing agents and form cations.

30. (c) In astronomy the horizon is the horizontal plane through (the eyes of) the observer. It is the fundamental plane of the horizontal coordinate system, the locus of points that have an altitude of zero degrees. While similar in ways to the geometrical horizon, in this context a horizon may be considered to be a plane in space, rather than a line on a picture plane.

31. (c) The Sutlej is sometimes known as the Red River. It is the easternmost tributary of the Indus River. Its source is Lake Rakshastal in Tibet. From there, it flows at first west-northwest for about 260 kilometres (160 mi) to the Shipki La pass, entering India in Himachal Pradesh state. It then turns slightly, heading west-southwest for about 360 kilometres (220 mi) to meet the Beas River near Makhu, Firozpur district, Punjab state.

32. (a) Limonite is an iron ore consisting of a mixture of hydrated iron(III) oxide-hydroxides in varying composition.

33. (c) Black revolution is related to self dependence in petroleum/crude oil.

34. (a) The thyroid also produces calcitonin, which plays a role in calcium homeostasis.

35. (c) Plasmodesmata (singular: plasmodesma) are microscopic channels which traverse the cell walls of plant cells and some algal cells, enabling transport and communication between them. Plasmodesmata evolved independently in several lineages, and species that have these structures.

36. (a) The aim of statistical mechanics is the interpretation and prediction of the observed macroscopic properties of matter in terms of the mechanical properties of the constituent molecules and the nature of the interaction among them. It is restricted to the non-equilibrium statistical mechanics of non-reacting gases that is to the theory of transport phenomena.

37. (d)

38. (a) The Potomac River is located along the mid-Atlantic coast of the United States and flows into the Chesapeake Bay. The river (main stem and North Branch) is approximately 405 miles (652 km) long, with a drainage area of about 14,700 square miles (38,000 km²). The river forms part of the borders between Maryland and Washington, D.C., on the left descending bank and West Virginia and Virginia on the river's right descending bank.

39. (b)

40. (d) The watt is a derived unit of power in the International System of Units, named after the Scottish engineer James Watt. The unit defined as one joule per second, measures the rate of energy conversion or transfer.

41. (b) Baglihar Dam, also known as Baglihar Hydroelectric Power Project, is a run-of-the-river power project on the Chenab River in the southern Doda district of the Indian state of Jammu and Kashmir. The project is estimated to cost USD $1 billion. The first phase of the Baglihar Dam was completed in 2004. With the second phase completed on 10 October 2008, Prime Minister Manmohan Singh of India dedicated the 900-MW Baglihar hydroelectric power project to the nation.

42. (d) The head of the femur articulates with the acetabulum in the pelvic bone forming the hip joint, while the distal part of the femur articulates with the tibia and patella forming the knee joint. By most measures the femur is the strongest bone in the body. The femur is also the longest bone in the body.

43. (c) The US team of scientists found the mechanism in the hypothalamus- which is located deep inside the brain- and showed that it is responsible for the ageing process. Scientists carried out a series of experiments to find that they could extend the lives of mice by a fifth, without the problems such as animals suffering from muscle weakness, bone loss or memory problems associated with old age.

44. (b) The visible surface of the Sun, the photosphere, is the layer below which the Sun becomes opaque to visible light. Above the photosphere visible sunlight is free to propagate into space, and its energy escapes the Sun entirely.

45. (c) The Suez Canal is an artificial sea-level waterway in Egypt, connecting the Mediterranean Sea and the Red Sea.

46. (c) Seoul is the capital of South Korea. Pyongyang is the capital of North Korea.

47. (a) The reason of algae float to the surface during the day & sink at night is due to photosynthesis. In Day time, the algae is producing oxygen. When enough Oxygen is produced during the day , it gets trapped in bubbles and it can lift the clumps up to the surface. In night, this oxygen is consumed and CO_2 is produced. So algae sinks.

48. (d) Berlin is the capital city of Germany. Berlin is located in northeastern Germany on the River Spree, it is the center of the Berlin-Brandenburg Metropolitan Region.

49. (a) In Indonesia the 'splash and burn agriculture' is called as jhoom cultivation.

50. (b) Theory of natural rights gave birth to the French Revolution and the Revolution in America.

51. (d) The 38th parallel north is a circle of latitude that is 38 degrees north of the Earth's equatorial plane. It crosses Europe, the Mediterranean Sea, Asia, the Pacific Ocean, North America, and the Atlantic Ocean. The 38th parallel north formed the border between North and South Korea prior to the Korean War.

52. (a) The branch of science that studies cells is called Cytology.

53. (a) Kaziranga National Park is a national park in the Golaghat and Nagaon districts of the state of Assam, India. A World Heritage Site, the park hosts two-thirds of the world's great one-horned rhinoceroses.

3   Miscellaneous (Defence/Sports/ Current Affairs & Others)

1. The winner of the highest number of gold medals in an Olympic game is   *[2011-I]*
   - (a) Mark Spitz
   - (b) Matt Biondi
   - (c) Michael Phelps
   - (d) Jenny Thompson
2. 'Agha Khan Cup' is associated with the game of *[2011-I]*
   - (a) Football
   - (b) Hockey
   - (c) Badminton
   - (d) Cricket
3. Usain Bolt, the 100 meters race world record holder, is from which country ?   *[2011-I]*
   - (a) Jamaica
   - (b) U.S.A.
   - (c) Canada
   - (d) Nigeria
4. Only two cricket players have taken 10 wickets in an innings. One is Anil Kumble. The other is   *[2011-I]*
   - (a) Richard Hadlee
   - (b) Muttiah Muralidharan
   - (c) Jim Laker
   - (d) Andy Roberts
5. The highest Indian gallantry award which could be given in peace time is   *[2011-I]*
   - (a) Ashok Chakra
   - (b) Param Vir Chakra
   - (c) Kirti Chakra
   - (d) Param Vishisht Seva Medal
6. The most successful Satellite Launch Vehicle of Indian Space Programme to launch commercial satellites is known as   *[2011-I]*
   - (a) SLV
   - (b) ASLV
   - (c) PSLV
   - (d) GSLV
7. The name of indigenously built Light Combat Aircraft is   *[2011-I]*
   - (a) Tejas
   - (b) Chakra
   - (c) Vajra
   - (d) Trishul
8. Who authored the book 'Train to Pakistan'?   *[2011-I]*
   - (a) Salman Rushdie
   - (b) Khushwant Singh
   - (c) Mulk Raj Anand
   - (d) Vikram Seth
9. The famous classical dance form of Andhra Pradesh is   *[2011-I]*
   - (a) Kathakali
   - (b) Kuchipudi
   - (c) Mohini Attam
   - (d) Yakshaagna
10. 'Borlaug Award' is given every year to an Indian scientist for outstanding contribution in the field of   *[2011-I]*
    - (a) Medicine
    - (b) Space
    - (c) Applied Science
    - (d) Agriculture
11. UNHCR, an organisation of United Nations, was established to provide/promote   *[2011-I]*
    - (a) Primary Education
    - (b) Health and Culture
    - (c) Relief
    - (d) Protection to refugees
12. 'Duckworth Lewis Rule' is used in the game of *[2011-II]*
    - (a) Lawn Tennis
    - (b) Cricket
    - (c) Basketball
    - (d) Rugby
13. Dronacharya award is given for outstanding contribution in the field of   *[2011-II]*
    - (a) Sports
    - (b) Sarv Shiksha Abhiyan
    - (c) Anganwadi
    - (d) Music
14. The first Olympic Games were held in 1896 at   *[2011-II]*
    - (a) Rome
    - (b) Athens
    - (c) Paris
    - (d) London
15. Indigenously build supersonic cruise missile is known as   *[2011-II]*
    - (a) Brahmos
    - (b) Prithvi
    - (c) Nag
    - (d) Astra
16. Defence Services Staff College is located at   *[2011-II]*
    - (a) Khadakvasala
    - (b) Secunderabad
    - (c) Dehradun
    - (d) Wellington
17. Who authored the book "Freedom at Midnight"? *[2011-II]*
    - (a) Salman Rushdie
    - (b) Charles Dickens
    - (c) Mahatma Gandhi
    - (d) Larry Collins and Dominique Lapierre
18. Who was the first Indian woman to climb Mount Everest ?   *[2011-II]*
    - (a) Junko Tabei
    - (b) Bachendri Pal
    - (c) Dola Banerjee
    - (d) Sanamacha Chanu
19. The United Nations Organisations responsible to maintain international peace & security, was established on 24 October in the year   *[2011-II]*
    - (a) 1920
    - (b) 1945
    - (c) 1939
    - (d) 1942
20. Yoga sutra was written by   *[2012-I]*
    - (a) Vatsyayana
    - (b) Patanjali
    - (c) Bhartrihari
    - (d) Maharshi Mahesh
21. The pioneer of Atomic energy in India is
    - (a) Homi J Bhabha
    - (b) Vikram Sarabhai
    - (c) C.V. Raman
    - (d) C.K. Naidu
22. Which one of the following statements regarding FIFA World Cup 2010 is not correct ?   *[2012-I]*
    - (a) South Africa became the first host nation to fail to qualify for the tournament's second round.
    - (b) The tournament was the culmination of a qualification process that began in August 2007.
    - (c) This is the first time that the tournament was hosted by an African nation.
    - (d) Zakumi, the official mascot for the FIFA World Cup, 2010 is an African bush elephant.

23. The first Indian to win the World Amateur Snooker Championship is *[2012-I]*
(a) Om Agarwal (b) Geet Sethi
(c) Michael Ferreira (d) Wilson Jones

24. The first person to win the Arjuna award for badminton is *[2012-I]*
(a) Pullela Gopichand (b) Prakash Padukone
(c) Nandu Natekar (d) Farook Engineer

25. The sport which requires the largest field is *[2012-I]*
(a) Football (b) Cricket
(c) Hockey (d) Polo

26. The National Institute of Oceanography is located at *[2012-I]*
(a) Trivandrum (b) Panaji
(c) Cochin (d) Mangalore

27. With which sport is Lewis Hamilton associated ? *[2012-II]*
(a) Golf (b) Hockey
(c) Billiards (d) F – 1

28. From which country does the top seeded Tennis player Rafael Nadal hail from ? *[2012-II]*
(a) France (b) Germany
(c) Spain (d) Russia

29. Which Indian Boxer won the gold medal in 60 kg category in Asian game and became the youngest to win a boxing gold for India ? *[2012-II]*
(a) Vijendra Singh (b) Vikas Krishan
(c) Ranjan Sodhi (d) Somdev

30. In 2010 Leander Paes in partnership with Cara Black won the mixed doubles title of *[2012-II]*
(a) Australian Open Tennis Championship
(b) Wimblendon Open Tennis Championship
(c) Both of the above
(d) None of the above

31. Nuclear Submarine Akula has been handed over to India recently by *[2012-II]*
(a) France (b) Germany
(c) USA (d) Russia

32. Who is the author of book 'The Fragrance of Forgotten Years' ? *[2012-II]*
(a) David Omand (b) Bilkees Latif
(c) Pranab Bardhan (d) Jagat S. Mehta

33. MNREGA stands for *[2012-II]*
(a) Mahatma Gandhi National Revenue Engagement Guarantee Association
(b) Maharaja National Revenue Employment Guarantee Act
(c) Mahanagar National Rural Employment Guarantee Act
(d) Mahatma Gandhi National Rural Employment Guarantee Act

34. Wayne Rooney, the famous footballer, hails from which country ? *[2013-I]*
(a) Italy (b) Brazil
(c) Argentina (d) England

35. The official song 'Waka Waka' of FIFA World Cup held in the year 2010 at South Africa was sung by which popular singer ? *[2013-I]*
(a) Madonna (b) Destiny Child
(c) Shakira (d) Rehanna

36. In the year 2011, the ace badminton player Saina Nehwal was honoured with which sports award ? *[2013-I]*
(a) Dronacharya award
(b) Rajiv Gandhi Khel Ratna award
(c) Arjun award
(d) None of these

37. Karrar is the unmanned bomber aircraft of *[2013-I]*
(a) Iraq (b) Iran
(c) Turkey (d) Pakistan

38. Who is the author of book 'Keeping the Faith: Members of a Parliamentarian'? *[2013-I]*
(a) David Omand (b) Raja Shehadeh
(c) Raghav Bahl (d) Somnath Chatterjee

39. Who is the cricketer bestowed with an honorary commission in the Territorial Army ? *[2013-I]*
(a) Sachin Tendulkar (b) Kapil Dev
(c) Virendra Sehwag (d) Harbhajan Singh

40. NREGA stands for *[2013-I]*
(a) National Revenue Engagement Guarantee Association
(b) National Revenue Employment Guarantee Act
(c) National Rural Employment Guarantee Association
(d) National Rural Employment Guarantee Act

41. Which of the following is not an agency of UN ? *[2014-I]*
(a) World Bank
(b) International Atomic Energy Agency
(c) Universal Postal Union
(d) None of the above

42. Which kind of missile is BRAHMOS ? *[2014-I]*
(a) Medium range ballistic missile
(b) Supersonic cruise missile
(c) Short range tactical missile
(d) Ultrasonic cruise missile

43. Which Indian sportsperson was appointed as 'Messenger of Peace' in 2001 by the UN ? *[2014-I]*
(a) Prakash Padukone (b) Vishwanathan Anand
(c) Sachin Tendulkar (d) Vijay Amritraj

44. Indian Women's hockey team secured which of the following position in Asian Champions Trophy 2013 ? *[2014-I]*
(a) First (b) Second
(c) Third (d) Fourth

45. Which among the following is not a gallantry medal ? *[2014-I]*
(a) Ashok Chakra (b) Arjuna Award
(c) Param Vir Chakra (d) Shaurya Chakra

46. Indian Institute of Science, Bangalore was founded by *[2014-I]*
(a) CV Raman (b) Jamsetji Tata
(c) Vikram Sarabhai (d) None of these

47. Who is the author of 'Train to Pakistan':- *[2014-II]*
(a) Arun Shourie (b) J.N. Dixit
(c) Khushwant Singh (d) Ismat Chugtai

48. The commonwealth Games Relay Baton has traditionally contained ? *[2014-II]*
(a) sand from the last host city
(b) a message from the Head of the Commonwealth
(c) The commonwealth Games Motto
(d) sand from each competing nation

49. When is the World Poetry Day recognized by the UNESCO observed ? *[2014-II]*
(a) 02 February
(b) 30 December
(c) 21 March
(d) 14 February

50. Who was the first Commander in chief of Indian Air Force in Independent India ? *[2014-II]*
(a) Gen KM Kariyappa
(b) Field Marshal Sam Manekshaw
(c) Major Stringer Lawrence
(d) Thomas Walker Elmhirst

51. Who was the first woman to climb Mount Everest ? *[2014-II]*
(a) Junko Tabei
(b) Tenzing Norgay
(c) Aarti Pradhan
(d) Bachendri Pal

52. Who founded the Asiatic Society of Bengal in Kolkata? *[2014-II]*
(a) Warren Hastings
(b) John Shore
(c) Sir William Jones
(d) Lord Cornwallis

53. The youngest mountain range in the world is:- *[2014-II]*
(a) Himalayas
(b) Alps
(c) Andes
(d) Rockies

54. Who amongst the following in the author of the book 'A Bend in the River? *[2015-I]*
(a) Chetan Bhagat
(b) VS Naipaul
(c) Kiran Desai
(d) Anita Desai

55. 'Long Walk to Freedom' is a book written by *[2015-I]*
(a) Sonia Gandhi
(b) LK Advani
(c) Nelson Mandela
(d) Benazir Bhutto

56. Which sports personality has been awarded the honorary rank of Group Captain by the IAF? *[2015-I]*
(a) Kapil Dev
(b) Sania Mirza
(c) Saina Nehwal
(d) Sachin Tendulkar

57. Which county among the following has been declared Ebola-free by WHO? *[2015-I]*
(a) Sierra leone
(b) Liberia
(c) Nigeria
(d) Guinea

58. How many Gold medals did India win in the Incheon Asian Games held in Oct 2014? *[2015-I]*
(a) 10
(b) 11
(c) 12
(d) 8

59. Who has been appointed as the new Finance Secretary of India? *[2015-I]*
(a) Arvind Mayaram
(b) Rajiv Mehrishi
(c) Kaushik Basu
(d) Dinesh Gupta

60. Which among the following is India's first long range subsonic cruise missile? *[2015-I]*
(a) Agni II
(b) Prithvi
(c) Dhanush
(d) Nirbhay

61. The highest civilian award of India 'Bharat Ratna' has been awarded to only two foreigners so far. One of them is Nelson Mandela. The other is *[2015-I]*
(a) Marshal Tito
(b) Mikhail Gorbachev
(c) Khan Abdul Ghaffar Khan
(d) Abdul Wali Khan

62. Sir CV Raman was awarded Nobel Prize for his work connected with which of the following phenomenon of radiation? *[2015-I]*
(a) Scattering
(b) Diffraction
(c) Interference
(d) Polarisation

63. In which city is headquarters of Asian Development Bank located? *[2015-I]*
(a) Manila
(b) Singapore
(c) Bangkok
(d) Jakarta

64. K-15 missile is *[2015-I]*
(a) Submarine launched Ballistic Missile (SLBM)
(b) Inter Continental Ballistic Missile (ICBM)
(c) Medium Range Ballistic Missile (MRBM)
(d) Short Range Ballistic Missile (SRBM)

65. India agreed to UN Chief Ban ki-Moon's offer to remain as a member of the advisory board of one of the following recently. *[2015-I]*
(a) UNCCT
(b) UNICEF
(c) UNEP
(d) UNCTAD

66. Who was the first Indian to win an individual medal in Olympics? *[2015-I]*
(a) Milkha Singh
(b) PT Usha
(c) Karnam Malleshwari
(d) KD Jadhav

67. Which of the following Intercontinental Ballistic Missiles (ICBMs) is under development in India? *[2015-I]*
(a) Agni-I
(b) Agni-II
(c) Agni-IV
(d) Agni-VI

68. Who among the following was adjudged as the Most Valuable Plaer of the 17th Asian Games held at Incheon, South Korea? *[2015-I]*
(a) Mary Kom of India
(b) Kosuke Hagino of Japan
(c) Ning Zetao of China
(d) None of these

Hints & Solutions

1. (c) Michael Fred Phelps (born June 30, 1985) is an American swimmer and 14-time Olympic gold medallist (the most by any Olympian), who currently holds seven world records in swimming. He holds the record for the most gold medals won at a single Olympics; a total of eight, surpassing Mark Spitz, also a swimmer. Overall, Phelps has won 16 Olympic medals: six gold and two bronze at Athens in 2004, and eight gold at the 2008 Summer Olympics in Beijing.

2. (a) The Agha Khan Gold Cup was played in Dhaka, East Pakistan(Bangladesh) which invited top club sides from leading football playing nations to compete.

3. (a) Usain St. Leo Bolt (born 21 August 1986) is a Jamaican sprinter widely regarded as the fastest person ever.

4. (c) Jim Laker and Anil Kumble are the only two players who have taken 10 wickets in an innings. James "Jim" Charles Laker (9 February 1922 - 23 April 1986) was a cricketer who played for England in the 1950s. Laker was the first player to take all 10 wickets in a Test match innings, ten for 53 in the Australians' second innings of the fourth Ashes Test at Old Trafford in 1956 (the only other bowler to take all 10 wickets is Anil Kumble of India in 1999).

5. (a) The Ashoka Chakra is the peace time equivalent of the Param Vir Chakra, and is awarded for the "most conspicuous bravery or some daring or pre-eminent valour or self-sacrifice" other than in the face of the enemy.

6. (c) PSLV- The Polar Satellite Launch Vehicle, commonly known by its abbreviation PSLV, is an expendable launch system developed and operated by the Indian Space Research Organisation (ISRO).

7. (a) The HAL Tejas is a 4+ generation, multirole light fighter developed by India.

8. (b) Train To Pakistan is a historical novel by Khushwant Singh, published in 1956. It recounts the Partition of India in August 1947.

9. (b) Kuchipudi is a Classical Indian dance from Andhra Pradesh, In9dia.

10. (d) The Borlaug Award is an award recognition conferred by a fertilizer company, Coromandel International, for outstanding Indian scientists for their research and contributions in the field of agriculture and environment. The award was created in 1972 and named in honour of Nobel Laureate Norman E. Borlaug. It carries a cash prize of Rs 500,000, a gold medal, and a citation.

11. (d) The Office of the United Nations High Commissioner for Refugees (UNHCR), also known as the UN Refugee Agency, is a United Nations agency mandated to protect and support refugees at the request of a government or the UN itself and assists in their voluntary repatriation, local integration or resettlement to a third country. Its headquarters are in Geneva, Switzerland and is a member of the United Nations Development Group.

12. (b) The Duckworth-Lewis method is a mathematical formulation designed to calculate the target score for the team batting second in a limited overs cricket match interrupted by weather or other circumstances.

13. (a) Dronacharya Award is an award presented by the government of India for excellence in sports coaching.

14. (b) The 1896 Summer Olympics, officially known as the Games of the I Olympiad, was a multi-sport event held in Athens, Greece, from 6 to 15 April 1896.

15. (a) The BrahMos has been developed as a joint venture between the Defence Research and Development Organization (DRDO) of India and the Federal State Unitary Enterprise NPO Mashinostroyenia (NPOM) of Russia under BrahMos Aerospace. The missile is named after two rivers, the Brahmaputra and the Moskva.

16. (d) One of the oldest military institutions in India, it was founded in 1905 as the Army Staff college in Deolali (near Bombay), relocated to its present home in Wellington Cantonment in The Nilgiris District of Tamil Nadu, India.

17. (d) Freedom at Midnight (1975) is a book by Larry Collins and Dominique Lapierre. It describes the events in the Indian independence movement in 1947-48, beginning with the appointment of Lord Mountbatten of Burma as the last viceroy of British India, and ending with the death and funeral of Mahatma Gandhi.

18. (b) Bachendri Pal (born 24 May 1954) is an Indian mountaineer, who in 1984 became the first Indian woman to reach the summit of Mount Everest.

19. (d)

20. (b) Yoga sutra was written by Patanjali.

21. (a) Homi J. Bhabha was the eminent scientist who played a key role in the development of the Indian atomic energy program. He is also considered as the father of India's nuclear program. He also established the Atomic Energy Commission of India in 1948.

22. (d) The official mascot for the 2010 World Cup was Zakumi, an anthropomorphised African leopard with green hair, presented on 22 September 2008.

23. (d) "Wilson Jones" was the first to win the world amateur billiards title. He won this title in 1958, he won it in Sydney, Australia. He was awarded the Arjuna Award in 1962, the Padma Shri Award in 1965, and the Dronacharya Award in 1996.

24. (c) The first successful Badminton players to win the award was N.M. Natekar who won it in 1961 and Ms. Meena Shah followed him to win it in the very next year in 1962.

25. (d) The playing field is 300 yards (274 metres) long by 160 yards (146 metres) wide, the approximate area of nine American football fields. The playing field is carefully maintained with closely mowed turf providing a safe, fast playing surface. Goals are posts which are set eight yards apart, centred at each end of the field.

26. (b) The National Institute of Oceanography (NIO) is one of 37 constituent laboratories of the CSIR - Council of Scientific and Industrial Research, an autonomous research organization in India. The institute has its headquarters in the coastal state of Goa i.e. Panaji, and regional centres in Kochi, Mumbai and Vizag.

27. (d) Lewis Carl Davidson Hamilton, MBE is a British Formula One racing driver from England, currently racing for the Mercedes AMG team. He is the 2008 Formula One World Champion. Hamilton was born in Stevenage, Hertfordshire.

28. (c) Rafael "Rafa" Nadal Parera (born 3 June 1986) is a Spanish professional tennis player and the current world No. 1. Nadal has won 13 Grand Slam singles titles, the 2008 Olympic gold medal in singles, a record 27 ATP World Tour Masters 1000 and a record 15 ATP World Tour 500 tournaments.

29. (a)

30. (b) Leander Paes and Cara Black won the last senior title of Wimbledon 2010 by beating Wesley Moodie and Lisa Raymond 6-4 7-6 (7-5) in the mixed doubles.

31. (d)

32. (b)

33. (d) Act offers to guarantee hundred days of wage-employment in a year to a rural household.

34. (d) Wayne Mark Rooney is an English footballer who plays as a forward for Manchester United and the England national team. Aged nine, Rooney joined the youth team of Everton, for whom he made his professional debut in 2002 at the age of 16.

35. (c) The official song of the 2010 World Cup "Waka Waka" was performed by the Colombian singer Shakira and the band Freshlyground from South Africa, and is sung in both English and Spanish. The song is based on a traditional African soldiers' song, "Zangalewa".

36. (b) Saina Nehwal was awarded the "Rajiv Gandhi Khel Ratna award" which is India's highest award for excellence in the field of sports, following her terrific achievements in badminton in the year 2010.

37. (b) Karrar is an unmanned combat air vehicle produced for the military of Iran. According to reports, the UCAV can bomb targets at high speed. It is the first long-range unmanned aerial drone manufactured in Iran. The long-range drone was unveiled on August 23, 2010 - one day after the activation of the nuclear reactor in Bushehr.

38. (d)

39. (b) On 24 September 2008 Kapil Dev joined the Indian Territorial Army and was commissioned as a Lieutenant Colonel by General Deepak Kapoor, Chief of the Army Staff. He joined as an honorary officer.

40. (d) It is an Indian law that aims to guarantee the 'right to work' and ensure livelihood security in rural areas by providing at least 100 days of guaranteed wage employment in a financial year to every household whose adult members volunteer to do unskilled manual work.

41. (b) The World Bank is a United Nations international financial institution that provides loans to developing countries for capital programs. The World Bank is a component of the World Bank Group, and a member of the United Nations Development Group.

The International Atomic Energy Agency (IAEA) is an international organization that seeks to promote the peaceful use of nuclear energy, and to inhibit its use for any military purpose, including nuclear weapons. The IAEA was established as an autonomous organization on 29 July 1957. Though established independently of the United Nations through its own international treaty, the IAEA Statute, the IAEA reports to both the United Nations General Assembly and Security Council.

The Universal Postal Union is a specialized agency of the United Nations that coordinates postal policies among member nations, in addition to the worldwide postal system.

42. (b) BrahMos is a supersonic cruise missile that can be launched from submarines, ships, aircraft or land. It is a joint venture between Republic of India's Defence Research and Development Organisation (DRDO) and Russian Federation's NPO Mashinostroeyenia who have together formed BrahMos Aerospace Private Limited. It is the world's fastest cruise missile in operation. The missile travels at speeds of Mach 2.8 to 3.0. The land-launched and ship-launched versions are already in service, with the air and submarine-launched versions currently in the testing phase.

43. (d) On 9 February 2001 Vijay Amritraj was appointed UN Messenger of Peace. He has been a committed advocate to people in need, devoting his time to raising awareness on the issues of drugs and HIV/AIDS and in raising funds to fight the spread of AIDS worldwide.

44. (b) Indian women's hockey team had to be content with a silver medal in third Asian Champions Trophy after losing to hosts Japan by a solitary goal in the summit clash of the event at Kakamigahara, Japan.

45. (b) The Arjuna Awards were instituted in 1961 by the government of India to recognize outstanding achievement in National sports. The award carries a cash prize of ₹ 500,000, a bronze statuette of Arjuna and a scroll.

46. (b) Indian Institute of Science (IISc) is a public university for scientific research and higher education located in Bengaluru (formerly Bangalore), India. Established in 1899 with active support from Jamshetji Tata it is also locally known as the "Tata Institute".[3] It acquired the status of a Deemed University in 1958. IISc is widely regarded as India's finest institution in its field, and has made significant contribution to advanced computing, space, and nuclear technologies.

47. (c) Train To Pakistan is a historical novel by Khushwant Singh, published in 1956. It recounts the Partition of India in August 1947. Instead of depicting the Partition in terms of only the political events surrounding it, Singh digs into a deep local focus, providing a human dimension which brings to the event a sense of reality, horror, and believability.

48. (b) The Queen's Baton Relay is one of the great traditions of the Commonwealth Games, having started at the Games in Cardiff, Wales, in 1958. The Baton is now as much a part of the Commonwealth Games tradition as the torch is part of the Olympics. The relay traditionally begins with a commencement ceremony at Buckingham Palace, London, which coincides with the city's Commonwealth Day festivities. There Her Majesty Queen Elizabeth II entrusts the baton containing Her 'message to the athletes' to the first honorary relay runner. The relay concludes at the Opening Ceremony, as the final relay runner hands the baton back to Her Majesty, or Her representative, and the message is read aloud. At that moment the Games begin.

49. (c) In November 1999, UNESCO designated World Poetry Day to be held on March 21 each year. The organization recognized the important role of poetry in the arts and in cultures throughout the world and over time. It also wanted the day to promote the efforts of small publishers with regard to publishing poetry.

50. (d) Air Marshal Sir Thomas Walker Elmhirst was the first Commander-in-Chief of the Indian Air Force. He was Air Chief from 15 August 1947 to 21 February 1950. It was Air Marshal Elmhirst, who insisted that the Indian Air Force be an independent service under no control of the Army.

51. (a) Junko Tabei is a Japanese mountain-climber who, on May 16, 1975, became the first woman to reach the summit of Mount Everest.

52. (c) The Asiatic Society was founded by Sir William Jones on 15 January 1784 in a meeting presided over by Sir Robert Chambers, the Chief Justice of the Supreme Court at the Fort William in Calcutta, then capital of the British Raj, to enhance and further the cause of Oriental research.

53. (a) Himalayas is one of the youngest mountain ranges in the world, situated in the northern border of India and spread across six Asian countries -India, Pakistan, Bhutan, Afghanistan, China and Nepal. The Himalayas contains some of the highest peaks in the world that includes Mount Everest, Karakoram and Kanchenjunga.

54. (b)

55. (c)

56. (d)

57. (c) Nigeria is considered free of Ebola transmission by WHO.

58. (b) India won 57 medals (11 gold, 10 silver, 36 bronze).

59. (b)

60. (d) Nirbhay is the first Indian long-range subsonic cruise missile developed by Defence Research & Development Organisation (DRDO). This missile can be launched from multiple platforms like, air, land. Nirbhay missile's flight test was successfully completed in October 2014.

61. (c) Khan Abdul Gaffar Khan was another foreigner who received Bharat Ratna. He was the foremost 20th-century leader of the Pashtuns (a Muslim ethnic group of Pakistan and Afghanistan), who became a follower of Mahatma Gandhi and was called the "Frontier Gandhi."

62. (a) Sir Chandrasekhara Venkata Raman, was an Indian physicist, whose ground breaking work in the field of light scattering earned him the 1930 Nobel Prize for Physics. He discovered that, when light traverses a transparent material, some of the deflected light changes in wavelength. This phenomenon is now called Raman scattering and is the result of the Raman Effect.

63. (a) The Asian Development Bank is a regional development bank established on 22 August 1966 which is headquartered in Metro Manila, Philippines, to facilitate economic development in Asia.

64. (a) K-15 Sagarika is a nuclear-capable submarine-launched ballistic missile with a range of 700 kilometres (435 mi). It belongs to the K Missile family and forms a part of India's nuclear triad, and will provide retaliatory nuclear strike capability.

65. **(a)** India agreed to remain a member of the UNCCT at the offer of UN Chief Ban Ki Moon. The UNCCT was established in 2011 within the United Nations Counter-Terrorism Implementation Task Force (CTITF), under the leadership of the CTITF, to assist in meeting capacity-building needs of Member States, and to strengthen United Nations' counter-terrorism expertise. The Centre engages with the over 30 CTITF entities with expertise on a broad spectrum of counter terrorism related issues.

66. **(d)** Khashaba Dadasaheb Jadhav (born January 15, 1926-August 14, 1984) was an Indian athlete. He is best known as a wrestler who won a bronze medal at the 1952 Summer Olympics in Helsinki.

67. **(d)** Agni-VI is an intercontinental ballistic missile being developed by the Defence Research and Development Organisation (DRDO) for the use of the Indian Armed Forces. Agni-VI will be a three-stage intercontinental ballistic missile, which is in the hardware development phase, after its design phase was completed.

68. **(b)** Kosuke Hagino, 20, won medals in all seven events he competed in, winning gold in the men's 200m freestyle, 200m and 400m individual medleys, and the 800m freestyle relay, in addition to one silver in the 400m freestyle and two bronze medals in the 100m and 200m backstroke events.

Practice Set

Time: 2 hrs.   *Max. Marks: 300*

SECTION-A : VERBAL ABILITY IN ENGLISH

DIRECTIONS (Qs. 1 - 3) : *Read the following passage carefully and answer the questions given below it :*

One day an army group won a land battle against the enemy. The commander feared that the enemy's powerful air force might bomb his camp that night in revenge. So, he ordered all lights to be put out at 7:00 pm. At midnight the commander went round inspecting the camp. Seeing a light in a tent, he entered it. His son, an officer under him, was writing a letter. The son explained that he was writing to his mother about his brave deeds in battle. The commander told his son to add to his letter that by the time his mother received the letter he would have been shot dead for indiscipline.

1. The commander went round the camp at midnight because he
   (a) was too tired from the day's battle to go to sleep
   (b) wished to check if his soldiers had obeyed his order
   (c) was too worried about the next day's battle
   (d) wished to check if enemies had entered his camp
2. The commander entered his son's tent because he
   (a) wished to see and talk to his son
   (b) suspected that enemies had entered his tent
   (c) wished to send a message to his wife
   (d) had to punish any soldier who disobeyed his order
3. The son was writing a letter because he
   (a) wanted to write to his mother about his father's brave deeds in battle
   (b) loved his mother so much that he had to write to her
   (c) was eager to tell his mother about his own deeds
   (d) did not care for orders, since his father was the commander

DIRECTION (Qs. 4 - 8) : *Select the most appropriate word from the options against each number :*

One fine morning a (4) man knocked at the doors of the home for the aged run by nuns. He told the nun in charge that as he was (5) to Delhi, he wanted to leave his servant-maid to the (6) of the nuns. He assured the nun of sending some money every month (7) she was an orphan. The nun (8) her saying that she had got an excellen master.

4. (a) gentle   (b) bad
   (c) nice   (d) good
5. (a) moved   (b) shifted
   (c) changed   (d) transferred
6. (a) care   (b) home
   (c) custody   (d) protection
7. (a) because   (b) and
   (c) though   (d) if
8. (a) loved   (b) praised
   (c) consoled   (d) condoled

DIRECTION (Qs. 9 - 10) : *Choose the one which best expresses the meaning of the given word and mark it in the Answer Sheet.*

9. Wily
   (a) Angry   (b) Wise
   (c) Stupid   (d) Cunning
10. Temerity
    (a) Paucity   (b) Verity
    (c) Audacity   (d) Simplicity

DIRECTION (Qs. 11 - 13) : *Choose the word opposite in meaning to the given word and mark it in the Answer Sheet.*

11. Fabricate
    (a) Unearth   (b) Construct
    (c) Demolish   (d) Renovate
12. Gregarious
    (a) Sociable   (b) Societal
    (c) Unsociable   (d) Solitary
13. Pragmatic
    (a) Indefinite   (b) Vague
    (c) Optimistic   (d) Idealistic

DIRECTION (Qs. 14 - 18) : *Each of these questions has an idiomatic expression followed by four options. Choose the one closest to its meaning.*

14. In the blues:
    - (a) Being colourful
    - (b) Melancholy and low spirited
    - (c) Behave like a lord
    - (d) Cheerful and happy

15. See eye to eye:
    - (a) State at each other
    - (b) Agree
    - (c) Depend on
    - (d) Make an effort

16. Talk shop:
    - (a) Talk about one's profession
    - (b) Talk about shopping
    - (c) Ridicule
    - (d) Treat lightly

17. Bad blood:
    - (a) Infected blood
    - (b) Ill-feeling
    - (c) Unfaithful
    - (d) Suspicion

18. Wear one's heart on one's sleeve:
    - (a) Lure passionately
    - (b) Do the right thing
    - (c) Show one's feelings
    - (d) Be intimate

DIRECTIONS (Qs. 19-22) : *In the following questions, a word has been spelt in four different ways, one of which is correct. Choose the correctly spelt word.*

19. (a) Dysentary   (b) Dysantery
    (c) Dysentry   (d) Dysentery
20. (a) Rejevanation   (b) Rejuvenation
    (c) Rejvenation   (d) Rejuenation
21. (a) accomodate   (b) acommodate
    (c) accommodate   (d) accommodat
22. (a) vegeterian   (b) vegetarian
    (c) vegetarean   (d) vegitarean

DIRECTIONS (Qs. 23-25) : *In each of the following sentences four words or phrases have been underlined. Only one underlined part in each sentence is not acceptable in Standard English, Pick up the part a, b, c or d.*

23. I have seen <u>as bad or</u> worse scenes of <u>disorder</u> at the
             a   b

    English fair <u>than</u> in <u>any other</u> Australian mining town.
          c   d

24. The officers are <u>now</u> <u>perfectly</u> happy fishing, boating,
          a   b

    shooting, <u>playing cricket</u> and <u>other sports</u> .
          c   d

25. While in conversation <u>with a</u> high military officer
          a

    he told me that at <u>the headquarters</u> nothing <u>was known</u> .
      b   c   d
    The subject should come before the verb.

26. 465 coins consists of 1 rupee, 50 paise and 25 paise coins. Their values are in the ratio 5 : 3 : 1. The number of each type of coins respectively is
    - (a) 155, 186, 124
    - (b) 154, 187, 124
    - (c) 154, 185, 126
    - (d) 150, 140, 175

27. A car covers four successive 6 km stretches at speeds of 25 kmph, 50 kmph, 75 kmph and 150 kmph respectively. Its average speed over this distance is
    - (a) 25 kmph
    - (b) 50 kmph
    - (c) 75 kmph
    - (d) 150 kmph

28. Kabir buys an article with 25% discount on its marked price. He makes a profit of 10% by selling it at ₹ 660. The marked price is
    - (a) ₹ 600
    - (b) ₹ 685
    - (c) ₹ 700
    - (d) ₹ 800

29. In a class of 250 students, 75.8% took French and 49.4% took Latin. How many students took both French and Latin ?
    - (a) 189.0
    - (b) 123.0
    - (c) 63.0
    - (d) 90.0

30. A is 3 times more efficient than B. Hence, he takes 60 days less in painting a room. In how many days, work will be completed, if A and B both work together ?
    - (a) 30 days
    - (b) 45 days
    - (c) $22\frac{1}{2}$ days
    - (d) $17\frac{1}{2}$ days

31. In a family, a couple has a son and daughter. The age of the father is three times that of his daughter and the age of the son is half of his mother. The wife is nine years younger to her husband and the brother is seven years older than his sister. What is the age of the mother ?
    - (a) 40 years
    - (b) 45 years
    - (c) 50 years
    - (d) 60 years

32. The monthly income of Komal and Asha are in the ratio of 4 : 3. Their monthly expenses are in the ratio of 3 : 2. However, both save ₹ 600 per month. What is their total monthly income ?
    - (a) ₹ 8,400
    - (b) ₹ 5,600
    - (c) ₹ 4,200
    - (d) ₹ 2,800

33. A worker reaches his factory 3 minutes late if his speed from his house to the factory is 5 km/hr If he walks at a speed of 6 km/hr, then he reaches the factory 7 minutes early. The distance of the factory from his house is
    - (a) 4 km
    - (b) 5 km
    - (c) 6 km
    - (d) 7 km

34. One local and another express train were proceeding in the same direction on parallel tracks at 29 km/hour and 65 km/hour respectively. The driver of the former noticed that it took exactly 16 seconds for the faster train to pass by him. What is the length of the faster train ?
    - (a) 60 m
    - (b) 120 m
    - (c) 160 m
    - (d) 240 m

35. A gardener increased the area of his rectangular garden by increasing its length by 40% and decreasing its width by 20%. The area of the new garden
(a) has increased by 20%.
(b) has increased by 12%.
(c) has increased by 8%.
(d) is exactly the same as the old area.

36. There are two candidates Bhiku and Mhatre for an election. Bhiku gets 65 % of the total valid votes. If the total votes were 6,000, what is the number of valid votes that the other candidate Mhatre gets if 25 % of the total votes were declared invalid ?
(a) 1575   (b) 1625
(c) 1675   (d) 1525

37. A sum of ₹5,000 lent on simple interest amounts to ₹5,700 in two years. If the rate of interest is increased by four percentage, then what would the sum amount to in the same period ?
(a) ₹5,980   (b) ₹6,100
(c) ₹5,900   (d) ₹6,300

38. Mira's expenditure and savings are in the ratio 3 : 2. Her income increases by 10%. Her expenditure also increases by 12%. By how much % do her savings increase ?
(a) 7%   (b) 9%
(c) 10%   (d) 13%

39. The difference between the simple interest and the compound interest compounded annually at the rate of 12% per annum on Rs 5000 for two years will be :
(a) ₹47.50   (b) ₹63
(c) ₹45   (d) ₹72

40. A pipe can fill a cistern in 6 hours. Due to a leak in its bottom, it is filled in 7 hours. When the cistern is full, in how much time will it be emptied by the leak ?
(a) 42 hours   (b) 40 hours
(c) 43 hours   (d) 45 hours

41. A man in a train notices that he can count 21 telephone posts in one minute. If they are known to be 50 metres apart, then at what speed is the train travelling ?
(a) 45 km/h   (b) 60 km/h
(c) 63 km/h   (d) 65 km/h

42. A and B run a 5 km race on a round course of 400 m. If their speeds be in the ratio 5 : 4, how often does the winner pass the other?
(a) $4\frac{1}{2}$ times   (b) $2\frac{3}{4}$ times
(c) $3\frac{1}{2}$ times   (d) $2\frac{1}{2}$ times

43. Which of the following pair of fractions adds up to a number greater than 5 ?
(a) $\dfrac{13}{5}, \dfrac{11}{6}$ (b) $\dfrac{11}{4}, \dfrac{8}{3}$
(c) $\dfrac{7}{3}, \dfrac{11}{5}$ (d) $\dfrac{5}{3}, \dfrac{3}{4}$

44. If the fractions $\dfrac{9}{13}, \dfrac{2}{3}, \dfrac{8}{11}, \dfrac{5}{7}$ are arranged in ascending order, then the correct sequence is :
(a) $\dfrac{9}{13}, \dfrac{2}{3}, \dfrac{8}{11}, \dfrac{5}{7}$ (b) $\dfrac{2}{3}, \dfrac{9}{13}, \dfrac{5}{7}, \dfrac{8}{11}$
(c) $\dfrac{2}{3}, \dfrac{8}{11}, \dfrac{5}{7}, \dfrac{9}{13}$ (d) $\dfrac{5}{7}, \dfrac{8}{11}, \dfrac{2}{3}, \dfrac{9}{13}$

45. A cistern has three pipes, A, B and C. The pipes A and B can fill it in 4 and 5 hours respectively and pipe C can empty it in 2 hours. If the pipes are opened in an order at 1, 2 and 3 A.M., when will the cistern be empty?
(a) 3 P.M.   (b) 7 P.M.
(c) 4 P.M.   (d) 5 P.M.

SECTION-C : REASONING & MILITARY APTITUDE

46. Identify the diagram that best represents the relationship among the classes given below :

Liquids, Milk, River water

(a) 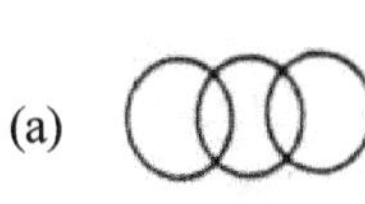   (b) 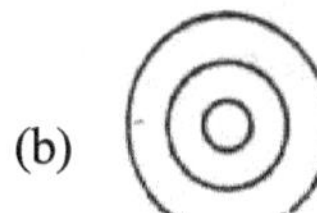

(c)    (d) 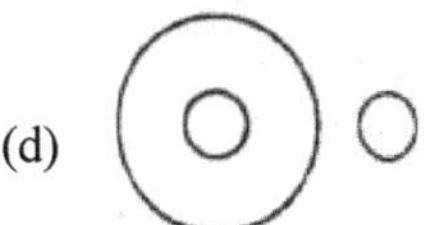

47. Identify the diagram that best represents the relationship among milk, goat, cow, hen?

Answer figures :

(a) 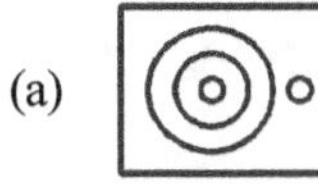   (b) 

(c)    (d) 

48. Identify the figure which best represents the relationship among Tree, Plant, and House.

Answer figures :

(a) 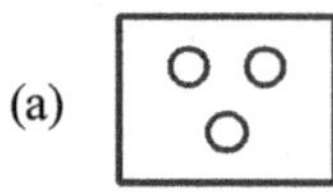   (b) 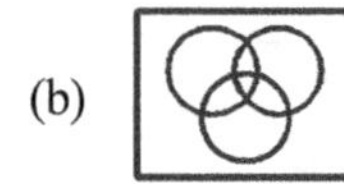

(c)    (d) 

49. Identify the diagram which represent the relationship among the following :- Capsules, Antibiotics, Injection.

(a)    (b) 

(c) 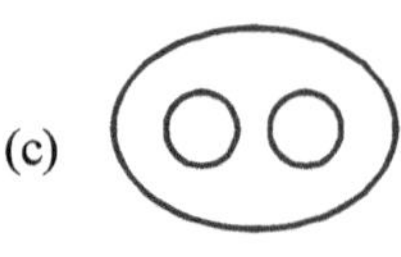   (d) 

50. Identify the diagram which represents the best relationship among athletes, football players and cricket-players.

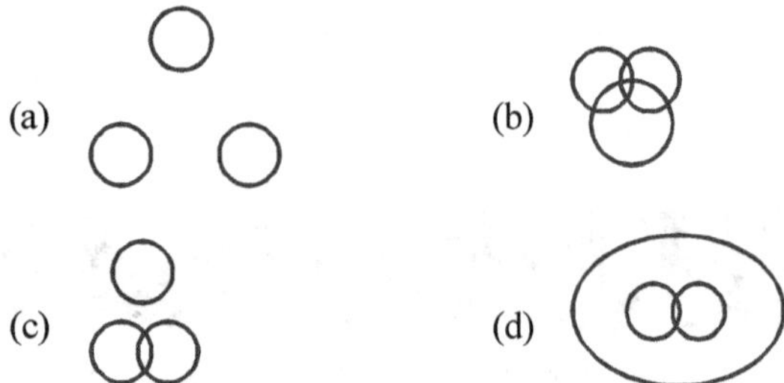

(a)   (b)

(c)   (d)

DIRECTIONS (Qs. 51-55) : *In each of the following questions, four words have been given out of which four are alike in some manner, while the fourth one is different. Choose the word which is different from the rest.*

51. (a) Pear (b) Apple
(c) Litchi (d) Orange

52. (a) Chameleon (b) Crocodile
(c) Alligator (d) Locust

53. (a) Cumin (b) Groundnut
(c) Cinnamon (d) Pepper

54. (a) Sleet (b) Mist
(c) Hailstone (d) Vapour

55. (a) Zinc (b) Iron
(c) Aluminium (d) Mercury

DIRECTIONS (Qs. 56-60) : *In each of the following questions find out the alternative which will replace the question mark.*

56. Microphone : Loud :: Microscope : ?
(a) Elongate (b) Investigate
(c) Magnify (d) Examine

57. Poles : Magnet :: ? : Battery
(a) Cells (b) Power
(c) Terminals (d) Energy

58. Cassock : Priest :: ? : Graduate
(a) Cap (b) Tie
(c) Coat (d) Gown

59. Ornithologist : Bird :: Archealogist : ?
(a) Islands (b) Mediators
(c) Archealogy (d) Aquatic

60. Cloth : Mill :: Newspaper : ?
(a) Editor (b) Reader
(c) Paper (d) Press

DIRECTIONS (Qs. 61-65) : *choose the most appropriate answer:*

61. Which one of the following is always in 'Sentiment'?
(a) Cruelty (b) Insight
(c) Neutrality (d) Emotion

62. Controversy always involves
(a) Dislike (b) Injustice
(c) Disagreement (d) Passion

63. What is found necessarily in newspaper?
(a) Date (b) Advertisement
(c) News (d) Editor

64. If we are going early in the morning towards the south the sun will be visible at our left:
(a) Always (b) Never
(c) Often (d) Sometimes

65. Which one of the following is always associated with 'justice'?
(a) Hypocrisy (b) Legitimate
(c) Magnanimity (d) Diminutiveness

DIRECTIONS (Qs. 66-69) : *Two Sets of the figures are given. One set of Question-figures and another set is of Answer-figures. Question-figures are arranged in a sequence. One figure from the Answer figures is to be selected such that it can be placed after the series of Question-figures. Find the correct Serial number of the selected Answer-figure.*

66. **Question-Figures**

Answer-Figures

(a)   (b)   (c)   (d)

67. **Question-Figures**

 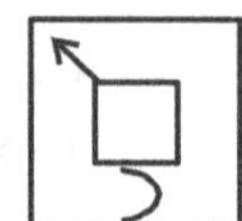 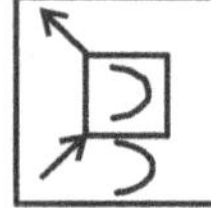 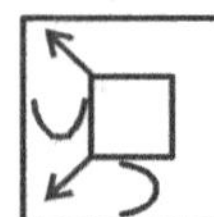 

Answer-Figures

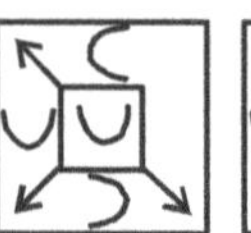 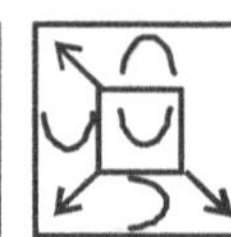 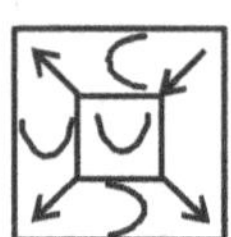 

(a)   (b)   (c)   (d)

68. **Question-Figures**

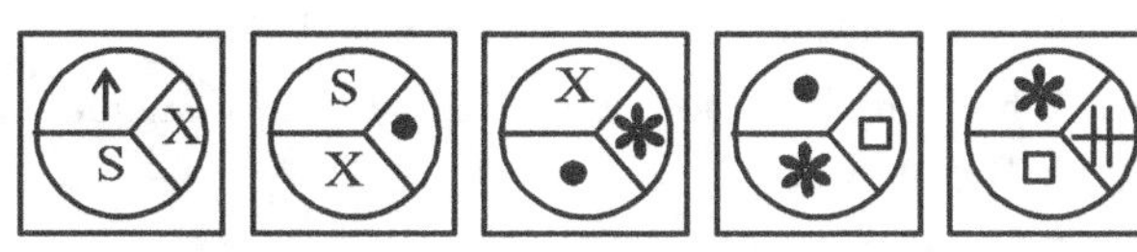

Answer-Figures

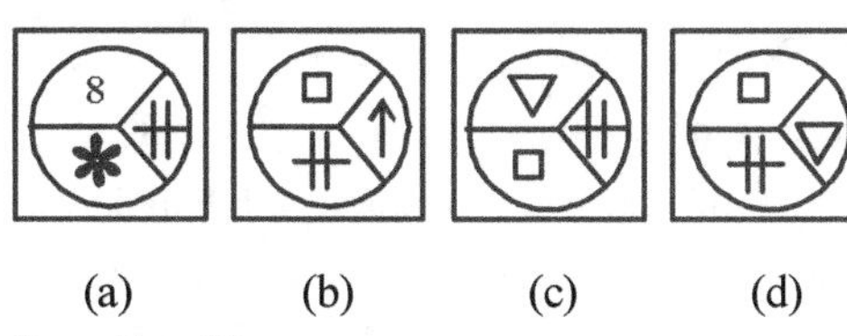

(a)   (b)   (c)   (d)

69. **Question-Figures**

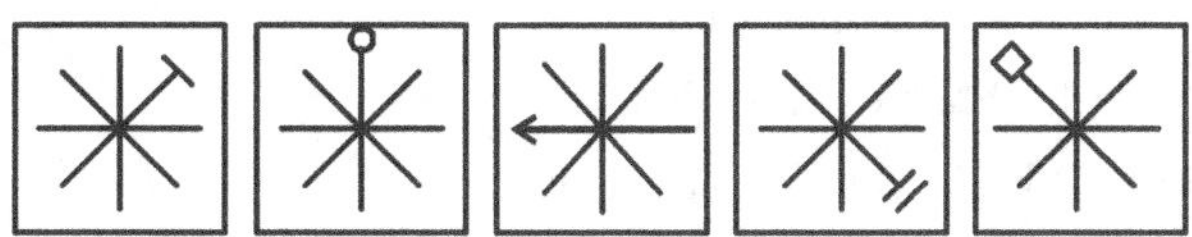

Answer-Figures

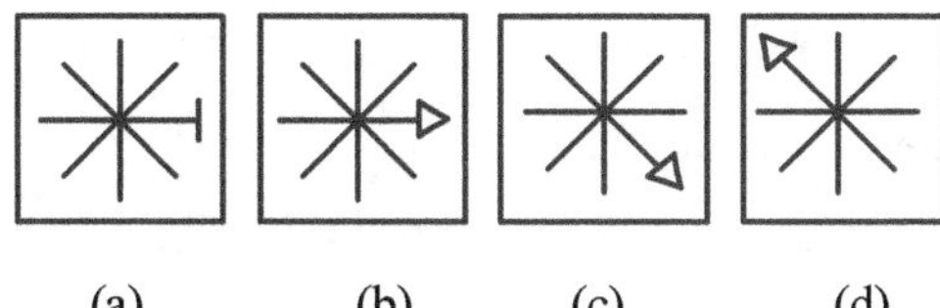

(a)   (b)   (c)   (d)

DIRECTIONS (Qs. 70 - 72): *In the following questions there is some relationship between the two figure on the left of (::) the same relationship exists between the two terms on the right, of which one is missing. Find the missing one from the given alternative.*

70. **Question-Figures**

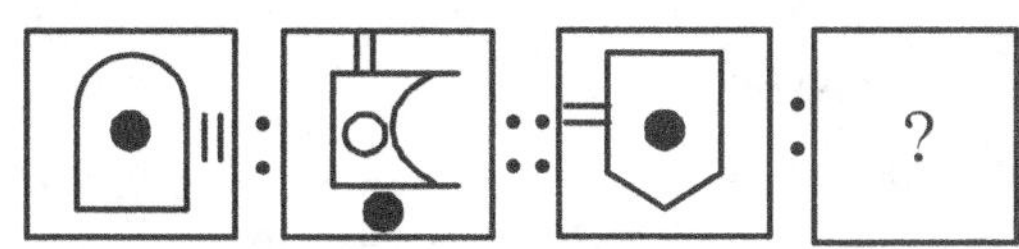

Answer-Figures

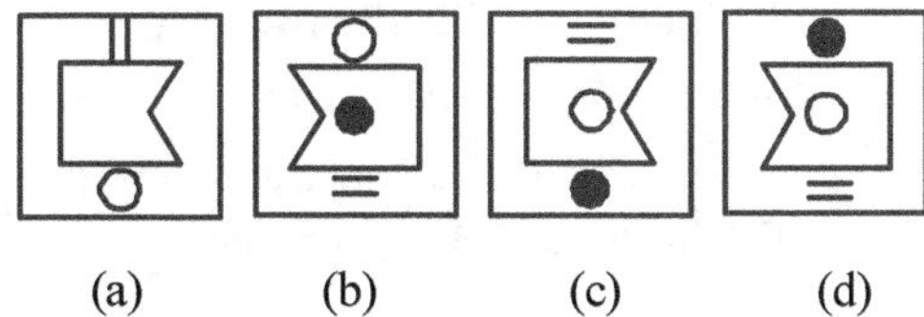

(a)   (b)   (c)   (d)

71. **Question-Figures**

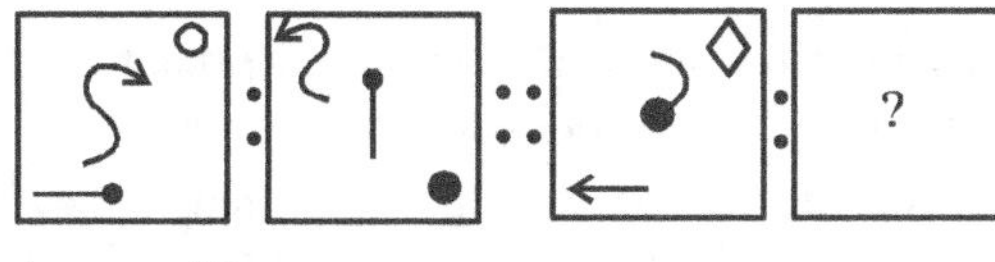

Answer-Figures

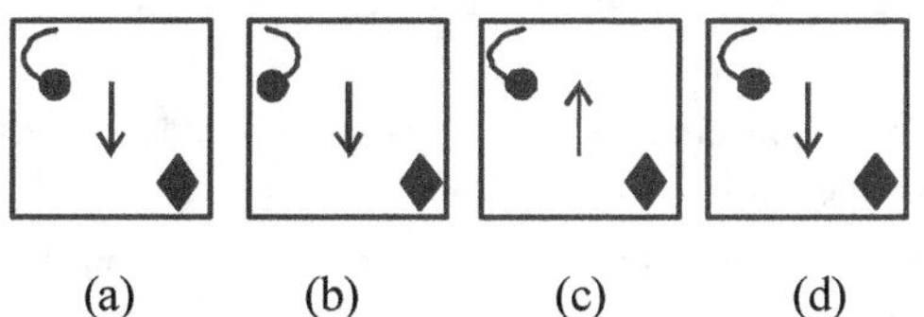

(a)   (b)   (c)   (d)

72. **Problem-figures:**

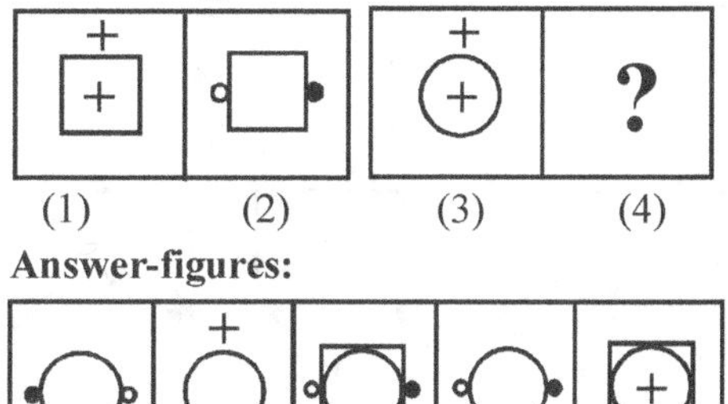

(1)   (2)   (3)   (4)

Answer-figures:

(a)   (b)   (c)   (d)   (e)

DIRECTIONS (Qs. 73 - 76) : *In each of the following questions four figures are given. One of these figures does not fit with the rest of the figures. Find out that correct serial number.*

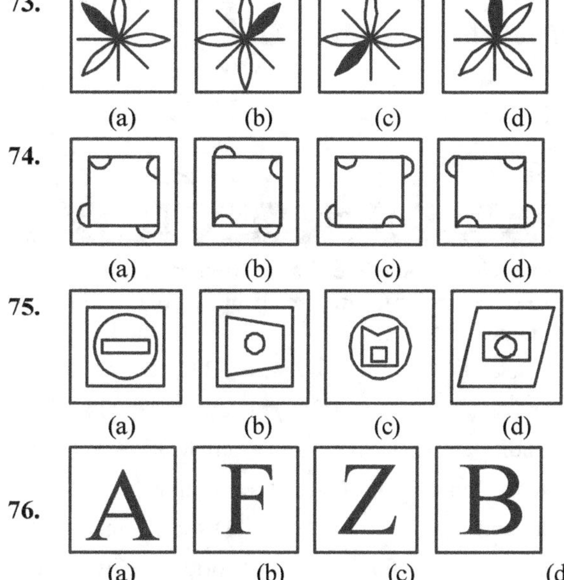

73.

(a)   (b)   (c)   (d)

74.

(a)   (b)   (c)   (d)

75.

(a)   (b)   (c)   (d)

76. A   F   Z   B

(a)   (b)   (c)   (d)

DIRECTIONS (Qs. 77 - 80) : *In each of the questions, there is a big figure at the top having a vacant chamber. Identify one figure from the given choices which will fit into the vacant chamber.*

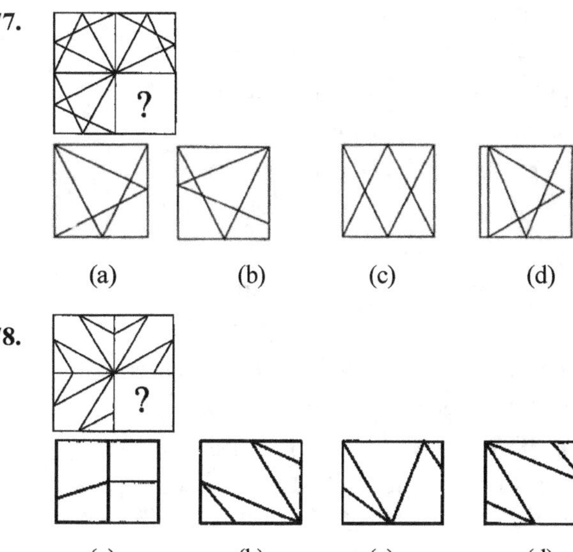

77.

(a)   (b)   (c)   (d)

78.

(a)   (b)   (c)   (d)

79. 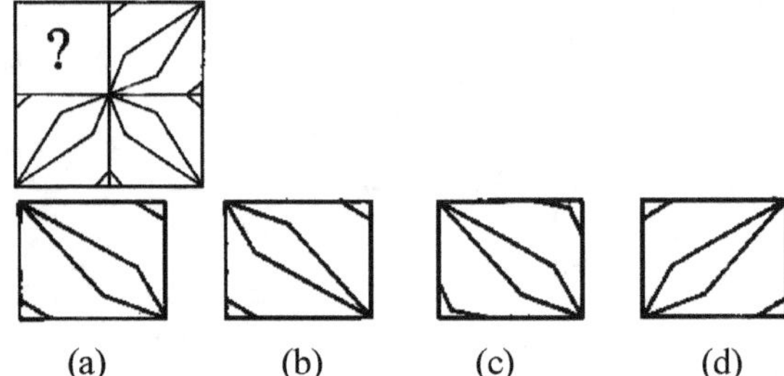

80. 

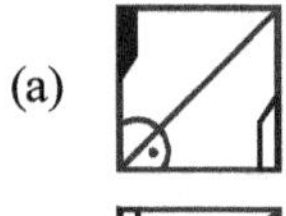 (a)

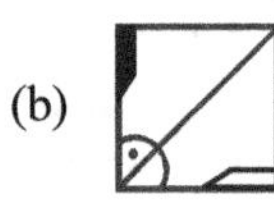 (b)

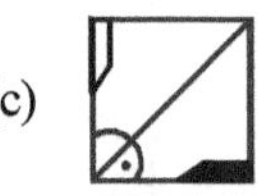 (c)

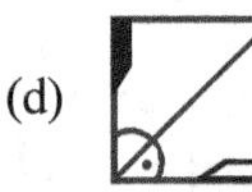 (d)

SECTION-D : GENERAL AWARENESS

81. Under which Article of the Constitution can an individual move to the Supreme Court directly in case of any violation of Fundamental Rights ?

- (a) Article 31
- (b) Article 32
- (c) Article 28
- (d) Article 29

82. The Dandi March of Gandhi-is an example of

- (a) Non-Coopefation
- (b) Direct Action
- (c) Boycott
- (d) Civil Disobedience

83. Which one of the following inscriptions relate to the Chalukya king, Pulakesin II ?

- (a) Nasik
- (b) Maski
- (c) Hathigumpha
- (d) Aihole

84. The filtration unit of kidney is

- (a) yellow fiber
- (b) axon
- (c) nephron
- (d) neuron

85. Yeast is an important source of

- (a) protein
- (b) vitamin B
- (c) invertase
- (d) vitamin C

86. The longest river of peninsular India is

- (a) Godavari
- (b) Krishna
- (c) Kaveri
- (d) Narmada

87. Minorities Rights Day is observed in India on

- (a) 18th December
- (b) 23rd December
- (c) 5th September
- (d) 1st December

88. "Sattriya Nritya" recognised as a classical dance form of India by the Sangeet Natak Akademi only in 2000, originated from

- (a) Tripura
- (b) Assam
- (c) Karnataka
- (d) Gujarat

89. Which one of the following National Park/Sanctuary is not in Rajasthan ?

- (a) Sariska National Park
- (b) Sambar Wildlife Sanctuary
- (c) Rajaji National Park
- (d) Rhanthambore National Park

90. Which of the following is associated with Panchayati Raj ?

- (a) Nanavati Commission
- (b) Balwant Rai Mehta Committee
- (c) Librahan Commission
- (d) Shah Commission

91. 'Pehli Udaan' is a name given to

- (a) Launching of Air Asia in India
- (b) SBI's Savings Account Scheme for children
- (c) Proposed Bullet Train in India
- (d) Satellite sent to Mars

92. Jean Tirole has won Nobel Prize in which of the below category?

- (a) Literature
- (b) Physics
- (c) Chemistry
- (d) Economics

93. What does 'Ozone Layer' absorb?

- (a) γ-rays
- (b) Infrared rays
- (c) Ultraviolet rays
- (d) X-rays

94. Who among the following is the author of "The scatter here is too great"?

- (a) Kedarnath Singh
- (b) Bilal Tanweer
- (c) Deepti Kapoor
- (d) Mahesh Rao

95. The Pilotless target aircraft, fabricated at the Aeronautical Development Establishment, Bengaluru, is:

- (a) Lakshya
- (b) Cheetah
- (c) Nishant
- (d) Arjun

96. Which of the following statements are true about the impact of Alexander's invasion of India?

- (a) Alexander destroyed the power of petty states in the north
- (b) The invasion opened up four distinct routes by land and sea
- (c) Greek settlements such as Buoukephala on the Indus were established
- (d) His invasion helps as to build Indian chronology for subsequent events on a definite basis.

97. The Blue Revolution is related with

    (a) Fish production

    (b) Food grain production

    (c) Oilseed production

    (d) Milk production

98. Which one of the following is not a line of demarcation between two countries ?

    (a) Durand Line   (b) Mac Mahon Line

    (c) Plimsoll Line   (d) Maginot Line

99. Who among the following first propounded the idea of Basic Education?

    (a) Jawahar Lal Nehru   (b) Raja Ram Mohan Roy

    (c) Mahatma Gandhi   (d) Dayanand Saraswati

100. Which of the following Countries is the host for the 2016 Olympic Games?

    (a) South Africa   (b) Netherlands

    (c) Brazil   (d) Italy

RESPONSE SHEET

1. ⓐⓑⓒⓓ	2. ⓐⓑⓒⓓ	3. ⓐⓑⓒⓓ	4. ⓐⓑⓒⓓ	5. ⓐⓑⓒⓓ
6. ⓐⓑⓒⓓ	7. ⓐⓑⓒⓓ	8. ⓐⓑⓒⓓ	9. ⓐⓑⓒⓓ	10. ⓐⓑⓒⓓ
11. ⓐⓑⓒⓓ	12. ⓐⓑⓒⓓ	13. ⓐⓑⓒⓓ	14. ⓐⓑⓒⓓ	15. ⓐⓑⓒⓓ
16. ⓐⓑⓒⓓ	17. ⓐⓑⓒⓓ	18. ⓐⓑⓒⓓ	19. ⓐⓑⓒⓓ	20. ⓐⓑⓒⓓ
21. ⓐⓑⓒⓓ	22. ⓐⓑⓒⓓ	23. ⓐⓑⓒⓓ	24. ⓐⓑⓒⓓ	25. ⓐⓑⓒⓓ
26. ⓐⓑⓒⓓ	27. ⓐⓑⓒⓓ	28. ⓐⓑⓒⓓ	29. ⓐⓑⓒⓓ	30. ⓐⓑⓒⓓ
31. ⓐⓑⓒⓓ	32. ⓐⓑⓒⓓ	33. ⓐⓑⓒⓓ	34. ⓐⓑⓒⓓ	35. ⓐⓑⓒⓓ
36. ⓐⓑⓒⓓ	37. ⓐⓑⓒⓓ	38. ⓐⓑⓒⓓ	39. ⓐⓑⓒⓓ	40. ⓐⓑⓒⓓ
41. ⓐⓑⓒⓓ	42. ⓐⓑⓒⓓ	43. ⓐⓑⓒⓓ	44. ⓐⓑⓒⓓ	45. ⓐⓑⓒⓓ
46. ⓐⓑⓒⓓ	47. ⓐⓑⓒⓓ	48. ⓐⓑⓒⓓ	49. ⓐⓑⓒⓓ	50. ⓐⓑⓒⓓ
51. ⓐⓑⓒⓓ	52. ⓐⓑⓒⓓ	53. ⓐⓑⓒⓓ	54. ⓐⓑⓒⓓ	55. ⓐⓑⓒⓓ
56. ⓐⓑⓒⓓ	57. ⓐⓑⓒⓓ	58. ⓐⓑⓒⓓ	59. ⓐⓑⓒⓓ	60. ⓐⓑⓒⓓ
61. ⓐⓑⓒⓓ	62. ⓐⓑⓒⓓ	63. ⓐⓑⓒⓓ	64. ⓐⓑⓒⓓ	65. ⓐⓑⓒⓓ
66. ⓐⓑⓒⓓ	67. ⓐⓑⓒⓓ	68. ⓐⓑⓒⓓ	69. ⓐⓑⓒⓓ	70. ⓐⓑⓒⓓ
71. ⓐⓑⓒⓓ	72. ⓐⓑⓒⓓ	73. ⓐⓑⓒⓓ	74. ⓐⓑⓒⓓ	75. ⓐⓑⓒⓓ
76. ⓐⓑⓒⓓ	77. ⓐⓑⓒⓓ	78. ⓐⓑⓒⓓ	79. ⓐⓑⓒⓓ	80. ⓐⓑⓒⓓ
81. ⓐⓑⓒⓓ	82. ⓐⓑⓒⓓ	83. ⓐⓑⓒⓓ	84. ⓐⓑⓒⓓ	85. ⓐⓑⓒⓓ
86. ⓐⓑⓒⓓ	87. ⓐⓑⓒⓓ	88. ⓐⓑⓒⓓ	89. ⓐⓑⓒⓓ	90. ⓐⓑⓒⓓ
91. ⓐⓑⓒⓓ	92. ⓐⓑⓒⓓ	93. ⓐⓑⓒⓓ	94. ⓐⓑⓒⓓ	95. ⓐⓑⓒⓓ
96. ⓐⓑⓒⓓ	97. ⓐⓑⓒⓓ	98. ⓐⓑⓒⓓ	99. ⓐⓑⓒⓓ	100. ⓐⓑⓒⓓ

ANSWERS & SOLUTIONS

1. (b) The commander had ordered the lights to be put off by 7 : 00 pm, he took a round to check if his soldiers had obeyed his orders or not.

2. (d) Refer to the last two lines of the passage.

3. (c) As written in the passage.

4. (a)   5. (d)   6. (c)   7. (a)   8. (c)

9. (d) 'Wily' means 'cunning' which also means skillful or clever.

10. (c) 'Audacity' best expresses the meaning of 'temerity' which also means 'arrogance'

11. (c) Fabricate means make up something artificial or untrue while demolish means destroy completely which is just opposite.

12. (c) Gregarious denotes tending to form a group with others of the same species and unsociable is the opposite.

13. (d) Pragmatic means concerned with practical matters while idealislic means bounded with limits.

14. (b) 'Blues' refer to bad moods, melancholy, low spirit, ill temper.

15. (b) Seeing eye to eye means approving of each other or agreeing with each other.

16. (a) This means to talk about one's profession in a dry, boring way.

17. (b) Bad - blood reefers to the element of animosity in a person and, thus, ill - feeling.

18. (c) This means to express openly one's desires or emotions.

19. (b)   20. (d)   21. (c)   22. (b)

23. (a) The underlined portion should be deleted.

24. (d) and indulging in other sports.

25. (b) I was told

26. (a) The ratio of number of coins = 5 : 6 : 4

$$\therefore \text{ The number of one rupee coins } = \frac{465}{5+6+4} \times 5 = 155$$

$$\text{The number of 50 paise coins } = \frac{465}{5+6+4} \times 6 = 186$$

$$\text{The number of 25 paise coins } = \frac{465}{5+6+4} \times 4 = 124$$

27. (b)
$$\text{Average Speed} = \frac{\text{Total Distance Covered}}{\text{Total Time Taken}}$$

$$= \frac{6+6+6+6}{\frac{6}{25}+\frac{6}{50}+\frac{6}{75}+\frac{6}{150}} \Rightarrow \frac{24}{6\left[\frac{1}{25}+\frac{1}{50}+\frac{1}{75}+\frac{1}{150}\right]}$$

$$= \frac{24 \times 300}{6 \times 24} \Rightarrow 50 \text{ km/hr}$$

28. (d) Let the marked price be ₹ x.

$$\because \text{ C.P.} = (x - 25\% \text{ of } x) = \frac{3}{4}x$$

$$\Rightarrow \text{ S.P.} = \left(\frac{3x}{4} + 10\% \text{ of } \frac{3x}{4}\right) = \frac{33}{40}x$$

$$\text{But, } \frac{33}{40}x = 660 \Rightarrow x = 800.$$

29. (c)

$$A \cup B = A + B - A \cap B$$
$$\Rightarrow 100 = 75.8 + 49.4 - A \cap B$$
$$\Rightarrow A \cap B = 125.2 - 100 = 25.2$$

Students who took both 25.2% of 250 = 63.0 (Approx)

30. (c) Let A takes 'n' days to paint the room.
So B will take 3n days to paint the room.
$$\Rightarrow 3n - n = 60$$
or n = 30
$$\Rightarrow A = 30, B = 90$$

$$\text{A \& B will do } \frac{1}{30} + \frac{1}{90} = \frac{4}{90} = \frac{2}{45} \text{ work in a day}$$

$$\text{So they will complete the work in } \frac{45}{2} = 22\frac{1}{2} \text{ days}$$

31. (d) Let the mother's age be y years.
$$\therefore \text{ The age of father} = (y + 9) \text{ years}$$

$$\text{The age of son} = \frac{y}{2} \text{ years}$$

$$\text{The age of daughter} = \left(\frac{y}{2} - 7\right) \text{years}$$

Now according to the given condition,

$$(y+9) = 3\left(\frac{y}{2} - 7\right)$$

$$\Rightarrow \qquad y+9 = \frac{3y - 42}{2}$$

$$\Rightarrow \qquad 2y + 18 = 3y - 42$$

$$\Rightarrow \qquad y = 60 \text{ years}$$

32. (c) Let monthly income of Komal and Asha be $4x$ and $3x$ Also, let Monthly expenses of Komal and Asha be $3y$ and $2y$.
Now, $4x - 3y = 600$ ......(i)
            $3x - 2y = 600$ .....(ii)
Solving (i) and (ii), $x = 600$ and $y = 600$
$\therefore$ Total monthly income = $(4 + 3)(600) = ₹ 4200$

33. (b) Let the worker takes t min originally and distance of the factory from his house be x.

Now,
$$x = \frac{(t+3)5}{60} = \frac{(t-7)6}{60}$$

$$\frac{(t+3)5}{60} = \frac{(t-7)6}{60}$$
$$5t+15 = 6t-42$$
$$t = 57$$

$\therefore$
$$x = \frac{(57+3)5}{60} = 5 \text{ km.}$$

34. (c) Relative speed of faster train with respect to the slower train $= \dfrac{(65-29)\times1000}{3600} = 10$ m/s

$\therefore$ Length of the faster train = Relative speed × time taken
$$= 10 \times 16 = 160 \text{ m}$$

35. (b) Let initial dimensions be, l & b $\therefore$ Final length is $1.4\,l$ Final breadth is $0.8\,b$

$\therefore$ Final area is $= 1.4\,l \times 0.8\,b$
$$= 1.12\,lb = lb + 12\% \text{ of } lb$$

$\therefore$ Area is increased by 12%.

Alternate Method : $+40-20+\dfrac{40\times(-20)}{100}$

$= 20 - 8 = 12\%$

Therefore, the area of the new garden increased by 12%

36. (a) Total votes $= 6000$
Invalid votes $= 25\%$ of 6000
$\therefore$ Valid votes $= 75\%$ of $6000 = 4500$
Bhiku gets $= 65\%$ of $4500 = 2925$ votes
$\therefore$ Mhatre gets $= 4500 - 2925 = 1575$ votes.

37. (b) S.I. $= 5700 - 5000 = ₹\,700$

$\therefore R = \dfrac{\text{S.I.} \times 100}{\text{Principal} \times \text{Time}} = \dfrac{700 \times 100}{5000 \times 2} = 7\%$ per annum

New rate $= 11\%$

$\therefore$ S.I. $= \dfrac{5000 \times 11 \times 2}{100} = ₹\,1100$

$\therefore$ Amount $= ₹\,(5000 + 1100) = ₹\,6100$

38. (a) Suppose her income is 5. So his expenditure after 12% increase becomes 3.36 and income after 10% increase becomes 5.5. Net increase in saving is 0.14. So percentage increase in savings is 7 per cent.

39. (d) Required difference

$$= \left[5000\left(1+\frac{12}{100}\right)^2 - 5000 \right] - \frac{5000 \times 12 \times 2}{100}$$

$$= 5000\left(\frac{28}{25} \times \frac{28}{25} - 1\right) - 1200$$

$$= 5000\left(\frac{784 - 625}{625}\right) - 1200 = ₹\,72$$

40. (a) Part of the capacity of the cistern emptied by the leak in one hour $= \left(\dfrac{1}{6} - \dfrac{1}{7}\right) = \dfrac{1}{42}$ of the cistern.

The whole cistern will be emptied in 42 hours.

41. (b) Distance between the 1st and 21st posts
$$= (21-1) \times 50 = 1000 \text{ m}$$
Therefore, the speed of train $= 1$ km/min $= 60$ km/h

42. (d) Given, ratio of speeds of A and B is $5:4$.
$\therefore$ B makes 4 rounds when A makes 5 rounds.
Now, distance covered by A in 5 rounds
$$= \left(5 \times \frac{400}{1000}\right) = 2\,\text{km}$$
and distance covered by B in 4 rounds
$$= \left(4 \times \frac{400}{1000}\right) \text{km} = 1.6\,\text{km}$$

It is clear that in 5 hours, A passes B only once. (i.e., 1 time).

In other words, in covering 2 km, A pases B 1 time.

$\therefore$ In covering 5 km, A passes B in $\left(\dfrac{1}{2} \times 5\right)$ times

i.e., $2\dfrac{1}{2}$ times.

43. (b) Let us check each of the options here starting with (a)

(a) $\dfrac{13}{5} + \dfrac{11}{6} = \dfrac{133}{30} < 5$

(b) $\dfrac{11}{4} + \dfrac{8}{3} = \dfrac{65}{12} > 5$

44. (b) Correct asecending order is

$$\frac{2}{3} < \frac{9}{13} < \frac{5}{7} < \frac{8}{11}$$

45. (d) Part of the tank filled in 2 hours $= \dfrac{1}{2} + \dfrac{1}{5} = \dfrac{7}{10}$

Part of the tank emptied in an hour when all three are opened $= \dfrac{1}{4} + \dfrac{1}{5} - \dfrac{1}{2} = -\dfrac{1}{20}$

$\therefore$ Time taken $= \dfrac{7}{10} \times 20 = 14$ hours

It means 5 p.m.

46. (c)

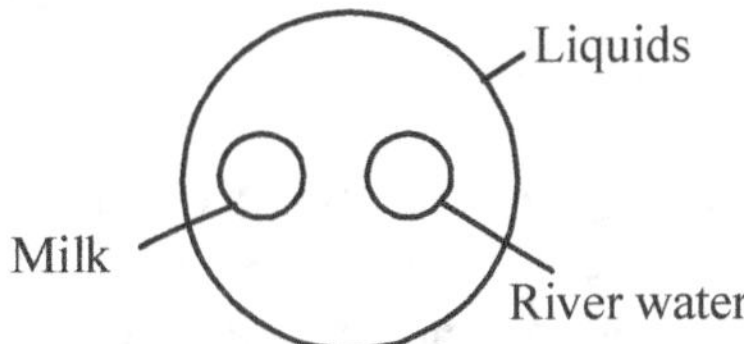

47. **(c)**

48. **(c)**
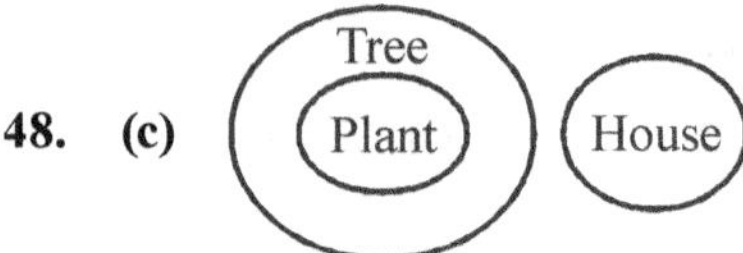

49. **(c)** Capsules are different from injection but both are uses as antibiotics.

50. **(b)** Some athletes may be football players and vice-versa.
Some athletes may be cricket players and vice-versa.
Some athletes may be both football players and cricket players.
Some cricket players may be football players and vice-versa.

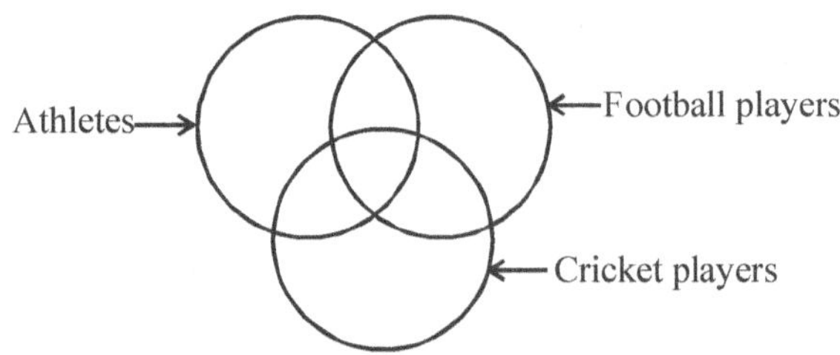

51. **(d)** Orange is the only citrus fruit in the group.

52. **(d)** All except Locust are reptiles, while locust is an insect.

53. **(b)** All except Groundnut are spices.

54. **(d)** All except Vapour are different forms of precipitation.

55. **(d)** Mercury is the only liquid metal in the group.

56. **(c)** As Microphone makes sound louder similarly Microscope makes the object magnified.

57. **(c)** As magnet has poles similarly battery has terminals.

58. **(a)** Priest wears cassock while Graduate wears gown.

59. **(c)** As Ornithologist is a specialist of Birds similarly Archealogist is a specialist of Archealogy.

60. **(d)** As Cloth is made in a Mill, similarly Newspaper is printed in press.

61. **(d)** Sentiment is a feeling especially based on emotions.

62. **(c)** Disagreement always creates controversy.

63. **(c)** A news paper always consists news.

64. **(a)** Early in the morning the sun is in the direction of east. If we are going towards the south, our face will be in the direction of South and our left hand will be in the direction of east.
Hence if we go early in the morning towards the south the sun will always be visible at our left.

65. **(b)**

66. **(b)** By visualizing the figure, we get option (b) is correct.

67. **(a)** By visualizing the figure, we get option (a) is correct.

68. **(d)** By visualizing the figure, we get option (d) is correct.

69. **(b)** Each time line rotates in $+45°, +90°, +135°, +180°, +225°$ clockwise direction. Hence, option (b) is correct.

70. **(d)** By visualizing the figure, we get option (d) is correct.

71. **(a)** By visualizing the figure, we get option (a) is correct.

72. **(d)**

73. **(d)** By visualizing the figure, we get option (d) is correct.

74. **(a)** In each figure semicircle is in inside the square and placed diagonally opposite to each other. Hence option (a) is not fit to the pattern.

75. **(c)** By visualizing the figure, we get option (c) is correct.

76. **(a)** Going by mirror image, we get option (a) is correct.

77. **(a)**   **78.** **(d)**   **79.** **(a)**

80. **(d)**
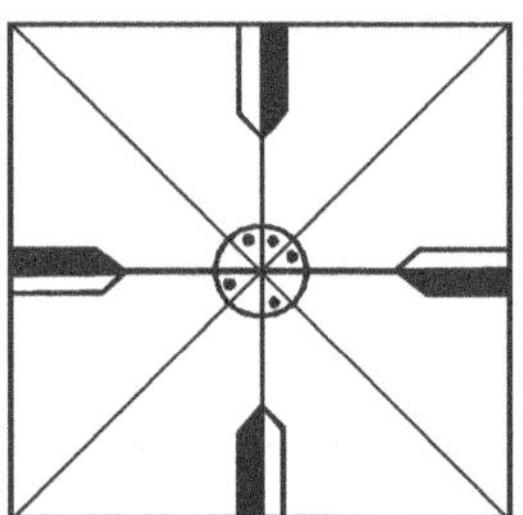

81. **(b)** Under Article 32 of the Constitution, an individual can directly move to the Supreme Court in Case of any violation of fundamental rights. Fundamental Rights are those rights which are essential for the growth of an individual's personality and are enjoyed by every citizen irrespective of caste, color, creed, race and sex.

82. **(d)** The Dandi March of Gandhi was an important part of the Indian Independence Movement.It was a direct action campaign of tax resistance and non-violent protest against British saltmonopoly and triggered the wider Civil Disobedience Movement.

83. **(d)** Aihole inscription is found at Aihole in Karnataka state India, was written by the Ravikriti,court poet of Chalukya king,Pulakeshin II who reigned from 610 to 642 CE.The poetic verses of Ravikirti,in praise of the king, can be read in the Meguti temple,dated 634CE.

84. **(c)** The filtration unit of kidney is known as nephron. Kidneys filter the nitrogenous waste products of the body through nephron and throw them out in the form of urine. Kidneys and skin are the chief organs of excretion.

85. **(b)** Yeast is an important source of vitamin B. Yeasts is eukaryotic microorganisms classified in the kingdom Fungi, with 1,500 species (estimated to be 1% of all fungal species). Yeasts are unicellular, although some species with yeast forms may become multicellular through the formation of strings of connected budding cells known as pseudohyphae, or false hyphae, as seen in most molds.

86. **(a)** Godavari is the longest river of peninsular India. From its source to the Eastern Ghats, the Godavari River flows through gentle, somewhat monotonous terrain, along the way receiving the Darna, Purna, Manjra, Pranhita, and Indravati rivers. Upon entering the Eastern Ghats region, however, the river flows between steep and precipitous banks, its width contracting until it flows through a deep cleft only 600 feet (180 metres) wide, known as the Gorge.

87. (a) Minorities Rights Day is observed in India in 18th December. National Commission for Minorities celebrated Minorities Rights Day on 18 December 2012. Minorities Rights Day is celebrated on 18th December every year. The day is celebrated to protect rights of the minorities communities as well as bringing the better understanding among religious minorities in India.

88. (b) "Sattriya Nritya" is a classical dance form of India and has originated in Assam. Sattriya or Sattriya Nritya , is one among the eight principal classical Indian dance traditions. In the year 2000, the Sattriya dances of Assam received recognition as one of the eight classical dance forms of India.

89. (c)   90. (b)   91. (b)

92. (d) Jean Tirole has won Nobel Prize for his analysis of market power and regulation.

93. (c) The ozone layer is a layer in Earth's atmosphere that absorbs most of the Sun's UV radiation. It contains relatively high concentrations of ozone (O_3), although it is still very small with regard to ordinary oxygen, and is less than ten parts per million, the average ozone concentration in Earth's atmosphere being only about 0.6 parts per million. The ozone layer is mainly found in the lower portion of the stratosphere from approximately 20 to 30 kilometres (12 to 19 miles) above Earth, though the thickness varies seasonally and geographically.

94. (b) Bilal Tanweer has been awarded with Shakti Bhatt First Book Prize- 2014 for his novel "The scatter here is too great".

95. (a)   96.   (c)

97. (a) The Blue Revolution is related with fish production.

98. (c) Plimsol line is not a line of demarcation between two countries.

99. (c) The first major attempt in curriculum reconstruction in India was made in 1937 when Gandhiji propounded the idea of Basic Education.

100. (c)

Practice Set

Time: 2 hrs.   *Max. Marks: 300*

SECTION-A : VERBAL ABILITY IN ENGLISH

DIRECTION (Qs. 1 - 5) : *Select the most appropriate word from the options against each number :*

Auctions are public __(1)__ of goods, conducted by an __(2)__ auctioneer. He encourages buyers to __(3)__ higher prices and finally names the __(4)__ bidder as the buyer of the goods. This is called 'knocking down' the goods, for when the bidding ends the auctioneer __(5)__ a small hammer on a table in front of him.

1. (a) sale   (b) marketing
   (c) promotion   (d) viewing
2. (a) authoritative   (b) allowed
   (c) authentic   (d) approved
3. (a) bid   (b) buy
   (c) get   (d) bargain
4. (a) smartest   (b) highest
   (c) biggest   (d) strongest
5. (a) bangs   (b) thrashes
   (c) smashes   (d) hits

DIRECTIONS (Qs. 6 - 8) : *Choose the word which is nearest in meaning to the given word :*

6. Apprise :
   (a) Praise   (b) Inform
   (c) Conceal   (d) Assess
7. Periodic :
   (a) Infrequent   (b) Continuous
   (c) Occasional   (d) Regular
8. Gruesome :
   (a) Sullen   (b) Hideous
   (c) Exhausting   (d) Insulting

DIRECTIONS (Qs. 9 - 11) : *Choose the word which is nearly opposite in meaning to the given word :*

9. Knack :
   (a) Talent   (b) Dullness
   (c) Dexterity   (d) Balance
10. Pernicious :
    (a) Prolonged   (b) Ruinous
    (c) Ruthless   (d) Beneficial
11. Opulence :
    (a) Luxury   (b) Transparency
    (c) Weath   (d) Poverty

DIRECTIONS (Qs. 12 - 16) : *Read the following passage carefully and answer the questions given below it :*

Freedom has assuredly given us a new status and new opportunities. But it also implies that we should discard selfishness, laziness and all narrowness of outlook. Our freadom suggests toil and creation of new values for old ones. We should so discipline ourselves as to be able to discharge our new responsibilities satisfactorily. If there is any one thing that needs to be stressed more, than any other in the new set-up, it is that we should put into action our full, capacity, each one of us in productive effort - each one of us in his own sphere, however humble. Work, unceasing work, should now be our watch-word. Work is wealth, and service is happiness. Nothing else is. The greatest crime in India today is idleness. If we root out idleness, all our difficulties, including even conflicts, will gradually disappear.

12. Anyone can free himself from the clutches of difficulties, if he
    (a) eliminates narrow outlook
    (b) fulfils his responsibilities
    (c) discards idleness
    (d) discharges his obligations
13. What has freedom undeniably offered to the citizens of India ?
    (a) New opportunities   (b) New outlook
    (c) New responsibilities   (d) New values

14. One thing needs to be stressed more than anything else in this new set-up. It is that people should
   - (a)   discard narrowness of outlook
   - (b)   discipline themselves suitably
   - (c)   work to their full capacity
   - (d)   substitute old values with new ones

15. Work should be the motto of our citizens.
   - (a)   Resourceful   (b)   Incessant
   - (c)   Productive   (d)   Ingenious

16. Nothing else can give us joy except
   - (a)   service   (b)   idleness
   - (c)   wealth   (d)   freedom

DIRECTIONS (Qs. 17 - 21) : *In the following questions, four alternatives are given for the Idiom/Phrase underlined. Choose the alternative which best expresses the meaning of the Idiom/ Phrase and mark it in the Answer Sheet.*

17. To be above board.
   - (a)   To have a good height
   - (b)   To be honest in any business deal
   - (c)   Having no debts
   - (d)   To try to be beautiful

18. To cry wolf.
   - (a)   To listen eagerly   (b)   To give false alarm
   - (c)   To turn pale   (d)   To keep off starvation

19. He is on the wrong side of seventy.
   - (a)   more than seventy years old
   - (b)   less than seventy years old
   - (c)   seventy years old
   - (d)   eighty years old

20. To have an axe to grind.
   - (a)   a private end to serve
   - (b)   to fail to arouse interest
   - (c)   to have no result
   - (d)   to work for both sides

21. To drive home.
   - (a)   To find one's root
   - (b)   To return to place of rest
   - (c)   Back to original position
   - (d)   To emphasise

DIRECTIONS (Qs. 22 - 25) : *In the following questions four words are given in each question, out of which only one word is correctly spelt. Find the correctly spelt word and indicate it in the Answer-Sheet by blackening the appropriate rectangle [■].*

22. (a)   garulous   (b)   garrulous
        (c)   garullous   (d)   garrullous

23. (a)   marquee   (b)   markue
        (c)   marquei   (d)   marquie

24. (a)   puissant   (b)   puiscant
        (c)   puiscent   (d)   puissent

25. (a)   disconncerting   (b)   disconserting
        (c)   discuncerting   (d)   disconcerting

SECTION-B : NUMERICAL ABILITY

26. Divide 50 into two parts so that the sum of their reciprocals is 1/12.
   - (a)   28, 22   (b)   35, 15
   - (c)   20, 30   (d)   24, 36

27. Rakesh got 273 marks in an examination and scored 5% more than the pass %. If Lokesh got 312 marks, then by what % above the pass mark did he pass the examination?
   - (a)   20%   (b)   27%
   - (c)   25%   (d)   15%

28. A man sold an article at a loss of 20%. If he sells the article for ₹ 12 more, he would have gained 10%. The cost price of the article is
   - (a)   ₹ 60   (b)   ₹ 40
   - (c)   ₹ 30   (d)   ₹ 22

29. What is the least fraction which, when added to or subtracted from $\dfrac{29}{12} + \dfrac{15}{16}$, will make the result a whole number ?
   - (a) $\dfrac{21}{38}$ (b) $\dfrac{31}{38}$
   - (c) $\dfrac{31}{48}$ (d) $\dfrac{17}{48}$

30. Among the goods purchased by a trader, two-fifth were sold at 20% loss, and the reamaining were sold at a profit. If on the whole 10% profit is made, what per cent of profit did the trader make on the remaining goods ?
   - (a)   15%   (b)   20%
   - (c)   30%   (d)   40%

31. Two equal sums of money were invested, one at 4% and the other at 4.5%. At the end of 7 years, the simple interest received from the latter exceeded to that received from the former by Rs 31.50. Each sum was :
   - (a)   Rs 1,200   (b)   Rs 600
   - (c)   Rs 750   (d)   Rs 900

32. Three brothers A, B and C divided a sum among them selves and their mother in the ratio 3 : 3 : 3 : 4. If their mother got ₹ 5,000 more than each son, how much amount did all the three brothers get ?
   - (a)   ₹ 15,000   (b)   ₹ 65,000
   - (c)   ₹ 30,000   (d)   ₹ 45,000

33. A train 100 metres long meets a man going in opposite Directions at 5 km/hr and passes him in $7\dfrac{1}{5}$ seconds. What is the speed of the train in km/hr ?
   - (a)   45 km/hr   (b)   60 km/hr
   - (c)   55 km/hr   (d)   50 km/hr

34. If $x + y > 5$ and $x - y > 3$, then which of the following gives all possible values of x ?
   - (a) $x > 3$ (b) $x > 4$
   - (c) $x > 5$ (d) $x < 5$

35. After having spent 35% of the money on machinery, 40% on raw material and 10% on staff, a person is left with Rs 60,000. The total amount of money spent on machinery and raw material is :

(a) Rs 1,76,000 (b) Rs 1,70,000
(c) Rs 3,00,000 (d) Rs 3,40,000

36. An aeroplane travels distances 2500 km, 1200km and 500km at the rate of 500 km/hr, 400 km/hr, and 250 km/hr, respectively. The average speed is

(a) 420 km/hr (b) 405 km/hr
(c) 410 km/hr (d) 575 km/hr

37. The population of a village is 10,000. If the population increases by 10% in the first year, by 20% in the second year and due to mass exodus, it decreases by 5 % in the third year, what will be its population after 3 years ?

(a) 13,860 (b) 11,540
(c) 12,860 (d) 12,540

38. A plane left 30 min later than its scheduled time to reach its destination 1500 km away. In order to reach in time it increases its speed by 250 km/h. What is its original speed ?

(a) 1000 km/h (b) 750 km/h
(c) 600 km/h (d) 800 km/h

39. X and Y can do a piece of work in 30 days. They work together for 6 days and then X quits and Y finishes the work in 32 more days. In how many days can Y do the piece of work alone ?

(a) 30 days (b) 32 days
(c) 34 days (d) 40 days

40. The ratio of two numbers is 3 : 4. If 5 is added to both the numbers, the ratio becomes 4 : 5. The product of the numbers added to the sum of the squares of the numbers is

(a) 950 (b) 925
(c) 700 (d) 725

41. A cistern has a leak which would empty it in 8 hours. A tap is turned on which admits 6 litres a minute into the cistern and it is now emptied in 12 hours. The cistern can hold

(a) 7860 litres (b) 6840 litres
(c) 8640 litres (d) None of these

42. If a% of x is equal to b% of y, then c% of y is what % of x ?

(a) c% (b) $\dfrac{ac}{b}$%

(c) $\dfrac{bc}{a}$% (d) abc%

43. In a class, the average score of girls in an examination is 73 and that of boys is 71. The average score of the whole class is 71.8. The percentage of the girls in the class is :

(a) 60% (b) 40%
(c) 1.8% (d) 18%

44. Two numbers are such as that square of one is 224 less than 8 times the square of the other. If the numbers are in the ratio

of 3 : 4, they are:

(a) 12, 16 (b) 6, 8
(c) 9, 12 (d) None of these

45. A train 300 m long is running at a speed of 90 km/hr. How many seconds will it take to cross a 200 m long train running in the opposite direction at a speed of 60 km/hr ?

(a) $7\dfrac{1}{5}$ (b) 60

(c) 12 (d) 20

DIRECTIONS (Qs. 46 - 47) : *Complete the series.*

46. YVP, WTN, URL, ?

(a) SPJ (b) TQLS
(c) VSP (d) SRJ

47. BD, FH, JL, NP, ?

(a) PQ (b) RS
(c) SU (d) RT

48. If A = 1, ACE = 9, then ART = ?

(a) 29 (b) 38
(c) 10 (d) 39

49. If A = 26, SUN = 27, then CAT = _________

(a) 27 (b) 72
(c) 57 (d) 58

50. If O = 16, FOR = 42, then what is FRONT equal to?

(a) 61 (b) 65
(c) 73 (d) 78

DIRECTIONS (Qs. 51-55): *Choose the word which is least like the other words in the group.*

51. (a) Skull (b) Appendix
(c) Pelvis (d) Fibula

52. (a) Island (b) Coast
(c) Harbour (d) Oasis

53. (a) Tonnes (b) Quintals
(c) Kilometres (d) Kilograms

54. (a) Tomato (b) Carrot
(c) Ginger (d) Potato

55. (a) Verse (b) Rhyme
(c) Couplet (d) Rhetoric

DIRECTIONS (Qs. 56-60) : *In each of the following questions find out the alternative which will replace the question mark.*

56. Ice : Coldness :: Earth : ?

(a) Weight (b) Jungle
(c) Gravitation (d) Sea

57. Physician : Treatment :: Judge : ?

(a) Punishment (b) Judgement
(c) Lawyer (d) Court

58. Flow : River :: Stagnant : ?

(a) Rain (b) Stream

(c) Pool   (d) Canal

59. Country : President :: State : ?

(a) Governor   (b) M.P

(c) Legislator   (d) Minister

60. Melt : Liquid :: Freeze : ?

(a) Ice   (b) Condense

(c) Solid   (d) Force

DIRECTIONS (Qs. 61-63) : *Consider the statement and assumptions that follow. Which of these assumption is/are implicit in the statement*

61. Statement: The situation of this area still continues to be tense and out of control. People are requested to be in their homes only.

Assumptions:

I. There had been some serious incidents.

II. People will not go to the office.

III. Normalcy will be restored shortly.

(a) Only I is implicit

(b) Only I and II are implicit

(c) Only I and III are implicit

(d) All are implicit

62. Statement: To improve the employment situation in India, there is a need to recast the present educational system towards implementation of scientific discoveries in daily life.

Assumptions:

I. The students after completing such education may be able to earn their livelihood.

II. This may bring meaning of education in the minds of the youth.

III. The state may earn more revenue as more and more people will engage themselves in self-employment.

(a) Only I and II are implicit

(b) Only III is implicit

(c) Only I and III are implicit

(d) None of these

63. Pramod decided to get the railway reservation in May, for the journey he wants to make in July, to Madras.

Assumptions:

I. The railways issues reservations two months in advance.

II. There are more than one trains to Madras.

III. There will be vacancy in the desired class.

(a) Only I is implicit

(b) Only II and III are implicit

(c) Only I and III are implicit

(d) All are implicit

DIRECTIONS (Qs. 64 & 65) : *Each of the question below has a set of 4 statements. Each statement has 3 segments. Choose the alternative where the third segment can be logically deduced, using both the preceding two, but not just from one of them.*

64. (A) To forgive is divine. Divine facts are rare. Forgiveness is rare.

(B) G is the brother of A and the father of L. B is the wife of A. L is the daughter of G.

(C) Pepsi contains added flavour. Coke contains permitted colours. Pepsi and Coke are cold drinks.

(D) Some beer is wine and some beer is vodka. All wine is vodka. All beer must be vodka or wine.

(a) Only A   (b) A & B

(c) C & A   (d) Only D

65. (A) All Jadoo is Magic. Some magic is witchcraft. Some Jadoo is witchcraft.

(B) Floor C is two storeys above floor D. Floor E & A are adjacent and above the floor C. In the Storey complex, Floor D is the ground Floor.

(C) In the Kingdom of Lemon Grass, Tom Yarn is 400 km from Jom Yarn. Tom Kha is 300 km from Jom Yorn, and away from Tom Yarn. Tom Kha and Tom Yarn are 700 km apart.

(D) Ford 1 km is a josh machine. Hyundai Santro is the complete family car. There is little josh in Santro.

(a) A & C   (b) Only B

(c) A & D   (d) B & C

DIRECTIONS (Qs. 66 - 69) : In each of the following questions, figure X is given with a part missing. Choose the alternative which will complete the missing part.

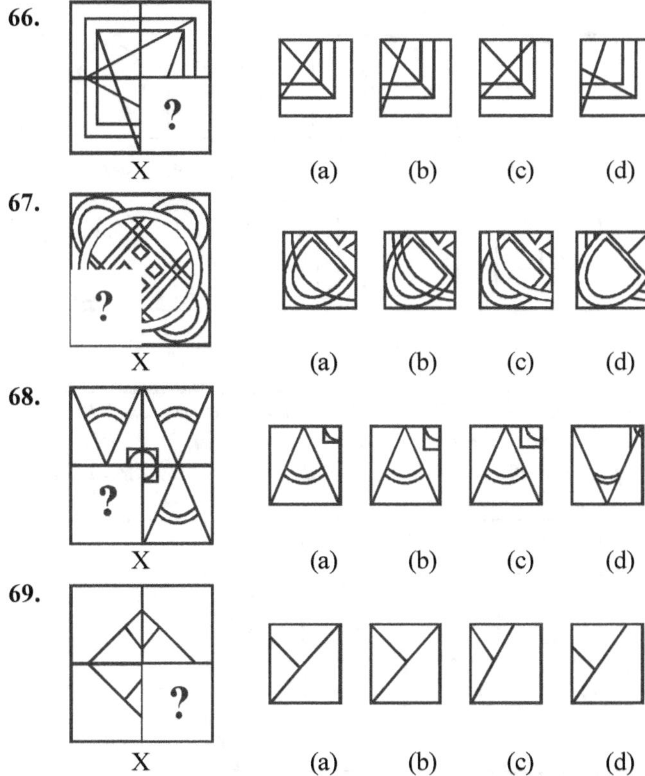

66. X   (a)   (b)   (c)   (d)

67. X   (a)   (b)   (c)   (d)

68. X   (a)   (b)   (c)   (d)

69. X   (a)   (b)   (c)   (d)

DIRECTIONS (Qs. 70 - 73) : In each of the questions, a part of the figure is given. Select one from the given four figures in which that part is embedded.

70. 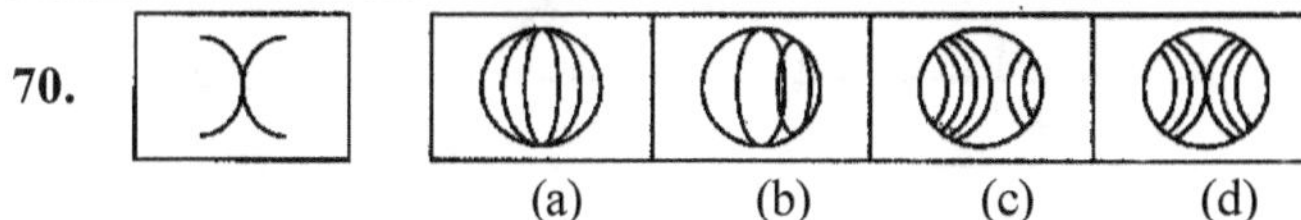

(a)   (b)   (c)   (d)

71. 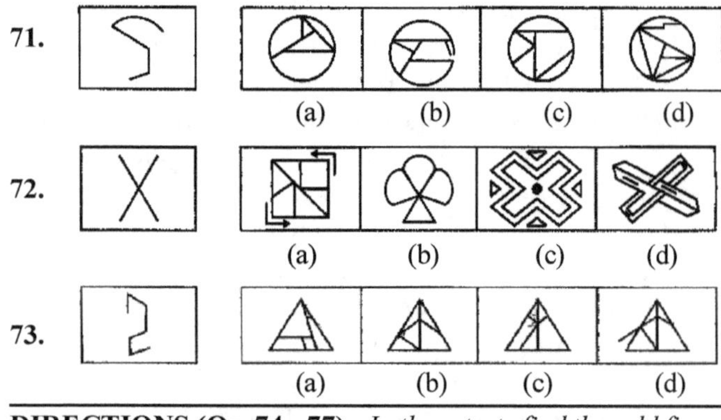

72.

73.

(a) (b) (c) (d)

DIRECTIONS (Qs. 74 - 77) : *In these tests find the odd figure out.*

74. 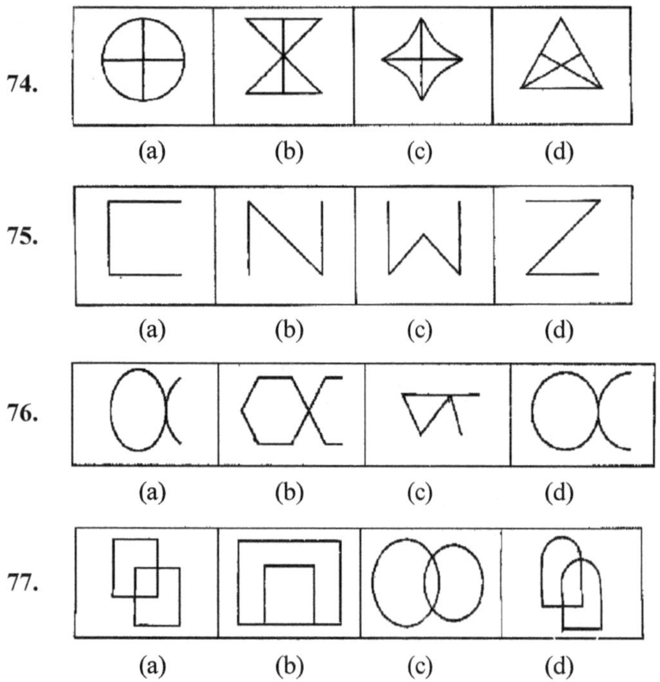

(a) (b) (c) (d)

75.

(a) (b) (c) (d)

76.

(a) (b) (c) (d)

77. 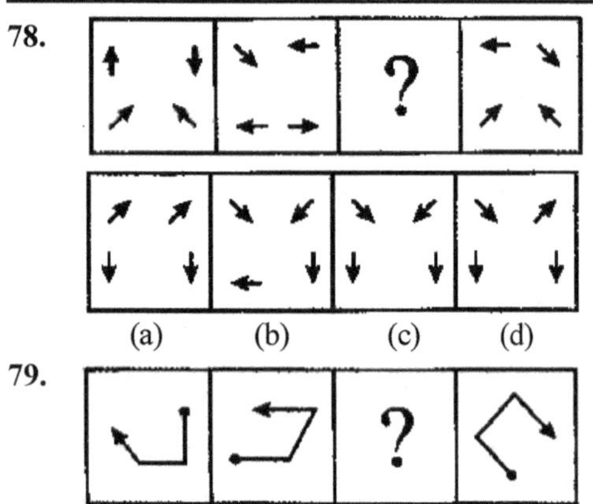

(a) (b) (c) (d)

DIRECTIONS (Qs. 78 - 80) : *In each of the questions, which one of the four numbered figures from the right side row will replace the question mark in the left side row so as to maintain the sequence ?*

78.

(a) (b) (c) (d)

79.

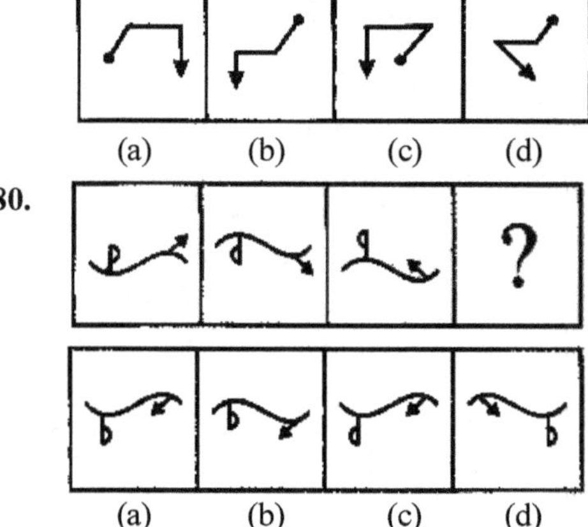

(a) (b) (c) (d)

80.

(a) (b) (c) (d)

81. In context to India's defence structure 'Agni missile' is _______ .
- (a) Surface-to-air
- (b) Air-to-air
- (c) Air-to-surface
- (d) Surface-to-surface

82. The programme of 'Operation Flood' was concentrated on
- (a) increasing irrigation facilities.
- (b) flood control.
- (c) increasing the milk production.
- (d) increase the flood grains production.

83. Article 324 of the Indian Constitution deals with the
- (a) imposition of President's Rule in States.
- (b) appointment of Finance Commission.
- (c) powers and functions of the Chief Election Commissioner.
- (d) functions of the Union Public Service Commission.

84. The founder of the Lodi Dynasty was
- (a) Bahlul Lodi
- (b) Sikandar Shah Lodi
- (c) Jalal Khan Lodi
- (d) Ibrahim Lodi

85. Which General, who commanded the British forces against the Americans in their War of Independence later became Governor-General of India ?
- (a) Dalhousie
- (b) William Bentinck
- (c) Wellesley
- (d) Cornwallis

86. The Constitutional Amendment Act that has introduced safeguards against the misuse of proclamation of national emergency is the
- (a) 42nd Amendment Act
- (b) 43rd Amendment Act
- (c) 44th Amendment Act
- (d) 45th Amendment Act

87. The Fundamental Rights can be suspended by the
- (a) Governor
- (b) President
- (c) Law Minister
- (d) Prime Minister

88. Prithvi Raj Chauhan was defeated in the Second Battle of Tarain by
- (a) Mahmud Ghazni
- (b) Muhammad Ghori
- (c) Qutbuddin Aibak
- (d) Yalduz

89. The city of Prayag was named Allahabad - the city of Allah by
    (a) Aurangzeb   (b) Akbar
    (c) Shahjahan   (d) Bahadur Shah Zafar
90. Which one of the following wars decided the fate of the French in India ?
    (a) Battle of Plassey
    (b) Battle of Wandiwash
    (c) First Carnatic War
    (d) Battle of Buxar
91. Which one of the following is a warm ocean current ?
    (a) Gulf Stream   (b) Kurile
    (c) Canary   (d) Labrador
92. The main advantage of Rain Water Harvesting (RWH) is
    (a) Avoid soil erosion
    (b) Recharge ground water
    (c) Avoid floods
    (d) Reduce the loss of water
93. Who was the first posthumous recipient of Bharat Ratna?
    (a) M.G. Ramachandran (b) B.R. Ambedkar
    (c) K. Kamraj   (d) Lal Bahadur Shastri
94. Which day is observed as "International Day of Non-Violence"
    (a) 1 st May   (b) 2 nd October
    (c) 24 th October   (d) 30 th January

95. Lakshmibai National Institute of Physical Education (LNIPE) is in:
    (a) Patiala   (b) Gwalior
    (c) Indore   (d) Jhansi
96. Amuktamalyada is the work of :
    (a) Krishnadeva Raya   (b) Vachcharaj
    (c) Kharavela   (d) Allasani Peddana
97. Yakshagana is a folk dance-drama of:
    (a) Maharashtra   (b) Karnataka
    (c) Gujarat   (d) W. Bengal
98. The 'Panch Prayag' which connotes the five sacred river confluences is in the state of ___________.
    (a) Himachal Pradesh   (b) Madhya Pradesh
    (c) Uttarakhand   (d) Andhra Pradesh
99. The 'Yashsvini Health Insurance' scheme is associated with which of the following states?
    (a) Punjab   (b) Karnataka
    (c) Tamil Nadu   (d) Andhra Pradesh
100. Which of the following pairs is incorrect ?
    (a) Amirkhusro – Sarod
    (b) Bhim Sen Joshi – Vocal music
    (c) Utpal Dutt – Films
    (d) Shambhu Maharaj – Kathak

RESPONSE SHEET

1. ⓐⓑⓒⓓ	2. ⓐⓑⓒⓓ	3. ⓐⓑⓒⓓ	4. ⓐⓑⓒⓓ	5. ⓐⓑⓒⓓ
6. ⓐⓑⓒⓓ	7. ⓐⓑⓒⓓ	8. ⓐⓑⓒⓓ	9. ⓐⓑⓒⓓ	10. ⓐⓑⓒⓓ
11. ⓐⓑⓒⓓ	12. ⓐⓑⓒⓓ	13. ⓐⓑⓒⓓ	14. ⓐⓑⓒⓓ	15. ⓐⓑⓒⓓ
16. ⓐⓑⓒⓓ	17. ⓐⓑⓒⓓ	18. ⓐⓑⓒⓓ	19. ⓐⓑⓒⓓ	20. ⓐⓑⓒⓓ
21. ⓐⓑⓒⓓ	22. ⓐⓑⓒⓓ	23. ⓐⓑⓒⓓ	24. ⓐⓑⓒⓓ	25. ⓐⓑⓒⓓ
26. ⓐⓑⓒⓓ	27. ⓐⓑⓒⓓ	28. ⓐⓑⓒⓓ	29. ⓐⓑⓒⓓ	30. ⓐⓑⓒⓓ
31. ⓐⓑⓒⓓ	32. ⓐⓑⓒⓓ	33. ⓐⓑⓒⓓ	34. ⓐⓑⓒⓓ	35. ⓐⓑⓒⓓ
36. ⓐⓑⓒⓓ	37. ⓐⓑⓒⓓ	38. ⓐⓑⓒⓓ	39. ⓐⓑⓒⓓ	40. ⓐⓑⓒⓓ
41. ⓐⓑⓒⓓ	42. ⓐⓑⓒⓓ	43. ⓐⓑⓒⓓ	44. ⓐⓑⓒⓓ	45. ⓐⓑⓒⓓ
46. ⓐⓑⓒⓓ	47. ⓐⓑⓒⓓ	48. ⓐⓑⓒⓓ	49. ⓐⓑⓒⓓ	50. ⓐⓑⓒⓓ
51. ⓐⓑⓒⓓ	52. ⓐⓑⓒⓓ	53. ⓐⓑⓒⓓ	54. ⓐⓑⓒⓓ	55. ⓐⓑⓒⓓ
56. ⓐⓑⓒⓓ	57. ⓐⓑⓒⓓ	58. ⓐⓑⓒⓓ	59. ⓐⓑⓒⓓ	60. ⓐⓑⓒⓓ
61. ⓐⓑⓒⓓ	62. ⓐⓑⓒⓓ	63. ⓐⓑⓒⓓ	64. ⓐⓑⓒⓓ	65. ⓐⓑⓒⓓ
66. ⓐⓑⓒⓓ	67. ⓐⓑⓒⓓ	68. ⓐⓑⓒⓓ	69. ⓐⓑⓒⓓ	70. ⓐⓑⓒⓓ
71. ⓐⓑⓒⓓ	72. ⓐⓑⓒⓓ	73. ⓐⓑⓒⓓ	74. ⓐⓑⓒⓓ	75. ⓐⓑⓒⓓ
76. ⓐⓑⓒⓓ	77. ⓐⓑⓒⓓ	78. ⓐⓑⓒⓓ	79. ⓐⓑⓒⓓ	80. ⓐⓑⓒⓓ
81. ⓐⓑⓒⓓ	82. ⓐⓑⓒⓓ	83. ⓐⓑⓒⓓ	84. ⓐⓑⓒⓓ	85. ⓐⓑⓒⓓ
86. ⓐⓑⓒⓓ	87. ⓐⓑⓒⓓ	88. ⓐⓑⓒⓓ	89. ⓐⓑⓒⓓ	90. ⓐⓑⓒⓓ
91. ⓐⓑⓒⓓ	92. ⓐⓑⓒⓓ	93. ⓐⓑⓒⓓ	94. ⓐⓑⓒⓓ	95. ⓐⓑⓒⓓ
96. ⓐⓑⓒⓓ	97. ⓐⓑⓒⓓ	98. ⓐⓑⓒⓓ	99. ⓐⓑⓒⓓ	100. ⓐⓑⓒⓓ

ANSWERS & SOLUTIONS

1.	(a)	2.	(d)	3.	(a)	4.	(b)
5.	(a)	6.	(b)	7.	(d)	8.	(b)
9.	(b)	10.	(d)	11.	(d)	12.	(c)
13.	(a)	14.	(c)	15.	(b)	16.	(a)

17. (b) If somebody is above board, he/she is honest in any business deal.

18. (b) To cry wolf means that someone is giving false alarm.

19. (a) If somebody is on the right/ wrong side of 30/ 40 etc that means he/she is younger/ older than 30/ 40 etc.

20. (a) If you have an axe to grind; that means you have a private end to serve.

21. (d) If you drive something home, that means you are making something completely clear to someone. She didn't have to drive the point home. The movie had done that.

22. (b) Garrulous

23. (a) Marquee

24. (a) Puissant

25. (d) Disconcerting

26. (c)
$$\frac{1}{x}+\frac{1}{50-x}=\frac{1}{12}$$
$$x^2-50x+600=0$$
$$x^2-30x-20x+600=0$$
$$x(x-30)-20(x-30)=0$$
$$x=30, 20$$

27. (a) Let passing marks be represented by p.
$$p \times 1.05 = 273$$
$$p = 260$$

Lokesh passing $\% = \frac{312-260}{260} \times 100 = 20\%$

28. (b) $S.P = C.P\left(\frac{80}{100}\right) \Rightarrow S.P = \frac{4}{5}C.P$ ...(1)

$S.P + 12 = C.P\left(\frac{110}{100}\right) \Rightarrow S.P = \frac{11}{10}C.P - 12$ ...(2)

From eqn. (1) and (2)

$$\frac{4}{5}C.P = \frac{11}{10}C.P - 12$$

$$\Rightarrow \frac{11}{10}C.P - \frac{4}{5}C.P = 12 \Rightarrow C.P = ₹40$$

29. (d) $\frac{29}{12}+\frac{15}{16}=\frac{116+45}{48}=\frac{161}{48}$

Therefore, $\frac{161}{48}+\frac{31}{48}=\frac{192}{48}=4$ = a whole number

And $\frac{161}{48}-\frac{17}{48}=3$ = whole number

Between $\frac{31}{48}$ and $\frac{17}{48}$; $\frac{17}{48}$ is the least fraction.

Clearly, the least fraction among the given fractions in options is $\frac{17}{48}$.

30. (c) Let number of goods = 100

C.P of each article = ₹ 1

$\therefore$ S.P. of $\frac{2}{5} \times 100 = 40$ article $= ₹\left(40 \times \frac{80}{100}\right) = ₹32.$

Total S.P. = ₹110.

$\therefore$ S.P. of remaining 60 articles $= ₹(110-32) = ₹78$

$\therefore$ Required percentage gain $= \frac{18}{60} \times 100 = 30\%$

31. (d) Let each sum be Rs x. Then
Difference of S.I. = Rs 31.50

$$\frac{x \times 4\frac{1}{2} \times 7}{100} - \frac{x \times 4 \times 7}{100} = 31.50$$

or $\frac{7x}{100} \times \frac{1}{2} = \frac{63}{2}$ or $x = $ Rs 900

32. (d) Let the total amount be x.
Sum of the ratios = 3 + 3 + 3 + 4 = 13

$\therefore \left(\frac{4}{13}-\frac{3}{13}\right) \times x = 5000$

$\therefore x = ₹65000$

$\therefore$ Amount of three brothers

$= \frac{9}{13} \times 65000 = ₹45000$

33. (a) Let speed of train = x km/hr
Distance travelled by train
= Relative speed of train × Time

$100\,m = (x+5)\,km/hr \times \frac{36}{5}$ seconds

$\frac{100}{1000}\,km = (x+5) \times \left(\frac{36}{5} \times \frac{1}{3600}\right)$ hrs

$\Rightarrow \qquad x+5 = 50$

$\therefore \qquad x = 45\,km/hr$

34. (b) $x + y > 5$ ....(i)

$x - y > 3$ ....(ii)

Adding inequations (i) and (ii), we get

$2x > 8$ i.e. $x > 4$

35. (c) Let the original money be Rs 100.

Money spent on machinery = Rs 35

Money spent on raw material = Rs 40

Money spent on staff = Rs 10

Money left = $100 - 85$ = Rs 15

If money left is Rs 15, the original money = 100

So, if money left is 60,000, the original money

$= \dfrac{100}{15} \times 60,000 = \text{Rs.} 400000$

Money spent on machinery and raw material

$= 400000 \times 75\% = $ Rs 300000

36. (a) Given, distances are 2500 km, 1200 km and 500 km.

Given, speeds are 500 km/h, 400 km/h and 250 km/h

$\therefore$ Total time $= \dfrac{2500}{500} + \dfrac{1200}{400} + \dfrac{500}{250}$

$= 5 + 3 + 2 = 10$ hr.

$\therefore$ Average speed $= \dfrac{\text{Total distance}}{\text{Total time}}$

$= \dfrac{2500 + 1200 + 500}{10} = \dfrac{4200}{10}$

$= 420$ km/hr

37. (d) Population after 1st year $= \dfrac{110}{100} \times 10,000 = 11000$

Population after 2nd year $= 11000 \times \dfrac{120}{100} = 13200$

Population after 3rd year $= 13200 \times \dfrac{95}{100} = 12,540$

Hence, population after 3rd year = 12, 540.

38. (b) Let the original time be T hours and original speed be x km/h

$\dfrac{1500}{x} = T$ \qquad ...(i)

$\dfrac{1500}{x + 250} = T - \dfrac{30}{60}$ \qquad ...(ii)

Solving equation (i) and (ii), we get

Speed of plane $= x = 750$ or -1000 (not possible)

$\therefore \quad x = 750$ km/h

39. (d) $(x + y)$'s 6 days' work $= \left(\dfrac{1}{30} \times 6\right) = \dfrac{1}{5}$.

Remaining work $= \left(1 - \dfrac{1}{5}\right) = \dfrac{4}{5}$

Now, $\dfrac{4}{5}$ work is done by y in 32 days.

Whole work will be done by y in $\left(32 \times \dfrac{5}{4}\right) = 40$ days.

40. (b) According to the question $\dfrac{3x + 5}{4x + 5} = \dfrac{4}{5}$

$15x + 25 = 16x + 20$

$\Rightarrow \quad x = 25 - 20 = 5$

$\therefore \quad$ Numbers are 15 and 20

$\therefore \quad$ Required answer $= 15 \times 20 + 15^2 + 20^2 = 925$

41. (c) In 1 hour, empty part $= \dfrac{1}{8}$ th.

When tap is turned on, then

empty part in 1 hour $= \dfrac{1}{12}$ th .

$\therefore \quad$ Part of cistern emptied, due to leakage in

1 hour $= \dfrac{1}{8} - \dfrac{1}{12} = \dfrac{3 - 2}{24} = \dfrac{1}{24}$ th

Now, In 1 min, cistern fill = 6 lit

$\therefore \quad$ In $\dfrac{1}{60}$ hr, cistern fill = 6 lit.

$\therefore \quad$ Cistern can hold $= 6 \times 60 \times 24$ litre = 8640 litre.

42. (b) $\dfrac{ax}{100} = \dfrac{by}{100} \Rightarrow \dfrac{y}{x} = \dfrac{a}{b}$

$\dfrac{\dfrac{cy}{100}}{x} \times 100 = \dfrac{cy}{x} = \dfrac{ca}{b}$

43. (b) Let the number of boys and girls be x and y, respectively.

Then, the total score of boys = 71x

and the total score of girls = 73y

Now, average score = 71. 8

$\therefore \quad \dfrac{71x + 73y}{x + y} = 71.8$

$\Rightarrow \quad 71x + 73y = 71.8x + 71.8y \quad \Rightarrow \quad 0.8x = 1.2y$

$\Rightarrow \quad \dfrac{x}{y} = \dfrac{1.2}{.8} = \dfrac{3}{2}$

$\Rightarrow \quad$ % of girls in the class $= \dfrac{2}{5} \times 100 = 40\%$

44. (b) Given, ratio of numbers is 3 : 4

$\therefore \quad$ The numbers are 3x and 4x.

Now, according to the question

$16x^2 = 8(3x)^2 - 224$

$\Rightarrow \quad 16x^2 = 72x^2 - 224 \quad \Rightarrow \quad 56x^2 = 224$

$\Rightarrow \quad x = 2$

$\therefore \quad$ Required numbers = 6, 8

45. **(c)** Relative speed $= 90 + 60 = 150$ km/hr.

Total distance to be covered $= 300 + 200 = 500$ m

Time required $= \dfrac{500}{150 \times 1000} \times 3600 = 12$ sec.

46. **(a)** 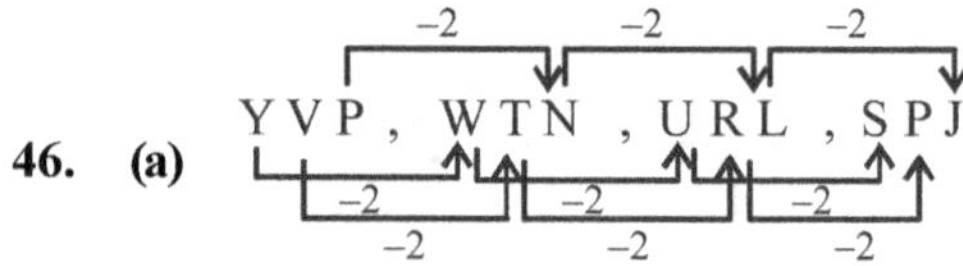

47. **(d)** 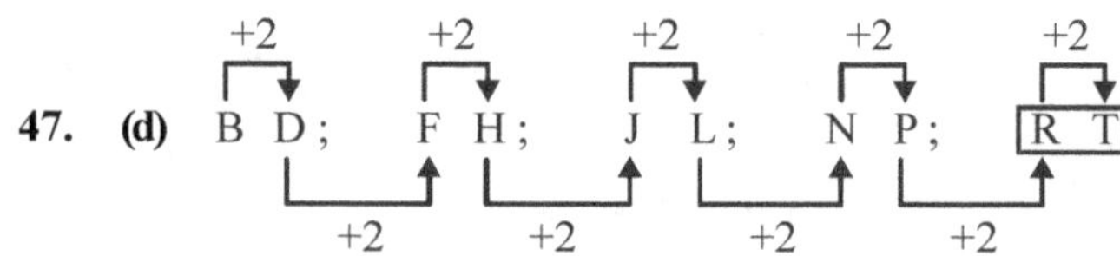

48. **(d)** $A = 1,$ $A + C + E = 1 + 3 + 5 = 9$

$A + R + T = 1 + 18 + 20 = 39$

49. **(c)** Reverse place value of $A = 26$

$SUN = (8 + 6 + 13) = 27$

$\therefore$ $CAT = (24 + 26 + 7) = 57$

50. **(d)** $O = 16,$ $FOR = 42$

$F = 6 + 1$ $= 7$

$R = 18 + 1$ $= 19$

$O = 15 + 1$ $= 16$

$N = 14 + 1$ $= 15$

$T = 20 + 1$ $= 21$

$\overline{78}$

Then, $FRONT = 78$

51. **(b)** All except Appendix are bones, while appendix is an organ.

52. **(d)** All except Oasis are features related to sea, while oasis is related to desert.

53. **(c)** All others are units for measuring weights.

54. **(a)** All except Tomato grow underground.

55. **(d)** All except Rhetoric are terms associated with poetry.

56. **(c)** As effect of Ice is coldness similarly the effect of Earth is gravitation.

57. **(b)** As Physician does the treatment similarly Judge delivers the judgement.

58. **(c)** As Water of a River flows similarly water of Pool is Stagnant.

59. **(a)** As President is the nominal head of a country, similarly Governor is the nominal head of a State.

60. **(c)** As on melting, liquid is formed similarly on freezing solid is formed.

61. **(b)** The statement mentions that situation in the area is tense. So, I is implicit. Since people have been requested not to go out and remain in homes for safety, so II is implicit. It cannot be inferred when the normalcy will be restored. So, III is not implicit.

62. **(a)** The statement mentions that such education can improve employment situation. So, both I and II are implicit. Nothing about the aspect of revenue collection is mentioned in the statement. So, III is not implicit.

63. **(a)** Clearly, since Pramod decides to get the reservation in May for the journey in July, so I is implicit. The number of trains to Madras or the position of vacancies in different classes cannot be deduced from the given statement. So, neither II nor III is implicit.

64. **(a)** 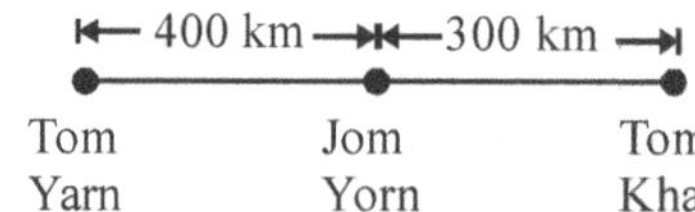

We see that forgiveness is divine and divine facts are rare. So, forgiveness is rare.

65. **(d)** In (a), the middle term 'magic' is not distributed. Therefore no deduction of mediate inference can be established. For (b) first two Statements, we see that the pattern of 5 storeys is as given.

E	→ 4th	(5th storey)
A	→ 3rd	(4th storey)
C	→ 2nd	(3rd storey)
–	→ 1st	(2nd storey)
D	→ Ground	(1st storey)

Clearly, D is the ground floor.

As per the first two statements, the position of cities is as follows:

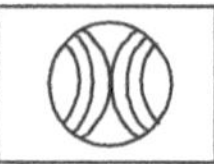

Tom	Jom	Tom
Yarn	Yorn	Kha

Clearly, Tom Kha and Tom Yarn are 700 km apart.

66. **(d)**   **67.** **(c)**   **68.** **(a)**   **69.** **(d)**

70. **(d)**   This figure comes in

71. **(b)**   **72.** **(b)**   **73.** **(b)**

74. **(d)** This figure not makes four equal or similar parts like others.

75. **(c)** This figure use four spokes but others use only three.

76. **(a)** 'Oval' is not a standard figure.

77. **(b)** Small figure partially covered by the big one.

78. **(c)**   **79.** **(c)**   **80.** **(a)**   **81.** **(d)**

82. **(c)** Operation Flood in India, a project of the National Dairy Development Board (NDDB) was the world's biggest dairy development program which made India, a milk-deficient nation, the largest milk producer in the world, surpassing the USA in 1998, with about 17 percent of global output in 2010-11, which in 30 years doubled the milk available per person, and which made dairy farming India's largest self-sustainable rural employment generator. All this was achieved not merely by mass production, but by production by the masses.

83. **(c)** powers and functions of the chief Election Commissioner

84. **(a)** Bahlul Khan Lodi was the founder of Lodi dynasty of the Delhi Sultanate in India upon the abdication of the last claimant from the previous Sayyid rule.

85. **(b)** Lieutenant-General Lord William Henry Cavendish-Bentinck, GCB, GCH, PC, known as Lord William Bentinck, was a British soldier and statesman. He served as Governor-General of India from 1828 to 1835.

86. **(c)**

87. **(b)** The Fundamental Rights can be suspended during the Emergency under Article 359 of the Constitution by the President of India.

88. **(b)** 1191 - First Battle of Tarain in which Prithviraj Chauhan defeated Mohd. Ghori.1192 - Second Battle of Tarain in which Mohd.Ghori defeated Prithviraj Chauhan.

89. **(b)** Emperor Akbar named Prayag as Allahabad - City of God- also called Allahabad in 1575 AD. The city of Allahabad is situated at the confluence of three rivers - Ganga, Yamuna and the invisible Saraswati. Every 12th year when the waters are felt to be especially purifying, Allahabad holds a much greater festival called Kumbh Mela. Built by Emperor Akbar in 1583 AD, the Allahbad fort stands on the banks of the river Yamuna near the confluence site i.e SANGAM.

90. **(b)** Battle of Wandiwash decided the fate of French in India. Battle of Wandiwash, (Jan. 22, 1760), in the history of India, a confrontation between the French, under the comte de Lally, and the British, under Sir Eyre Coote. It was the decisive battle in the Anglo-French struggle in southern India during the Seven Years' War (1756-63).

91. **(a)** Gulf Stream is a warm ocean current. It flows along the North America and drifts towards western Europe, thus raising the temperature of western coast considerably.

92. **(b)** Recharging of ground water is the main advantage of rain water harvesting. Rainwater harvesting provides an independent water supply during regional water restrictions and in developed countries is often used to supplement the main supply. It provides water when there is a drought, can help mitigate flooding of low-lying areas, and reduces demand on wells which may enable ground water levels to be sustained.

93. **(d)** Lal Bahadur Shastri was the first posthumous recipient of Bharat Ratna in 1966. Lal Bahadur Shastri was the third Prime Minister of the Republic of India and a leader of the Indian National Congress party. Shastri joined the Indian independence movement in the 1920s.

94. **(b)**　　　**95.** **(b)**　　　**96.** **(a)**　　　**97.** **(b)**

98. **(c)** The Panch Prayag the five sacred river confluence is in the state of Uttarakhand. The five prayags are Vishnu Prayag, Nand Prayag, Karn Prayag, Rudra Prayag and Dev Prayag.

99. **(b)** Yashsvini is a health insurance scheme for the members of the cooperative bodies in Karnataka.

100. **(a)**

INSTRUCTIONS

1. This practice set comprises four sections. **Section A** : Verbal Ability in English; **Section B** : Numerical Ability; **Section C** : Reasoning and Military Aptitude; **Section D** : General Awareness.
2. The set will consist of 100 questions and each questions will be of 3 marks.
3. Each questions have four options, of which one is correct. The students are advised to read all the options thoroughly.
4. There is **one-third negative** marking in the set.

Time: 2 hrs.   *Max. Marks: 300*

SECTION-A : VERBAL ABILITY IN ENGLISH

DIRECTIONS (Qs. 1 - 4) : *Read the following passage carefully and answer the questions given below it:*

Over four hundred years after his death, scholars are still travelling the mysteries of Michelangelo's art. Recently one mystery that was revealed was that his famous drawing of a pensive Cleopatra included a hidden drawing of a different Cleopatra on the reverse side. This hidden Cleopatra shows a tormented woman, whose eyes stare out at the viewer and whose mouth is open, screaming in horror. The two images, drawn on two sides of the same paper, can be viewed simultaneously. A second mystery concerns Michelagelo's architectural plan for the dome of St. Peter's Basilica in Rome. Did he intend for the dome to look like the model he built between 1558 and 1561 ? Or did he change his mind after building the model and decide to elevate the <u>dome</u> in the way it is today? Scholars do not agree on the answer. A third mystery about one of the greatest artists who ever lived was why he destroyed hundreds or thousands of his drawings before he died. Did he feel they were unimportant? Did he want posterity to see only his finished products?

1. The dome of St. Peter's Basilica:
   - (a) bears no relation to the one in the model
   - (b) was destroyed after the model was built
   - (c) is raised more than the one in the model
   - (d) follows the plan of the model
2. According to the passage, Michelangelo is :
   - (a) a private person
   - (b) one of the greatest artists in the world
   - (c) the most famous architect in Rome
   - (d) screaming in horror
3. Why did Michelangelo destroy so many drawings before he died?
   - (a) Nobody knows
   - (b) They were unimportant
   - (c) They were only drafts
   - (d) He had changed the drawings
4. Which of the following is meaning to word 'dome' as used in passage?
   - (a) Floor
   - (b) Arched part of ceiling
   - (c) Foot
   - (d) None of these

DIRECTIONS (Qs. 5 - 8) : *Select the most appropriate word from the options against each number :*

Experienced climber Aron Ralston set out on a __5__ hiking adventure, which proved to be a __6__ event. Despite it being a common safety practice amongst climbers to inform others when undertaking unaccompanied hiking trips, Aron had not __7__ anyone of his plans. During his climbing adventure Aron's right arm became pinned against the canyon wall by a 360 kg boulder. Aron was unable to free himself, and after six days of being __8__ he made the decision to break the bones in his forearm and then amputate his arm below the elbow. Once free he made his way down a cliff and walked 8 km to seek assistance. Aron survived.

5. Which of these fits gap 7?
   - (a) authorised
   - (b) alerted
   - (c) signalled
   - (d) cautioned
6. Which of these fits gap 5?
   - (a) supervised
   - (b) solo
   - (c) team
   - (d) shared
7. Which of these fits gap 8?
   - (a) suppressed
   - (b) captive
   - (c) trapped
   - (d) entangled
8. Which of these fits gap 6?
   - (a) beath-taking
   - (b) fail-safe
   - (c) stimulating
   - (d) life-changing

DIRECTIONS (Qs. 9 - 14) : *Choose the word which can be substituted for the given words/sentence :*

9. That which has a double meaning
   - (a) doubtless
   - (b) uncertain
   - (c) controversial
   - (d) ambiguous
10. Incapable of making errors
    - (a) infallible
    - (b) incorrigible
    - (c) impervious
    - (d) inexplicable

11. Governed by a sense of duty
    (a) conscious   (b) sensible
    (c) intelligent   (d) conscientious
12. The depository where state records and documents are preserved
    (a) museum   (b) library
    (c) emporium   (d) archive
13. That which is no longer fashionable or in use
    (a) unused   (b) ancient
    (c) obsolete   (d) old
14. Murder of a king
    (a) homicide   (b) fratricide
    (c) regicide   (d) parricide

DIRECTIONS (Qs. 15 - 20) : *Which word or words explains the meaning of the following idioms :*

15. To turn over a new leaf
    (a) To change completely one's course of action
    (b) To shift attention to new problems
    (c) To cover up one's faults by wearing new marks
    (d) To change the old habits and adopt new ones
16. To wrangle over an ass's shadow
    (a) To act in a foolish way
    (b) To quarrel over trifles
    (c) To waste time on petty things
    (d) To do something funny
17. All Agog
    (a) Everybody   (b) All ready
    (c) Restless   (d) Almighty
18. To take with a grain of salt
    (a) To take with some reservation
    (b) To take with total disbelief
    (c) To take whole heartedly
    (d) To take seriously
19. Hobson's choice
    (a) Feeling of insecurity
    (b) Accept or leave the other
    (c) Feeling of strength
    (d) Excellent choice
20. To take through one's hat
    (a) To speak fluently
    (b) To talk nonsense
    (c) To talk wisdom
    (d) To speak at random

DIRECTIONS (Qs. 21 - 25) : *Choose the correct spelling of the given word.*

21. (a) Efflorascence   (b) Efflorescence
    (c) Effllorescence   (d) Eflorescence
22. (a) Aliennate   (b) Allienate
    (c) Alienate   (d) Alienatte
23. (a) Forefiet   (b) Forefeit
    (c) Forfeit   (d) Forfiet
24. (a) Comemorate   (b) Commemmorate
    (c) Momemmorate   (d) Commemorate
25. (a) Exemple   (b) Exampel
    (c) Example   (d) Exampal

SECTION-B : NUMERICAL ABILITY

26. The prize money of ₹ 1,800 is divided among 3 students A, B and C in such a way that 4 times the share of A is equal to 6 times the share of B, which is equal to 3 times the share of C. Then A's share is
    (a) ₹ 400   (b) ₹ 600
    (c) ₹ 700   (d) ₹ 800
27. The average of 5 consecutive numbers is n. If the next two numbers are also included, the average of the 7 numbers will
    (a) increase by 2   (b) increase by 1
    (c) remain the same   (d) increase by 1.4
28. The compound interest on a certain sum for two years is ₹ 618, whereas the simple interest on the same sum at the same rate for two years is ₹ 600. The ratio of interest per annum is
    (a) 18%   (b) 9%
    (c) 6%   (d) 3%
29. If the numerator and the denominator of a proper fraction are increased by the same quantity, then the resulting fraction is :
    (a) always greater than the original fraction
    (b) always less than the original fraction
    (c) always equal to the original fraction
    (d) None of these
30. Out of 40 boys in a class, average weight of 30 is 60 kg and the average weight of the remaining is 56 kg. The average weight (in kilogram) of the whole class is
    (a) 58.5   (b) 58
    (c) 57   (d) 59
31. A CD was sold at a profit of $12\frac{1}{2}\%$. If it had been sold at a profit of 15%, it would have gained him ₹ 10 more. The cost prices of CD is (in ₹)
    (a) 450   (b) 500
    (c) 400   (d) 550
32. Mr. X's salary is increased by 20%. On the increase, the tax rate is 10% higher. The percentage increase in his tax liability is :
    (a) 20   (b) 22
    (c) 23   (d) cannot be determined
33. Half the girls and one-third of the boys of a college reside in the hostel. What fractional part of the student body is hostle dwellers if the total number of girls in the college is 100 and is $\frac{1}{4}$ of the total student strength ?
    (a) $\frac{3}{5}$ (b) $\frac{5}{8}$
    (c) $\frac{2}{5}$ (d) None of these

34. A train covers 180 km distance in 4 hours. Another train covers the same distance in 1 hour less. What is the difference in the distances covered by these trains in one hour ?
    (a) 45 km
    (b) 9 km
    (c) 40 km
    (d) None of these

35. A man sells an article at 5% profit. If he had bought it at 5% less and sold it for ₹ 1 less, he would have gained 10%. The cost price of the article is :
    (a) ₹ 200
    (b) ₹ 150
    (c) ₹ 240
    (d) ₹ 280

36. A bag contains ₹ 216 in the form of one rupee, 50 paise and 25 paise coins in the ratio of 2 : 3 : 4. The number of 50 paise coins is :
    (a) 96
    (b) 144
    (c) 114
    (d) 141

37. A can do 50% more work as B can do in the same time. B alone can do a piece of work in 20 hours. A, with help of B, can finish the same work in how many hours ?
    (a) 12
    (b) 8
    (c) $13\frac{1}{3}$
    (d) $5\frac{1}{2}$

38. Anil calculated that it will take 45 minutes to cover a distance of 60 km by his car. How long will it take to cover the same distance if the speed of his car is reduced by 15 km/hr?
    (a) 36 min
    (b) 55.38 min
    (c) 48 min
    (d) 40 min

39. A trader has a weighing balance that shows 1,200 gm for a kilogram. He further marks up his cost price by 10%. Then the net profit percentage is
    (a) 32%
    (b) 23%
    (c) 31.75%
    (d) 23.5%

40. ₹ 6500 were divided equally among a certain number of persons. Had there been 15 more persons each would have got ₹ 30 less. Find the original number of persons.
    (a) 45
    (b) 50
    (c) 55
    (d) 48

41. A number of friends decided to go on a picnic and planned to spend ₹ 96 on eatables. Four of them, did not turn up. As a consequence, the remaining ones had to contribute ₹ 4 each extra. The number of those who attended the picnic was ?
    (a) 8
    (b) 16
    (c) 12
    (d) 24

42. Ravi's salary is 150% of Amit's salary. Amit's salary is 80% of Ram's salary. What is the ratio of Ram's salary to Ravi's salary ?
    (a) 1 : 2
    (b) 2 : 3
    (c) 5 : 6
    (d) 6 : 5

43. ₹ 5,887 is divided between Shyam and Ram, such that Shyam's share at the end of 9 years is equal to Ram's share at the end of 11 years, compounded annually at the rate of 5%. The share of Shyam is

(a) ₹ 2,088
(b) ₹ 2,000
(c) ₹ 3,087
(d) None of these

44. The average monthly salary of employees, consisting of officers and workers, of an organisation is ₹ 3000. The average salary of an officer is ₹ 10000 while that of a worker is ₹ 2000 per month. If there are a total 400 employees in the organisation, find the number of officers.
    (a) 50
    (b) 60
    (c) 80
    (d) 40

45. A car owner buys petrol at ₹ 7.50, ₹ 8.00 and ₹ 8.50 per litre for three successive years. What approximately is his average cost per litre of petrol if he spends ₹ 4000 each year ?
    (a) ₹ 8
    (b) ₹ 9
    (c) ₹ 7.98
    (d) ₹ 8.50

SECTION-C : REASONING & MILITARY APTITUDE

DIRECTIONS (Qs 46- 48) : *Choose the most appropriate word.*

46. 'Rabbit' is related to 'Burrow' in the same way as 'Lunatic' is related to:
    (a) Prison
    (b) Cell
    (c) Barrack
    (d) Asylum

47. 'Smoke' is related to 'Pollution' in the same way as 'War' is related to:
    (a) Victory
    (b) Treaty
    (c) Defeat
    (d) Destruction

48. Walk' is related to 'Run' in the same way as 'Breeze' is related to:
    (a) Cold
    (b) Dust
    (c) Wind
    (d) Air

DIRECTIONS (Qs 49-50) : *Each of the following questions has a group. Find out which one of the given alternatives will be another member of the group or of that class.*

49. Wheat, Barley, Rice
    (a) Food
    (b) Agriculture
    (c) Farm
    (d) Gram

50. Clutch, Brake, Horn
    (a) Car
    (b) Scooter
    (c) Accident
    (d) Steering

DIRECTIONS (Qs 51 - 55) : *In each word of the following questions consists of pair of words bearing a relationship among these, from amongst the alternatives, pick up the pair that best illustrate a similar relationship.*

51. Thermometer : Temperature
    (a) Millimeter : Scale
    (b) Length : Breadth
    (c) Solar Energy : Sun
    (d) Cardiograph : Heart rate

52. Sound : Muffled
    (a) Moisture : Humid
    (b) Colour : Faded
    (c) Despair : Anger
    (d) Odour : Pungent

53. Platform : Train
   (a) Aeroplane : Aerodrome   (b) Hotel : Tourist
   (c) Quay : Ship   (d) Footpath : Traveller

54. Scales : Fish
   (a) Bear : Fur   (b) Woman : Dress
   (c) Skin : Man   (d) Tree : Leaves

55. Numismatist : Coins
   (a) Jeweller : Jewels
   (b) Cartographer : Maps
   (c) Philatelist : Stamps
   (d) Geneticist : Chromosomes

DIRECTIONS (Qs. 56 - 60) : *The following questions are based on the patterns of three circles as shown in the following diagrams. Each question has an item group having relationship with a particular pattern of circles. Find out which item group is related to which pattern of circles.*

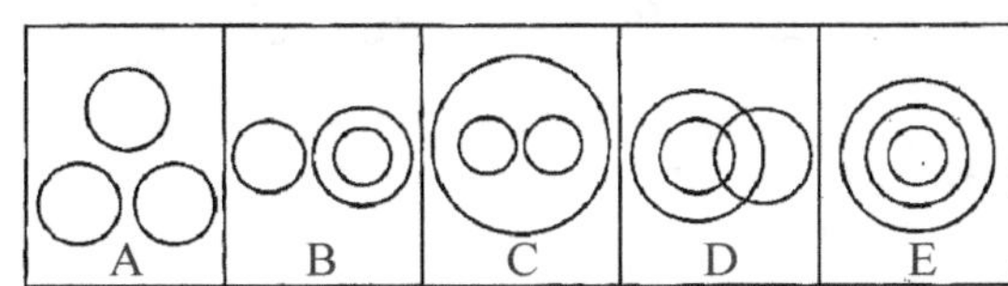

56. Mammals, Cows, Crows
   (a) E   (b) B
   (c) C   (d) D

57. Women, Mothers, Engineers
   (a) E   (b) C
   (c) D   (d) A

58. Family, Sons, Daughters
   (a) E   (b) B
   (c) C   (d) A

59. Colour, Cloth, Merchant
   (a) A   (b) B
   (c) C   (d) D

60. Konark, Pushkar, India
   (a) E   (b) D
   (c) C   (d) B

DIRECTIONS (Qs 61 & 62) : *In these questions find the odd word/number/ letters/number pair from the given alternatives.*

61. (a) LPXOY   (b) RQST
   (c) FBDLX   (d) MPONL

62. (a) 14 - 16   (b) 56 - 64
   (c) 77 - 88   (d) 80 - 93

63. Question figures

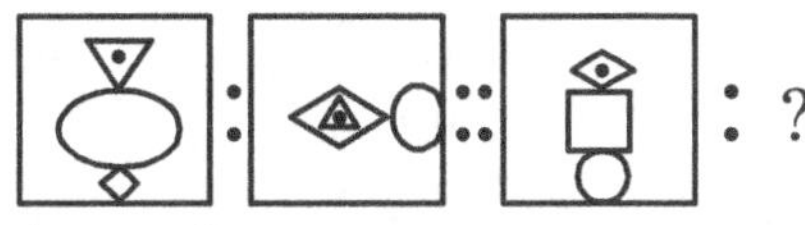

Answer figures

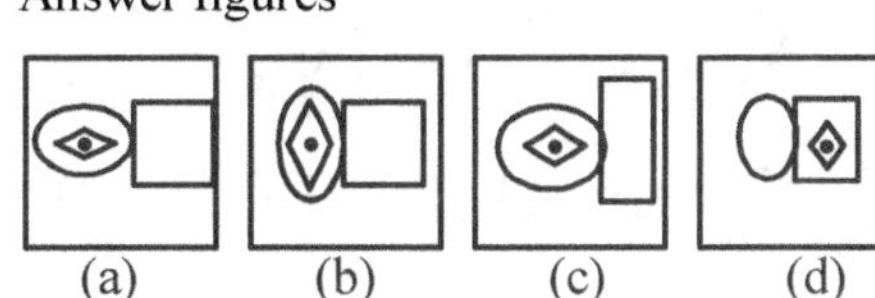

64. In the following questions number of letters skipped in between adjacent letters in the series increased by one.

Which of the following series observe the rule ?
   (a) KORYBGJ   (b) LMEYTPK
   (c) KMPTYEL   (d) KPTYELM

DIRECTIONS (Qs. 65) : *Find the odd number / letters / number pair from the given alternatives.*

65. (a) Pathology   (b) Geology
   (c) Cardiology   (d) Radiology

DIRECTIONS (Qs. 66-70) : *Find out which of the alternatives (a), (b), (c) and (d) can be formed from the pieces given in box 'X'.*

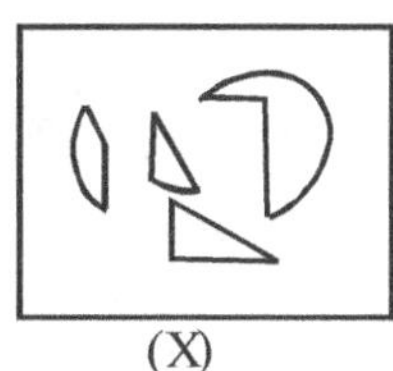

(X)

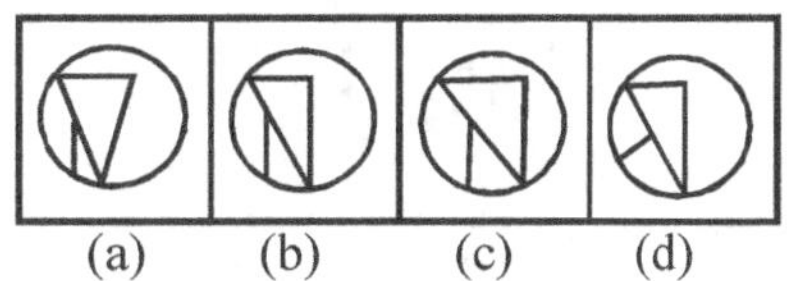

(a)   (b)   (c)   (d)

67.

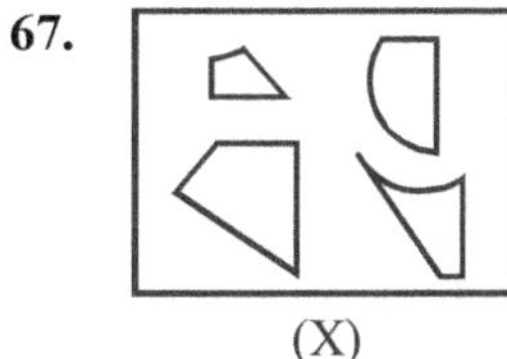

(X)

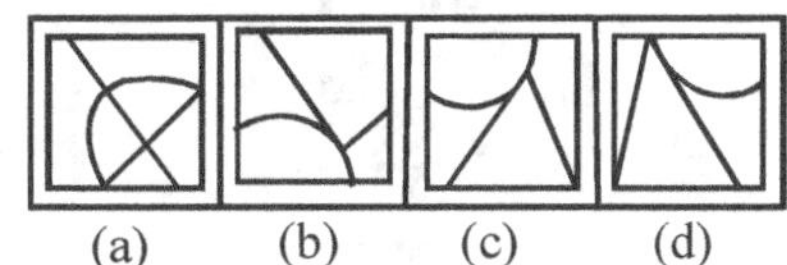

(a)   (b)   (c)   (d)

68.

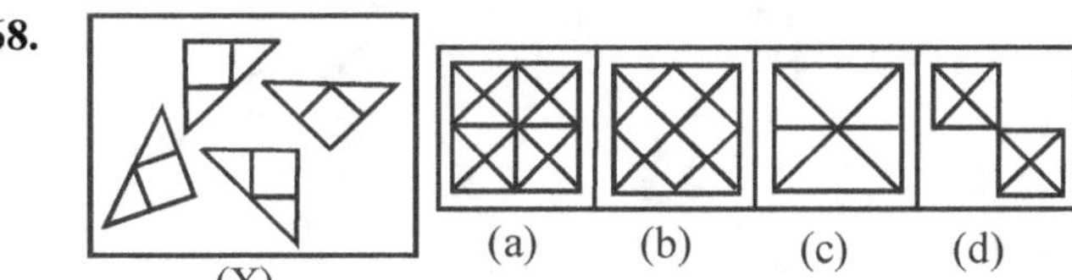

(X)   (a)   (b)   (c)   (d)

69.

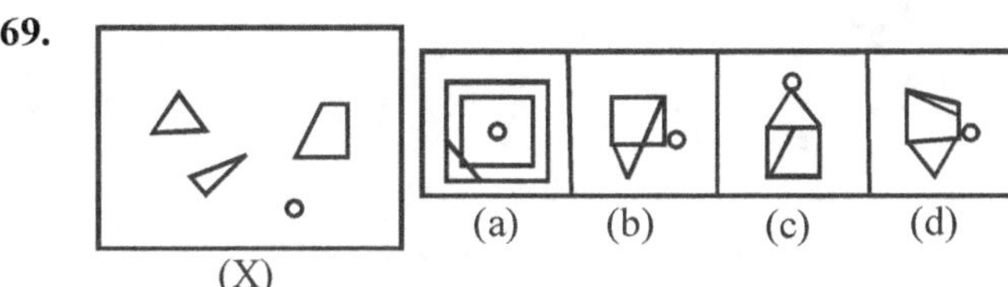

(X)   (a)   (b)   (c)   (d)

70.

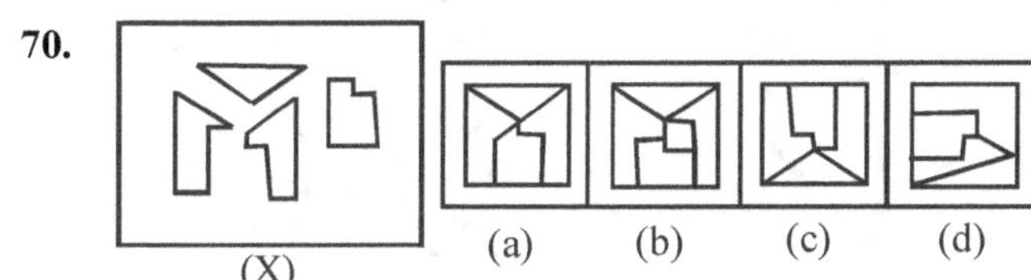

(X)   (a)   (b)   (c)   (d)

DIRECTIONS (Qs 71 - 75) : *In each of the following questions, a part of the figure is missing. Find out from the given option (a), (b), (c) or (d) the right figure to fit in the missing figure (x).*

71.

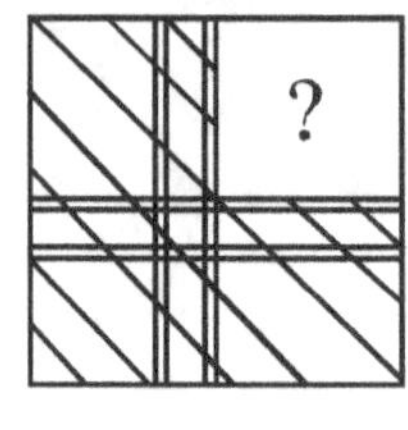

(X)

(a) 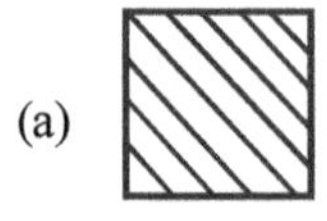   (b) 

(c) 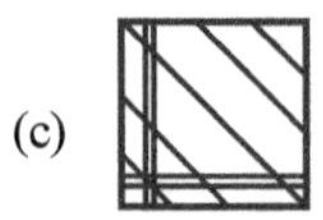   (d) 

72.

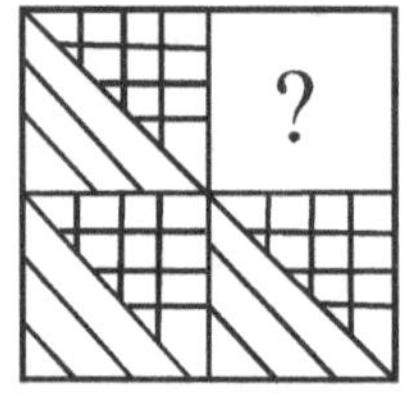

(X)

(a)    (b) 

(c)    (d) 

73.

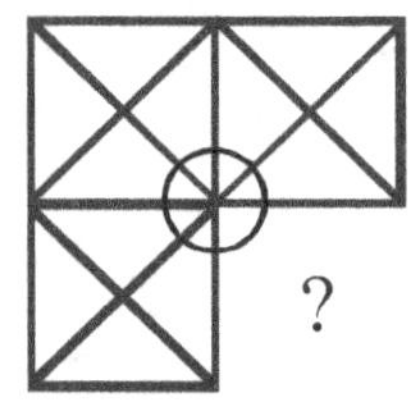

(X)

(a)    (b) 

(c) 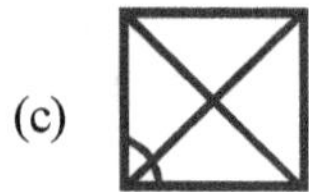   (d) 

74.

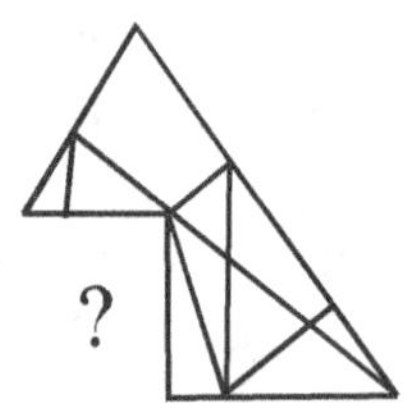

(X)

(a) 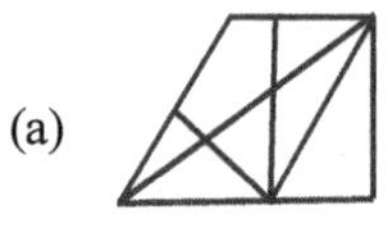   (b) 

(c) 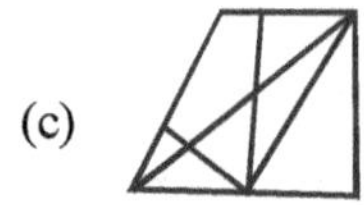   (d) 

75.

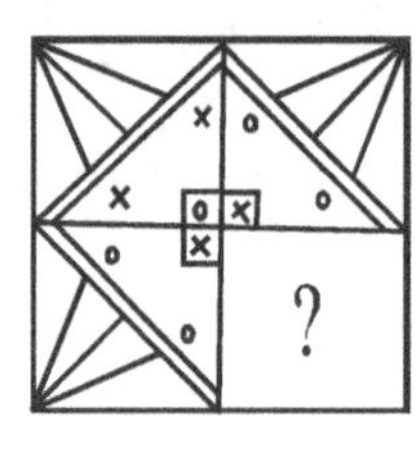

(X)

(a) 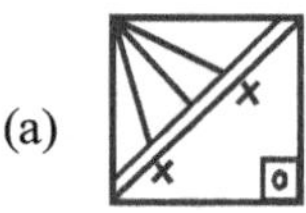   (b) 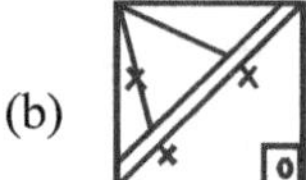

(c) 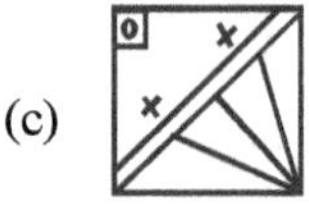   (d) 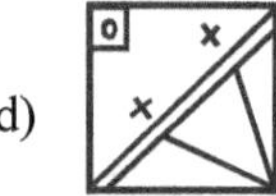

DIRECTIONS (Qs 76 - 80) : *From amongst the figures marked (1), (2), (3) and (4), select the figure which satisfies the same conditions of placement of the dots as in figure (X).*

76.

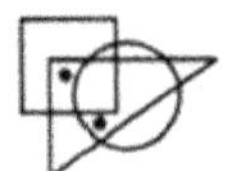  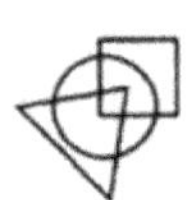 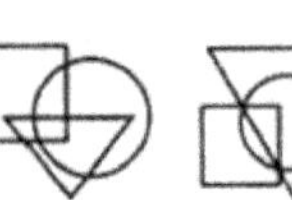

(X)   (1)   (2)   (3)   (4)

(a) 1   (b) 2
(c) 3   (d) 4

77.

   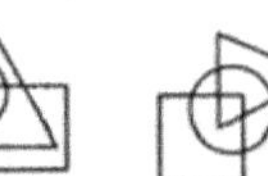 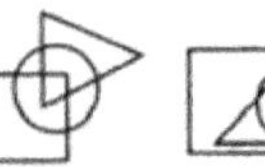

(X)   (1)   (2)   (3)   (4)

(a) 1   (b) 2
(c) 3   (d) 4

78. Select the figure which satisfies the same conditions of placement of the dots as in Figure-X.

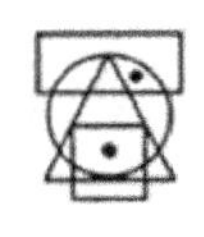 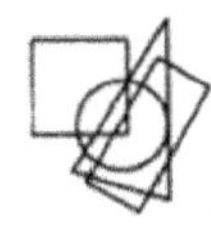 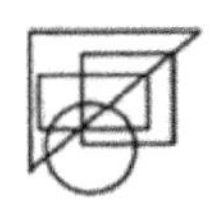 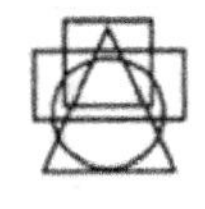 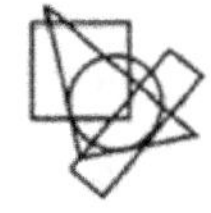

   (X)   (1)   (2)   (3)   (4)

(a) 1   (b) 2

(c) 3   (d) 4

79.

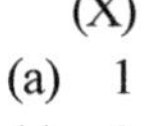 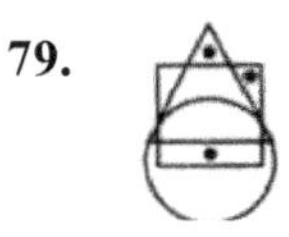 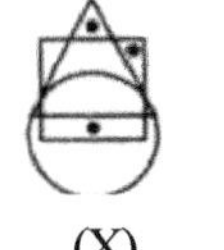     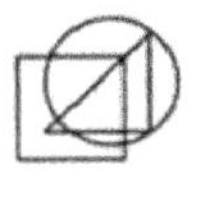 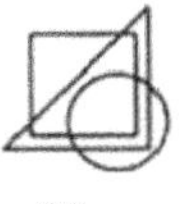

   (X)   (1)   (2)   (3)   (4)

(a) 1   (b) 2

(c) 3   (d) 4

80.

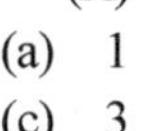 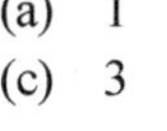 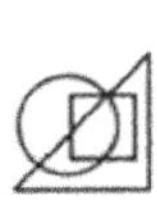  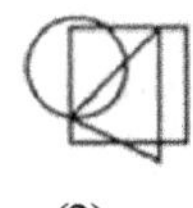 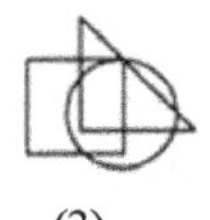 

   (X)   (1)   (2)   (3)   (4)

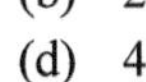

(a) 1   (b) 2

(c) 3   (d) 4

SECTION-D : GENERAL AWARENESS

81. How many members can be nominated to both the Houses of the Parliament by the President ?

(a) 14   (b) 16

(c) 10   (d) 12

82. Presidential form of government consists of the following :

(a) Popular election of the President

(b) No overlap in membership between the executive and the legislature

(c) Fixed term of office

(d) All of the above

83. Who among the following introduced the Mansabdari system ?

(a) Jahangir   (b) Shah Jahan

(c) SherShah   (d) Akbar

84. Moraines are formed in

(a) Monsoon region   (b) River deltas

(c) Arid regions   (d) Glacial regions

85. An employment situation where the marginal productivity of agricultural labour is zero is known as :

(a) Seasonal unemployment

(b) Cyclical unemployment

(c) Disguised unemployment

(d) Disguised unemployment

86. Longest cell in human body is:

(a) Blood cell   (b) Bone cell

(c) Nerve cell   (d) Muscle cell

87. Which is NOT the name of the missile developed by the Defense Research and Development Organisation (DRDO)?

(a) Shaurya   (b) Pinaka

(c) Brahmos   (d) Agni

88. 'New Horizons' spacecraft was launched by NASA to Study which of the following Planet?

(a) Mars   (b) Pluto

(c) Jupiter   (d) Mercury

89. Which of the following is known as 'Seven Pagodas'?

(a) Mahabalipuram temple   (b) Karle caves

(c) Chaityas   (d) Elephanta caves

90. Who is the author of the book India 2020?

(a) Nibal Singh   (b) R.K. Narayan

(c) Sidney Shelton   (d) Dr. A.P.J.Abdul Kalam

91 When is the World Population Day observed?

(a) May 31   (b) October 4

(c) December 10   (d) July 11

92. The Government of India has decided to set up National Cultural Audio-Visual Archives at

(a) Jodhpur   (b) Vadodara

(c) Jalandhar   (d) Ernakulam

93. Deendayal Antyodaya Yojana, launched on September 25, 2014 is related to—

(a) Skill Development in rural and urban areas

(b) Poverty Alleviation in rural areas

(c) Enhancement of livelihood of the poorest among poor

(d) None of the above

94. The study of lake is called

(a) Topology   (b) Hydrology

(c) Limnology   (d) Potomology

95. Which countries are separated by the McMahon line?

(a) India and Bangladesh

(b) India and Pakistan

(c) China and Tibet

(d) India and China

96. The 'Chipko Movement' is related to

(a) Wildlife preservation

(b) Scientific agriculture

(c) Forest conservation

(d) Deforestation

97. Israel built "Spike", which has been decided to be bought by India is a/an

(a) Radar system   (b) Anti- aircraft missile

(c) Stealth ship   (d) Anti tank missile

98. With how many permanent members of United Nations Security Council India has civil nuclear pact signed?

(a) Two   (b) Three

(c) Four   (d) Five

99. What is the name given to military exercises conducted between India and Nepal?

(a) Surya Kiran   (b) Malabar

(c) Indra   (d) Varuna Exercise

100. The union government has announced a nationwide scheme "Rashtriya Gokul Mission" which aims to

(a) Eliminate diseases of cattle

(b) Increase milk production

(c) Curb slaughtering of cattle

(d) Protect the indigenous breed of cows

ANSWERS & SOLUTIONS

1. **(c)** This also is a factual question. Refer to the line "Did he intend for the dome to look like the model he built..... elevate the dome in the way it is today ?" This line clearly suggests that the dome is raised more than the medal.

2. **(b)** This is an inference question. This should be solved by elimination. (a) is not the answer because the passage does not state the in Michelangelo was a private person, it only question if he was a private person. (b) is obviously implicit in the passage (c) is not suggested by the passage. He did some architectural work in Rome, which is considered great but the passage does not directly deem Michelangelo as the greatest arched of Rome (d) is absolutely wrong and is not in any way suggested by in passage.

3. **(a)** Because the passage raises many questions about the fact that Michelangelo destroyed many of his paintings but cause is not mentioned in the passage.

4. **(b)**

5. **(c)** In the gap 7, 'Aron had not signalled anyone' is the right option. Other options simply do not fit in here.

6. **(b)** 'Solo' means 'any activity that is performed alone without assistance' which Aron did. Other options 'supervised' means under observation or under the direction of a superintendent or overseer, team means form a team and shared means have in common; held or experienced in common.

7. **(c)** In the gap 7, the word 'trapped' is the right option while suppressed means kept from public knowledge by various means; captive means a person who is confined; especially a prisoner of war and entangled means deeply involved especially in something complicated.

8. **(d)** In the context of paragraph, the 'life-changing' may rightly be fit in here as it changed Aaron's life with the amputation of one of his arms. Other options are not relevant.

9. **(d)** Ambiguous means having more than one possible meaning.

10. **(a)** If someone or something is infallible, that means they are incapable of failure or error.

11. **(d)** Conscientious is the one who is guided by or in accordance with conscience or sense of duty and right and wrong.

12. **(d)**

13. **(c)** Obsolete means no longer in use

14. **(c)** regicide means the act of killing a king.

15. **(d)**   16. **(b)**   17. **(c)**   18. **(a)**

19. **(b)**   20. **(b)**   21. **(b)**   22. **(c)**

23. **(c)**   24. **(d)**   25. **(c)**

26. **(b)** $4A = 6B \Rightarrow 2A = 3B \Rightarrow A:B = 3:2$

$B = 3C \Rightarrow 2B = C \Rightarrow B:C = 1:2$

$$
\begin{array}{ccc}
A & : B & : C \\
3 & : 2 & \\
& 1 & : 2 \\
\hline
3 & : 2 & : 4
\end{array}
$$

A's share $= \dfrac{3}{(3+2+4)} \times 1800 = \dfrac{3}{9} \times 1800 = 600$

27. **(b)** Let the numbers be $n-2, n-1, n, n+1$ and $n+2$. Their average $= n$.

Next two consecutive numbers are $n+3$ and $n+4$.

Therefore the average of 7 consecutive numbers

$$= \frac{(n-2)+(n-1)+n+(n+1)+(n+2)+(n+3)+(n+4)}{7}$$

$$= \frac{5n+2n+7}{7} = n+1$$

28. **(c)** Let P be the Principal amount and r be the rate of interest

C.I − S.I $= 618 - 600 = 18$

$$P\left[\left(1+\frac{r}{100}\right)^2 - 1\right] - \frac{P \times r \times 2}{100} = 18$$

$$P\left(\frac{r}{100}\right)^2 = 18 \qquad \ldots(1)$$

Also, we have $\dfrac{2\,Pr}{100} = 300 \Rightarrow Pr = 30000$

Put value of Pr in (1)

we get, r = 6, rate = 6%

29. **(a)** Let us take a proper fraction, such as $\dfrac{1}{2}$.

Now, the new fraction $= \dfrac{1+2}{2+2} = \dfrac{3}{4}$

Thus, $\dfrac{3}{4} > \dfrac{1}{2}$

30. (d) Average weight of 30 = 60 kg

$\Rightarrow$ Sum of weight of 30 boys = 1800

Average weight of 10 = 56 kg

$\Rightarrow$ Sum of weight of 10 boys = 560

Average weight of the whole class

$$= \frac{\text{Sum of weight of all boys}}{40}$$

$$= \frac{\text{sum of weight of 30 boys + sum of weight of 10 boys}}{40}$$

$$= \frac{60 \times 30 + 56 \times 10}{40} = 59 \text{kg}$$

31. (c) **Ist case :**

$$\text{S.P} = \frac{100 \times \text{Profit\%}}{100} \times \text{C.P.} \Rightarrow \text{S.P.} = \frac{100 + \frac{25}{2} \times \text{C.P}}{100}$$

$$\Rightarrow \text{S.P} = \frac{112.5}{100} \text{CP} \qquad \text{...(1)}$$

IInd case :

$$\text{S.P} = \frac{100 + \text{Profit \%}}{100} \times \text{C.P.} \Rightarrow (\text{S.P} + 10) = \frac{100 + 15}{100} \times \text{C.P.}$$

$$\Rightarrow \quad (\text{S.P} + 10) = \frac{115}{100} \text{C.P} \qquad \text{...(2)}$$

Dividing equation (1) by (2)

$$\frac{\text{S.P}}{\text{S.P} + 10} = \frac{112.5}{100} (\text{C.P}) \times \frac{100}{115(\text{C.P})}$$

$$\text{S.P} = \left(\frac{112.5}{115}\right)(\text{S.P} + 10)$$

$$115\,\text{S.P} = 112.5\,\text{SP} + 1125$$

$$\text{S.P} = 450$$

$$\therefore \quad \text{C.P} = \frac{\text{S.P} \times 100}{112.5} = \frac{450 \times 100}{112.5} = 400$$

32. (b) Let the salary of Mr 'X' is Rs x and % of tax he has to pay = y

So tax payable = $\dfrac{xy}{100}$

On increase in salary, his salary becomes = $1.2x$

% of tax he has to pay on increased salary = $1.1y$

So, tax payable on increased salary

$$= \frac{1.1y \times 0.2x}{100} = \frac{0.22xy}{100}$$

Total tax payable on new salary = $\dfrac{xy}{100} + \dfrac{0.22xy}{100}$

$\therefore$ % increase in tax liability

$$= \frac{\left(\dfrac{0.22xy}{100} + \dfrac{xy}{100} - \dfrac{xy}{100}\right)}{\dfrac{xy}{100}} \times 100 = 22\%$$

33. (d) Total no. of students = 400; No. of girls = 100

$\therefore$ No. of boys = 300

No. of hostel dwellers = $\dfrac{1}{2} \times 100 + \dfrac{1}{3} \times 300 = 150$

$\therefore$ Required fraction = $\dfrac{150}{400} = \dfrac{3}{8}$

34. (d) First train's speed is 45km/hr.

$$\left(\text{Using speed} = \frac{\text{Distance}}{\text{Time}}\right)$$

Second train's speed is 60km/hr.

Difference in the distance covered by these trains in 1 hr. is 15 km.

35. (a) Let the CP of the article be ₹ x.

Then, SP = ₹ $\dfrac{105x}{100}$

Now, new CP = ₹ $\dfrac{95x}{100}$ and new SP = $\dfrac{105x}{100} - 1$

According to the question

$$\frac{105x}{100} - 1 - \frac{95}{100} = \frac{10 \times 95x}{100 \times 100}$$

$\therefore\ x = ₹\,200$

36. (b) Let the no. of one rupee, 50 paise and 25 paise coins be 2x, 3x and 4x respectively.

According to question,

$$₹\left(2x + \frac{3x}{2} + \frac{4x}{4}\right) = ₹\,216$$

$$\Rightarrow \frac{8x + 6x + 4x}{4} = 216$$

$\therefore\ x = 48$

$\therefore$ Number of 50 paise coins = 48 × 3 = 144

37. (b) In one hr. B finishes $\dfrac{1}{20}$ of the work.

In one hr. A finishes $\dfrac{1}{20} \times \dfrac{3}{2} = \dfrac{3}{40}$ of the work.

A+B finish $\dfrac{2+3}{40} = \dfrac{1}{8}$ of the work in 1 hr.

Both of them will take 8 hrs. to finish the work.

38. (b) $D = S \times T$

$60 = S \times \left(\dfrac{45}{60}\right) hr$

$S = \dfrac{60 \times 60}{45} \Rightarrow 80 km/hr$

Now, new speed $= 80 - 15 = 65\, km/hr.$

$\therefore\quad$ Time $= \dfrac{\text{Distance}}{\text{Speed}} = \dfrac{60}{65} hr.$

or $\dfrac{60}{65} \times 60\, min = 55.38\, min.$

Hence, Time to taken by car to travel same distance is 55.38 min.

39. (a) The trader professes to sell 1200 kg but sells only 1000 kg.

So profit $= 20\%$

Markup $= 10\%$

Total profit $= 10 + 20 + \dfrac{10 \times 20}{100} = 32\%$

40. (b) Let the original no. of persons be x.

Then, $\dfrac{6500}{x} = \dfrac{6500}{x+15} + 30$

or $\dfrac{6500}{x} = \dfrac{6500 + 30x + 450}{x+15}$

or $x^2 + 15x - 3250 = 0$

or $x = 50$

41. (a) Let initial number of friends to attend picnic = x.

$\therefore \dfrac{96}{x} + 4 = \dfrac{96}{x-4}$ ....(1)

where $(x-4)$ attended the picnic.

On solving with the help of options from (a) to (d) we find x = 12 suits the equation (1).

Hence the no. of friends who attended the picnic is 8.

42. (c) Let the salary of Ram be ₹ 100.

Then, salary of Amit = ₹ 80

and salary of Ravi = 150% of 80 = ₹ 120

Ratio of Ram's salary to Ravi's salary = 100 : 120 = 5 : 6

43. (c) Let Shyam's share be x

According to question

$x\left(1+\dfrac{5}{100}\right)^9 = (5887 - x)\left(1+\dfrac{5}{100}\right)^{11}$

$\dfrac{x}{5887 - x} = \left(1+\dfrac{5}{100}\right)^2$

$\dfrac{x}{5887 - x} = 1.1025$

$x = ₹\, 3087.$

44. (a) Average monthly salary of employees = 3000

Let the number of officer = n_1

and the number of workers = n_2

$10000\, n_1 + 2000\, n_2 = 400 \times 3000$

$10n_1 + 2n_2 = 1200$

$n_1 + n_2 = 400$

$\Rightarrow 10n_1 + 2n_2 = 1200$

$\underline{\quad\; 2n_1 + 2n_2 = 800\quad}$

$8n_1 = 400$

$n_1 = \dfrac{400}{8} = 50$

Number of employee = 50

45. (c) Let average cost of petrol per litre be ₹ x

$\therefore\quad x = \dfrac{12000}{\dfrac{4000}{7.5} + \dfrac{4000}{8} + \dfrac{4000}{8.5}}$

$= \dfrac{12000}{4000\left(\dfrac{1}{7.5}+\dfrac{1}{8}+\dfrac{1}{8.5}\right)} = \dfrac{3}{\dfrac{10}{75}+\dfrac{1}{8}+\dfrac{10}{85}} = \dfrac{3}{\dfrac{2}{15}+\dfrac{1}{8}+\dfrac{2}{17}}$

$= \dfrac{6120}{767} = ₹\, 7.98$ per litre

46. (d) As the dwelling place of 'Rabbit' is 'Burrow' in the same way the dwelling place of 'Lunatic' is 'Asylum'.

47. (d) As 'smoke' leads to 'pollution' in the same way "War" leads to 'destruction'.

48. (c) As fast mode of 'Walk' is 'Run' in the same way fast mode of 'Breeze' is 'Wind'.

49. **(d)** All the terms given in the question are cereals and gram is also one of the cereals.

50. **(d)** All these are parts of a vehicle.

51. **(d)** As temperature is measured from a thermometer in the same way heart rate is measured with cardiograph.

52. **(b)** Second is the process of gradual disappearances of the first.

53. **(c)** Second is the place where first stops.

54. **(c)** As scales from an outer layer of fish similarly skin form an outer layer of man.

55. **(c)** As Numismatist collects coins similarly Philatelist collects stamps.

56. **(b)** 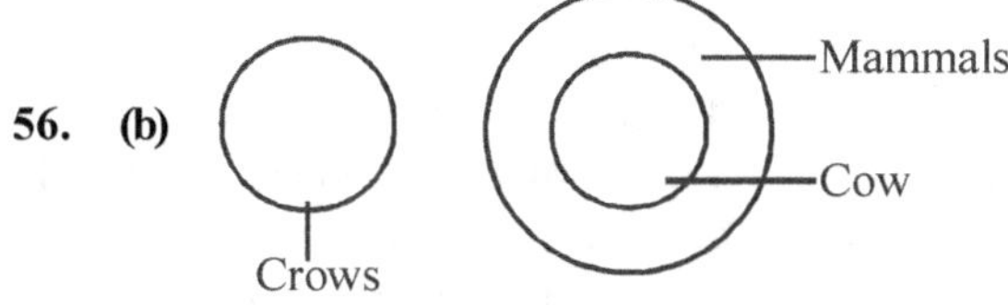

57. **(c)** 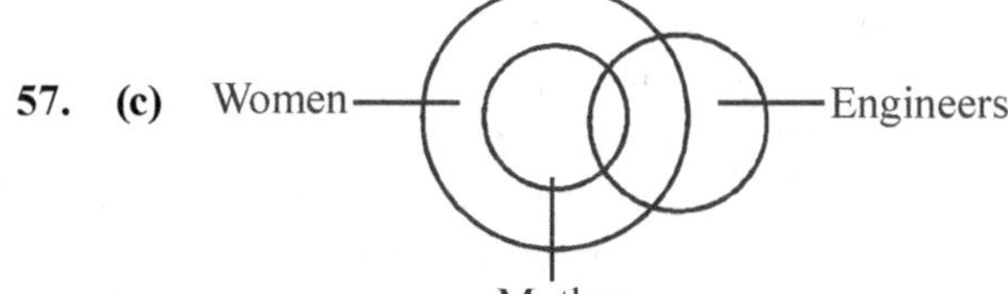

58. **(c)** 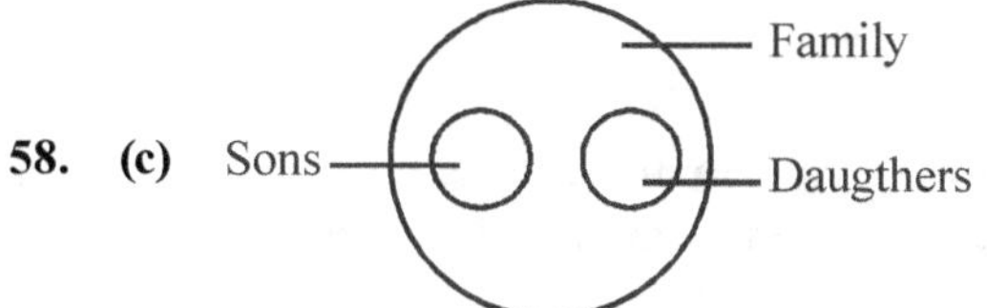

59. **(d)** 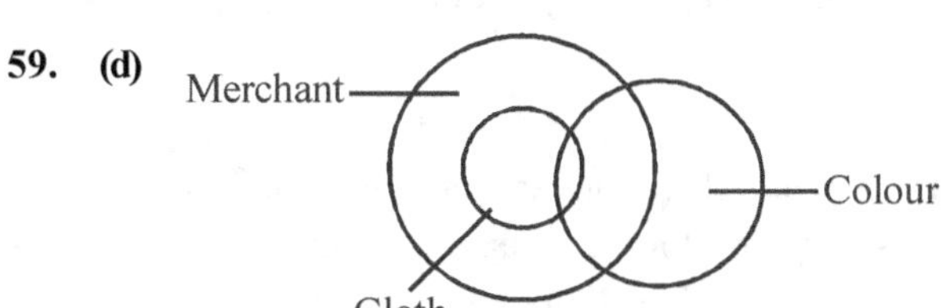

60. **(c)** 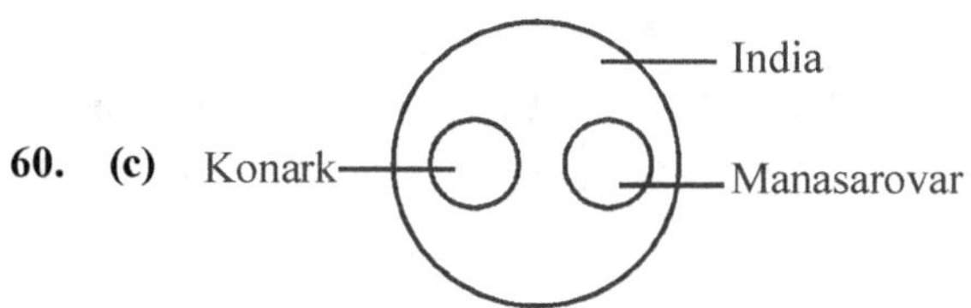

61. **(b)** Except (b) all others have five letters.

62. **(d)** Except (d) in both number in all others pairs are divided by same number.

63. **(a)** The middle element adjecents to the right side line after rotating 90° anti-clockwise. The bottom element goes up on the top and becomes enlarge. The top element becomes the inner figure of bottom element.

64. **(c)** By options :
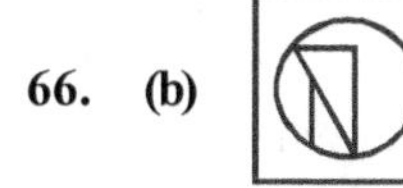
$$K \xrightarrow{+2} M \xrightarrow{+3} P \xrightarrow{+4} T \xrightarrow{+5} Y \xrightarrow{+6} E \xrightarrow{+7} L$$

65. **(b)** As all terms given in question are medical terms except geology.

66. **(b)** 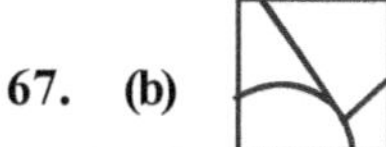

67. **(b)** 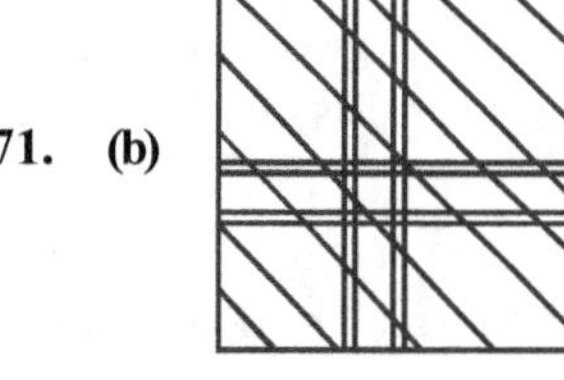

68. **(b)**

69. **(c)**

70. **(c)**

71. **(b)** 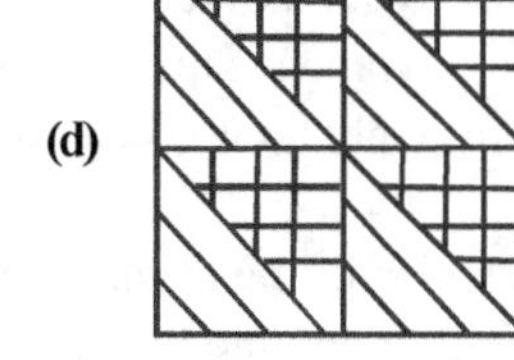

72. **(d)** 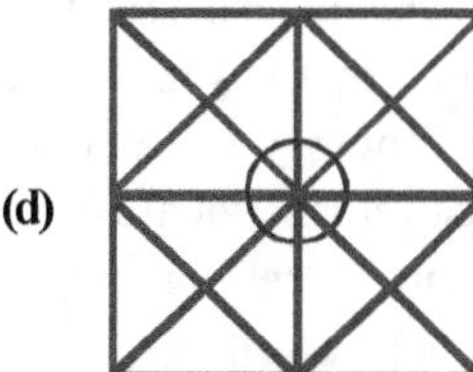

73. **(d)** 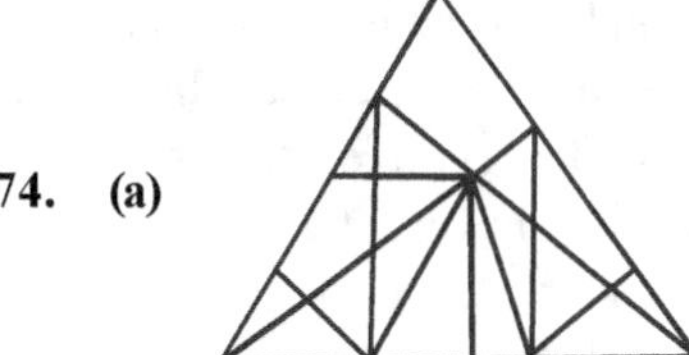

74. **(a)** 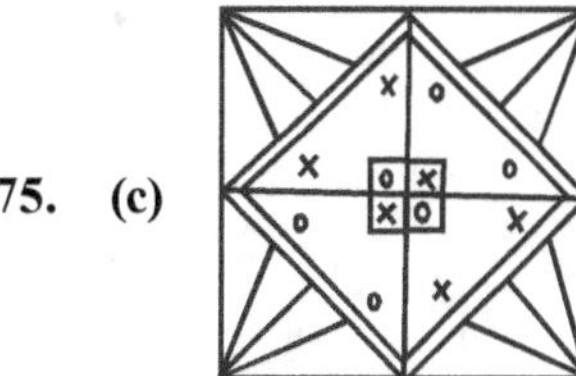

75. **(c)**

76. **(c)** In fig. (X), one of the dots lies in the region common to the square and the triangle and another dot lies in the region common to the circle and the triangle. In each of the alternatives (1), (2) and (4), the region common to the square and the triangle lies within the circle. Therefore, in each of these figures, there is no region common to the square and the triangle only. Only the alternative (3) consists of a region common to the square and the triangle only and another region common to the circle and the triangle only. Hence, fig. (3) is the answer.

77. **(c)** In fig. (X), one of the dots lies in the region common to the circle and the triangle only, another dot lies in the circle alone and the third dot lies in the region common to the circle and the square only. In fig. (1) there is no region common to the circle and the triangle only, in fig. (2), there is no region common to the circle and the square and in fig. (4), there is no region which lies in the circle alone. Only, fig. (3) consists of all the three types of regions.

78. **(d)** In fig. (X), one of the dots lies in the region common to the circle and the rectangle only and the other dot lies in the region common to the circle, the square and the triangle only. In each of the figures (1) and (2), there is no region common to the circle and the rectangle only. In fig. (3), there is no region common to the circle, the square and the triangle only. Only fig. (4) consists of both the types of regions.

79. **(a)** In fig. (X), one of the dots lies in the square alone, another dot lies in the triangle alone and the third dot lies in the region common to the circle and the square. In fig. (2) there is no region that lies in the square alone, in fig. (3) there is no region that lies in the triangle alone and in fig. (4) there is no region that lies in the region common to the circle and the square only. Only fig. (1) consists of all the three types of regions.

80. **(c)** In fig. (X), one of the dots lies in the square alone, another dot lies in the region common to the square and the triangle only and the third dot lies in the region common to the circle and the triangle. In fig. (1), there is no region which lies in the square alone. In each of the figures (2) and (4), there is no region common to the circle and the triangle only. Only, fig. (3) consists of all the three types of regions.

81. **(a)** According to the Indian Constitution, 14 members can be nominated to both the houses of parliament by the President. This is the legislative power of the President where he nominates 12 members to the Rajya Sabha and if not adequately represented 2 Anglo-Indian members to the Lok Sabha.

82. **(d)** A presidential system is a republican system of government where a head of government is also head of state and leads an executive branch that is separate from the legislative branch. The United States, for instance, has a presidential system. Popular election of President, no overlap in membership and fixed term of office are the main criteria of Presidential form of Government.

83. **(d)** Akbar introduced the Mansabdari system. This system came under the military reforms of Akbar. Under this system each officer was assigned a rank(mansab). Varying from 10 to 10,000, the mansab carried the Zat(the personal status and salary) and Sawar (the number of cavalry men to be maintained.

84. **(d)** Moraines are formed in glacial regions. Moraine is accumulation of rock debris (till) carried or deposited by a glacier. The material, which ranges in size from blocks or boulders (usually faceted or striated) to sand and clay, is unstratified when dropped by the glacier and shows no sorting or bedding.

85. **(c)**

86. **(c)**

87. **(d)** Agni is a surface to surface missile developed in India under Integrated Guided Missile Programme.

88. **(b)**

89. **(a)** Mahabalipuram temple is known as 'Seven-Pagodas'.

90. **(d)**

91. **(d)**

92. **(a)** Ministry of Culture and the Rupayan Sansthan has signed an MoU to set up a National Cultural Audio-Visual Archives in Jodhpur with the aim to preserve cultural heritage of the country.

93. **(a)**   **94.** **(c)**   **95.** **(d)**   **96.** **(d)**

97. **(d)**   **98.** **(c)**   **99.** **(a)**   **100.** **(d)**

4 Practice Set

INSTRUCTIONS

1. This practice set comprises four sections. **Section A** : Verbal Ability in English; **Section B** : Numerical Ability; **Section C** : Reasoning and Military Aptitude; **Section D** : General Awareness.
2. The set will consist of 100 questions and each questions will be of 3 marks.
3. Each questions have four options, of which one is correct. The students are advised to read all the options thoroughly.
4. There is **one-third negative** marking in the set.

Time: 2 hrs.   *Max. Marks: 300*

SECTION-A : VERBAL ABILITY IN ENGLISH

DIRECTION (Qs. 1 - 5) : *Read the following passage carefully and answer the questions given below it :*

Patriotism is a very complex feeling, built up out of primitive instincts and highly intellectual convictions. There is love of home and family and friends, making us peculiarly anxious to preserve our own country from <u>invasion</u>. There is the mild instinctive liking for compatriots as against foreigners. There is pride, which is bound up with the success of the community to which we feel that we belong. There is a belief, suggested, by pride but reinforced by history, that one's own nation represents a great tradition and stands for ideals that are important to the human race. But besides all these, there is another element, at once nobler and more open to attack, an element of worship, of willing sacrifice, of joyful merging of the individual life in the life of the nation. This religious element in patriotism is essential to the strength of the State, since it enlists the best that is in most men on the side of national sacrifice.

1. A suitable title for the passage could be :
(a) Elements of Patriotism
(b) Historical Development of a Nation
(c) The role of Religion and History in Patriotism
(d) Religion and Patriotism

2. Describing the element of worship "Open to attack", the author implies that it :
(a) is unnecessary
(b) leads to national sacrifice
(c) has no historical basis
(d) cannot be justified on rational grounds

3. The tone of the passage can best be described as :
(a) critical   (b) descriptive
(c) persuasive   (d) analytical

4. Which of the following can clearly be grouped under "intellectual convictions" the author mentions in the opening sentence?
(a) Love of family
(b) Love of compatriots
(c) The element of worship
(d) None of the above

5. Which one of the following statements is false?
(a) We tend to like our own countrymen better than we like foreigners
(b) Nations always stand for ideals that are important to the human race
(c) It is the religious element in patriotism that motivates us for sacrificing ourselves for our nation
(d) Our pride of the community is bound with the community's success

DIRECTION (Qs. 6 - 8) : *Choose the word which is nearest in meaning to the given word :*

6. DISCOMFIT
(a) litigate   (b) ease
(c) conflict   (d) frustrate

7. WRATH
(a) violence   (b) anger
(c) hatred   (d) displeasing

8. ABSTINENCE
(a) synchronic   (b) torrential
(c) restraint   (d) gluttony

DIRECTION (Qs. 9 - 10) : *Choose the word which is nearly opposite in meaning to the given word.*

9. Insipid
(a) Tasty   (b) Colourful
(c) Colourless   (d) Dull

10. Relinquish
(a) Relish   (b) Continue
(c) Vanish   (d) Quench

DIRECTIONS (Qs. 11 - 15) : *In each of the following questions, find out which part has an error.*

11. Hasan plays (a) / both-cricket and billiards (b) /at the national level. (c) / No error. (d)

12. More you (a) / think of it, (b) / the worse it becomes.(c) / No error. (d)

13. My father gave me (a) / a pair of binocular (b) / on my birthday. (c) / No error. (d)

14. Kalidas is (a) / a Shakespeare (b) /of India. (c) / No error. (d)

15. The teacher as well as his students, (a) / all left (b) / for the trip. (c) / No error. (d)

DIRECTIONS (Qs. 16 - 20) : *Pick up the most effective word from the given words to fill in the blanks to make the sentence meaningfully complete.*

16. The human mind seems to have built-in _________against original thought.
    (a) prejudices   (b) ideas
    (c) interests   (d) safeguards

17. The statue _________ a global symbol of freedom
    (a) stands against   (b) stands to
    (c) stands for   (d) stands as

18. A child is the future of a family _________ nation.
    (a) just as   (b) as a
    (c) like a   (d) as well as of a

19. If strict security measures were taken, the tragedy might have been _________
    (a) restrained   (b) averted
    (c) removed   (d) controlled

20. The deceased left _______ children.
    (a) behind   (b) for
    (c) with   (d) by

DIRECTIONS (Qs. 21 - 25) : *Which word or words explains the meaning of the following idioms :*

21. To take through one's hat
    (a) To speak fluently
    (b) To talk nonsense
    (c) To talk wisdom
    (d) To speak at random

22. To snap one's fingers
    (a) To speak abruptly
    (b) To accept immediately
    (c) To grasp eagerly
    (d) To become contemptuous of

23. To take the bull by the horns
    (a) To punish a person severly for his arrogance
    (b) To grapple courageously witha difficulty that lies in our way
    (c) To handle it by fierce attack
    (d) To bypass the legal process and take action according-ing to one's own whims.

24. To be in abeyance
    (a) To be in trouble
    (b) Dual minded
    (c) In a fighting mood
    (d) Insuspense

25. To cast pearls before a swine
    (a) To spend recklessly
    (b) To spend a lot of money on the unkeep of domestic hogs
    (c) To waste monkey over trifles
    (d) To offer to a person a thing which he cannot appreciate.

SECTION-B : NUMERICAL ABILITY

26. A student was asked to divide a number by 6 and add 12 to the quotient. He, however, first added 12 to the number and then divided it by 6, getting 112 as the answer. The correct answer should have been :
    (a) 122   (b) 118
    (c) 114   (d) 124

27. One-fourth of Nikhil's money is equal to one-sixth of Yogesh's money. If both together have Rs 600, what is the difference between their amounts ?
    (a) ₹ 160   (b) ₹ 240
    (c) ₹ 200   (d) ₹ 120

28. Ram spends 20% of his monthly income on his household expenditure, 15% of the rest on books, 30% of the rest on clothes and saves the rest. On counting, he comes to know that he has finally saved ₹ 9,520. Find his monthly income.
    (a) ₹ 15,000   (b) ₹ 10,000
    (c) ₹ 20,000   (d) None of these

29. The price of petrol is increased by 25%. How much per cent must a car owner reduce his consumption of petrol so as not to increase his expenditure on petrol ?
    (a) 50%   (b) 30%
    (c) 25%   (d) 20%

30. If books bought at prices ranging from ₹ 150 to ₹ 300 are sold at prices ranging from ₹ 250 to ₹ 350, what is the greatest possible profit that might be made in selling 15 books ?
    (a) ₹ 3,000   (b) Cannot be determined
    (c) ₹ 750   (d) ₹ 4,250

31. The average of 30 numbers is 40 and that of other 40 numbers is 30. The average of all the numbers is
    (a) 34.5   (b) $34\frac{2}{7}$
    (c) 35   (d) 34

32. A man sold two articles at ₹ 375 each. On one, he gains 25% and on the other, he loses 25%. The gain or loss% on the whole transaction is :
    (a) 6%   (b) $4\frac{1}{6}\%$
    (c) 7%   (d) $6\frac{1}{4}\%$

33. In a school, the ratio of boys to girls is 4 : 3 and the ratio of girls to teachers is 8 : 1. The ratio of student to teachers is :
   (s) 56 : 3 (b) 55 : 1
   (c) 49 : 3 (d) 56 : 1

34. R and S start walking each other at 10 AM at the speeds of 3 km/hr and 4 km/hr respectively. They were initially 17.5 km apart. At what time do they meet ?
   (a) 2 : 30 PM (b) 11 : 30 AM
   (c) 1 : 30 PM (d) 12 : 30 PM

35. The length and breadth of a square are increased by 30% and 20% respectively. The area of the rectangle so formed exceeds the area of the square by:
   (a) 46% (b) 66%
   (c) 42% (d) 56%

36. The average weight of 12 crewmen in a boat is increased by $\frac{1}{3}$ kg, when one of the crewmen whose weight is 55 kg is replaced by a new man. What is the weight of that new men ?
   (a) 58 (b) 60
   (c) 57 (d) 59

37. A sum of ₹ 8,000 lent on simple interest amounts to ₹ 8,800 in two years. If the rate of interest is decreased by two percentage, then what would the sum amount to in the same period ?
   (a) ₹ 8,680 (b) ₹ 8,480
   (c) ₹ 8,280 (d) ₹ 8,340

38. Two trains are 2 km apart and their lengths are 200 m and 300 m. They are approaching towards each other with a speed of 20 m/s and 30 m/s, respectively. After how much time will they cross each other ?
   (a) 50 s (b) 100 s
   (c) 25/3 s (d) 150 s

39. When the price of a radio was reduced by 20%, its sale increased by 80%. What was the net effect on the sale?
   (a) 44% increase (b) 44% decrease
   (c) 66% increase (d) 75% increase

40. A and B run a 5 km race on a round course of 400 m. If their speeds be in the ratio 5 : 4, how often does the winner pass the other ?
   (a) $4\frac{1}{2}$ times (b) $2\frac{3}{4}$ times
   (c) $3\frac{1}{2}$ times (d) $2\frac{1}{2}$ times

41. Two pipes P and Q would fill a cistern in 24 and 32 minutes, respectively. Both pipes are kept open. When should the first pipe be turned off so that the cistern may be just filled in 16 minutes ?
   (a) After 10 minutes (b) After 12 minutes
   (c) After 14 minutes (d) None of these

42. If the length of a certain rectangle is decreased by 4 cm and the width is increased by 3 cm, a square with the same area as the original rectangle would result. The perimeter of the original rectangle (in centimetres) is :
   (a) 44 (b) 46
   (c) 48 (d) 50

43. A, B, C together earn ₹ 1450 and spend 60%, 65% and 70% of their salaries respectively. If their savings are in the ratio 14 : 21 : 15, the salary of B is
   (a) ₹ 500 (b) ₹ 600
   (c) ₹ 450 (d) ₹ 750

44. Rahul can row a certain distance downstream in 6 hours and return the same distance in 9 hours. If the speed of Rahul in still water is 12 km/hr, find the speed of the stream.
   (a) 2 km/hr (b) 2.4 km/hr
   (c) 3 km/hr (d) Data inadequate

45. Two trains, 130 m and 110 m long, are going in the same direction. The faster train takes one minute to pass the other completely. If they are moving in opposite directions, they pass each other completely in 3 seconds. Find the speed of each train.
   (a) 38 m/sec, 36 m/sec (b) 42 m/sec, 38 m/sec
   (c) 36 m/sec, 42 m/sec (d) None of these

SECTION-C : REASONING & MILITARY APTITUDE

DIRECTIONS (Qs. 46-50): *In each of the following questions, certain pairs of words are given, out of which the words in all pairs except one, bear a certain common relationship. Choose the pair in which the words are differently related.*

46. (a) Newspaper : Editor (b) Film : Director
    (c) Stamps : Philatelist (d) Book : Author

47. (a) Steel : Utensils (b) Bronze : Statue
    (c) Duralumin : Aircraft (d) Iron : Rails

48. (a) Fish : Pisciculture (b) Birds : Horticulture
    (c) Bees : Apiculture (d) Silkworm : Sericulture

49. (a) Principal : School (b) Soldier : Barrack
    (c) Artist: Troupe (d) Singer : Chorus

50. (a) Cow : Fodder (b) Crow : Carrion
    (c) Poultry : Farm (d) Vulture : Prey

DIRECTIONS (Qs. 51-55): *In each of the following questions, five words have been given out of which four are alike in some manner, while the fifth one is different. Choose the word which is different from the rest.*

51. (a) Inch (b) Foot
    (c) Yard (d) Quart

52. (a) Mercury (b) Bromine
    (c) Aluminium (d) Sodium

53. (a) Mariana (b) Nigar
    (c) Angel (d) Gersoppa

54. (a) Arc (b) Diagonal
    (c) Tangent (d) Radius

55. (a) Granite (b) Lignite
    (c) Peat (d) Anthracite

DIRECTIONS (Qs. 56 - 60): *Three words in bold letters are given in each questions, which have something in common among themselves. Out of the four given alternatives, choose the most appropriate description about these three words.*

56. Spinach : Fenugreek : Celery

    (a) These are cactus plants.

    (b) These are wild flowers.

    (c) These are wild plants.

    (d) These are leafy vegetables.

57. Pulpit : Pews : Steeple

    (a) They are connected with a glacier valley.

    (b) They are connected with church.

    (c) The terms are connected with race-course.

    (d) They are parts of a plant.

58. Petrol : Phosphorus : Cooking gas

    Options:

    (a) They are fuels.

    (b) They are highly inflammable.

    (c) They can't be sold without permit.

    (d) India has to import them.

59. Chlorine : Fluorine : Iodine

    (a) These are names of inert gases.

    (b) These are gases at room temperature.

    (c) These are transition elements.

    (d) These are halogens.

60. Species : Genera : Family

    (a) These are biological terms.

    (b) These give information about living things for classification.

    (c) These are traits of animal kingdom.

    (d) These are groups of animals.

DIRECTION (Qs. 61- 65) : *In each of the following questions, select a figure from amongst the four alternatives which when placed in the blank space of figure (X) would complete the pattern.*

61.

(X)

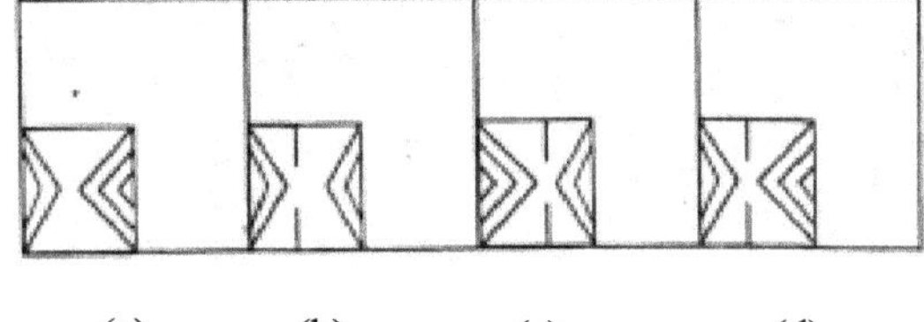

(a)　　　(b)　　　**(c)**　　　(d)

62.

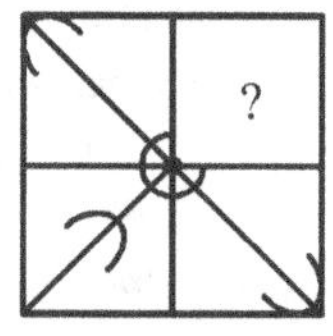

(X)

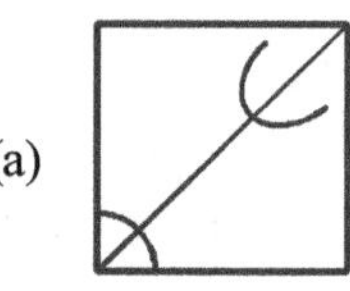　　　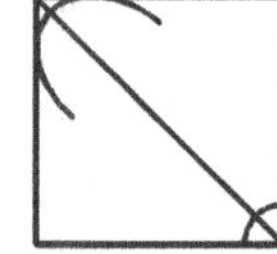

(a)　　　(b)

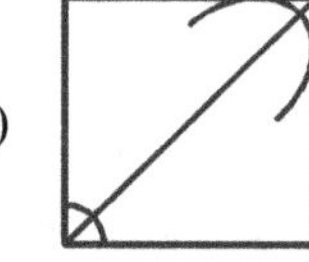　　　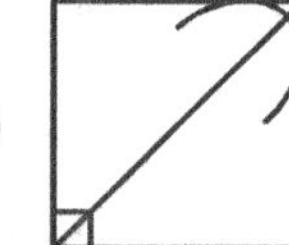

(c)　　　(d)

63

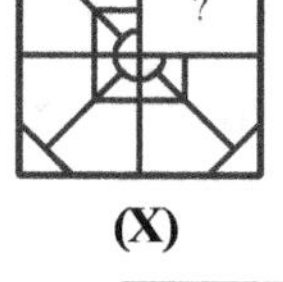

(X)

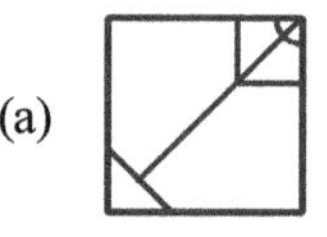　　　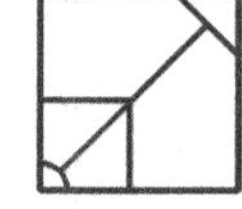

(a)　　　(b)

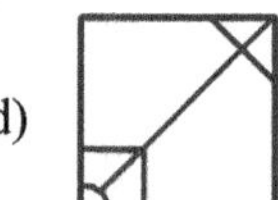

(c)　　　(d)

64.

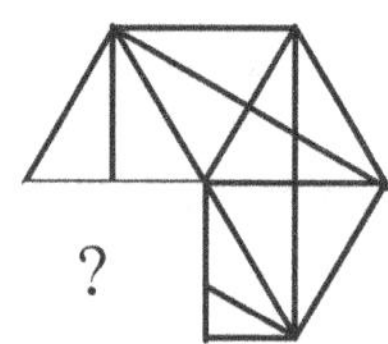

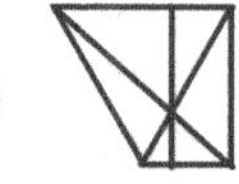

(a)　　　(b)

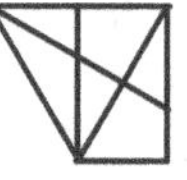　　　

(c)　　　(d)

65.

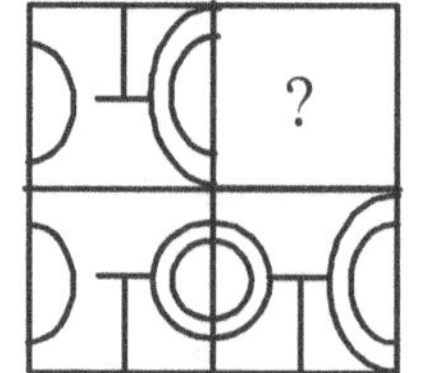

(a)　　　(b)

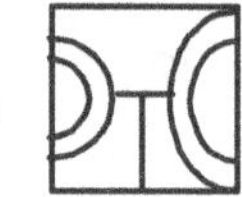　　　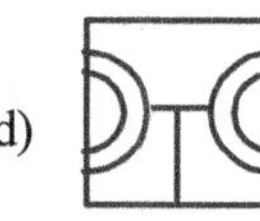

(c)　　　(d)

DIRECTIONS (Qs. 66-70): *In each of the following questions there is a specific relationship between the first and second figure. The same relationship exists between the third and fourth figure which will replace the blank column. Select the term from the alternatives given.*

66.

67.

68.

69.

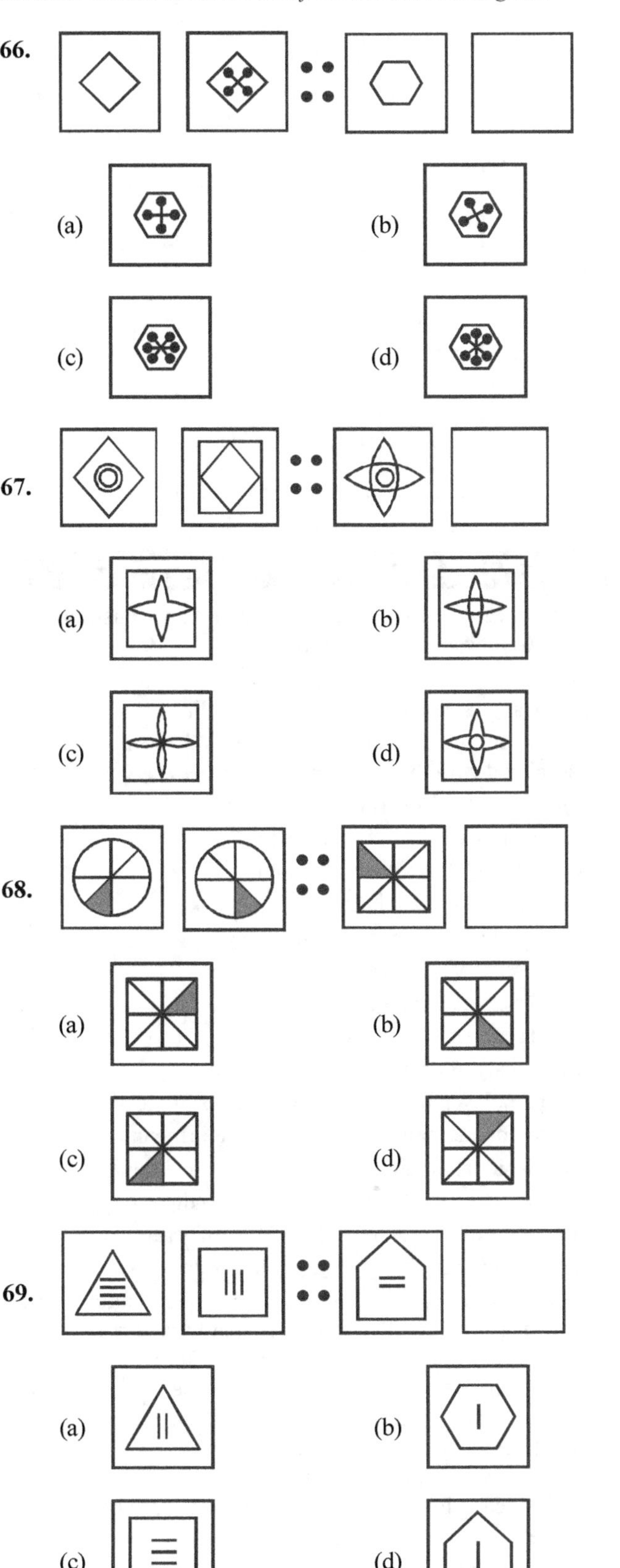

70.

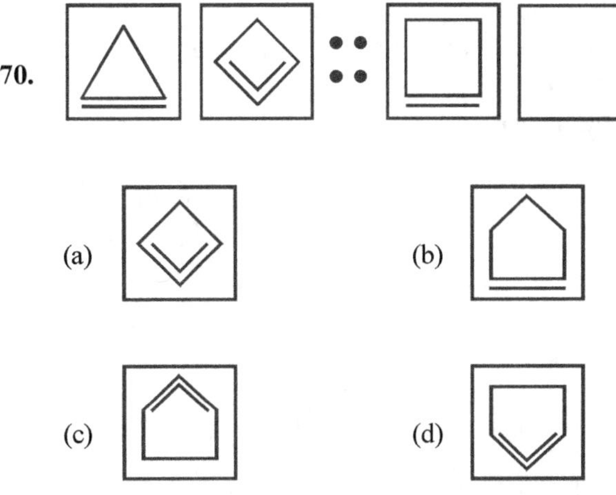

(a)   (b)

(c)   (d)

DIRECTIONS (Qs. 71- 75) : *In each of the following questions there are four figures which are alike in some respect and one is different from others. Find out the odd figure in each questions and indicate your answer.*

71.

(a)   (b)   (c)   (d)

72.

(a)   (b)   (c)   (d)

73.

(a)   (b)   (c)   (d)

74.

(a)   (b)   (c)   (d)

75.

(a)   (b)   (c)   (d)

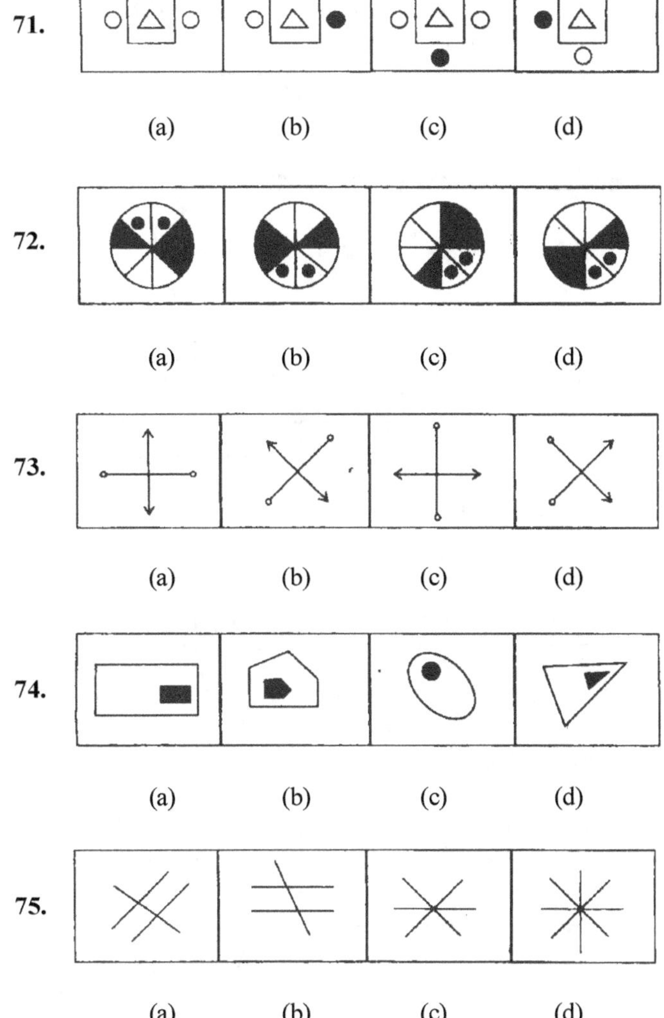

DIRECTION (Qs. 76 - 80) : *Each of the following questions consists of five problem figures marked A, B, C, D and E. From the answer figures marked* (a), (b), (c) *and* (d) *select a figure which will continue the series.*

76. Problem Figures

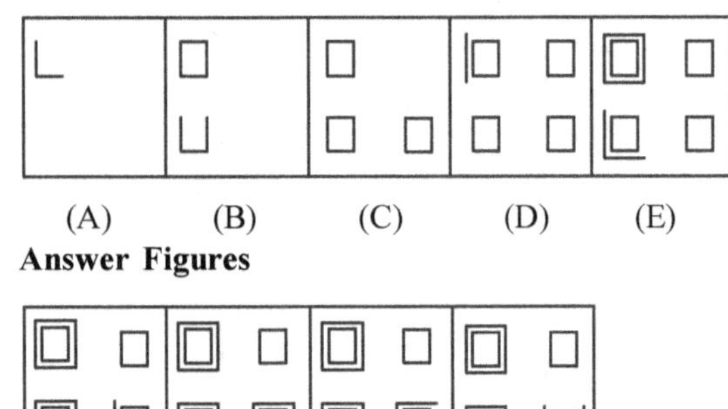

(A) (B) (C) (D) (E)

Answer Figures

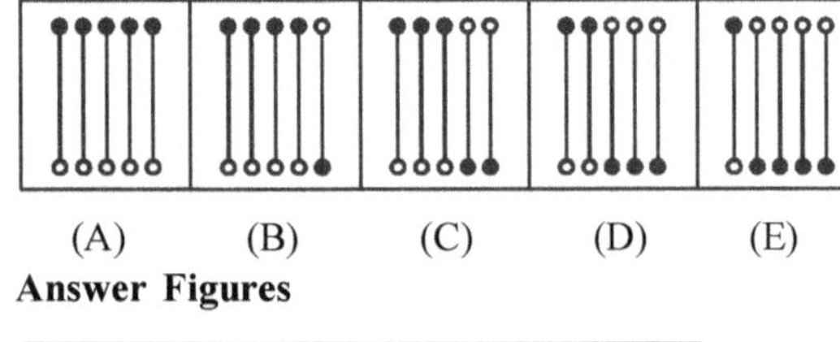

(a) (b) (c) (d)

77. Problem Figures

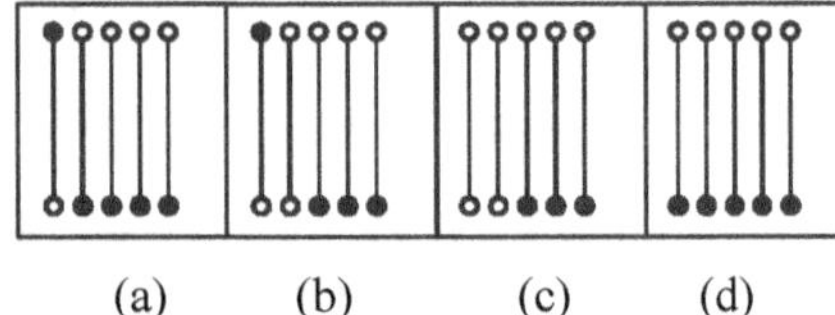

(A) (B) (C) (D) (E)

Answer Figures

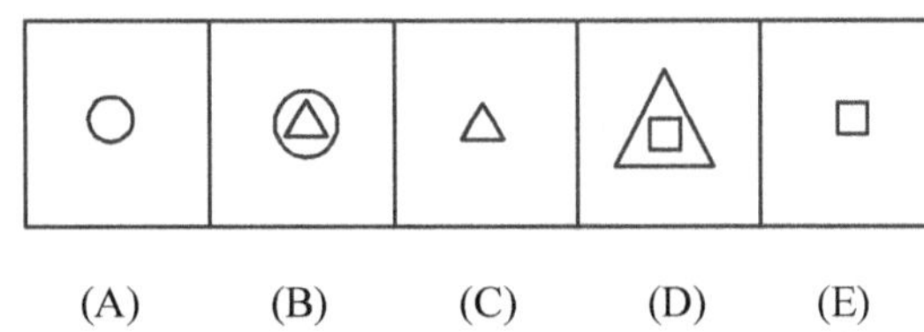

(a) (b) (c) (d)

78. Problem Figures

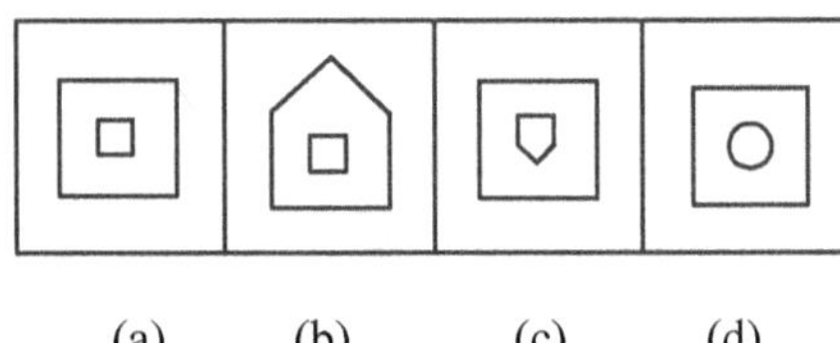

(A) (B) (C) (D) (E)

Answer Figures

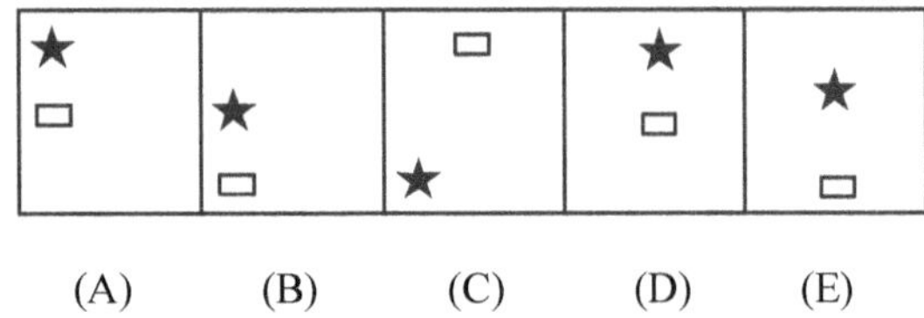

(a) (b) (c) (d)

79. Problem Figures

(A) (B) (C) (D) (E)

Answer Figures

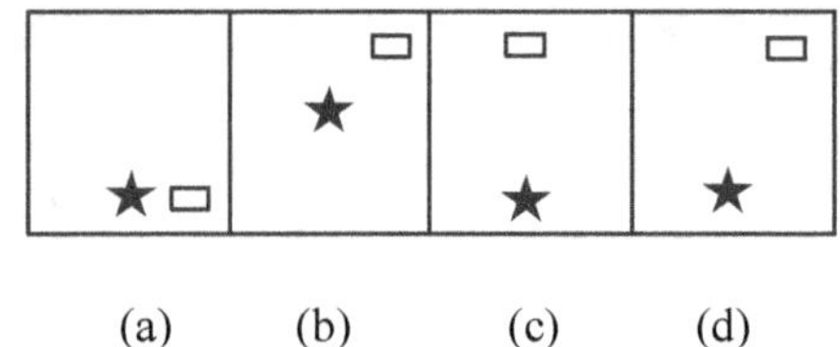

(a) (b) (c) (d)

80. Problem Figures

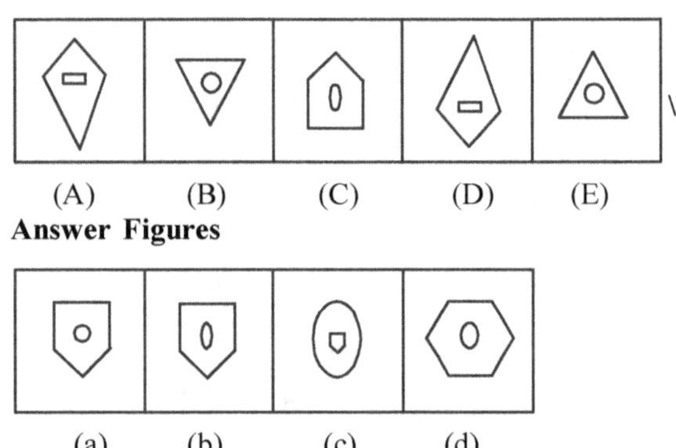

(A) (B) (C) (D) (E)

Answer Figures

(a) (b) (c) (d)

SECTION-D : GENERAL AWARENESS

81. The concept of Concurrent List in Indian Constitution is borrowed from the Constitution of
 (a) U.S.A. (b) Japan
 (c) Canada (d) Australia

82. Which one of the following cities and the personalities associated with their establishment is ***wrongly*** matched ?
 (a) Calcutta - Robert Clive
 (b) Pondicherry - Francis Martin
 (c) Ahmedabad - Ahmad Shah I
 (d) Madras - Francis Day

83. The Crimean War came to an end by the
 (a) Treaty of St. Germain
 (b) Treaty of Trianon
 (c) Treaty of Versailles
 (d) Treaty of Paris

84. The Himalayan mountain range is an example of
 (a) Fold mountain (b) Volcanic mountain
 (c) Residual mountain (d) Block mountain

85. The depletion of Ozone layer is mainly due to
 (a) Chlorofluorocarbons (b) Volcanic eruptions
 (c) Aviation fuels (d) Radioactive rays

86. The use of which of the following regional languages was popularised by the Bhakti leader, Shankaradeva ?
 (a) Bengali (b) Brijbhasha
 (c) Avadhi (d) Assamese

87. Which part of the plant is used as 'saffron'?
 (a) Petals (b) Stamens
 (c) Style and Stigma (d) Sepals

88. Suspended colloidal particles in the water can be removed by the process of :
 (a) Filtration (b) Adsorption
 (c) Absorption (d) Coagulation

89. When and by whom were the Asokan inscriptions deciphered for the first time ?
    - (a) 1787 - John Tower
    - (b) 1825 - Charles Metcalfe
    - (c) 1837 - James Prinsep
    - (d) 1810 - Harry Smith

90. Which gupta emperor is said to have founded Nalanda University?
    - (a) Skandagupta
    - (b) Buddhagupta
    - (c) Purugupta
    - (d) Kumaragupta I

91. Other than Annie Besant, who among the following also launched a Home Rule Movement in India?
    - (a) Aurobindo Ghosh
    - (b) Bal Gangadhar Tilak
    - (c) Gopal Krishna Gokhale
    - (d) Moti Lal Nehru.

92. Three-tier system of Panchayati Raj consists of
    - (a) Gram Panchayat, Panchayat Samiti, Block Samiti
    - (b) Gram Panchayat, Block Samiti, Zila Parishad
    - (c) Gram Panchayat, Panchayat Samiti, Zila Parishad
    - (d) None of these

93. 'Sarva Siksha Abhiyan' is aimed at the education of which of the following?
    - (a) Engineering and technical education
    - (b) Education of girls upto graduation level
    - (c) College education
    - (d) Education of children between 6-14 years

94. 'Apna Khet, Apna Kaam', a new scheme under MNREGA has been initiated in which state?
    - (a) Punjab
    - (b) Rajasthan
    - (c) Uttra Pradesh
    - (d) Madhya Pradesh

95. Which of the following places is famous for Chikankari work, which is a traditional art of embroidery?
    - (a) Lucknow
    - (b) Hyderabad
    - (c) Jaipur
    - (d) Mysore

96. The second highest Gallantry award is
    - (a) Mahavir Chakra
    - (b) Vir Chakra
    - (c) Arjuna Award
    - (d) Ashok Chakra

97. The highest peace time gallantry award is
    - (a) Ashok Chakra
    - (b) Param Vir Chakra
    - (c) Kirti Chakra
    - (d) Vir Chakra

98. Who has authored the recently released book - "India and the Global Financial Crisis"?
    - (a) Y. V. Reddy
    - (b) Shankar Acharya
    - (c) Rakesh Mohan
    - (d) C. Rangarajan

99. Which of the following is a pair names of the same game?
    - (a) Soccer - Football
    - (b) Golf - Polo
    - (c) Billiards - Carrom
    - (d) Volleyball – Squash

100. Which zone of a candle flame is the hottest ?
    - (a) Dark innermost zone
    - (b) Outermost zone
    - (c) Middle luminous zone
    - (d) Central zone

ANSWERS & SOLUTIONS

1. **(a)** To find a suitable title one should first find the central theme of the passage-Patriotism of the four given options (a) is the most appropriate because the other three options only talk about a particular idea discussed in the passage whereas none of them receives role importance all of them are mentioned and discuss therefore a general title elements of patriotism will include all failure and well be the most appropriate title for the given passage

2. **(d)** "Open to attack" would mean it can be questioned or criticized. Coopering this meaning to the given options (a) is not necessarily true, (b) is wrong, (c) is also not necessarily true, (d) on the other hand is nearest to this meaning. Even in the larger sense of the passage (d) is the most possible answer.

3. **(d)** Thus can be done through elimination (a) is incorrect, passage is not critical of any thing, it is rather bent more positively towards patriotism. (B) is also incorrect because there is no description as such of a process. (c) is not true because the author is only giving an analysis of several elements of patriotism and not persuading the reader to believe anything persay. Thus (d) is the correct answer.

4. **(d)** This also will be done through elimination. "Intellectual conviction" will means beliefs regarding matters of the intellect. None of the options given are intellectual matters, they are rather feelings. Therefore the answer is (d).

5. **(c)** The element of "willing sacrifice" as mentioned in the line "But besides all these,...... Of willing sacrifice, of joyful merging of the individual life in life of nation" does not necessarily emerge from the religious element. Both element of worship and the passage does not suggest that the former motivates the latter.

6. **(d)** If you are discomfited by something, it causes you to feel slightly embarrassed or confused. In other words, it, frustrates you.

7. **(b)** Wrath is extreme anger.

8. **(c)** If you abstain from something, you deliberately do not do it. Abstinence, however, is a particular kind of abstaining —that from alcoholic drink, sex etc, often for health or religious reasons. If you abstain from drinking, you do not get drunk. Abstinence does not refer to "drink" only,

9, **(a)** The opposite of 'insipid' is 'tasty'. The word 'insipid' means dull, boring or colorless.

10. **(b)** The opposite of 'relinquish' is 'continue'. Relinquish means to 'give up'.

11. **(d)**

12. **(a)** Add 'the' before 'more'. Here the sentence consists of two clauses- Principal and Subordinate, where the Principal clause should be given more stress by adding 'the' before 'more'.

13. **(b)** Delete 'pair of' before binocular because the word 'binocular' itself suggests a pair.

14. **(b)** 'a' should be replaced with 'the'. Here Kalidas is not Shakespeare but he is compared to Shakespeare.

15. **(b)** Delete 'all' before 'left'. Here the usage of 'all' is superfluous as 'the teacher as well as his students' itself signifies everyone.

16. **(a)** The word 'prejudice' will fill in the blank because here it means something or opinion which is not based on reason or experience and hence it seems to get conflicted with original thoughts.

17. **(d)** The phrase 'stands as' will fill in the blank because it means to signify.

18. **(d)** The phrase 'as well as of a' will fill in the blank as children are considered to shape the future of a nation along with carrying the goodwill of a family.

19. **(b)** The word 'averted' will fill in the blank. It is also the synonym for the word 'avoid' and hence it can be understood that if strict measures were taken then the tragedy would have been avoided.

20. **(a)** The word 'behind' will fill in the blank. The sentence means that the deceased (the person who recently died), left behind him two young children.

21. **(b)**   **22.** **(d)**   **23.** **(b)**

24. **(d)**   **25.** **(d)**

26. **(a)** Let the number be x. Then, as per the operation undertook by the student, we have

$$\frac{x+12}{6} = 112 \implies x = 660$$

Hence, the correct answer $= \dfrac{660}{6} + 12 = 122$

27. **(d)** Let Nikhil has ₹ x and Yogesh has ₹ y
According to question

$$\frac{1}{4}x = \frac{1}{6}y \qquad \text{...(i)}$$

and $x + y = 600$ ...(ii)

From equation (i) and (ii), we get
Nikhil has ₹ $x = $ ₹ 240
and Yogesh has ₹ $y = $ ₹ 360
Difference between their amounts ₹ $360 - ₹\,240 = ₹\,120$

28. **(c)** Let Ram's monthly income be ₹ 100

Household expenditure $= 100 \times \dfrac{20}{100} = 20$

Rest income $= 100 - 20 = 80.$

Books expenditure $= 80 \times \dfrac{15}{100} = 12.$

Rest income $= 80 - 12 = 68.$

Clothes expenditure $= 68 \times \dfrac{30}{100} = 20.4$

Rest saved income $= 68 - 20.4 = 47.6$

But finally saved income $= 9520$

$\therefore \quad \dfrac{47.6}{100} \times x = 9520 \Rightarrow x = 20,000$

Hence, Ram's monthly income $= 20,000$.

29. **(d)** Required consumption to be reduced

$= \dfrac{25 \times 100}{100 + 25} = \dfrac{25 \times 100}{125} = 20\%$

30. **(a)** Least cost price $= ₹(150 \times 15) = ₹2250$

Greatest selling price $= ₹(350 \times 15) = ₹5250$

Required profit $= ₹(5250 - 2250) = ₹3000$

31. **(b)** Sum of 30 numbers $= 30 \times 40 = 1200$

Sum of 40 numbers $= 40 \times 30 = 1200$

Average of 70 numbers $= \dfrac{1200 + 1200}{70} = \dfrac{2400}{70} = 34\dfrac{2}{7}$

32. **(d)** In such type of question,

Required % loss $= \dfrac{(25)^2}{100}\%$

$= \dfrac{625}{100}\% = 6.25\% = 6\dfrac{1}{4}\%$

33. **(a)**

boys	:	girls		girls	:	teacher
4	:	3		8	:	1

So, boys : girls : teacher

4	:	3		
		8	:	1
32	:	24	:	3

So, Student : teacher

$\Rightarrow$ (boys + girls) : teacher

$(32 + 24) : 3$

$56 : 3$

34. **(d)** Since they are moving in opposite direction, therefore their relative speed will be $4 + 3 = 7$ km/hr.

Time $= \dfrac{d}{s} = \dfrac{17.5}{7} = 2.5$ hrs.

(where d is distance and s is speed).

$\therefore$ They should meet at 12.30 PM.

35. **(d)** Let the side of square $= $ 'x'

Area of square $= x^2$

New length of rectangle $= \dfrac{130}{100}x$

New Breadth of rectangle $= \dfrac{120}{100}x$

Hence, Area of so formed rectangle $= \dfrac{130}{100} \times \dfrac{120}{100} \times x^2$

$= \dfrac{156}{100}x^2$

Therefore, area of rectangle exceeds the area of square by 56%

36. **(d)** Weight of new crewmen

$=$ Replace man weight $+$ [No. of crew mewn $\times$ increased average]

$= 55 + 12 \times \dfrac{1}{3} = 59$ kg

37. **(b)** S.I. $= 8800 - 8000 = ₹800$

$\therefore R = \dfrac{\text{S.I.} \times 100}{\text{Principal} \times \text{Time}} = \dfrac{800 \times 100}{8000 \times 2} = 5\%$ per annum

New rate $= 3\%$

$\therefore$ S.I. $= \dfrac{8000 \times 3 \times 2}{100} = ₹480$

$\therefore$ Amount $= ₹(8000 + 4800) = ₹8480$

38. **(a)** Relative velocity $= 20 + 30 = 50$ m/s.

Distance $= 2.5$ kms. $= 2500$ m.

$t = 2500/50 = 50$ s.

39. **(a)** Let the original price be x and sale be of y units.

Then, the revenue collected initially $= x \times y$

Now, new price $= 0.8x$, new sale $= 1.8y$

Then, new revenue collected $= 1.44xy$

% increase in revenue $= \dfrac{0.44xy}{xy} \times 100 = 44\%$

40. **(d)** Given, ratio of speeds of A and B is $5 : 4$.

$\therefore$ B makes 4 rounds when A makes 5 rounds.

Now, distance covered by A in 5 rounds

$= \left(5 \times \dfrac{400}{1000}\right) = 2$ km

and distance covered by B in 4 rounds

$= \left(4 \times \dfrac{400}{1000}\right)$ km $= 1.6$ km

It is clear that in 5 hours, A passes B only once. (i.e., 1 time).

In other words, in covering 2 km, A pases B 1 time.

$\therefore$ In covering 5 km, A passes B in $\left(\dfrac{1}{2} \times 5\right)$ times

i.e., $2\dfrac{1}{2}$ times.

41. **(b)** Work of pipe P in 16 minutes $= \dfrac{1}{24} \times 16 = \dfrac{2}{3}$

Similarly, work of pipe Q in 16 minutes $= \dfrac{1}{32} \times 16 = \dfrac{1}{2}$

$\therefore$ Remaining work of pipe Q $= 1 - \dfrac{1}{2} = \dfrac{1}{2}$

Now, Time taken by pipe P $= \dfrac{1}{2} \times 24 = 12$ minutes.

Hence, first pipe (i.e P) should be turned off after 12 minutes.

42. **(d)** Let the length and breadth of the rectangle be x and y cm, respectively.

Then, $(x-4)(y+3) = xy \Rightarrow 3x - 4y = 12$ ....(i)

Also, $(x-4) = (y+3)$ [sides of square]

$\Rightarrow x - y = 7$ ....(ii)

From (i) and (ii),

$x = 16$ and $y = 9$

Perimeter of the original rectangle $= 2(x+y) = 50$ cm

43. **(b)** Let the salaries of A, B and C are x, y and z respectively.

$x + y + z = 1450$ ...(i)

$14 : 21 : 15 = 40\%$ of $x : 35\%$ of $y : 30\%$ of z

$\dfrac{14}{21} = \dfrac{40x}{35y} \Rightarrow x = \dfrac{35 \times 14 \, y}{21 \times 40}$

$\dfrac{21}{15} = \dfrac{35y}{30z} \Rightarrow \dfrac{15 \times 35y}{21 \times 30} = z$

Put these value in eqn (i)

$\dfrac{35 \times 14y}{21 \times 40} + y + \dfrac{55 \times 35y}{21 \times 30} = 1450$

$0.583y + y + 0.833y = 1450$

$2.416y = 1450$

$\therefore y = \dfrac{1450}{2.416} = ₹\,600.08$

44. **(b)** Let the speed of the stream be x km/hr and distance travelled be S km. Then,

$\dfrac{S}{12+x} = 6$ and $\dfrac{S}{12-x} = 9$

$\Rightarrow \dfrac{12-x}{12+x} = \dfrac{6}{9} \Rightarrow 108 - 9x = 72 + 6x$

$\Rightarrow 15x = 36 \Rightarrow x = \dfrac{36}{15} = 2.4$ km / hr.

45. **(b)** Let the Speed of faster train be x and speed of slower train be y.

Now, when both the train move in same direction their relative speed $= x - y$

Now, total distance covered $= 130 + 110 = 240$

Now, distance = speed × time

$\therefore 240 = (x-y) \times 60$ ($\because 1\min = 60\sec$)

$\Rightarrow x - y = 4$ ...(1)

When the trains move in opposite direction then their relative speed $= x + y$

$\therefore 240 = (x+y) \times 3$

$\Rightarrow 80 = x + y$ ...(2)

on solving eq^n (1) and (2), we get x = 42 m/sec and y = 38 m/sec

46. **(c)** In all other pairs, first is prepared by the second.

47. **(d)** In all other pairs, first is the alloy used to make the second. (Iron is not an alloy but a metal.)

48. **(b)** In all other pairs, second is the name given to artificial rearing of the first.

49. **(a)** In all other pairs, second is a collective group of the first.

50. **(c)** In all other pairs, second is the food over which the first feeds.

51. **(d)** All except Quart are units of measuring distances.

52. **(b)** All except Bromine are metals, while bromine is a non-metal.

53. **(a)** All except Mariana are waterfalls, while Mariana is a trench.

54. **(b)** All except Diagonal are terms associated with circle.

55. **(a)** All except Granite are different types of coal, while granite is a rock.

56. **(d)** These are leafy vegetables.

57. **(b)** They are connected with church.

58. **(b)** They are highly inflammable.

59. **(d)** These are halogens.

60. **(b)** These give information about living things for classification.

61. **(d)**

62. **(a)**

63. **(b)**

64. **(c)** 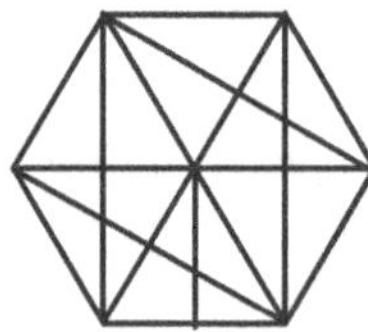

65. **(a)** 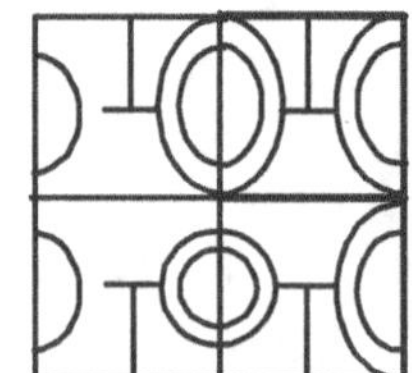

66. **(d)** As 4 dots are formed with intersecting lines in the 4 sided figure so 6 dots will form with intersecting lines in the 6 sided figure. Again the dots will be in the middle of each side as in Figure 2.

67. **(a)** A box surrounds the figure and the inner figure is removed, only boundary is left.

68. **(c)** Shaded position is moved 45 degrees in anticlockwise direction.

69. **(b)** Outer figure one side is increased and inner lines one line is decreased and line position also change from vertical to horizontal.

70. **(d)** One side is increased in the figure and outer line taken inside and kept down opening upwards in 'V' shape.

71. **(b)** All the figures have shaded circle placed opposite to each other. Hence (b) is odd one out.

72. **(b)** In every shaded sector have three unshaded sector between them. Hence, (b) is odd one out.

73. **(d)** All images have double sided arrow except the last one.

74. **(c)** Every figure have some sides except (c).

75. **(d)** Each images have 3 lines intersecting while (d) have 4 lines intersecting.

76. **(d)** Five line segments are added in each step to complete the squares in an ACW direction.

77. **(d)** One of the pins gets inverted in each step. The pins gets inverted sequentially from right to left.

78. **(c)** In one step, the existing element enlarges and a new element appears inside this element. In the next step, the outer element is lost

79. **(d)** In each step, both the elements move one space (each space is equal to half-a-side of the square boundary) downwards. Once any of the two elements reaches the lowermost position, then in the next step, it reaches the uppermost position in the next column to the right.

80. **(b)** Similar figure repeats in every third step and each time a figure reappears it gets vertically inverted.

81. **(d)** The concept of Concurrent List in Indian Constitution is borrowed from the Constitution of Australia. The Concurrent List or List-III is a list of 52 items(though the last item is numbered 47) given in Part XI of the Constitution of India, concerned with relations between the Union and States. This part is divided between legislative and administrative powers. The legislative section is divided into three lists: Union List, State List and Concurrent List.

82. **(a)** Calcutta with Robert Clive is wrongly matched. Lord Curzon was associated with Calcutta. Lord Curzon felt that the Bengal province was too big to be administered efficiently and so he wanted to split it into two provinces, one of which had Dacca as its capital.

83. **(d)** The Crimean War came to an end by the treaty of Paris. Crimean War, (October 1853-February 1856), war fought mainly on the Crimean Peninsula between the Russians and the British, French, and Ottoman Turkish, with support from January 1855 by the army of Sardinia-Piedmont.The resulting Treaty of Paris, signed on March 30, 1856, guaranteed the integrity of Ottoman Turkey and obliged Russia to surrender southern Bessarabia, at the mouth of the Danube.

84. **(a)** The Himalayan Mountain Range is an example of fold mountain.They are known as fold mountains because the mountains extend for 2500 km in length in a series of parallel ridges or folds and consist of three folds namely Himadri, Himachal, Shiwalik.

85. **(a)** The depletion of Ozone layer is mainly due to chlorofluorocarbons. A chlorofluorocarbon is an organic compound that contains only carbon, chlorine, and fluorine, produced as a volatile derivative of methane, ethane, and propane. They are also commonly known by the DuPont brand name Freon.

86. **(d)** Sankaradeva was an erudite scholar, a prolific writer, a versatile saint-poet of unlimited merit, a lyricist of universal acceptance, a musician of high calibre, a pioneer in the field of Assamese prose, drama and dramatic performances, a painter and above all the greatest religious teacher-preacher-leader of the medieval Vaisnava movement in Assam which is rightly known as the Sankaradeva Movement.

87. **(c)** Saffron, a spice derived from the dried stigmas of the saffron crocus. (crocus sativus) a small plant about a foot tall. Each flower has three female parts. (stigmas) two male parts. (stamens) each stigmas is red or dark red in color towards the top and yellow towards the bottom of the stigma, where it is attached to the flower.

88. **(d)**   **89.** **(c)**   **90.** **(d)**

91. **(b)** Two home Rule leagues were started in 1915-16 – one under the leadership of Lokmanya Tilak at Poona and other under the leadership of Anne Basent and S. Subramanya Iyer at Madras.

92. **(c)** Three-tier system of Panchayati Raj consists of Gram Panchayat, Panchayat Samiti and Zila Parishad.

93. **(d)** 'Sarva Siksha Abhiyan' is aimed at the education of children between 6-14 years.

94. **(b)**   **95.** **(a)**   **96.** **(a)**

97. **(a)**   **98.** **(a)**   **99.** **(a)**

100. **(c)** Middle luminous zone of a candle flame is the hottest.

Practice Set

1. This practice set comprises four sections. **Section A** : Verbal Ability in English; **Section B** : Numerical Ability; **Section C** : Reasoning and Military Aptitude; **Section D** : General Awareness.
2. The set will consist of 100 questions and each questions will be of 3 marks.
3. Each questions have four options, of which one is correct. The students are advised to read all the options thoroughly.
4. There is **one-third negative** marking in the set.

Time: 2 hrs. *Max. Marks: 300*

SECTION-A : VERBAL ABILITY IN ENGLISH

DIRECTIONS (Qs. 1 - 5) : *Read the following passages carefully and answer the questions given below it :*

A man found a cocoon of a butterfly. One day a small opening appeared; he sat and watched the butterfly for several hours as it struggled to force its body through that little hole. Then it seemed to stop making any progress.

Then the man decided to help the butterfly, so he took a pair of scissors and snipped off the remaining bit of the cocoon. The butterfly then emerged easily. But it had a swollen body and small, shrivelled wings. The man continued to watch the butterfly because he expected that, at any moment, the wings would enlarge and expand to be able to support the body, which would contract in time.

Neither happened! It never was able to fly.

What this man in his kindness and haste did not understand was that the restricting cocoon and the struggle required for the butterfly to get through the tiny opening were nature's way of forcing fluid from the body of the butterfly into its wings.

Sometimes struggles are exactly what we need in our life.

1. What did the man find?
   - (a) a coconut
   - (b) a coco plum
   - (c) a cocoon
   - (d) a coco palm
2. What did the man see one day?
   - (a) One day he saw a wide opening appear
   - (b) One day he saw a large opening appear
   - (c) One day he saw a small insect go inside the opening
   - (d) One day he saw a small opening appear
3. What did the man do to help the butterfly?
   - (a) The man took a pair of scissors and snipped off the whole of the cocoon.
   - (b) The man took a pair of scissors and snipped off the remaining bit of the cocoon.
   - (c) The man took a hammer and cracked the remaining bit of the cocoon.
   - (d) The man took a needle and snipped off the remaining bit of the cocoon.
4. What happened after the man had snipped off the remaining bit of the cocoon?
   - (a) The butterfly died instantly
   - (b) The butterfly flew in to the air
   - (c) The butterfly emerged easily
   - (d) The butterfly thanked the man
5. What did the man not understand in his kindness and haste?
   - (a) It was nature's way of forcing fluid from the body of the butterfly into its wings.
   - (b) It was nature's way of forcing liquid from the body of the butterfly into its wings.
   - (c) It was nature's way of forcing mobile from the body of the butterfly into its wings.
   - (d) It was nature's way of forcing fluid from the wings of the butterfly into its body.

DIRECTIONS (Qs. 6 - 11) : *Find out which part of a sentence has an error :*

6. It was he who / came running in the house /
      (a)   (b)

   with the news about the earthquake. / No Error.
            (c)   (d)
7. Her mother does not approve of / her to go to the party /
           (a)   (b)

   without dressing formally. / No Error.
        (c)   (d)
8. Riding across the battle field / the famous Bhishm /
           (a)   (b)

saw a large number of dead warriors. / No Error.
                (c)   (d)

9. My Aunt / was first / to get a degree / No Error.
   (a)   (b)   (c)   (d)

10. Padmini had not rarely missed /
          (a)

a dance performance or festival since /
          (b)

she was eight years old. / No Error.
     (c)   (d)

11. Krupa and Kavya studied / in the Delhi Public School /
       (a)   (b)

and so does Kamya. / No Error.
     (c)   (d)

DIRECTIONS (Qs. 12 - 15) : *Select the most appropriate word from the options against each number :*

I peered at the river through a gap in the roots of the strangler fig. The thick branches of the tree __12__ me without really protecting me. I noticed the gentlest of ripples in the water and then something __13__ began to emerge from its depths. An enormous head upon a slender neck rose about the surface. I looked into the beast's cold, reptilian eyes. I could sense no mind or soul behind them. I had to refrain from letting out a frightened __14__! The time for retreating into the depths of the forest had arrived and I knew that it was __15__ .

12. (a) either sooner rather than later
    (b) either now or never
    (c) neither now or never
    (d) neither sooner nor later

13. (a) magnificent yet terrifying
    (b) frightening yet scary
    (c) wonderful yet grand
    (d) amazing yet astonishing

14. (a) "Phew!"   (b) "Aah!"
    (c) "Aha!"   (d) "Ouch!"

15. (a) were hiding   (b) hiding
    (c) hidden   (d) was hiding

DIRECTIONS (Qs. 16 - 20) : *Choose the word/words which complete the sentence :*

16. Let us quickly __________ .
    (a) muddle   (b) huddle
    (c) hurdle   (d) puddle

17. Rajesh's car wasn't __________ Ramesh's, so we were too exhausted by the time we reached home.

(a) such comfortable   (b) as comfortable as
(c) comfortable enough   (d) so comfortable that

18. I don't suppose that Pramod will be elected __________ how hard he struggles as he is not completely supported by the committee.
    (a) although   (b) seeing as
    (c) no matter   (d) however

19. Regular exercise is conducive __________ heath.
    (a) in   (b) to
    (c) for   (d) of

20. Can you please __________ my web site just before I publish it ?
    (a) find out   (b) go through
    (c) set out   (d) look up

DIRECTIONS (Qs. 21 & 22): *Choose the word which is nearest in meaning to the given word.*

21. ANIMATE
    (a) kill   (b) dead
    (c) energise   (d) calm

22. NIGGARDLY
    (a) penurious   (b) generous
    (c) liberal   (d) nimbus

DIRECTIONS (Qs. 23 - 25) : *Choose the word which is nearly opposite in meaning to the given word.*

23. INDIGENTLY
    (a) richly   (b) awfully
    (c) completely   (d) diligency

24. AUDACITY
    (a) quivering   (b) patricide
    (c) bravado   (d) cowardice

25. ELEVATION
    (a) depression   (b) deflation
    (c) depreciation   (d) recession

SECTION-B : NUMERICAL ABILITY

26. If $3x - \dfrac{1}{4y} = 6$, then the value of $4x - \dfrac{1}{3y}$ is
    (a) 2   (b) 4
    (c) 6   (d) 8

27. A shopkeeper marks an article at a price which gives a profit of 25%. After allowing certain discount, the profit reduces to $12\dfrac{1}{2}\%$. The discount percent is
    (a) 12%   (b) 12.5%
    (c) 10%   (d) 20%

28. The smallest positive integer which when multiplied by 392, gives a perfect square is
    (a) 2   (b) 3
    (c) 5   (d) 7

29. If A : B = 6 : 7 and B : C = 8 : 9. Find the value of C : A?

(a) $\dfrac{9}{6}$ (b) $\dfrac{16}{21}$

(c) $\dfrac{21}{16}$ (d) $\dfrac{6}{9}$

30. Out of a group of swans, 7/2 times the square root of the number is playing on the shore of the pond. The two remaining are inside the pond. What is the total number of swans?

(a) 10   (b) 14

(c) 12   (d) 16

31. Anthony got 30% of the maximum marks in an examination and failed by 10 marks. However, Amar who took the same examination, got 40% of the total marks and got 15 more than the passing marks in the examination. What were the passing marks in the examination ?

(a) 35   (b) 250

(c) 75   (d) 85

32. The length of the ractangular field is increased by 25%. By what per cent must the width be reduced so that the area in each case remains the same?

(a) 15%   (b) 17%

(c) 18%   (d) 20%

33. A machine is sold at a profit of 10%. Had it been sold for ₹40 less, there would have been a loss of 10%. What was the cost price ?

(a) ₹320   (b) ₹200

(c) ₹225   (d) ₹250

34. A train 100 metres long moving at a speed of 50 km/hr. crosses a train 120 metres long coming from opposite direction in 6 sec. The speed of the second train is

(a) 60 km/hr.   (b) 82 km/hr.

(c) 70 km/hr.   (d) 74 km/hr.

35. A shopkeeper marks up his goods to gain 35%. But he allows 10% discount for cash payment. His profit on the cash transaction in percentage, is

(a) $13\dfrac{1}{2}$ (b) 25

(c) $21\dfrac{1}{2}$ (d) $31\dfrac{1}{2}$

36. Dhiraj purchased 150 kg of rice. He sold $\dfrac{1}{3}$rd of it at 10% loss. At what per cent of profit must he sell the remaining rice so that he can make 10% profit on the whole ?

(a) 20%   (b) 15%

(c) 10%   (d) None of these

37. The average monthly salary of employees, consisting of officers and workers, of an organisation is ₹ 3000. The average salary of an officer is ₹ 10,000 while that of a worker is ₹ 2000 per month. If there are total 400 employees in the organisation, find the number of officers. *[Feb. 2007]*

(a) 60   (b) 50

(c) 80   (d) 40

38. A man gains 10% by selling a certain article for a certain price. If he sells it at double the price, then the profit made is:

(a) 120%   (b) 60%

(c) 100%   (d) 80%

39. A 4 cm cube is cut into 1 cm cubes. Find the percentage decrease in surface area.

(a) 200%   (b) 94%

(c) 400%   (d) 300%

40. In what time will ₹ 500 give ₹ 50 as interest at the rate of 5% per annum on simple interest ?

(a) 2 years   (b) 3 years

(c) 4 years   (d) 5 years

41. What is the missing figure in the expression given below ?

$$\dfrac{16}{7}\times\dfrac{16}{7}-\dfrac{*}{7}\times\dfrac{9}{7}+\dfrac{9}{7}\times\dfrac{9}{7}=1$$

(a) 1   (b) 7

(c) 4.57   (d) 32

42. If the ratio of boys to girls in a class is B and the ratio of girls to boys is G, then 3 (B + G) is :

(a) equal to 3   (b) less than 3

(c) more than 3   (d) less than $\dfrac{1}{3}$

43. In a mixture of 45 litres, the ratio of milk and water is 4 : 1. How much water must be added to make the mixture ratio 3 : 2 ?

(a) 72 litres   (b) 24 litres

(c) 15 litres   (d) 1.5 litres

44. Two men starting from the same place walk at the rate of 5 km/h and 5.5 km/h respectively. What time will they take to be 8.5 km apart, if they walk in the same direction?

(a) 16 h   (b) 8 h 30 min

(c) 4h / 5min   (d) 17 h

45. If the cost of 12 pencils is equal to the selling price of 10 pencils, the profit percent in the transaction is :

(a) $16\dfrac{1}{3}\%$ (b) $22\dfrac{1}{2}\%$

(c) 20%   (d) 25%

SECTION-C : RASONING AND MILITARY APTITUDE

DIRECTIONS (Qs 46 -50) : *The words in the bottom row are related in the same way as the words in the top row. For each item, find the word that completes the bottom row of words.*

46.

ant	Fly	bee
hamster	squirrel	?

(a) Spider   (b) mouse

(c) rodent   (d) cat

47. Tadpole   Frog   Amphibian
Lamb   Sheep   ?
- (a) Animal
- (b) Wool
- (c) Farm
- (d) mammal

48. Snow   Mountain   Ski
Warmth   Lake   ?
- (a) Sand
- (b) Wwim
- (c) Sunburn
- (d) Vacation

49. Walk   Skip   Run
Toss   Pitch   ?
- (a) Wwerve
- (b) Hurl
- (c) Jump
- (d) Dance

50. Rule   Command   Dictate
Doze   Sleep   ?
- (a) Snore
- (b) Govern
- (c) Awaken
- (d) Hibernate

DIRECTIONS (Qs 51 - 53) : *Three of the words will be in the same classification, the remaining one will not be. Your answer will be the one word that does NOT belong in the same classification as the others.*

51. Which word does NOT belong with the others?
- (a) book
- (b) index
- (c) glossary
- (d) chapter

52.
- (a) unimportant
- (b) trivial
- (c) insignificant
- (d) familiar

53.
- (a) biology
- (b) chemistry
- (c) theology
- (d) zoology

54. Yesterday I saw an ice cube which had already melted due to heat of a nearby furnace.
- (a) Always
- (b) Never
- (c) Often
- (d) Sometimes

55. What is always in worry?
- (a) Difficulty
- (b) Unrest
- (c) Non-cooperation
- (d) Poignancy

56. Which one of the following is always found in 'Remedy of fault'?
- (a) Punishment
- (b) Remedy
- (c) Fault
- (d) Scolding

57. A mirror always
- (a) Retracts
- (b) Distorts
- (c) Refracts
- (d) Reflects

58. Danger always involves
- (a) Enemy
- (b) Attack
- (c) Fear
- (d) Help

DIRECTIONS (Qs. 59 & 60) : *In each of the question below is given a statement followed by two assumptions numbered I and II. Consider the statement and the following assumptions and decide which of the assumptions is implicit in the statement.*

59. **Statement:** "If you trouble me, I will slap you." - A mother warns her child.

Assumptions:
- I. With the warning, the child may stop troubling her.
- II. All children are basically naughty.
- (a) Only assumption I is implicit
- (b) Only assumption II is implicit
- (c) Either I or II is implicit
- (d) Neither I nor II is implicit

60. **Statement:** The State government has decided to appoint four thousand primary school teachers during the next financial year.

Assumptions:
- I. There are enough schools in the state to accommodate four thousand additional primary school teachers.
- II. The eligible candidates may not be interested to apply as the government may not finally appoint such a large number of primary school teachers.
- (a) Only assumption I is implicit
- (b) Only assumption II is implicit
- (c) Either I or II is implicit
- (d) Neither I nor II is implicit

DIRECTIONS (Qs. 61 - 65) : *Which answer figure will complete the pattern in the question figure?*

61. **Question Figure :**

Answer Figures :

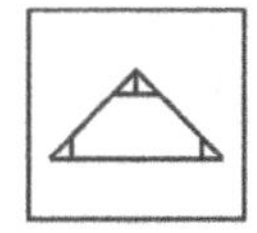 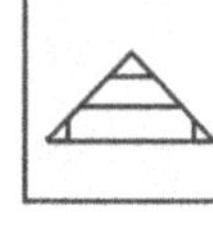 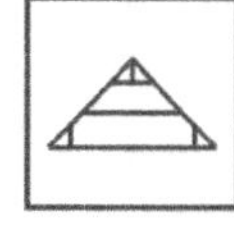 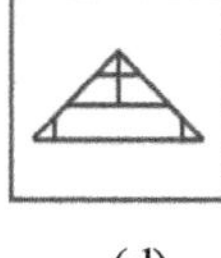

   (a)   (b)   (c)   (d)

62. **Question Figure :**

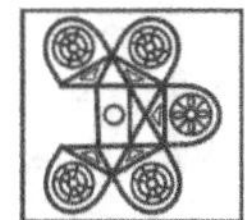

Answer Figures :

 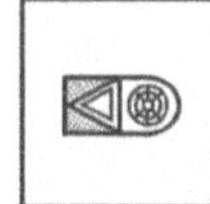 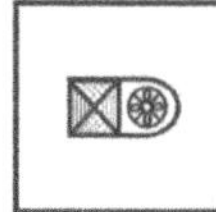 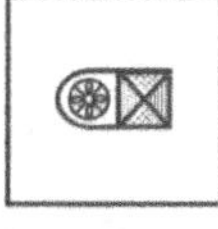

   (a)   (b)   (c)   (d)

63. **Question Figure :**

Answer Figures :

  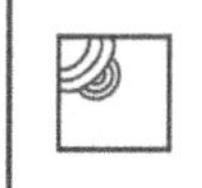 

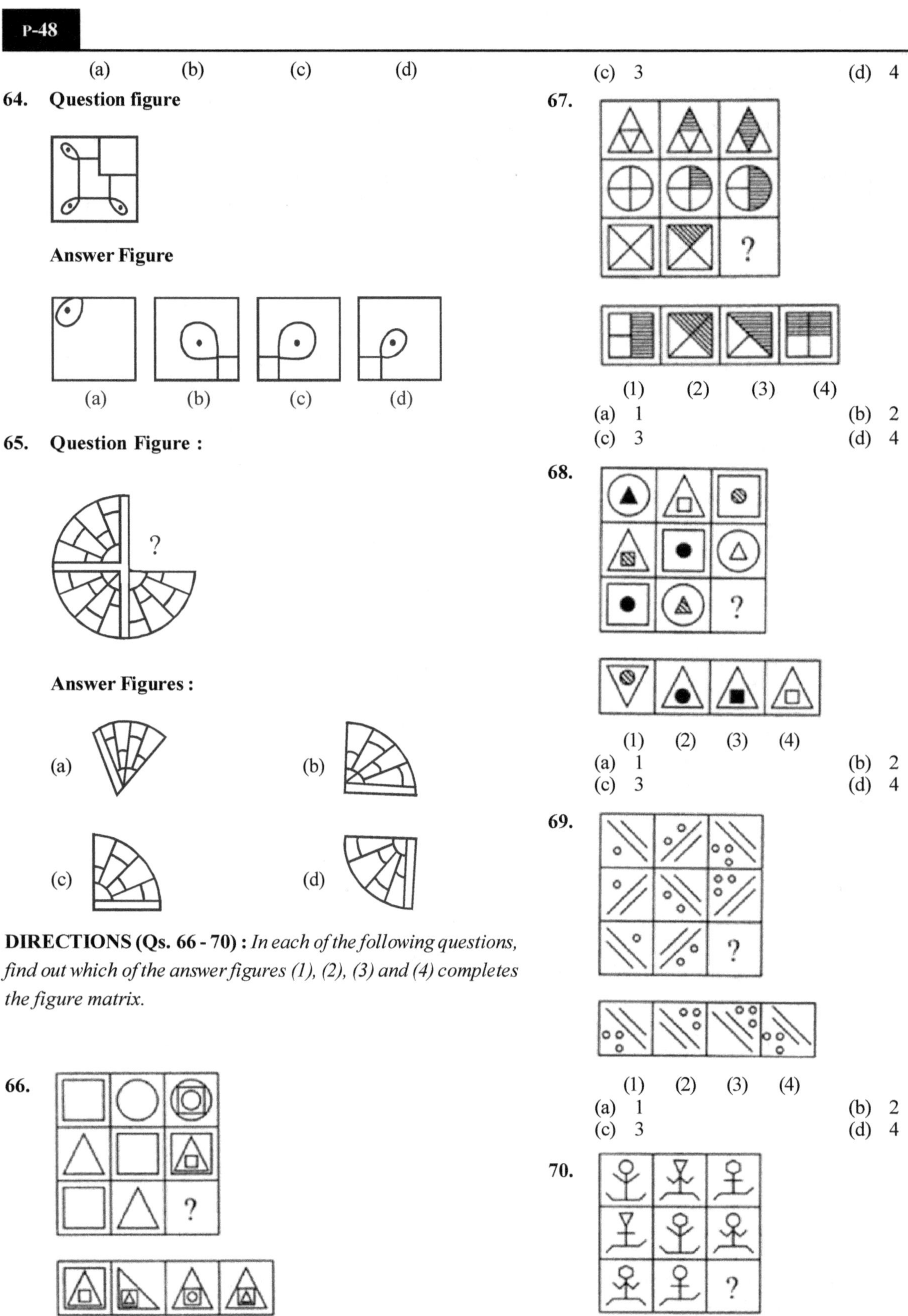

(a)   (b)   (c)   (d)

64. Question figure

Answer Figure

(a)   (b)   (c)   (d)

65. Question Figure :

Answer Figures :

(a)   (b)

(c)   (d)

DIRECTIONS (Qs. 66 - 70) : *In each of the following questions, find out which of the answer figures (1), (2), (3) and (4) completes the figure matrix.*

66.

    (1)   (2)   (3)   (4)

(a) 1   (b) 2

(c) 3   (d) 4

67.

    (1)   (2)   (3)   (4)

(a) 1   (b) 2

(c) 3   (d) 4

68.

    (1)   (2)   (3)   (4)

(a) 1   (b) 2

(c) 3   (d) 4

69.

    (1)   (2)   (3)   (4)

(a) 1   (b) 2

(c) 3   (d) 4

70.

    (1)   (2)   (3)   (4)

(a) 1 (b) 2
(c) 3 (d) 4

DIRECTIONS (Qs. 71-75) : *In there tests find which code matches the shape or pattern given at the end of each questions.*

71.

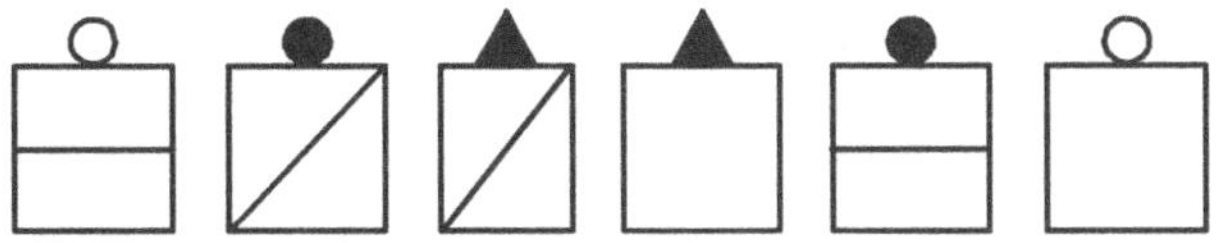

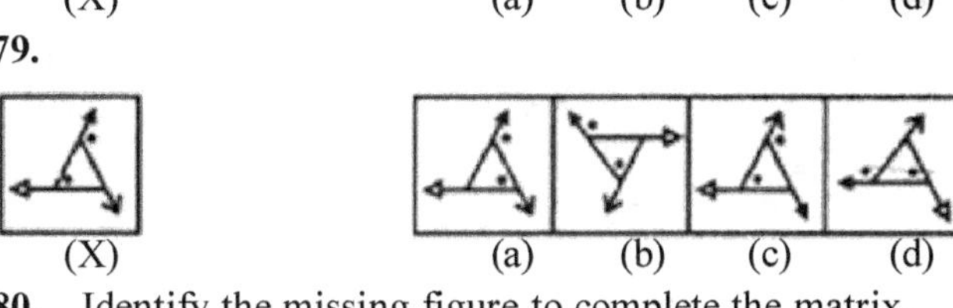

SL	OP	ON	TN	SP	?

(a) TP (b) SN
(c) TL (d) TN

72.

AC	TP	GL	GK	AG	?

(a) AG (b) TA
(c) GA (d) TG

73.

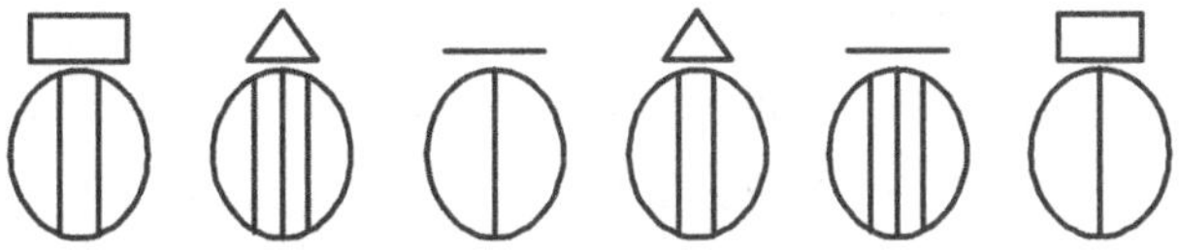

TK	GR	JS	TR	GS	?

(a) GK (b) JK
(c) RS (d) JR

74.

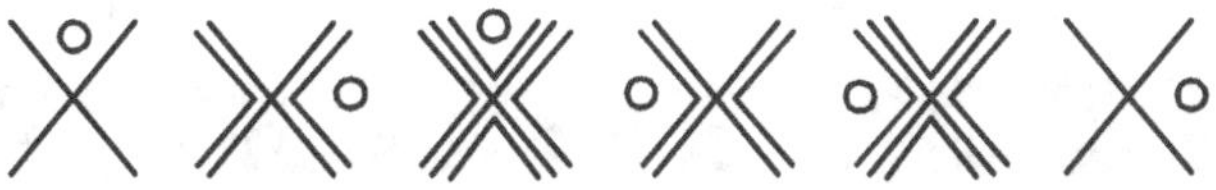

CF	TL	CP	EL	EP	?

(a) TF (b) LT
(c) TL (d) EL

75.

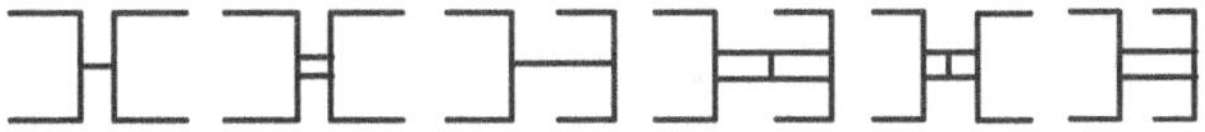

TK	KC	LP	PK	TP	?

(a) PC (b) PK
(c) TP (d) LT

DIRECTIONS (Qs. 76 - 79) : *In each of the following questions, find out how will the key figure (x) look lite after rotation.*

76.

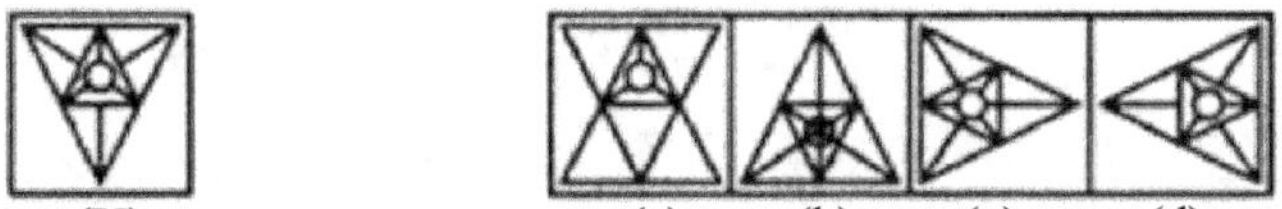

(X) (a) (b) (c) (d)

77.

(X) (a) (b) (c) (d)

78.

(X) (a) (b) (c) (d)

79.

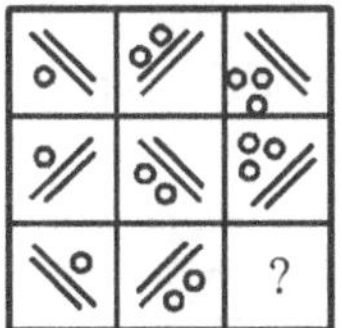

(X) (a) (b) (c) (d)

80. Identify the missing figure to complete the matrix.

Question figure :

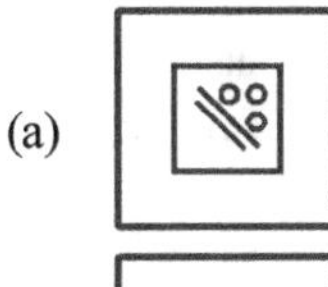

Answer figures :

(a) 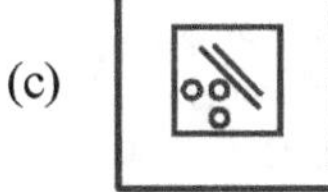   (b) 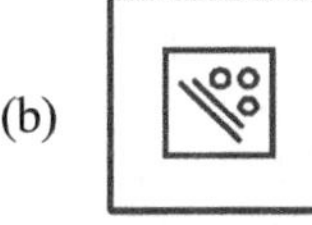

(c)    (d) 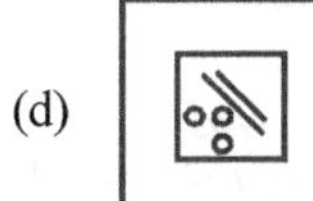

81. Hiuen Tsang visited the Pallava kingdom during the reign of ?
(a) Narasimhavarman I (b) Mahendravarman I
(c) Paramesvarvarman II (d) Nandivarman II

82. The first sermon of Buddha made at Saranath is called
(a) Dharmachakra Parivartan (b) Dharma Sansthapan
(c) Dharma Sabha (d) Maha Parinirvan

83. When Alexander invaded india, who were the rulers of Magadha ?
(a) Haryankas (b) Shishunagas
(c) Nandas (d) Maurya

84. Bhakta Tukaram was a contemporary of which Mughal emperor?
(a) Babar (b) Akbar
(c) Jahangir (d) Aurangzeb

85. Who founded the Fort William College at Calcutta?
(a) Lord Cornwallis (b) Lord Ellenborough
(c) Lord Macaulay (d) Lord Wellesley

86. Who abolished the Dual Government of Bengal?
(a) Cornwallis (b) Robert Clive
(c) Warren Hastings (d) John Macfersson

87. In 1930, Mahatma Gandhi started Civil Disobedience Movement from:
(a) Sevagram (b) Dandi
(c) Sabarmati (d) Wardha

88. Which comet appears every 76 years?
(a) Hailey's (b) Holme's
(c) Donati's (d) Alpha Centauri

89. The waterfall 'Victoria' is associated with the river
(a) Amazon (b) Missouri

   (c) St. Lawrence   (d) Zambezi

90. Which one of the following rights has been described by Dr. Ambedkar as 'The heart and soul of the constitution'?
   (a) Rights of Equality
   (b) Right to freedom
   (c) Right to property
   (d) Right to Constitutional Remedies

91. The electric charge is stored in a device called
   (a) Inductor   (b) Capacitor
   (c) Resister   (d) Transformer

92. The folk dance 'Chhau' belongs to
   (a) Odisha   (b) Uttarakhand
   (c) Jharkhand   (d) Assam

93. Which country is the winner of Davis Cup- 2014?
   (a) Serbia   (b) USA
   (c) Switzerland   (d) Russia

94. Who among the following players has received the Arjuna Award in 2014?
   (a) Manoj Kumar   (b) Mary Kom
   (c) M S Dhoni   (d) Sardar Singh

95. Dr. APJ Abdul Kalam was formally conferred the title of Honorary Professor by which of the following university?
   (a) Shanghai University
   (b) University of Hong Kong
   (c) Peking University
   (d) Tsinghua University

96. Richard Flanagan recently won Man Booker Prize for which of the following book?
   (a) The Narrow Road to the Deep North
   (b) The Sound of One Hand Clapping
   (c) Death of a River Guide
   (d) The Unknown Terrorist

97. Patrick Madiano has been awarded with Nobel Prize in which of the following category?
   (a) Medicine   (b) Economics
   (c) Physics   (d) Literature

98. Fertilization occurs normally in the
   (a) Cervix   (b) Vagina
   (c) Fallopian tube   (d) Uterus

99. Which one of the following correctly describes AGNI ?
   (a) A fighter plane   (b) A versatile tank
   (c) A long-range missile   (d) A long-range gun

100. According to a resolution adopted by the United Nations General Assembly, 'International Day of Peace' is observed every year on
   (a) September 1   (b) September 14

RESPONSE SHEET

1. ⓐⓑⓒⓓ	2. ⓐⓑⓒⓓ	3. ⓐⓑⓒⓓ	4. ⓐⓑⓒⓓ	5. ⓐⓑⓒⓓ
6. ⓐⓑⓒⓓ	7. ⓐⓑⓒⓓ	8. ⓐⓑⓒⓓ	9. ⓐⓑⓒⓓ	10. ⓐⓑⓒⓓ
11. ⓐⓑⓒⓓ	12. ⓐⓑⓒⓓ	13. ⓐⓑⓒⓓ	14. ⓐⓑⓒⓓ	15. ⓐⓑⓒⓓ
16. ⓐⓑⓒⓓ	17. ⓐⓑⓒⓓ	18. ⓐⓑⓒⓓ	19. ⓐⓑⓒⓓ	20. ⓐⓑⓒⓓ
21. ⓐⓑⓒⓓ	22. ⓐⓑⓒⓓ	23. ⓐⓑⓒⓓ	24. ⓐⓑⓒⓓ	25. ⓐⓑⓒⓓ
26. ⓐⓑⓒⓓ	27. ⓐⓑⓒⓓ	28. ⓐⓑⓒⓓ	29. ⓐⓑⓒⓓ	30. ⓐⓑⓒⓓ
31. ⓐⓑⓒⓓ	32. ⓐⓑⓒⓓ	33. ⓐⓑⓒⓓ	34. ⓐⓑⓒⓓ	35. ⓐⓑⓒⓓ
36. ⓐⓑⓒⓓ	37. ⓐⓑⓒⓓ	38. ⓐⓑⓒⓓ	39. ⓐⓑⓒⓓ	40. ⓐⓑⓒⓓ
41. ⓐⓑⓒⓓ	42. ⓐⓑⓒⓓ	43. ⓐⓑⓒⓓ	44. ⓐⓑⓒⓓ	45. ⓐⓑⓒⓓ
46. ⓐⓑⓒⓓ	47. ⓐⓑⓒⓓ	48. ⓐⓑⓒⓓ	49. ⓐⓑⓒⓓ	50. ⓐⓑⓒⓓ
51. ⓐⓑⓒⓓ	52. ⓐⓑⓒⓓ	53. ⓐⓑⓒⓓ	54. ⓐⓑⓒⓓ	55. ⓐⓑⓒⓓ
56. ⓐⓑⓒⓓ	57. ⓐⓑⓒⓓ	58. ⓐⓑⓒⓓ	59. ⓐⓑⓒⓓ	60. ⓐⓑⓒⓓ
61. ⓐⓑⓒⓓ	62. ⓐⓑⓒⓓ	63. ⓐⓑⓒⓓ	64. ⓐⓑⓒⓓ	65. ⓐⓑⓒⓓ
66. ⓐⓑⓒⓓ	67. ⓐⓑⓒⓓ	68. ⓐⓑⓒⓓ	69. ⓐⓑⓒⓓ	70. ⓐⓑⓒⓓ
71. ⓐⓑⓒⓓ	72. ⓐⓑⓒⓓ	73. ⓐⓑⓒⓓ	74. ⓐⓑⓒⓓ	75. ⓐⓑⓒⓓ
76. ⓐⓑⓒⓓ	77. ⓐⓑⓒⓓ	78. ⓐⓑⓒⓓ	79. ⓐⓑⓒⓓ	80. ⓐⓑⓒⓓ
81. ⓐⓑⓒⓓ	82. ⓐⓑⓒⓓ	83. ⓐⓑⓒⓓ	84. ⓐⓑⓒⓓ	85. ⓐⓑⓒⓓ
86. ⓐⓑⓒⓓ	87. ⓐⓑⓒⓓ	88. ⓐⓑⓒⓓ	89. ⓐⓑⓒⓓ	90. ⓐⓑⓒⓓ
91. ⓐⓑⓒⓓ	92. ⓐⓑⓒⓓ	93. ⓐⓑⓒⓓ	94. ⓐⓑⓒⓓ	95. ⓐⓑⓒⓓ
96. ⓐⓑⓒⓓ	97. ⓐⓑⓒⓓ	98. ⓐⓑⓒⓓ	99. ⓐⓑⓒⓓ	100. ⓐⓑⓒⓓ

ANSWERS & SOLUTIONS

1. **(c)** A cocoon
2. **(d)** One day he saw a small opening appear
3. **(b)** The man took a pair of scissors and snipped off the remaining bit of the cocoon.
4. **(c)** The butterfly emerged easily
5. **(a)** It was nature's way of forcing fluid from the body of the butterfly into its wings
6. **(b)**   7. **(b)**   8. **(d)**
9. **(b)**   10. **(a)**   11. **(c)**
12. **(b)** When you say 'either now or never', it means that you must do something immediately because you will not get another opportunity. Other options are simply out of context.
13. **(a)** When two pairs of words are connected with 'yet', they should usually be in contrast; despite anything to the contrary (usually following a concession); e.g. He was a stern yet fair master. Other options are just not relevant.
14. **(a)** In gap 11 the interjection 'phew!' rightly fits as it is used to express relief, fatigue, surprise, or disgust which is also the case here. Other options are out of context.
15. **(a)** Here 'were hiding' is the right form of the verb. Other options do not fit in here.
16. **(b)**   17. **(b)**   18. **(c)**
19. **(b)**   20. **(b)**
21. **(c)** As an adjective, animate simply means "having life". For example: Plants and animals are animate objects. If you animate something, you make it lively or more cheerful. Thus you put energy into it. In other words, you energise it.
22. **(a)** If someone is niggardly, he shows lack of generosity. Thus generous (b) would be its antonym. But we are looking for a synonym. None of the words is a fit synonym. In such cases we go for the word closest in meaning. Both penurious (very poor) and niggardly imply a lack of money, though in different senses.
23. **(a)** One who is indigent is very poor. The opposite of poor is rich.
24. **(d)** Audacity is audacious behaviour. If you are audacious, you take risks in order to achieve something. So it is a kind of bravery. Now, the opposite of bravery is cowardice.
25. **(a)** An elevation is a 'piece of ground that is higher (elevated) than the area around it. A depression in a surface is an area which is lower (depressed) than the parts surrounding it.

26. **(d)** $3x - \dfrac{1}{4y} = 6$ $3x = 6 + \dfrac{1}{4y}$

   Taking 3 common on both sides

   $$x = \dfrac{6}{3} + \dfrac{1}{4.3y} \Rightarrow x = 2 + \dfrac{1}{12y}$$

   Multiplying equation by 4 on both sides

   $$4x = 8 + \dfrac{1}{3y} \Rightarrow 4x - \dfrac{1}{3y} = 8$$

27. **(c)** **Short cut method :**

   $$\text{Net profit} = \text{Profit} + \text{Discount} + \dfrac{\text{Profit} \times \text{Discount}}{100}$$

   $$\dfrac{25}{2} = 25 - \text{Discount} - \dfrac{25 \times \text{Discount}}{100}$$

   ('–' to represent discount)

   $$\dfrac{25}{2} - 25 = \dfrac{-5}{4} \text{ Discount}$$

   $\therefore$ Discount % = 10%

28. **(a)** $392 \times 2 = 784 \Rightarrow (27)^2$

   Hence, 2 can be multiplied by 392 which gives perfect square.

29. **(c)** A : B = 6 : 7

   B : C = 8 : 9

   $$\Rightarrow \dfrac{A}{B} \times \dfrac{B}{C} = \dfrac{6}{7} \times \dfrac{8}{9} = \dfrac{48}{63}$$

   $$\therefore C : A = \dfrac{63}{48} = \dfrac{21}{16}$$

30. **(d)** From the given option only 16 is perfect square of 4.

   $\therefore$ According to the question,

   Total number of swans $= \dfrac{7}{2}\sqrt{16} + 2 = 14 + 2 = 16.$

31. **(d)** Let the max. marks be x.

   Then, according to question,

   $x \times 30\% + 10 = x \times 40\% - 15$

   $\Rightarrow x \times 10\% = 25$ or $x = 250$

   Therefore, passing marks $= 250 \times \dfrac{30}{100} + 10 = 85$

32. **(d)** Area remains same

$$25 - x - \frac{25x}{100} = 0$$

$$\Rightarrow x + \frac{x}{4} = 25$$

$$\Rightarrow 5x = 25 \times 4$$

$$\Rightarrow x = 20\%$$

33. **(b)** Let the cost price of machine be Rs 100
SP of machine at a profit of 10% = Rs 110
SP of machine at a loss of 10% = Rs 90
If SP is (110 – 90) = Rs 20 less then CP = Rs 100
Therefore, if SP is Rs 40 less then

$$CP = \frac{100}{20} \times 40 = Rs\ 200$$

34. **(b)** Let speed of the second train = x km/hr.
Relative speed of trains = $(50 + x)$ km/hr.
Distance travelled by trains = $(100 + 120)$ = 220 metres
Distance = Speed × Time

$$\left(\frac{220}{1000}\right) km = (50 + x)\ km/hr. \times \left(\frac{6}{3600}\right) hr$$

$$50 + x = \frac{220 \times 3600}{1000 \times 6}$$

$$50 + x = 132$$

$$x = 132 - 50 = 82\ km/hr$$

35. **(c)** Let the cost price be Rs 100.
∴ Marked price is Rs 135.
At 10% discount, the customer has to pay
= Marked price – discount = 135 – 13.5 = 121.5.

$$\therefore \% \text{ profit} = 21.5\% = 21\frac{1}{2}\%.$$

36. **(a)** Let the C.P. of 150 kg of rice be ₹150.
∴ S.P. of 50 kg of rice at 10%

$$loss\ = \frac{90}{100} \times 50 = ₹45$$

For 10% of gain on the whole.

$$S.P. = 150 \times \frac{110}{100} = ₹165$$

∴ 100 kg rice should be sold for ₹ 120.
∴ Per cent gain = 20

37. **(b)** Let the number of officers be x.
Number of workers = 400 – x

$$\Rightarrow 10000 \times x + 2000(400 - x) = 3000(400)$$

$$\Rightarrow 10000x + 800000 - 2000x = 12,00,000$$

$$\Rightarrow 4x = 600 - 400 = 200 \Rightarrow x = 50$$

∴ Number of officers = 50

38. **(a)** Let the cost price of an article be ₹ 100
then, S.P. = 100 + 10 = ₹ 110
If S.P. = 2 × 110 = ₹ 220

$$then,\ profit\ \% = \frac{(220 - 100)}{100} \times 100 = 120\%$$

39. **(b)** Surface area with side 4 cm = $6 \times 4^2 = 96$ cm^2
Now, surface area with side 1 cm = $6 \times 1^2 = 6$ cm^2
Decrease = 96 – 6 = 90 cm^2

$$Decrease\ \% = \frac{90}{96} \times 100 = 94\%$$

40. **(a)** Here, $50 = \frac{500 \times 5 \times t}{100} \Rightarrow t = 2$ years

41. **(d)** Let the missing figure in the expression be x.

$$\frac{16}{7} \times \frac{16}{7} - \frac{x}{7} \times \frac{9}{7} + \frac{9}{7} \times \frac{9}{7} = 1$$

$$\Rightarrow 16 \times 16 - 9x + 9 \times 9 = 7 \times 7$$

$$\Rightarrow 9x = 16 \times 16 + 9 \times 9 - 7 \times 7 = 256 + 81 - 49 = 288$$

$$\Rightarrow x = \frac{228}{9} = 32$$

42. **(c)** Let the number of boys be x and the number of girls be y.

$$Then,\ 3(B + G) = 3\left(\frac{x}{y} + \frac{y}{x}\right) = \frac{3(x^2 + y^2)}{xy},$$

Clearly, which is greater than 3.

$$\because\ [(a - b)^2 \geq 0 \Rightarrow a^2 + b^2 - 2ab \geq 0$$

$$\Rightarrow a^2 + b^2 \geq 2ab \Rightarrow \frac{a^2 + b^2}{ab} \geq 2\ ]$$

43. **(c)** Quantity of milk = $45 \times \frac{4}{5} = 36$ litres

Quantity of water = $45 \times \frac{1}{5} = 9$ litres

Let x litres of water be added to make the ratio 3 : 2

$$Then,\ \frac{36}{9 + x} = \frac{3}{2}$$

$$\Rightarrow 72 = 27 + 3x \Rightarrow x = 15\ litres$$

44. **(d)** Relative speed = 5.5 – 5 = 0.5 km/h.

$$Required\ time = \frac{8.5}{0.5} = 17h$$

45. **(c)** Let CP of 12 pencils = SP of 10 pencils = ₹ 1

Therefore, CP of 1 pencil = ₹ $\dfrac{1}{12}$ and

SP of 1 pencil = ₹ $\dfrac{1}{10}$

Profit on one pencil = $\dfrac{1}{10} - \dfrac{1}{12} = \dfrac{2}{120} = ₹ \dfrac{1}{60}$

% profit = $\dfrac{1/60}{1/12} \times 100 = 20\%$

46. **(b)** The three above the line are all insects. The hamster and squirrel are rodents, so the correct choice is b because the mouse is also a rodent. The other three choices are not rodents.

47. **(d)** The tadpole is a young frog; frogs are amphibians. The lamb is a young sheep; sheep are mammals. Animal (choice a) is incorrect because it is too large a grouping: Animals include insects, birds, mammals, reptiles, and amphibians. Choices b and c are incorrect because they are not part of the progression.

48. **(b)** The relationship above the line is that snow on a mountain creates conditions for skiing. Below the line, the relationship is that warmth at a lake creates conditions for swimming.

49. **(b)** Walk, skip, and run represent a continuum of movement: Skipping is faster than walking; running is faster than skipping. Below the line, the continuum is about throwing: Pitch is faster than toss; hurl is faster than pitch.

50. **(d)** The words above the line show a continuum: Command is more extreme than rule, and dictate is more extreme than command. Below the line, the continuum is as follows: Sleep is more than doze, and hibernate is more than sleep. The other choices are not related in the same way

51. **(a)** An index, glossary, and chapter are all parts of a book. Choice a does not belong because the book is the whole, not a part.

52. **(d)** The first three choices are all synonyms.

53. **(c)** Biology, chemistry, and zoology are all branches of science. Theology is the study of religion.

54. **(b)** Since the ice cube had already melted due to the heat of a nearby furnace so after this ice cannot remain as ice cube.

55. **(b)** worry involves to keep thinking about unpleasant things that creates always unsest.

56. **(c)**

57. **(d)** A mirror always has refeflection of an image.

58. **(c)** Danger always creates fear.

59. **(a)** The mother warns her child with the expectation that he would stop troubling her. So, I is implicit. The general nature of children cannot be derived from the statement. So, II is not implicit.

60. **(a)** Such decisions as given in the statement are taken only after taking the existing vacancies into consideration. So, I implicit while II isn't.

61 **(d)**

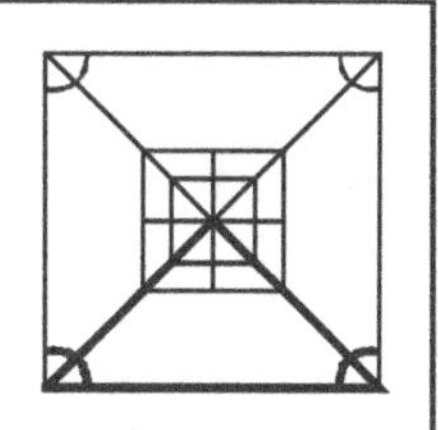

62. **(d)**

63. **(c)**

64. **(d)**

65. **(c)**

66. **(d)** In each row, the second figure forms the innermost and the outermost elements of the third figure and the first figure forms the middle element of the third figure.

67. **(b)** In each row, the second figure is obtained by shading one of the four parts of the first figure and the third figure is obtained by shading two out of the four parts of the first figure.

68. **(d)** In each row, there are three types of outer elements (circle, triangle and square), three types of inner elements (circle, triangle and square) and three types of shadings in the inner elements (black, white and lines).

69. **(b)** In each row, the second figure is obtained by rotating the first figure through 90°CW or 90° ACW and adding a circle to it. Also, the third figure is obtained by adding two circles to the first figure (without rotating the figure).

70. **(d)** There are 3 types of faces, 3 types of hands and 3 types of legs. Each type is used once in each row! So, the features not used in the first two figures of the third row would together form the missing figure.

71. **(c)**

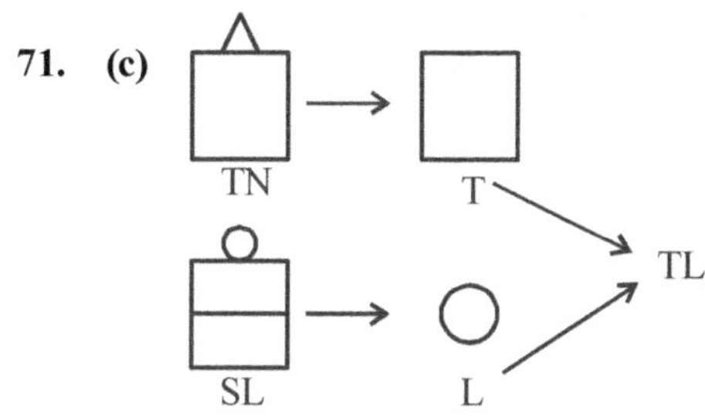

72. (d) 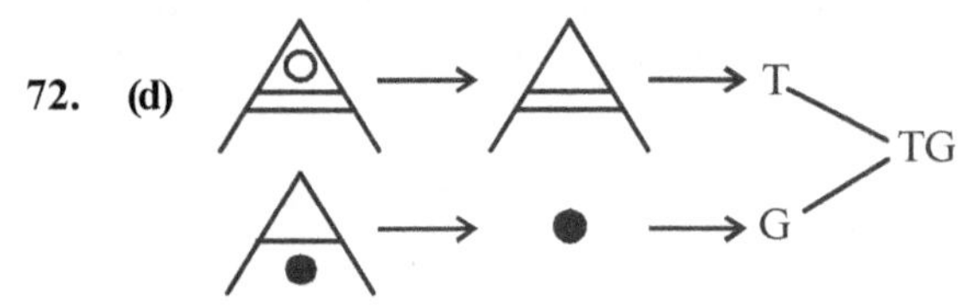

73. (b) 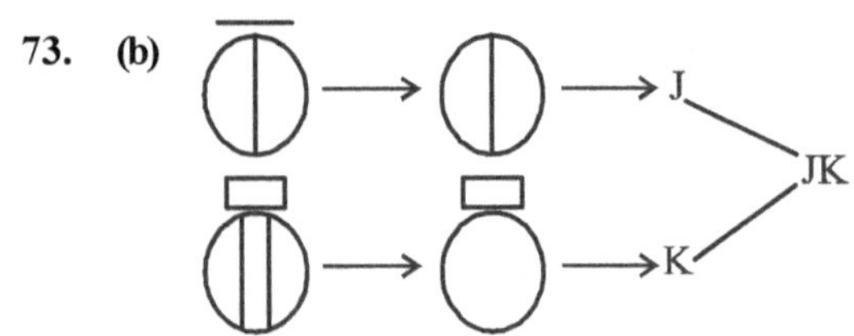

74. (a) 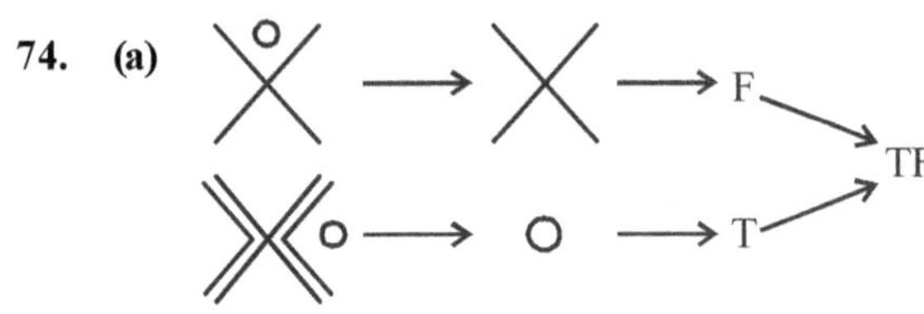

75. (a) 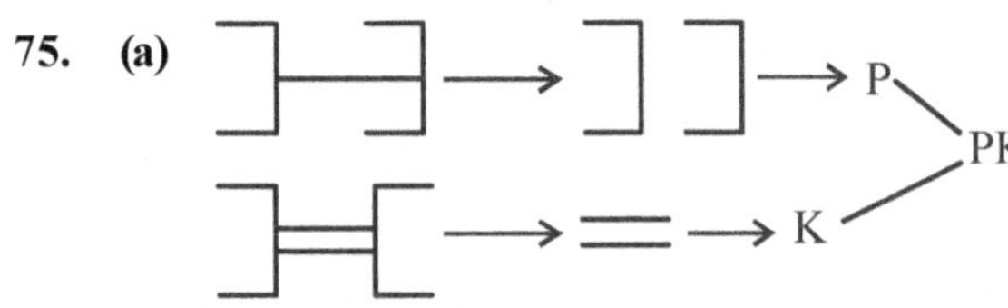

76. (d)
77. (d)
78. (b)
79. (d)
80. (a)
81. (a)
82. (a) The first sermon of Buddha made at Sarnath is called Dharmachakra Parivartan.

83. (c) When Alexander invaded India, Nandas were the rulers of Magadha.

84. (c) Best answer is c as Tukaram (1608–1650) was a Marathi Bhakti poet and a devotee of Lord Krishna. Time period of Jahangir was 1605-1627.

85. (d) Lord Wellesley founded Fort William College at Calcutta.

86. (c)

87. (c) On 12 March, 1930, Gandhi started his civil disobedience movement by starting Dandi March from Sabarmati Ashram in Gujarat and reached Dandi on 6 April 1930 and broke the salt law.

88. (a)

89. (d) Victoria waterfalls is associated with the river Zambezi which is situated in Africa.

90. (d) Right to 'constitutional Remedies' has been described by Dr. Ambedkar as "The heart and soul of the constitution.

91. (b) Capacitor is a device which stors electric charge.

92. (c)

93. (c) Switzerland defeated France by 3-1 to win Davis Cup-2014.

94. (a) Boxer Manoj Kumar received the Arjuna Award after he filed a case in the Delhi High Court.

95. (c) Peking University, one of the oldest Chinese universities. conferred the title of Honorary Professor to Dr.Kalam.

96. (a) The Narrow Road to the Deep North is set in the background of World War II and give details about life of Prisoners of War.

97. (d) Patrick Madiano who has been hailed as "Marcel Proust of our time" has been awarded with the Nobel Prize for Literature.

98. (c)   99. (c)   100. (c)

GENERAL KNOWLEDGE QUESTION BANK

1. Which one of the following Indus Valley Civilization sites gives evidence of a stadium?

   (a) Harappa   (b) Kalibangan

   (c) Mohenjodaro   (d) Dholavira

2. Indus Valley Civilization was discovered by:

   (a) Dayaram Sahni   (b) R. D. Banerji

   (c) Cunningham   (d) Wheeler

3. Who is the most important God in Rigaveda?

   (a) Agni   (b) Indra

   (c) Varun   (d) Vishnu

4. The expounder of Yoga philosophy was :

   (a) Patanjali   (b) Shankaracharya

   (c) Jaimini   (d) Gautam

5. The river most mentioned in Rigveda is :

   (a) Sindhu   (b) Sutudri

   (c) Saraswati   (d) Gandaki

6. The great law given of ancient time was :

   (a) Vatsyayana   (b) Ashoka

   (c) Manu   (d) Panini

7. Gautam Buddha attained Mahaparinirvana at

   (a) Kapilvastu   (b) Kushinagar

   (c) Bodhgaya   (d) Rajgriha

8. The most important source for the study of Mauryan history is

   (a) Mudrarakshasa   (b) Natural Historica

   (c) Devichandraguptam   (d) Arthashastra

9. Who was the mentor of Chandragupta Maurya?

   (a) Vishakhadutta   (b) Chanakya

   (c) Megasthenes   (d) Patanjali

10. During Gupta period, which deity was called Lokarka?

   (a) Sun   (b) Ganesha

   (c) Kumara   (d) Shiva

11. Which of the following was a strong centre of the Pasupatas during the time of Chandragupta II?

   (a) Mathura   (b) Kaushambi

   (c) Tripuri   (d) Udaigiri

12. The Chola rulers were generally the worshippers of

   (a) Shiva   (b) Vishnu

   (c) Sakti   (d) Kartikeya

13. The Seven Pagodas of Mahabalipuram are a witness to the art patronised by the

   (a) Pallavas   (b) Pandyas

   (c) Cholas   (d) Cheras

14. Who was the first ruler of the Slave dynasty?

   (a) Qutubuddin Aibak   (b) Iltutmish

   (c) Sultan Mahmud   (d) Balban

15. Who abolished Iqta system?

   (a) Qutubuddin Aibak   (b) Iltutmish

   (c) Balban   (d) Alauddin Khilji

16. The Turkish brought with them musical instruments.

   (a) Rabab and Sarangi   (b) Sitar and Flute

   (c) Veena and Tabla   (d) Tanpura and Mridanga

17. Amir Khusro wrote his famous masanavi 'Ashiqa' on the order of

   (a) Alauddin Khilji   (b) Khizra Khan

   (c) Rai Karan   (d) Rani Kamla Devi

18. The Sultan who desecrated the Puri Jagannath temple and Jwalamukhi temple at Kangra was

   (a) Balban   (b) Alauddin Khilji

   (c) Firoz Shah Tughlaq   (d) Sikandar Lodi

19. The famous poet Amir Khusro was associated with the court of

    (a) Qutubuddin Aibak   (b) Alauddin Khilji

    (c) Sikandar Lodi   (d) Akbar

20. Which of the following Sultans of Delhi was known as Lakh Bakhsh?

    (a) Qutubuddin Aibak   (b) Balban

    (c) Alauddin Khilji   (d) Jalaluddin Khilji

21. In the Sultanate period, the highest rural authority for land revenue was

    (a) Rawat   (b) Malik

    (c) Chaudhary   (d) Patwari

22. Coins of which Muslim ruler have been image of Devi Lakshmi?

    (a) Muhammad Ghori   (b) Iltutmish

    (c) Alauddin Khilji   (d) None of these

23. Before which of his important battles in India did Babur declare the abolition of Tamgha tax ?

    (a) Panipat   (b) Khanwa

    (c) Chanderi   (d) None of these

24. Who among the following had joined Akbar's Din-i-Ilahi?

    (a) Birbal   (b) Bhagwan Das

    (c) Man Singh   (d) Surjan Rai

25. Which one of the following had bestowed the title of Jagat Seth to Fatehchand?

    (a) Alivardi Khan   (b) Sirajuddaula

    (c) Mir Zafar   (d) Muhammad Shah

26. Who was the author of Humayun-nama?

    (a) Humayun   (b) Gulbadan Begam

    (c) Badauni   (d) Ahmad Yadgar

27. Mansabdari system of the Mughals had its origin in

    (a) Persia   (b) Arabia

    (c) Central Asia   (d) India

28. The offsprings of which Mughal emperor were born in a Sufi's Khanqah instead of the Mughal haram?

    (a) Humayun   (b) Akbar

    (c) Shahjahan   (d) Aurangzeb

29. Which one of the following was the first English ship that came to India?

    (a) Elizabeth   (b) Titanic

    (c) Red Dragon   (d) Mayflower

30. Which one of the following factories in Bengal was established by Portuguese?

    (a) Kasim Bazar   (b) Chinsura

    (c) Hoogly   (d) Srirampur

31. Which one of the following European trading companies adopted the "Blue Water Policy" in India?

    (a) Dutch company

    (b) French company

    (c) Portuguese company

    (d) British East India company

32. Where in India, did the Portuguese build their first fortress?

    (a) Cochin   (b) Goa

    (c) Anjidiv   (d) Cannanore

33. Where did the British East India Company open its first factory in India?

    (a) Masulipatanam   (b) Surat

    (c) Bharuch   (d) Mumbai

34. Who among the following introduced Cashewnut, Pineapple and Tobacco in India?

    (a) Dutch   (b) English

    (c) French   (d) Portuguese

35. Who was Sir George Oxenden?

    (a) First president of Council of Surat

    (b) First governor of Bombay

    (c) First president of Council of Madras

    (d) None of the above

36. The South Indian ruler who introduced sericulture as an agro-industry in his kingdom was

    (a) Tipu Sultan   (b) Hyder Ali

    (c) Krishnadeva Raya   (d) Rajaraja II

37. The statement, "We have crippled over enemy without making our friends too formidable", is associated with

    (a) Fourth Anglo-Mysore War

    (b) Third Anglo-Mysore War

    (c) Second Angle-Mysore War

    (d) First Anglo-Mysore War

38. To overthrow the British rule, Kuka Movement was organised in

    (a) Punjab   (b) Uttar Pradesh

    (c) Bihar   (d) Maharashtra

39. Who was the first Viceroy of India?

    (a) Lord Canning

    (b) Warren Hastings

    (c) Lord William Bentinck

    (d) Lord Curzon

40. Which one of the following is known as Mother of Indian Revolutionaries?

    (a) Annie Besant   (b) Sarojini Naidu

    (c) Madam Cama   (d) Usha Mehta

41. The Revolt of 1857 at Lucknow was led by

    (a) Begum Hazarat Mahal

    (b) Tantiya Tope

    (c) Rani Laxmi Bai

    (d) Nana Saheb

42. Who among the following British persons admitted the Revolt of 1857 as a national revolt?

    (a) Lord Dalhousie   (b) Lord Canning

    (c) Lord Ellenborough   (d) Disraelli

43. " Poverty and the Un-British Rule in India" was written by

    (a) Dadabhai Naoroji

    (b) Ramesh Chandra Dutta

    (c) Gopal Krishna Gokhle

    (d) Surendranath Banerjee

44. In which of the following movements, Vande Mataram was adopted slogan for agitation?

    (a) Revolt of 1857

    (b) Partition of Bengal in 1905

    (c) Non-cooperation Movement in 1920

    (d) Quit India Movement in 1942

45. Devi Chaudharani patronised a historic movement of Bengal. Find out the correct answer among the options given below:

    (a) Weavers Movement

    (b) Sanyasi Movement

    (c) Indigo Growers Movement

    (d) Swadeshi Movement

46. In which of the following sessions of Indian National Congress, the resolution of Swadeshi was adopted?

    (a) Madras Session 1903

    (b) Bombay Session 1904

    (c) Banaras Session 1905

    (d) Calcutta Session 1906

47. During which of the following movements, Vande Mataram became the theme song of the Indian National Movement?

    (a) Champaran Sataygrah

    (b) Swadeshi Movement

    (c) Anti-Rowlatt Act Agitation

    (d) Non-cooperation Movement

48. Who among the following was not associated with the Home Rule Movement?

    (a) C.R. Das   (b) S. Subramaniyam Iyer

    (c) Annie Besant   (d) Bal Gangadhar Tilak

49. The Ryotwari settlement of Madras was introduced by

    (a) Cornwallis   (b) Wingate

    (c) Clive   (d) Munro

50. Who started the socio-religious organization "Tattvabodhini Sabha" and its appended journal 'Tattvabodhini'?

    (a) Ram Mohan Roy

    (b) Radhakant Dev

    (c) Devendranath Tagore

    (d) Dwarkanath Tagore

51. Which planet takes the longest time to go around the sun?

 (a) Earth (b) Jupiter

 (c) Uranus (d) Neptune

52 The distance of Moon from the Earth is

 (a) 364 thousand kms. (b) 300 thousand kms.

 (c) 350 thousand kms. (d) 446 thousand kms.

53. The Earth becomes maximum distance from the sun on

 (a) January 30th (b) December 22nd

 (c) September 22nd (d) July 4th

54. Which one of the following planets is the brightest?

 (a) Mars (b) Mercury

 (c) Venus (d) Jupiter

55. The outermost layer of the sun is called

 (a) Chromosphere (b) Photosphere

 (c) Lithosphere (d) Corona

56. Which of the following planets is known as "Red Planet"?

 (a) Earth (b) Mars

 (c) Jupiter (d) Saturn

57. The last stage in the life cycle of a star is

 (a) Black Hole (b) Supernova

 (c) Red Giant (d) White Dwarf

58. Cycle of sun spots is

 (a) 9 years (b) 10 years

 (c) 11 years (d) 12 years

59. The Indian subcontinent was originally part of a huge mass called

 (a) Indian (b) Aryavarta

 (c) Angaraland (d) Gondwana land

60. The highest salinity is found in which of the following lakes?

 (a) Van Lake (b) Dead sea

 (c) Balkash lake (d) Baikal lake

61. Ox-bow lake is a feature formed by

 (a) River erosion in youthful stage

 (b) Transportation action of the river

 (c) River erosion in mature stage

 (d) Deposition in old stage of a river

62. Thunderstorms are associated with

 (a) Cumulus clouds (b) Cumulonimbus clouds

 (c) Cirrus clouds (d) Stratus clouds

63. Which one of the following is not related to plate Tectonic Theory?

 (a) Continental drift (b) Pole wandering

 (c) Transform fault (d) Sea floor spreading

64. Where is the Blind Valley found?

 (a) River valley region (b) Arid region

 (c) Karst region (d) Glacier region

65. The process of water vapour changing to the liquid state (water) is called

 (a) Sublimation (b) Transpiration

 (c) Condensation (d) Dew

66. The Coriollis Effect is produced by

 (a) pressure gradient

 (b) earth's revolution

 (c) earth's rotation

 (d) earth's rotation and revolution

67. Which of the following countries is the largest producer of diamond?

 (a) Australia (b) Venezuela

 (c) Russia (d) Botswana

68. Which of the following industries should be mainly located near the raw material areas?

 (a) Iron steel (b) Cotton textile

 (c) Ship building (d) Engineering

69. The 'Wheat Crescent' lies in

 (a) Australia (b) Argentina

 (c) Canada (d) U.S.A

70. In the U.S.A the cotton textile industry shifted from North Eastern states to the south because of

 (a) High labour cost (b) Low demand

 (c) Hilly terrain (d) Lack of coal

71. Which of the following countries is the highest producer of Uranium in Asia?

(a) China   (b) India

(c) Uzbekistan   (d) Indonesia

72. The lines of equal transport cost in the industrial location model of Alfred Weber are known as

(a) Isoline   (b) Isobar

(c) Isodapen   (d) Isotim

73. World's largest reserve of Uranium is found in

(a) Australia   (b) Brazil

(c) Canada   (d) South Africa

74. Silviculture is concerned with

(a) Making vines

(b) Growing plants saplings

(c) Growing spices

(d) Market gardening

75. The world's most active volcano is

(a) Cotapaxi   (b) Fujiyama

(c) Kilauea   (d) Vesuvius

76. The most urbanized country of the world is

(a) Germany   (b) Japan

(c) Singapore   (d) U.S.A

77. The demographic transition model was propounded by

(a) J. Clarke   (b) F.W. Notestien

(c) G.T. Trewartha   (d) J.J. Spengler

78. Which one of the following countries does not border the Caspian Sea?

(a) Azerbaijan   (b) Iran

(c) Iraq   (d) Kazakhstan

79. Which one of the following is the busiest ocean route in the world?

(a) Mediterranean Suez Route

(b) South Atlantic Route

(c) North Atlantic Route

(d) Pacific Ocean Route

80. The continental shelf is marked by an isobath line of

(a) 100 metres   (b) 200 metres

(c) 300 metres   (d) 350 metres

81. The Great Barrier Reef is located on the coast of

(a) Central Australia   (b) West Australia

(c) East Australia   (d) South Australia

82. Which country has the highest percentage of its geographical area under forests?

(a) China   (b) India

(c) Indonesia   (d) Japan

83. Doddabetta Peak is located in the

(a) Anaimalai   (b) Mahendragiri

(c) Nilgiris   (d) Shevaroys

84. Kaziranga Wildlife Sanctuary is in the state of

(a) Assam   (b) Tamilnadu

(c) Uttar Pradesh   (d) Kerala

85. The term 'operation flood' refers to

(a) Flood control

(b) Milk production

(c) Population control

(d) Foodgrain production

86. Which of the following cities has an astronomical observatory ?

(a) Simla   (b) Jaipur

(c) Amritsar   (d) Hyderabad

87. With which country does MacMahon Line form India's boundary ?

(a) Pakistan   (b) Afganistan

(c) China   (d) Bangladesh

88. Ganga is a result of the confluence of rivers —— .

(a) Bhagirathi and Alakananda at Dev Prayag

(b) Bhagirathi and Alakananda at Karan Prayag

(c) Bhagirathi and Alakananda at Gangotri

(d) Bhagirathi and Alakananda at Rudra Prayag

89. The group of stars arranged in a definite pattern is called

(a) Milky way (b) Constellation

(c) Andromeda (d) Solar system

90. Which of the following planets is smaller in size than the Earth?

(a) Venus (b) Uranus

(c) Saturn (d) Neptune

91. Which planet is called "Evening star"?

(a) Mars (b) Jupiter

(c) Venus (d) Saturn

92. What is the primary cause of the day and night ?

(a) Earth's annual motion

(b) Earth's daily motion

(c) Inclination of the earth's axis and its rotation

(d) Inclination of the earth's axis and its revolution

93. On which date is the earth in perihelion ?

(a) June 21 (b) Dec 22

(c) January 3 (d) July 4

94. The earth is in aphelion on

(a) June 21 (b) Dec. 22

(c) Sept. 23 (d) July 4

95. How much is the mass of the moon when compared with that of the earth ?

(a) 1/49 (b) 1/81

(c) 1/51 (d) 1/8

96. Greenwich mean time is ——————— IST.

(a) 5.5 hours ahead (b) 12 hours ahead

(c) 4.5 hours behind (d) 5.5 hours behind

97. How much time does the light from the nearest star take in reaching the earth ?

(a) 12 minutes (b) 4.3 minutes

(c) 4.3 hours (d) 4.3 years

98. The shortest route between two places is along the

(a) latitudes (b) longitudes

(c) rivers (d) direction of winds

99. The mouth of a volcano is known as

(a) Glacier (b) Cone

(c) Crater (d) Pipe

100. Telegraph plateau is a part of

(a) North Atlantic Ridge

(b) South Atlantic Ridge

(c) Indian Ocean Ridge

(d) South Pacific Ridge

101. Which one of the following is different from others?

(a) Canary current (b) Mozambique current

(c) Oyashio current (d) Falkland current

102. Rift valley is formed by

(a) Earthquake (b) Folding

(c) Faulting (d) All of these

103. Granite and Basalt are the examples of which of the following?

(a) Sedimentary rock (b) Metamorphic rock

(c) Igneous rock (d) Calcareous rock

104. Volcanic eruptions do not occurs in the

(a) Baltic sea (b) Black sea

(c) Caribbean sea (d) Caspian sea

105. What is the most important element of climate ?

(a) Rainfall (b) Temperature

(c) Pressure (d) Humidity

106. Roaring forties are the

(a) High velocity trade winds

(b) High velocity westerly winds

(c) High velocity polar winds

(d) High mangitude tidal waves due to high wind velocity

107. The Great Barrier Reef is located at the

(a) East Australian coast

(b) Andaman and Nicobar coast

(c) West Australian coast

(d) Mouth of Gulf and Cambay

108. Peanuts are the main crop of

(a) Georgia   (b) Gambia

(c) Ghana   (d) Guatemala

109. Monoculture is a distinct characteristic of

(a) Commercial grain farming

(b) Shifting cultivation

(c) Subsistence farming

(d) Organic farming

110. Plantation agriculture is practical mainly in the

(a) Arid region

(b) Mediterranean region

(c) Temperate region

(d) Tropical region

111. Teak and Sal are products of

(a) Tropical dry deciduous Forest

(b) Tropical Evergreen Forests

(c) Tropical Thorn Forests

(d) Alpine Forests

112. The natural rubber is obtained from the

(a) bark of trees   (b) fruit of trees

(c) roots to trees   (d) latex of trees

113. What is viticulture ?

(a) Cultivation of grapes (b) Growing small plants

(c) Growing tobacco   (d) Cultivation of spices

114. Silviculture is concerned with

(a) Making vines

(b) Growing plants saplings

(c) Growing spices

(d) Market gardening

115. Which crop is afflicted by the disease called red rot ?

(a) Rice   (b) Wheat

(c) Bajra   (d) Sugarcane

116. Horticulture is concerned with the

(a) growing of flowers and fruits

(b) rearing animals for meet and skins

(c) farming without crop rotaion

(d) cultivation of crops without any machinery etc.

117. What is white coal ?

(a) Petroleum

(b) Producing fuel from Thermal power

(c) Producing fuel from Chopped wood

(d) Producing fuel from Nuclear power

118. The deepest lake of the world is

(a) Pushkar lake   (b) Superior lake

(c) Victoria lake   (d) Baikal lake

119. 90° E Ridge lies in

(a) Atlantic ocean   (b) Indian ocean

(c) Pacific ocean   (d) Mediterranean ocean

120. What is meant by the term Midnight Sun?

(a) Twilight

(b) Rising sun

(c) Very bright moon

(d) Sun shining in the polar circle for long time.

121. Which article of the Indian Constitution provides for uniform civil code for the citizens?

(a) Article 42   (b) Article 44

(c) Article 46   (d) Article 48

122. The mention of the word 'justice' in the Preamble to the Constitution of India expresses

(a) social, political and religious justice

(b) social, economic and cultural justice

(c) social, economic and political justice

(d) economic and political justice

123. Which of the following amendments had reduced the age of the voters from 21 years to 18 years?

(a) 52nd amendment   (b) 60th amendment

(c) 61st amendment   (d) 62nd amendment

124. Which of the following schedules deals with the division of powers between union and states?

   (a) fourth schedule   (b) sixth schedule

   (c) seventh schedule   (d) ninth schedule

125. India has borrowed the concept of Fundamental Rights from the Constitution of

   (a) UK   (b) USA

   (c) Russia   (d) Ireland

126. Which Article of Indian Constitution is related with the Protection of the interests of the minorities?

   (a) Article 17   (b) Article 29

   (c) Article 30   (d) Article 31

127. Which schedule of Indian Constitution is related to Panchayti Raj ?

   (a) II Schedule   (b) VIII Schedule

   (c) X Schedule   (d) XI Schedule

128 Which one of the following committees recommended the inclusion of fundamental duties in the Indian Constitution?

   (a) Barua Committee   (b) Ramaswamy Committee

   (c) Sikri Committee   (d) Swarn Singh Committee

129. Which one of the following is not a part of the 'basic structure' of the Indian Constitution ?

   (a) Rule of law

   (b) Secularism

   (c) Republican form of government

   (d) Parliamentary form of government

130. What was the duration in the making of Indian Constitution ?

   (a) 1 Year 10 Months and 12 Days

   (b) 2 Years 10 Months and 5 Days

   (c) 2 Years 11 Months and 18 Days

   (d) 3 Years 6 Months and 7 Days

131. To be officially recognized by the speaker of Lok Sabha as an opposition group, a party or coalition of parties must have at least

   (a) 50 members

   (b) 60 members

   (c) 80 members

   (d) 1/3 of total members of the Lok Sabha

132. How many times has Financial Emergency been declared in India so far?

   (a) 5 times   (b) 4 times

   (c) once   (d) Never

133. Which one of the following taxes is levied and collected by the Union but distributed between union and states?

   (a) Corporation tax

   (b) Tax on income other than on agricultural income

   (c) Tax on railway fares and freights

   (d) Customs

134. Which of the following subjects lies in the concurrent list?

   (a) Agriculture   (b) Education

   (c) Police   (d) Defence

135. According to our Constitution, the Rajya Sabha

   (a) is dissolved once in two years.

   (b) is dissolved every five years.

   (c) is dissolved every six years.

   (d) is not subject of dissolution

136. If the position of President and Vice-President are vacant, who officiates as the President of India?

   (a) The Prime Minister

   (b) The Chief Justice of India

   (c) The Speaker of Lok Sabha

   (d) None of these

137. Voting right by the youth at the age of 18 years was exercised for the first time in the general election of

   (a) 1987   (b) 1988

   (c) 1989   (d) 1990

138 The Council of Ministers is collectively responsible to which of the following?

   (a) Prime Minister   (b) President

   (c) Rajya Sabha   (d) Lok Sabha

139. Right to vote is a

   (a) Social right   (b) Personal right

   (c) Political right   (d) Legal right

140. The speaker of the Lok Sabha can resign his office by addressing his resignation to

(a) The President

(b) The Prime Minister

(c) The Deputy Speaker of the Lok Sabha

(d) The Chief Justice of India

141. A committee appointed in 1977 to review working of the Panchayti Raj was chaired by

(a) Balwant Rai Mehta (b) Ashok Mehta

(c) K.N. Katju (d) Jagjivan Ram

142. Panchayati Raj in India represents:

(a) Decentralization of powers

(b) Participation of the people

(c) Community development

(d) All of these

143. 'National Rural Employment Guarantee Scheme' was launched initially in:

(a) 100 districts (b) 200 districts

(c) 330 districts (d) All the districts

144. When was the concept of the HDI introduced by the United Nations Development Programme?

(a) 1990 (b) 1991

(c) 1993 (d) 1995

145. In India, the first Municipal Corporation was set up in which one among the following?

(a) Calcutta (b) Madras

(c) Bombay (d) Delhi

146. Who is responsible to make changes in names and boundaries of the states?

(a) Prime Minister (b) Parliament

(c) Rajya Sabha (d) Governor

147. The Prime Minister launched on August 21, 2014, the "Digital India" campaign whose idea is to

(a) change India into an electronically empowered economy

(b) connect India digitally with other world's economies

(c) link all railways digitally

(d) display the government data and statistics by means of displayed digits

148. The mobile court in India is brainchild of:

(a) Justice Bhagwati

(b) Mr. Rajiv Gandhi

(c) Dr. A.P.J. Abdul Kalam

(d) Mrs. Pratibha Patil

149. Which one of the following Amendments of the Constitution of India deals with the issue of strengthening of the Panchayati Raj?

(a) 42nd (b) 44th

(c) 73rd (d) 86th

150. The disputes regarding the election of the President and Vice-President of India are decided by the-

(a) Parliament (b) Election Commission

(c) Supreme Court (d) High Court

151. Acting Chief Justice of the Supreme Court in India is appointed by the

(a) Chief Justice of Supreme Court

(b) Prime Minister

(c) President

(d) Law Minister

152. The system of Judicial Review exists in

(a) India only (b) U.K. only

(c) U.S.A only (d) India and U.S.A

153. The Supreme Court of India was set up by the

(a) Regulating Act, 1773

(b) Pitt's India Act, 1984

(c) Charter Act, 1813

(d) Charter Act, 1833

154. The first High/Supreme Court judge, who voluntarily made his assets public is

(a) Justice D.V.S. Kumar (b) Justice K. Chandra

(c) Justice K. Kannan (d) Justice V.C. Srivastava

155. Which of the following writs literally means 'we command'?

(a) Habeas Corpus (b) Mandamus

(c) Prohibition (d) Quo-Warranto

156. The 'Due Process of Law' is the characteristics of the judicial system of

(a) India   (b) France

(c) U.K.   (d) U.S.A

157. The number of judges can be modified in the Supreme Court by

(a) Presidential Order

(b) Supreme Court by Notification

(c) Parliament by Law

(d) Central Government by notification

158. Which High Court has jurisdiction over the State of Arunachal Pradesh?

(a) Guwahati   (b) Mumbai

(c) Kolkata   (d) Chandigarh

159. Which among the following Union Territory has a Judicial Commissioner?

(a) Pondicherry

(b) Andaman & Nicobar Islands

(c) Daman & Diu

(d) Lakshadweep

160. Which writ is issued by the High court to the lower courts to stop legal action?

(a) Habeas Corpus   (b) Prohibition

(c) Quo Warranto   (d) Certiorari

161. Scent sprayer is based on

(a) Charles's law

(b) Boyle's law

(c) Archimedes' principle

(d) Bernoulli's principle

162. At which temperature the centigrade and Fahrenheit scales are equal?

(a) $40°$ (b) $-40°$

(c) $37°$ (d) $94.6°$

163. The colour of the star is an indication of its

(a) distance from earth

(b) temperature

(c) luminosity

(d) distance from the sun

164. What is the source of electrical energy in an artificial satellite?

(a) Solar cell   (b) Mini nuclear reactor

(c) Dynamo   (d) Thermopile

165. The mirror used by a dentist to examine the teeth of patients is

(a) Concave   (b) Convex

(c) Plane   (d) Cylindrical

166. When water is heated from $0°C$ to $4°C$, its volume

(a) increases

(b) decreases

(c) first increases then decreases

(d) remains the same

167. Among the following radiations, which has the highest energy ?

(a) Visible   (b) X-ray

(c) Ultraviolet   (d) Infrared

168 A cut diamond sparkles because of its

(a) hardness

(b) high refractive index

(c) emission of light by the diamond

(d) absorption of light by the diamond

169. The lift of an air plane is based on

(a) Torricelli's theorem

(b) Bernoulli's theorem

(c) Law of gravitation

(d) Conservation of linear momentum

170. Compared to burn due to air at $100°C$, a burn due to steam at $100°C$ is

(a) less dangerous   (b) more dangerous

(c) equally dangerous   (d) None of these

171. The special technique used in ships to calculate the depth of ocean beds is

(a) LASER   (b) SONAR

(c) sonic boom   (d) reverberation

172. When a body is stationary, then

    (a) there is no force acting on it

    (b) the body is in vacuum

    (c) the force acting on it is not in contact with it

    (d) the net forces acting on it balances each other

173. The clouds float in the atmosphere because of their low

    (a) temperature   (b) velocity

    (c) pressure   (d) density

174. Sound cannot travel though

    (a) solids   (b) liquids

    (c) gases   (d) vacuum

175. Soap bubble looks coloured due to

    (a) dispersion   (b) reflection

    (c) interference   (d) Any one of these

176. Solder is an alloy of

    (a) tin and lead

    (b) tin and copper

    (c) tin, copper and zinc

    (d) tin, lead and zinc

177. CNG used in automobiles to check pollution, mainly consists of

    (a) CH_4 (b) CO_2

    (c) N_2 (d) H_2

178. 'Acid rain' is caused due to air-pollution by

    (a) carbon dioxide

    (b) carbon monoxide

    (c) methane

    (d) nitrous oxide and sulphur dioxide

179. A device used for the measurement of radioactivity is

    (a) Mass spectrometer   (b) Cyclotron

    (c) Nuclear reactor   (d) G.M. counter

180. Which has maximum calorific value?

    (a) Fat   (b) Protein

    (c) Carbohydrate   (d) Amino acid

181. Alum purifies muddy water by

    (a) Absorption   (b) Dialysis

    (c) Emulsification   (d) Coagulation

182 Which one among the following is used as a moderator in nuclear reactors?

    (a) Ozone   (b) Heavy hydrogen

    (c) Heavy water   (d) Hydrogen peroxide

183. Commonly used antiseptic 'Dettol' is a mixture of

    (a) o-chlorophenoxylenol + terepineol

    (b) o-cresol + terepineol

    (c) phenol + terepineol

    (d) chloroxylenol + terepineol

184. Cinnabar is an ore of

    (a) Hg   (b) Cu

    (c) Pb   (d) Zn

185. Which one of the following mixtures is homogeneous?

    (a) Starch and sugar

    (b) Methanol and water

    (c) Graphite and charcoal

    (d) Calcium carbonate and calcium bicarbonate

186. Who of the following is known as the Father of Biology?

    (a) Darwin   (b) Lamarck

    (c) Aristotle   (d) Theophrastus

187. Who is called the Father of Taxonomy?

    (a) Aristotle   (b) Carolus Linnaeus

    (c) Theophrastus   (d) Lamarck

188. Which of the following is used as an ornamental plant?

    (a) *Psilotum*   (b) *Lycopodium*

    (c) *Selaginella*   (d) *Pteris*

189. Which of the following gas is necessary for the process of photosynthesis?

    (a) O_2 (b) CO

    (c) N_2 (d) CO_2

190. The water and mineral salts are transported to the various organs by which of the following?

  (a) Xylem   (b) Phloem

  (c) Cortex   (d) Cambium

191. Turpentine oil is extracted from

  (a) Nettle   (b) *Cycas*

  (c) Teak   (d) *Pine*

192. Bamboo is classified as

  (a) Tree   (b) Grass

  (c) Shrub   (d) Herb

193. Which one of the following is a rich source of iron?

  (a) Carrot   (b) Pea

  (c) Rice   (d) Spinach

194. Kuttu flour is obtained from

  (a) *Tapioca*   (b) *Fagopyrum*

  (c) *Plantago*   (d) *Eleusine*

195. Which of the following harmones contains Iodine ?

  (a) Thyroxine   (b) Testosterone

  (c) Insulin   (d) Adrenaline

196. Which organelle in the cell, other than nucleus contains DNA ?

  (a) Centriole   (b) Golgi apparatus

  (c) Lysosome   (d) Mitrochondrion

197. Who discovered genetic material ?

  (a) Crick and Watson

  (b) Avery Mclood

  (c) Friedrich Miescher

  (d) Federik Meischer

198. The phenomenon of genetic mutation can not occur in

  (a) DNA   (b) RNA

  (c) chromosome   (d) ribosome

199. The study related to the fishes is called

  (a) Cryptology   (b) Sicrotology

  (c) Ichthyology   (d) Lepidopterology

200 The scientist who firstly explained about the blood circulation

  (a) A. Leeuwenhoek   (b) William Harvey

  (c) J.G. Mendel   (d) Ronald Ros

201. Which of the following is not a water pollutant ?

  (a) Zinc   (b) Copper

  (c) Nickel   (d) Sulphur dioxide

202. Eco-Mark is given to the Indian products that are

  (a) Pure and unadulterated

  (b) Rich in proteins

  (c) Environment-friendly

  (d) Economically viable

203. The United Nations Convention on climate change ratified by more than 50 countries became effective on

  (a) March 21, 1994   (b) May 21, 1995

  (c) June 21, 1996   (d) June 21, 1999

204. The orderly sequence of change in the vegetation of an area over time is described as

  (a) biomes   (b) succession

  (c) trophic level   (d) climax

205. Which one of the following trees is considered to be an environmental hazard ?

  (a) Babool   (b) Amaltas

  (c) Neem   (d) Eucalyptus

206. Solar radiation plays the most important role in the

  (a) Carbon cycle   (b) Oxygen cycle

  (c) Water cycle   (d) Nitrogen cycle

207. Endangered species are listed in

  (a) Dead Stock Book   (b) Red Data Book

  (c) Live Stock Book   (d) None of these

208. Mangrove forests in Asia are largely concentrated in

  (a) India   (b) Malaysia

  (c) Indonesia   (d) Philippines

209. Which one of the following is not related to water pollution ?

  (a) Eutrophication

  (b) Nitrification

  (c) Biological Oxygen Demand (BOD)

  (d) Oil slicks

210. Which one of the following is designated as the "lungs of the world" ?

(a) Mangrove forests

(b) Mid-latitude mixed forests

(c) Taiga forests

(d) Equatorial evergreen forests

211. What term denotes the organisms getting their food from others ?

(a) Heterotrophs   (b) Autotrophs

(c) Producers   (d) Synthesizers

212. Supersonic jet causes pollution by thinning of

(a) O_3 layer   (b) C_2 layer

(c) SO_2 layer   (d) O_2 layer

213. The concept of carbon credit originated from which one of the following ?

(a) Kyoto protocol   (b) Earth summit

(c) Doha round   (d) Montreal Protocol

214. Which one of the following energy is most utilized in biomass ?

(a) Atomic energy   (b) Solar energy

(c) Geothermal energy   (d) Tidal energy

215. Which one of the following is not included under the basic component of the environment ?

(a) Abiotic component   (b) Biotic component

(c) Energy component   (d) Spatial component

216. The use of fossil fuels is responsible for the increase in the amount of which gas in the atmosphere ?

(a) Nitrogen   (b) Carbondioxide

(c) Ozone   (d) Argon

217. Which one of the following is not helpful in maintaining ecological stability?

(a) Ecosystem complexity

(b) Ecosystem diversity

(c) Ecosystem uniformity

(d) Homeostatic mechanism

218. A pesticide which is a chlorinated hydrocarbon is sprayed on a food crop. The food chain is: Food crop – Rat – Snake – Hawk. In this food chain, the highest concentration of the pesticide would accumulate in which one of the following ?

(a) Food crop   (b) Rat

(c) Snake   (d) Hawk

219. Earth summit was held in

(a) Chicago

(b) Copenhagen

(c) Rio de Janeiro

(d) London

220. The use of microorganism metabolism to remove pollutants such as oil spills in the water bodies is known as

(a) biomagnification

(b) bioremediation

(c) biomethanation

(d) bioreduction

221. With which sport the term' Caddie' is associated?

(a) Polo   (b) Golf

(c) Bridge   (d) Billiards

222. Who is the highest wicket taker in the world in one day cricket?

(a) Kapil Dev

(b) Muthia Muralitharan

(c) Wasim Akram

(d) Anil Kumble

223. The famous player 'Ronaldo' is associated with which of the following games?

(a) Table Tennis   (b) Football

(c) Hockey   (d) Volleyball

224. First youth Olympic games was held in

(a) Japan   (b) China

(c) North Korea   (d) Singapore

225. 'Subroto Cup' is associated with

(a) Badminton   (b) Cricket

(c) Chess   (d) Football

226. India reached the final of the Davis Cup for the first time in

(a) 1965   (b) 1966

(c) 1970   (d) 1971

227. 'Dipeeka Kumari' is known for her outstanding performance in which of the following?

(a) Boxing   (b) Athletics

(c) Basketball   (d) Archery

228. Wankhede Stadium is situated in

(a) Mumbai   (b) Delhi

(c) Lucknow   (d) Bangalore

229. National Sports Day is celebrated on

(a) 29th Aug.   (b) 4th Dec.

(c) 14th Nov.   (d) 28th Oct.

230. The term 'bogey' is associated with

(a) Cricket   (b) Chess

(c) Golf   (d) Baseball

231 Which of the following trophies is not concerned with Football?

(a) Durand Trophy   (b) Rovers Cup

(c) Euro Cup   (d) Ranji Trophy

232. In which Indian state did the game of 'Polo' originates?

(a) Nagaland   (b) Manipur

(c) Mizoram   (d) Kerala

233. When did the Wimbledon Grand Slam Tennis tournament start?

(a) 1857   (b) 1877

(c) 1897   (d) 1898

234. The sportsperson 'Soma Biswas' is associated with

(a) Sailing   (b) Hockey

(c) Golf   (d) Athletics

235. Which one of the following countries had hosted the first winter Paralympic Games?

(a) Sweden   (b) France

(c) Soviet Union   (d) China

236. Gagan Narang, whose name has been recommended for 'Rajiv Gandhi Khel Ratna Award' is a famous

(a) Motor Car Racer   (b) Cricketer

(c) Air Rifle Shooter   (d) Footballer

237. What is the number of players in Polo and Water-polo respectively?

(a) 2 and 5   (b) 7 and 9

(c) 4 and 7   (d) 6 and 5

238. Among the following which one is not a football club?

(a) Arsenal   (b) Aston villa

(c) Chelsea   (d) Monte Carlo

239. Duleep Trophy is associated with the game of

(a) Hockey   (b) Badminton

(c) Football   (d) Cricket

240. How many players are there in Kho-Kho?

(a) 9   (b) 10

(c) 8   (d) 7

241. What is the National Game of Russia?

(a) Chess   (b) Hockey

(c) Table Tennis   (d) Baseball

242. 'Blue Riband Cup' is associated with

(a) Rugby Football   (b) Netball

(c) Horse Racing   (d) Chess

243. Which county did Ravi Shastri play for?

(a) Glamorgan   (b) Leicestershire

(c) Gloucestershire   (d) Lancashire

244. India won its first Olympic hockey gold in...?

(a) 1928   (b) 1932

(c) 1936   (d) 1948

245. The number of medals won by Indian in the 2010 Commonwealth Games-

(a) 107   (b) 101

(c) 105   (d) 98

246. In which year did Milkha Singh win the first National title in the 400 m race?

    (a) 1955   (b) 1956

    (c) 1957   (d) 1970

247. Who was the 1st ODI captain for India?

    (a) Bishen Singh Bedi   (b) Ajit Wadekar

    (c) Vinoo Mankad   (d) Nawab Pataudi

248. First Olympic Games were held in-

    (a) 776 BC.   (b) 798 BC.

    (c) 876 BC.   (d) 898 BC.

249. Which football hero was nicknamed "The Sundance Kid"?

    (a) Jim Forrest Kiick   (b) Troy Aikman

    (c) Brett Favre   (d) Joe Montana

250. The Flamingo Festival is celebrated in________?

    (a) Andhra Pradesh (b) Karnataka

    (c) Kerala   (d) Jammu & Kashmir

251. Jnanpith Award is given for which field?

    (a) Journalism   (b) Music

    (c) Science   (d) Literature

252. Highest award given to civilian in India is

    (a) Bharat Ratna   (b) Padma Vibhushan

    (c) Sharam Award   (d) Padma Bhushan

253. Sports coaches receive which of the following awards?

    (a) Rajiv Gandhi Khel Ratna Award

    (b) Dronacharya Award

    (c) Arjuna Award

    (d) None of these

254. The second highest Gallantry award is

    (a) Mahavir Chakra   (b) Vir Chakra

    (c) Arjuna Award   (d) Ashok Chakra

255. Vachaspati Samman is given in the field of

    (a) Sanskrit Literature

    (b) Medical Science

    (c) Indian Philosophy

    (d) Hindi Literature

256. Which of the Gallantry award is exactly like Ashok Chakra?

    (a) Mahavir Chakra   (b) Kirti Chakra

    (c) Vir Chakra   (d) Shaurya Chakra

257. Which of the following famous financial journals of international repute confers 'Finance minister of the year' Award?

    (a) Dalal Street

    (b) Euromoney

    (c) Business Standard

    (d) Money Matters

258. Manav Seva Award has been instituted in the memory of

    (a) Rajiv Gandhi

    (b) Dr. Rajendra Prasad

    (c) Indira Gandhi

    (d) Acharya

259. The journalist who refused to accept 'Padma Bhushan' was?

    (a) Shekaran Nair

    (b) Khushwant Singh

    (c) Ratan Thiyam

    (d) Arun Shourie

260. Which among the following states has won the 10th National Award for Excellence work in Mahatma Gandhi National Rural Employment Guarantee Act (MGNREGA)?

    (a) Madhya Pradesh   (b) Karnataka

    (c) West Bengal   (d) Haryana

261 Admiral Gorshkov, the Soviet aircraft carrier imported by India is now named

    (a) INS Vikrant   (b) INS Vikramaditya

    (c) INS Virat   (d) INS Vishaal

262. Which of the following organizations has Sarvatra Sarvottam Suraksha as its slogan?

    (a) Border Security Forece

    (b) Sikh Light Infantry

    (c) Indian Air Force

    (d) National Security Guard

263. At which of the following places is the Headquarters of South Western Air Command located?

    (a)   Vadodara   (b)   Jodhpur

    (c)   Pune   (d)   Gandhinagar

264. Who of the following was the Chief of Army at the time of Indo-Pak war of 1971?

    (a)   General PP Kumaramangalam

    (b)   Field Marshall SHFJ Manekshaw

    (c)   General JN Chaudhari

    (d)   General KS Thimayya

265. Which of the following was the first aircraft inducted by the Indian Air Force (then Royal Indian Air Force) in 1932?

    (a)   de Havilland Tiger Moth

    (b)   Westland Wapiti

    (c)   Supermarine Spitfire

    (d)   Fairchild Packet

266. Which one among the following is the unit raised to protect the naval assets?

    (a)   Sagar Rakshak Bal   (b)   Sagar Suraksha Bal

    (c)   Sagar Prahari Bal   (d)   Sagar Nigrani Bal

267. Indian Army's counter-insurgency school is situated in

    (a)   Kanker   (b)   Srinagar

    (c)   Tezpur   (d)   Vairengte

268. Dhanush, a missile inducted into the Indian Navy

    (a)   is a customized and naval variant of Prithvi missile

    (b)   has a range of 700 km

    (c)   can be launched from an aircraft

    (d)   cannot carry nuclear warheads

269. The commando unit of the Indian Air Force is named

    (a)   Baaz   (b)   Garud

    (c)   MARCOS   (d)   Ghatak

270. On which of the following dates is the Navy Day celebrated in India?

    (a)   January 15   (b)   October 8

    (c)   December 4   (d)   February 1

271. Lt Commander Abhilash Tomy of the Indian Navy became the first Indian to complete a solo, unassisted, non-stop circumnavigation of the world in 2013. What was the name of the vessel used by him?

    (a)   INSV Mandovi   (b)   INSV Mhadei

    (c)   INS Abhimanyu   (d)   INS Abhay

272. At which of the following places is the Indian National Defence University being set up?

    (a)   Medak, Andhra Pradesh

    (b)   Amethi, Uttar Pradesh

    (c)   Gurgaon, Haryana

    (d)   Kasargod, Kerala

273. At which of the following places is the College of Defence Management located?

    (a)   Dehradun   (b)   Pune

    (c)   Secunderabad   (d)   Chennai

274. The highest official rank of Air Force is __________.

    (a)   Air Marshal   (b)   Supreme Marshal

    (c)   Air Chief Marshal   (d)   Chief of Air Force

275. DRDL stands for

    (a)   Defence Research and Development Laboratary

    (b)   Department of Research and Development Laboratory

    (c)   Differential Research and Documentation Laboratary

    (d)   None of the above

276. Who was the first Indian Chief of Army Staff of the Indian Army ?

    (a)   Gen. K.M. Cariappa

    (b)   Vice-Admiral R.(D) Katari

    (c)   Gen. Maharaja Rajendra Singhji

    (d)   None of the above

277. Which was the first missile boat of India?

    (a)   INS Vinash   (b)   INS Khukri

    (c)   INS Shakti   (d)   INS Ajay

278. Which was the first tanker naval ship in India?

    (a)   INS Vinash   (b)   INS Khukri

    (c)   INS Shakti   (d)   INS Ajay

279. Which was the first nuclear reactor in India?

    (a) Apsara   (b) CIRUS

    (c) Dhruva   (d) Kaiga

280. Who among the following is associated with first nuclear explosion in Pokhran?

    (a) (C)N.R. Rao   (b) Homi.J.Bhabha

    (c) Anil Kakodkar   (d) Raja Ramanna

281. When was UAV Nishant induct?

    (a) 1996   (b) 1998

    (c) 2000   (d) 2003

282. Which is the first indigenous aircraft of India?

    (a) HT-2

    (b) Mikoyan MiG-25

    (c) HF-25 MKI

    (d) Sukhoi Su-30 MKI

283. Which is the first trisonic aircraft of India?

    (a) HT-2   (b) Mikoyan MiG-25

    (c) HF-25 MKI   (d) Sukhoi Su-30 MKI

284. Which is the first tactical surface-to-surface missile of India?

    (a) Akash   (b) Trishul

    (c) Nag   (d) Prithvi

285. Which is the first long-range multiple-target missile in India?

    (a) Akash   (b) Agni

    (c) Brahmos   (d) Prithvi

286. When was INS Prahar inducted in Indian Navy?

    (a) 1991   (b) 1992

    (c) 1993   (d) 1997

287. Cryogenic engines are used in

    (a) rockets and spacecrafts

    (b) atomic reactors

    (c) defrost refrigerators

    (d) doing research connected with superconductivity.

288. What is the source of electrical energy in an artificial satellite?

    (a) Solar cells

    (b) Mini nuclear reactor

    (c) Dynamo

    (d) Thermopile

289. The fastest super computer of the world is

    (a) Param Yuva II   (b) Tianhe-2

    (c) IBM Road runner   (d) Titan

290. Which one of the following organisations is not related to science and technology ?

    (a) DST   (b) CSIR

    (c) ICSSR   (d) DAE

291. 'Satish Dhawan Space Centre' is located in

    (a) Vishakhapatnam   (b) Goa

    (c) Sriharikota   (d) Chennai

292. HAL is related to manufacturing of

    (a) Telecommunication equipments

    (b) Aircrafts

    (c) Space missiles

    (d) War missiles

293. If an apple is released from an orbiting spaceship, it will

    (a) fall towards the earth

    (b) move of a lower speed

    (c) move along with the spaceship at the same speed

    (d) move at a higher speed

294. Missile 'Astra' is a

    (a) land to land missile

    (b) land to air missile

    (c) air to air missile

    (d) water to land missile

295. When did India make first nuclear weapon explosion ?

    (a) 15th May, 1964   (b) 18th May, 1974

    (c) 11th May, 1989   (d) 13th May, 1998

296. Which one of the following is not a space satellite?

    (a) SLV-3   (b) RS-D1

    (c) IRS-1D   (d) INSAT-2D

297. Mobile IP provides two basic functions

    (a) route discovery and registration

    (b) agent discovery and registration

    (c) IP binding and registration

    (d) none of the above

298. Which is a satellite based tracking system that enables the determination of a person's position?

    (a) Bluetooth

    (b) WAP

    (c) Short message service

    (d) Global positioning system

299. The first operational remote sensing satellite from India was

    (a) IRS-P6   (b) P4

    (c) IRS 1A   (d) CARTOSAT 1

300 The fastest computer developed by the NASA is

    (a) Columbia   (b) Pleiades

    (c) Blue Gene   (d) Param

ANSWER KEY

1. (d)	**2.** (a)	**3.** (b)	**4.** (a)	**121.** (b)	**122.** (c)	**123.** (c)	**124.** (c)
5. (a)	**6.** (c)	**7.** (b)	**8.** (d)	**125.** (b)	**126.** (b)	**127.** (d)	**128.** (d)
9. (a)	**10.** (a)	**11.** (a)	**12.** (a)	**129.** (d)	**130.** (c)	**131.** (b)	**132.** (d)
13. (a)	**14.** (a)	**15.** (b)	**16.** (a)	**133.** (b)	**134.** (b)	**135.** (d)	**136.** (b)
17. (a)	**18.** (c)	**19.** (b)	**20.** (a)	**137.** (c)	**138.** (d)	**139.** (c)	**140.** (c)
21. (c)	**22.** (a)	**23.** (b)	**24.** (a)	**141.** (b)	**142.** (d)	**143.** (b)	**144.** (a)
25. (d)	**26.** (b)	**27.** (c)	**28.** (b)	**145.** (a)	**146.** (b)	**147.** (a)	**148.** (c)
29. (c)	**30.** (c)	**31.** (c)	**32.** (a)	**149.** (c)	**150.** (c)	**151.** (c)	**152.** (d)
33. (b)	**34.** (d)	**35.** (b)	**36.** (a)	**153.** (a)	**154.** (c)	**155.** (b)	**156.** (d)
37. (b)	**38.** (a)	**39.** (a)	**40.** (c)	**157.** (c)	**158.** (a)	**159.** (c)	**160.** (b)
41. (a)	**42.** (d)	**43.** (a)	**44.** (b)	**161.** (d)	**162.** (b)	**163.** (b)	**164.** (a)
45. (b)	**46.** (d)	**47.** (b)	**48.** (a)	**165.** (a)	**166.** (b)	**167.** (b)	**168.** (b)
49. (d)	**50.** (c)	**51.** (d)	**52.** (a)	**169.** (b)	**170.** (b)	**171.** (b)	**172.** (d)
53. (b)	**54.** (c)	**55.** (d)	**56.** (b)	**173.** (d)	**174.** (d)	**175.** (c)	**176.** (a)
57. (d)	**58.** (c)	**59.** (d)	**60.** (a)	**177.** (a)	**178.** (d)	**179.** (d)	**180.** (a)
61. (c)	**62.** (b)	**63.** (b)	**64.** (c)	**181.** (d)	**182.** (c)	**183.** (d)	**184.** (a)
65. (c)	**66.** (c)	**67.** (c)	**68.** (a)	**185.** (b)	**186.** (c)	**187.** (b)	**188.** (c)
69. (b)	**70.** (a)	**71.** (c)	**72.** (c)	**189.** (d)	**190.** (a)	**191.** (d)	**192.** (b)
73. (a)	**74.** (b)	**75.** (c)	**76.** (c)	**193.** (d)	**194.** (b)	**195.** (a)	**196.** (d)
77. (b)	**78.** (c)	**79.** (c)	**80.** (b)	**197.** (c)	**198.** (d)	**199.** (c)	**200.** (b)
81. (c)	**82.** (d)	**83.** (c)	**84.** (a)	**201.** (b)	**202.** (c)	**203.** (a)	**204.** (b)
85. (b)	**86.** (b)	**87.** (c)	**88.** (a)	**205.** (d)	**206.** (c)	**207.** (b)	**208.** (c)
89. (b)	**90.** (a)	**91.** (c)	**92** (b)	**209.** (b)	**210.** (d)	**211.** (a)	**212.** (a)
93. (c)	**94.** (d)	**95.** (b)	**96.** (d)	**213.** (a)	**214.** (b)	**215.** (d)	**216.** (b)
97. (d)	**98.** (b)	**99.** (c)	**100.** (a)	**217.** (c)	**218.** (d)	**219.** (c)	**220.** (b)
101. (b)	**102.** (c)	**103.** (c)	**104.** (a)	**221.** (b)	**222.** (b)	**223.** (b)	**224.** (d)
105. (b)	**106.** (b)	**107.** (a)	**108.** (b)	**225.** (d)	**226.** (b)	**227.** (d)	**228.** (a)
109. (a)	**110.** (d)	**111.** (a)	**112.** (d)	**229.** (a)	**230.** (c)	**231** (d)	**232.** (b)
113. (a)	**114.** (b)	**115.** (d)	**116.** (a)	**233.** (b)	**234.** (d)	**235.** (a)	**236.** (c)
117. (c)	**118.** (d)	**119.** (b)	**120.** (d)	**237.** (c)	**238.** (d)	**239.** (d)	**240.** (a)

241. (a)	**242.** (c)	**243.** (a)	**244.** (a)	**273.** (c)	**274.** (c)	**275.** (a)	**276.** (a)
245. (b)	**246.** (c)	**247.** (b)	**248.** (a)	**277.** (a)	**278.** (c)	**279.** (a)	**280.** (a)
249. (a)	**250.** (a)	**251.** (d)	**252.** (a)	**281.** (b)	**282.** (a)	**283.** (b)	**284.** (d)
253. (b)	**254.** (a)	**255.** (a)	**256.** (d)	**285.** (a)	**286.** (d)	**287.** (a)	**288.** (a)
257. (b)	**258.** (a)	**259.** (b)	**260.** (a)	**289.** (b)	**290.** (c)	**291.** (c)	**292.** (b)
261 (b)	**262.** (d)	**263.** (d)	**264.** (b)	**293.** (c)	**294.** (c)	**295.** (b)	**296.** (a)
265. (b)	**266.** (b)	**267.** (d)	**268.** (a)	**297.** (b)	**298.** (d)	**299.** (c)	**300.** (b)
269. (b)	**270.** (c)	**271.** (c)	**272.** (c)				

1. Which of the following days is National Technology Day observed?
   - (a) May 12
   - (b) May 10
   - (c) May 9
   - (d) May 11

2. Which country has been re-elected as observer to forum Arctic Council?
   - (a) China
   - (b) India
   - (c) Japan
   - (d) Russia

3. With reference to Basel Convention, consider the following statements:
   1. It aims to protect human health and the environment against the adverse effects of hazardous wastes.
   2. It was adopted by the Conference of Plenipotentiaries in Basel, Switzerland in 1989

   Which of the above statements is/are correct?
   - (a) 1 Only
   - (b) 2 Only
   - (c) Both 1 and 2
   - (d) Neither 1 nor 2

4. Consider the following statements with reference to Moderate Resolution Imaging Spectroradiometer:
   1. It is an earth observation payload launched on board with Terra Satellite.
   2. It is being monitored by SpaceX agency.

   Which of the above statements is/are correct?
   - (a) 1 Only
   - (b) 2 Only
   - (c) Both 1 and 2
   - (d) Neither 1 nor 2

5. With reference to World Customs Organisation, consider the following statements:
   1. It is an independent intergovernmental body.
   2. It aims to enhance the effectiveness and efficiency of Customs administrations.
   3. India chairs the Asia Pacific region of World Customs Organisation.

   Which of the above statements is/are correct?
   - (a) 1 and 3
   - (b) 1 and 2
   - (c) 1, 2 and 3
   - (d) 2 and 3

6. Consider the below statements with reference to Chilika Lake:
   1. It is the largest coastal lagoon in India located in Andhra Pradesh.
   2. It is designated as 'wetland of international importance under the Ramsar convention.

   Which of the above statements is/are correct?
   - (a) 1 Only
   - (b) 2 Only
   - (c) Both 1 and 2
   - (d) Neither 1 nor 2

7. Recently, The International Water Conference was held in:
   - (a) New Delhi
   - (b) Garland Texas
   - (c) Basel
   - (d) Paris

8. Name Kerala's largest temple festival, which held recently in May 2019?.
   - (a) Thrissur Pooram
   - (b) Vishu
   - (c) Onam
   - (d) Aranmula Boat Race

9. Which of the following animals may not survive climate change, according to a new study?
   - (a) Grizzly Bear
   - (b) Polar Bear
   - (c) White Tigers
   - (d) Bengal Tigers

10. By what percentage was India's industrial production in March 2019 declined?
    - (a) 10
    - (b) 1.0
    - (c) 0.1
    - (d) 0.01

11. In which of the following states the highest child mortality rate was reported?
    - (a) Assam
    - (b) West Bengal
    - (c) Goa
    - (d) Sikkim

12. Ireland parliament has recently become the second after _______ to declare a climate emergency.
    - (a) New Zealand
    - (b) Argentina
    - (c) USA
    - (d) Britain

13. Tariff on import to which of the following countries was raised by the US recently?
    - (a) Japan
    - (b) China
    - (c) Nepal
    - (d) Sri Lanka

14. Which country has reported the first case of monkeypox?
    - (a) Singapore
    - (b) Vietnam
    - (c) Indonesia
    - (d) Malaysia

15. Who is the publisher of world's first women's cricket magazine?
    - (a) Mithali Raj
    - (b) Yash Lahoti
    - (c) Smiriti Mandhana
    - (d) Harmanpreet Kaur

16. Which firm has developed artificial intelligence to create fashion models?
    - (a) DataGrid
    - (b) DataMatics
    - (c) Softonic
    - (d) DataMatrix

17. Read the following statements.
    I. Anand-based National Dairy Development Board (NDDB) has developed world's first complete parent-wise genome assembly of buffalo.
    II. The estimated population of buffaloes in the world is 224.4 million, of which 219 million (97.58%) are in Asia.

Choose the correct statement.

(a) Only I
(b) Only II
(c) Both I and II
(d) None of these

18. Read the following statements.

   I. Japan has opened the first stretch of a so-called electric highway.

   II. The system was built by Munich-based engineering firm Volkswagen AG, while Siemens AG's Scania trucks unit provided the vehicles.

   Choose the correct statement.

   (a) Only I
   (b) Only II
   (c) Both I and II
   (d) None of these

19. Read the following statements.

   I. A team of researchers working at the U.S. Department of Energy says it has created a kind of plastic that could lead to products that are 100 percent recyclable.

   II. The team works at the Department of Energy's Lawrence Berkeley National Laboratory in California.

   Choose the correct option.

   (a) Only I
   (b) Only II
   (c) Both I and II
   (d) None of these

20. Read the following statements.

   I. Engineers from the Indian Institute of Technology Bombay (IIT Bombay) have developed a microprocessor called AJIT.

   II. AJIT is a micro-processor.

   Choose the correct statement.

   (a) Only I
   (b) Only II
   (c) Both I and II
   (d) None of these

21. Who has recently been awarded the Presidential Medal of Freedom, US's highest civilian honour?

   (a) Dwayne Johnson
   (b) Lionel Messi
   (c) Tiger Woods
   (d) Rafael Nadal

22. Who has been honoured with the 2019 VK Krishna Menon Award in Journalism?

   (a) PV Bakshi Gaur
   (b) AK Sinha
   (c) VK Krishna Menon
   (d) GD Robert Govender

23. Which Indian has been reelected to the International Narcotics Control Board in May 2019?

   (a) Amartya Sen
   (b) Jagdish Bhagwati
   (c) Gita Gopinath
   (d) Jagjit Pavadia

24. Recently who has been appointed to the Supreme Court of Fiji's non-resident panel?

   (a) Justice AK Sikri
   (b) Justice MB Lokur
   (c) Justice Kurian Joseph
   (d) Justice Ranjan Gogoi

25. The exercise Varuna 19.1 is a navy exercise between India and which country?

   (a) Russia
   (b) France
   (c) Japan
   (d) Vietnam

26. Who has recently been designated as a global terrorist at the UN?

   (a) Dawood Ibrahim
   (b) Masood Azhar
   (c) Abdul Rauf Azhar
   (d) Hafiz Saeed

27. What is the theme of this year's International Workers Day?

   (a) Sustainable Pension for all: The Role of Social Partners
   (d) Sustainable Workers
   (c) Celebrating the International Labour Movement
   (d) Workers Sacrifices

28. Which country is first in the world to declare climate change emergency?

   (a) USA
   (b) UK
   (c) Russia
   (d) Canada

29. What is the theme of this year's World Press Freedom Day 2019?

   (a) Advancing Media and Journalism
   (b) Critical Minds For Critical Times
   (c) Media for Democracy: Journalism and Elections in Times of Disinformation
   (d) Media for Democracy: Elections and Journalism

30. Consider the following statements with reference to Mission Chandrayaan 2:

   1. The mission will be launched on board Geosynchronous Satellite Launch Vehicle- Mk III.

   2. It will be ISRO's second interplanetary mission to land a rover on any celestial body.

   3. It is a totally indigenous venture comprising of an orbiter, a lander and a rover.

   Which of the above statements is/are correct?

   (a) 1 and 2
   (b) 1, 2 and 3
   (c) 2 and 3
   (d) 1 and 3

31. Consider the following pairs:

   1. World Intellectual Property Day : April 26
   2. Labour Day : April 1
   3. Good Governance Day : December 26

   Which of the pairs given above is/are INCORRECTLY matched?

   (a) 1 and 2
   (b) 2 and 3
   (c) 1 and 3
   (d) 3 Only

32. Recently SEBI has barred which of the following from raising money from the securities for six months in a case related to the misuse of algorithmic trading.

   (a) BSE
   (b) NSE
   (c) MCX
   (d) NASDAQ

33. The term Superbugs relates to:

   (a) Strains of bacteria that are resistant to the majority of antibiotics commonly used today
   (b) A computer malware
   (c) The sophisticated supercomputer
   (d) None of the above

34. "Al Qaida and Taliban Sanctions Committee" of United Nations was in the news recently. Which of the following statements about this committee is/are true?

   1. It is also known as UNSC 1267 Committee.

   2. It consists only of 5 permanent members of UN Security Council.

Select the correct answer using the codes given below.

(a) 1 only (b) 2 only
(c) Both 1 & 2 (d) Neither 1 nor 2

35. Which of the following statements about World Press Freedom Prize is/are true?

1. It is conferred every year by UNESCO.

3. It is named in honour of Guillermo Cano Isaza, a Colombian journalist.

Select the correct answer using the codes given below.

(a) 1 only (b) 2 only
(c) Both 1 & 2 (d) Neither 1 nor 2

36. Which of the following institutions releases 'World's Press Freedom Index'?

(a) UNESCO

(b) Reporters Without Borders

(c) World Economic Forum

(d) International Press Institute

37. Recently, which of the following High Courts has started a Project titled "Zero Pendency Courts".

(a) Calcutta High Court (b) Madras High Court
(c) Bombay High Court (d) Delhi High Court.

38. Sovereign Internet bill was recently in news. It was passed by which of the following countries?

(a) India (b) USA
(c) China (d) Russia

39. Recently, government has released a postage stamp to commemorate the 750th birth anniversary of which spiritual icon?

(a) Manavala Mamunigal (b) Sri Vedanta Desikan
(c) Yamunacharya (d) Nathamuni

40. Which Institute has signed MoU with Principal Scientific Adviser (PSA) to government for setting up a Centre of Excellence for Waste to Wealth Technologies in India?

(a) IIT Kanpur (b) IIT Bombay
(c) IIT Delhi (d) IIT Madras

41. Which of the following cyclones has hit the Indian States of Odisha and West Bengal in May 2019?.

(a) Cyclone Hudhud (b) Cyclone Gaja
(c) Cyclone Phailin (d) Cyclone Fani

42. 16th ministerial meeting of Asia Cooperation Dialogue (ACD) was held in which country?

(a) Qatar (b) Japan
(c) Saudi Arabia (d) China

43. Which one of the following has recently facilitated the quick delivery of kidney for transplant?

(a) Airplane (b) Drone
(c) Artificial intelligence (d) None of these

44. **Read the following statements.**

I. Scientists have developed a smart suitcase that can help people with visual disabilities to navigate airport terminals safely.

II. The suitcase has been developed by the Carnegie Mellon University, Pittsburgh, Pennsylvania.

Choose the correct statement.

(a) I only (b) II only
(c) Both a & b (d) None of these

45. According to a latest finding, which of the following processes in brain can assist people who can't talk?

(a) Conversion of electric signals into speech

(b) Conversion of brain signals into speech

(c) Conversion of sound into brain signals

(d) Conversion of electric signals into brain signals

46. Read the following statements.

I. Stargazing technology could be used to detect cancer.

II. 3D medical X-ray machine is based on stargazing technology.

III. The US will be the first country to use stargazing technology to treat cancer.

Choose the correct option.

(a) I only (b) Both I and II
(c) I and III (d) I, II and III

47. India's growth in 2019-20 is forecasted to

(a) 8.5% (b) 7.3%
(c) 6.9% (d) 7.8%

48. Which of the following is the deadliest infectious disease in India?

(a) Tuberculosis (b) Cancer
(c) AIDS (d) Polio

49. The cyclone which recently affected eastern coast of India is called

(a) Mora (b) Komen
(c) Fani (d) Viyaru

50. Read the following statements.

I. A national climate emergency has been declared by the UK Parliament.

II. The United Nation's Paris Agreement aims at preventing global temperatures from reaching 3?C above pre-industrial levels by 2100.

III. Intergovernmental Panel on Climate Change focuses on limiting carbon monoxide emission.

Choose the correct option.

(a) I Only (b) I and II
(c) I and III (d) I, II and III

51. Who has recently been sworn in as Japan's new emperor and has ascended to the Chrysanthemum Throne?

(a) Zaruito (b) Burnavito
(c) Akihito (d) Naruhito

52. Recently, which country has declared 'Reiwa' as the name of its new imperial era?

(a) Brunei (b) Cambodia
(c) Japan (d) Denmark

53. Recently who has been conferred with the highest civilian award of France?

(a) A S Kiran (b) K Sivan
(c) Narendra Modi (d) Ram Nath Kovind

54. Who has been appointed as the first non-British President of the Marylebone Cricket Club?

   (a) Mahela Jayawardene   (b) Sachin Tendulkar

   (c) MS Dhoni   (d) Kumar Sangakkara

55. Recently, master Hirannaiah passed away. He was related to which field?

   (a) Theatre Artist   (b) Social Activist

   (c) Politicians   (d) Musician

56. Recently, ISRO launched the country's first electronic surveillance satellite, EMISAT. It was launched onboard__________.

   (a) PSLV-C45   (b) PSLV-C42

   (c) PSLV-C44   (d) PSLV-C43

57. What is the theme of Earth Hour 2019?

   (a) Change the way We Live

   (b) Switch off The Lights Worldwide

   (c) Connect2 Earth

   (d) Future Depends on Our Actions Today

58. India inks MoU with National Bank for Agriculture and Rural Development Consultancy Services (NABCONS) for setting up the India-Africa Institute of Agriculture and Rural development in which country?

   (a) South Africa   (b) Malawi

   (c) Uganda   (d) Kenya

59. Recently, Kandhamal Hladi got GI tag. It belongs to which state?

   (a) Maharashtra   (b) Andhra Pradesh

   (c) Odisha   (d) Kerala

60. Which country has unveiled the new name of its imperial era as "Reiwa"?

   (a) France   (b) Russia

   (c) Japan   (d) China

61. Consider the below statements with reference to Earth Hour:

1. It is an initiative of the World Wide Fund for Nature's.

2. The theme for 2019 is #Bee4ThePlanet.

Which of the above statements is/are correct?

   (a) 1 Only   (b) 2 Only

   (c) Both 1 and 2   (d) Neither 1 nor 2

62. Consider the below statements with reference to International Solar Alliance:

1. Recently Bolivia joined the International Solar Alliance.

2. The membership extended to all members of EU.

3. It is an outcome of Paris Declaration.

Which of the above statements is/are correct?

   (a) 1 and 2   (b) 1,2 and 3

   (c) 2 and 3   (d) 1 and 3

63. Consider the below statements with reference to anti-dumping duty.

1. It is a protectionist tariff that a domestic government imposes on foreign imports that it believes are priced below fair market value.

2. It will help to protect the foreign countries from domestic production.

Which of the above statements is/are correct?

64. With reference to Transport and Marketing Assistance, consider the below statements:

1. It aims at boosting manufacturing exports.

2. It provides financial assistance for transport and marketing of agricultural products.

3. It will promote Indian brands internationally for specified overseas market.

Which of the above statements is/are correct?

   (a) 1 and 2   (b) 2 and 3

   (c) 1, 2 and 3   (d) 1 and 3

65. Consider the following statements with reference to EMISAT Satellite:

1. It is an all-weather and all-terrain condition satellite.

2. It was launched on GSLV Mark III vehicle.

3. The satellite is aimed at electromagnetic spectrum measurement.

Which of the above statements is/are correct?

   (a) 1 and 2   (b) 1, 2 and 3

   (c) 2 and 3   (d) 1 and 3

66. Consider the following statements with reference to self regulatory organisation proposed by SEBI:

1. It will work as an independent body of SEBI.

2. It will take disciplinary actions apart from grievance redressal and dispute resolution of activities.

Which of the above statements is/are correct?

   (a) 1 only   (b) 2 only

   (c) both 1 and 2   (d) neither 1 nor 2

67. With reference to Café Scientifique initiative, consider the below statements:

1. It is a grassroots public science initiative of Karnataka.

2. It aims at empowering non-scientists to comfortably assess science and technology issues particularly those that impact social policy making.

Which of the above statements is/are correct?

   (a) 1 Only   (b) 2 Only

   (c) Both 1 and 2   (d) Neither 1 nor 2

68. Consider the below statements with reference to the State of Global Air 2019 report:

1. The report stated that China alone is responsible for over half of the total global attributable deaths from all air pollution in 2017.

2. The report has been released by United Nations Environment Programme.

Which of the above statements is/are correct?

   (a) 1 Only   (b) 2 Only

   (c) Both 1 and 2   (d) Neither 1 nor 2

69. Consider the following statements about State of Global Air 2019.

I. India and China together accounted for more than 70% of global 5 million deaths due to air pollution.

II. Air pollution is responsible for shortening life on average by 20 months around the globe.

Which of the above statements is/are correct?

(a) Only I
(b) Only II
(c) Both I and II
(d) Neither I nor II

70. What is the estimated population of chronically-hungry population in past three years as per Global Report on Food Crises-2019?

(a) 1 million
(b) 10 million
(c) 50 million
(d) 100 million

71. Recently (April 2019), in which of the following pairs of cities BS-VI norm fuel was introduced?

(a) Delhi & Noida
(b) Meerut & Delhi
(c) Alwar & Jaipur
(d) Hapur & Agra

72. The Centre for Cellular & Molecular Biology (CCMB) is located in which of the following cities?

(a) Kolkata
(b) New Delhi
(c) Hyderabad
(d) Bengaluru

73. Consider the following statements about first Nationwide 5G network in the world?

I. It was launched by United States.

II. SK Telecom, KT and LG Uplus were the top three telecom providers to start the 5G facility.

III. Initially the facility was provided to select customers.

Select the correct answer using the codes given below.

(a) Only I and II
(b) Only II and III
(c) Only I and III
(d) I, II and III

74. Recently, who has been conferred the highest civilian honour of UAE – Zayed medal?

(a) C Vidyasagar Rao
(b) Ram Nath Kovind
(c) Narendra Modi
(d) Arun Jaitley

75. Recently, who has taken over as the new ICC Chief executive?

(a) M N Chinayappa
(b) Manu Sawhney
(c) Dave Richardson
(d) K Srinivasan

76. Who has been named as the new World Bank president in April 2019?

(a) Jim Yong Kim
(b) Kristalina Georgieva
(c) David Malpass
(d) Christine Lagarde

77. Recently, who has become the first Indian to be elected as a member of the FIFA Executive Council?

(a) Shashank Manohar
(b) Kevin Richardson
(c) Dave Richardson
(d) Praful Patel

78. Who took charge as the new President of the Confederation of Indian Industry (CII) in April 2019?

(a) Sanjay Kirloskar
(b) Vikram Kirloskar
(c) Rakesh Bharti Mittal
(d) Shobana Kamineni

79. The 2019 UNESCO/Guillermo Cano Press Freedom Prize has been awarded to

(a) Liang Xiangyi and Claudia Mo

(b) Xiao Qiang and Gao Yu

(c) Wa Lone and Kyaw Soe Oo

(d) Choe Sang-Hun and Sohn Suk-hee

80. Which of the following ancient human species has been discovered by researchers in the Philippines which was previously unknown to science?

(a) Homo habilis
(b) Homo Luzonensis
(c) Homo erectus
(d) Homo floresiensis

81. Which one of the following countries equity market has overtaken Japan to be the world's third largest in value, behind only the U.S. and mainland China?

(a) Thailand
(b) India
(c) Australia
(d) Hong Kong

82. Consider the following statements with reference to Air Pollution levels of Indian cities:

1. Delhi is ranked sixth on the list.

2. As per the WHO list of most polluted cities, 14 of the 15 most polluted cities in the world are in India.

3. Kanpur in Uttar Pradesh is the most polluted city in the world.

Which of the above statements is/are correct?

(a) 1 and 2
(b) 1, 2 and 3
(c) 2 and 3
(d) 1 and 3

83. Which of the following universities scientists using powerful computer simulations have discovered the existence of the state known as the Chain-melted state?

(a) University of Edinburgh

(b) Hong Kong University of Science and Technology

(c) University of Oxford

(d) University of Cambridge

84. The Indian Space Research Organisation (ISRO) has signed an MoU with which institute to map, validate and protect smaller wetlands in the coastal region and restore them through coastal livelihood programmes?

(a) Central Marine Fisheries Research Institute

(b) Central Institute of Fisheries Education

(c) Central Institute of Fisheries Technology

(d) Indian Council of Agricultural Research

85. Recently, Trump Administration has announced its intent to designate the IRGC and its Quds Force as a foreign terrorist organisation (FTO) in accordance with Section 219 of the Immigration and Nationality Act. What is the full form of IRGC?

(a) International Risk Governance Council

(b) Islamic Revolutionary Guard Corps

(c) International Revolutionary Governance Council

(d) Indo–Islamic Revolutionary Guard Corps

86. Consider the following statements with reference to World Summit on the Information Society (WSIS) awards of the United Nations:

1. Utkarsh Bangla and Sabooj Sathi scheme won WSIS award.

2. WSIS Prizes, an international contest, was first held in 2012.

Which of the above statements is/are correct?

(a) 1 Only
(b) 2 Only
(c) Both 1 and 2
(d) Neither 1 nor 2

87. The "Utkarsh Bangla" and "Sabooj Sathi" which won the World Summit on the Information Society (WSIS) awards of the United Nations belong to which state?
   (a) Gujarat
   (b) Odisha
   (c) West Bengal
   (d) Maharastra

88. Who has been appointed Vice Chancellor of New Delhi's Jamia Millia Islamia, becoming the first woman to head the 99-year-old university?
   (a) Dr. Mariamma Varghese
   (b) Najma Akhtar
   (c) Inderjit Kaur
   (d) Ruchi Sinha

89. Which of the following institutes has topped the overall rankings of higher education institutions released by the Ministry of Human Resource Development?
   (a) Indian Institute of Technology, Madras
   (b) Indian Institute of Technology, Delhi
   (c) Banaras Hindu University, Varanasi
   (d) University of Hyderabad, Hyderabad

90. Who has recently been selected for the prestigious Saraswati Samman, 2018?
   (a) Ramli Bin Ibrahim
   (b) Pran Kishore Kaul
   (c) K Siva Reddy
   (d) Joyasree Goswami Mahanta

91. Who has become the first woman Chairman and Managing Director of the mini ratna-I category PSU Pawan Hans Limited?
   (a) Rajesh Kakkar
   (b) Usha Padhee
   (c) Arun Kumar
   (d) Sanjeev Kapoor

92. Name the person who has recently become the President of International Chamber of Commerce (ICC) India.
   (a) Narinder Biba
   (b) Mehsopuria
   (c) Vikramjit Singh Sahney
   (d) Bikram Singh

93. Graham Reid appointed as Indian Men's Hockey Team Chief Coach recently belongs to which country?
   (a) England
   (b) Belgium
   (c) Netherlands
   (d) Australia

94. Shiv Das Meena appointed as the Chairman cum Managing Director (CMD) to which of the following entities?
   (a) Marsh & McLennan Companies
   (b) National Buildings Construction Corporation (NBCC)
   (c) IPL Information Processing Limited
   (d) IBM Global Business Services

95. Who has recently been honoured with the Freedom of the City of London in recognition of his/ her work to promote insurance ties between India and the UK?
   (a) Alice G. Vaidyan
   (b) M. Sashikala
   (c) A.K. Das
   (d) Ravi Mital

96. Consider the following statements about Homo luzonensis.
   I. It is one of the recently discovered human species.
   II. It is discovered in one of the longest caves in Meghalaya.

Which of the above statements is/are correct?
   (a) Only I
   (b) Only II
   (c) Both I and II
   (d) Neither I nor II

97. Consider the following statements about the birth of a baby in Greece involving mitochondrial donation technique.
   I. It is one of the recently developed techniques involving three parents.
   II. In this technique, egg is provided by a female donor while mitochondria is provided by male.
   III. The technique is useful in the case of certain fertility problems.

Select the correct answer using the codes given below.
   (a) Only I and II
   (b) Only II and III
   (c) Only I and III
   (d) I, II and III

98. Recently British Prime Minister has expressed "deep regret" related to which of the following historical events?
   (a) World War II
   (b) Partition of India and Pakistan
   (c) Jallianwala Bagh massacre
   (d) The policy of British Colonialism

99. The United Nations Security Council (UNSC) has recently voted to end peace keeping operations in which of the following Latin American Country?
   (a) Paraguay
   (b) Chile
   (c) Peru
   (d) Haiti

100. Select the correct option for new state of matter discovered by scientists recently?
   (a) Chain melted state
   (b) Liquid-Liquid state
   (c) Solid-melted state
   (d) Solid–liquid condensate

101. Consider the following statements relating to Varuna Naval Exercise 2019?
   I. India and France will conduct their largest ever naval exercise 'Varuna'.
   II. The exercise has been christened 'Varuna' and will take place off Goa and Karwar from 1 May 2019.

Which of the above statement/statements are correct?
   (a) Only 1
   (b) Only 2
   (c) Both 1 and 2
   (d) Neither 1 nor 2

102. Consider the following statements with reference to Indian steel market.
   1. During the 2018-19 financial year, India's finished steel imports rose 4.7 percent to 7.84 million tonnes.
   2. The country's finished steel exports fell by 25% in the fiscal year that ended in March, 2019.

Which of the above statements is/are correct?
   (a) 1 only
   (b) 2 only
   (c) Both 1 and 2
   (d) Neither 1 nor 2

103. Which country launched its first satellite "Raavana 1" from NASA's Flight Facility on Virginia's east shore in space?
   (a) Myanmar
   (b) Malaysia
   (c) Bangladesh
   (d) Sri Lanka

104. Name the Nepal's first satellite which launched into space from the Virginia-based station of the National Aeronautics and Space Administration (NASA) in the US.
- (a) NepaliSat-1
- (b) NepaliSpace-1
- (c) Satellite N – 1
- (d) Nepali S – 1

105. Which of the following peacekeepers were honoured with UN Medal for their services in UN Mission in South Sudan (UNMISS)?
- (a) South Sudan Peacekeepers
- (b) US Peacekeepers
- (c) Indian Peacekeepers
- (d) Bangladesh Peacekeepers

106. Who has been honoured with the 2019 Pulitzer Prize in fiction category?
- (a) Jackie Sibblies Drury
- (b) David W. Blight
- (c) Jeffrey C Stewart
- (d) Richard Powers

107. Which of the following organisations releases World Press Freedom Index every year?
- (a) Reporters without Borders
- (b) United Nations
- (c) Thomson Reuters
- (d) World Peace Council

108. Which of the following countries is not a member of Asian Tea Alliance (ATA) which is a union of five tea-growing and consuming countries?
- (a) India
- (b) China
- (c) Indonesian
- (d) Myanmar

109. Which of the following research institutes has undertaken an indigenous genetic mapping effort to educate a generation of students on the "usefulness" of genomics?
- (a) Central Glass and Ceramic Research Institute
- (b) Central Inland Fisheries Research Institute
- (c) Council of Scientific and Industrial Research
- (d) National Institute of Biomedical Genomics

110. Which of the following countries researchers have printed the world's first 3D vascularised engineered heart using a patient's own cells and biological materials?
- (a) Japan
- (b) China
- (c) Israel
- (d) France

111. Liquid methane has recently been spotted on which satellite in the solar system?
- (a) triton
- (b) Titan
- (c) Ganymede
- (d) Callisto

112. What is the operational range of the India's first indigenously designed Sub-sonic Cruise Missile 'Nirbhay'?
- (a) 1500km
- (b) 1000km
- (c) 750km
- (d) 1250km

113. Who will chair the Inter-Ministerial Steering Committee of National Mission on Transformative Mobility and Battery Storage to finalise the framework for a Phased Manufacturing Program (PMP)?
- (a) Rajiv Kumar
- (b) Amitabh Kant
- (c) Yashwant Sinha
- (d) S.P. Gupta

114. Name the city where tech giant Google has launched the first African artificial Intelligence (AI) laboratory?
- (a) Monrovia, Liberia
- (b) Bamako, Mali
- (c) Abuja, Nigeria
- (d) Accra, Ghana

115. Name the combined immune deficiency disorder which is cured by gene therapy developed by HIV (Human Immunodeficiency Virus).
- (a) Bubble boy
- (b) Lupus
- (c) Inflammatory bowel disease
- (d) Multiple sclerosis

116. Which country's border trade route was suspended recently from Jammu & Kashmir LOC by Ministry of Home Affairs (MHA) of Indian government?
- (a) China
- (b) Bangladesh
- (c) Bhutan
- (d) Pakistan

117. Research team of which institute has identified a new method to detect breast and ovarian cancer recently?
- (a) IIT Delhi
- (b) IIT Kharagpur
- (c) IIT Roorkee
- (d) IIT Kanpur

118. Which country topped the World Press Freedom Index 2019 released by Reporters Without Borders, a non profitable organization?
- (a) Norway
- (b) Denmark
- (c) Sweden
- (d) Finland

119. Consider the following statements about LOC Trade that has been suspended by Ministry of Home Affairs (MHA) recently?
- I. LOC trade is allowed through Salamabad and Muzaffarabad Facilitation centers.
- II. The trade across LOC is meant to facilitate the exchange of goods between local populations across the border on daily basis.

Which of the statement(s) given above is/ are correct?
- (a) I only
- (b) II only
- (c) Both I and II
- (d) Neither I nor II

120. In the context of Cancer Preparedness (ICP) index 2019, consider the following statements:
- I. In overall ranking India ranks 19th with 75% score.
- II. India ranks 23rd for its national cancer control plan which is relatively poor.

Which of the statement(s) given above is/ are correct?
- (a) I only
- (b) II only
- (c) Both I and II
- (d) Neither I nor II

121. With reference to African artificial Intelligence (AI) laboratory, consider the following statements:
- I. To tackle Africa's challenges, Google has launched this in Accra, capital city of Ghana.
- II. The laboratory will use Artificial Intelligence technique to develop solutions in healthcare, education and agriculture.

Which of the statement(s) given above is/ are correct?
- (a) I only
- (b) II only
- (c) Both I and II
- (d) Neither I nor II

122. Consider the following statements about Quasi-Crypto currency that has been jointly launched by IMF and World Bank.

    I. It is also called as Learning Coin.

    II. It is also a real crypto currency but has no money value.

    Which of the statement(s) given above is/ are correct?

    (a) I only   (b) II only

    (c) Both I and II   (d) Neither I nor II

123. Consider the following statements about ETMONEY, financial service app.

    I. This app for financial services has been integrated with UPI as a payment method recently.

    II. The user can make the payment instantly within a few seconds by entering valid UPI ID

    Which of the statement(s) given above is/ are correct?

    (a) I only   (b) II only

    (c) Both I and II   (d) Neither I nor II

124. Consider the following statements about Gagandeep Kaur.

    I. She becomes the first Indian FRS.

    II. She is credited with the building of national rotavirus and typhoid surveillance networks.

    Which of the above statement(s) is/are correct?

    (a) Only I   (b) Only II

    (c) Both I and II   (d) Neither I nor II

125. Who holds the record for woman astronaut with longest single spaceflight?

    (a) Christina Koch   (b) Sunita Williams

    (c) Anne McClain   (d) Peggy Whitson

126. Recently Emperor of which of the following countries announced his decision to abdicate the throne to his son?

    (a) Swaziland   (b) Bhutan

    (c) Japan   (d) Brunei

127. Who has been appointed as new High commissioner to South Africa?

    (a) Jaideep Sarkar   (b) Suhel Ajaz Khan

    (c) O P Rawat   (d) Ruchi Ghanshyam

128. Consider the following statements about Volodymyr Zelensky.

    I. He is a famous Ukrainian Comedian.

    II. He has been elected as Next President of Ukraine.

    Which of the above statement(s) is/are correct?

    (a) Only I   (b) Only II

    (c) Both I and II   (d) Neither I nor II

129. Recently which of the following persons has been appointed as new Prime Minister of Mali?

    (a) Ibrahim Boubacar Keïta

    (b) Boubou Cisse

    (c) Soumeylou Boubèye Maïga

    (d) Abdoulaye Idrissa Maïga

130. 5th ABU Media Summit on Climate Action and Disaster Preparedness was held recently in Kathmandu, Nepal. ABU stands for

    (a) African Pacific Broadcasting Union

    (b) Atlantic Broadcasting Union

    (c) Asia Pacific Broadcasting Union

    (d) Australian Pacific Broadcasting Union

ANSWER KEY

1	(d)	18	(d)	35	(c)	52	(c)	69	(b)	86	(c)	103	(d)	120	(b)
2	(b)	19	(c)	36	(b)	53	(a)	70	(d)	87	(c)	104	(a)	121	(c)
3	(c)	20	(a)	37	(d)	54	(d)	71	(d)	88	(b)	105	(c)	122	(a)
4	(a)	21	(c)	38	(d)	55	(a)	72	(c)	89	(a)	106	(d)	123	(c)
5	(b)	22	(d)	39	(b)	56	(a)	73	(b)	90	(c)	107	(a)	124	(b)
6	(b)	23	(d)	40	(c)	57	(a)	74	(c)	91	(b)	108	(d)	125	(d)
7	(d)	24	(b)	41	(d)	58	(b)	75	(b)	92	(c)	109	(c)	126	(c)
8	(a)	25	(b)	42	(a)	59	(c)	76	(c)	93	(d)	110	(c)	127	(d)
9	(d)	26	(b)	43	(b)	60	(c)	77	(d)	94	(b)	111	(b)	128	(c)
10	(c)	27	(a)	44	(c)	61	(a)	78	(b)	95	(a)	112	(b)	129	(c)
11	(a)	28	(b)	45	(b)	62	(d)	79	(c)	96	(a)	113	(b)	130	(c)
12	(d)	29	(c)	46	(b)	63	(a)	80	(b)	97	(c)	114	(d)		
13	(b)	30	(d)	47	(b)	64	(b)	81	(d)	98	(c)	115	(a)		
14	(a)	31	(b)	48	(a)	65	(d)	82	(b)	99	(d)	116	(d)		
15	(b)	32	(b)	49	(c)	66	(d)	83	(a)	100	(a)	117	(c)		
16	(a)	33	(a)	50	(a)	67	(b)	84	(a)	101	(c)	118	(a)		
17	(c)	34	(a)	51	(d)	68	(d)	85	(b)	102	(a)	119	(d)		